D0783178

'Dennis, I have got something for you to do. It must be kept a secret, and it allows of no delay.'

Blind Love

BY

WILKIE COLLINS

With a Preface by
WALTER BESANT

and Illustrations by
A. FORESTIER

DOVER PUBLICATIONS, INC.
NEW YORK

Published in Canada by General Publishing Company, Ltd., 30 Lesmill Road, Don Mills, Toronto, Ontario.

Published in the United Kingdom by Constable and Company, Ltd., 10 Orange Street, London WC2H 7EG.

This Dover edition, first published in 1986, is an unabridged republication of the work first published in *The Illustrated London News* in 1889 and in book form by Chatto and Windus, London, in 1890.

Manufactured in the United States of America
Dover Publications, Inc., 31 East 2nd Street, Mineola, N.Y. 11501.

Library of Congress Cataloging in Publication Data

Collins, Wilkie, 1824–1889.
Blind love.

Reprint. Originally published: London : Chatto & Windus, Piccadilly, 1890.
I. Besant, Walter, Sir, 1836–1901. II. Title.
PR4494.B5   1986   823'.8   86-13419
ISBN 0-486-25189-6

PREFACE

*I*N the month of August 1889, and in the middle of the seaside holiday, a message came to me from Wilkie Collins, then, though we hoped otherwise, on his death-bed.

It was conveyed to me by Mr. A. P. Watt. He told me that his son had just come from Wilkie Collins: that they had been speaking of his novel, 'Blind Love,' then running in the 'Illustrated London News': that the novel was, unfortunately, unfinished: that he himself could not possibly finish it: and that he would be very glad, if I would finish it if I could find the time. And that if I could undertake this work he would send me his notes of the remainder. Wilkie Collins added these words: 'If he has the time I think he will do it: we are both old hands at this work, and understand it, and he knows that I would do the same for him if he were in my place.'

Under the circumstances of the case, it was impossible to decline this request. I wrote to say that time should be made, and the notes were forwarded to me at Robin Hood's Bay. I began by reading carefully and twice over, so as to get a grip of the story and the novelist's intention, the part that had already appeared, and the proofs so far as the author had gone. I then turned to the notes. I found that these were not merely notes such as I expected—simple indications of the plot and the development of events, but an actual detailed scenario, in which every incident, however trivial, was carefully laid down: there were also fragments of dialogue inserted at those places where dialogue was wanted to emphasise the situation and make it real. I was much struck with the writer's perception of the vast importance of dialogue in making the reader seize the scene. Description requires attention : dialogue rivets attention.

It is not an easy task, nor is it pleasant, to carry on another man's work : but the possession of this scenario lightened the work enormously. I have been careful to adhere faithfully and exactly to the plot, scene by scene, down to the smallest detail as it was laid down by the author in this book. I have altered nothing. I have preserved and incorporated every fragment of dialogue. I have used the very language wherever that was written so carefully as to show that it was meant to be used. I think that there is only one trivial detail where I had to choose because it was not clear from the notes what the author had intended. The plot of the novel, every scene, every situation, from beginning to end, is the work of Wilkie Collins. The actual writing is entirely his up to a certain point : from that point to the end it is partly his, but mainly mine. Where his writing ends and mine begins, I need not point out. The practised critic will, no doubt, at once lay his finger on the spot.

I have therefore carried out the author's wishes to the best of my ability. I would that he were living still, if only to regret that he had not been allowed to finish his last work with his own hand !

WALTER BESANT.

CONTENTS

THE STORY

FIRST PERIOD

SECOND PERIOD

THIRD PERIOD

ILLUSTRATIONS

BLIND LOVE

I

SOON after sunrise, on a cloudy morning in the year 1881, a special messenger disturbed the repose of Dennis Howmore, at his place of residence in the pleasant Irish town of Ardoon.

Well acquainted apparently with the way upstairs, the man thumped on a bed-room door, and shouted his message through it : 'The master wants you, and mind you don't keep him waiting.'

The person sending this peremptory message was Sir Giles Mountjoy of Ardoon, knight and banker. The person receiving the message was Sir Giles's head clerk. As a matter of course, Dennis Howmore dressed himself at full speed, and hastened to his employer's private house on the outskirts of the town.

He found Sir Giles in an irritable and anxious state of mind. A letter lay open on the banker's bed, his night-cap was crumpled crookedly on his head, he was in too great a hurry to remember the claims of politeness, when the clerk said 'Good morning.'

'Dennis, I have got something for you to do. It must be kept a secret, and it allows of no delay.'

'Is it anything connected with business, sir ? '

The banker lost his temper. 'How can you be such an infernal fool as to suppose that anything connected with business could happen at this time in the morning ? Do you know the first milestone on the road to Garvan ? '

'Yes, sir.'

'Very well. Go to the milestone, and take care that nobody sees you when you get there. Look at the back of the stone. If you discover an Object which appears to have been left in that situation on the ground, bring it to me; and don't forget that the most impatient man in all Ireland is waiting for you.'

Not a word of explanation followed these extraordinary instructions.

The head clerk set forth on his errand, with his mind dwelling on the national tendencies to conspiracy and assassination. His employer was not a popular person. Sir Giles had paid rent when he owed it; and, worse still, was disposed to remember in a friendly spirit what England had done for Ireland, in the course of the last fifty years. If anything appeared to justify distrust of the mysterious Object of which he was in search, Dennis resolved to be vigilantly on the look-out for a gun-barrel, whenever he passed a hedge on his return journey to the town.

Arrived at the milestone, he discovered on the ground behind it one Object only—a fragment of a broken tea-cup.

Naturally enough, Dennis hesitated. It seemed to be impossible that the earnest and careful instructions which he had received could relate to such a trifle as this. At the same time, he was acting under orders which were as positive as tone, manner, and language could make them. Passive obedience appeared to be the one safe course to take—at the risk of a reception, irritating to any man's self-respect, when he returned to his employer with a broken tea-cup in his hand.

The event entirely failed to justify his misgivings. There could be no doubt that Sir Giles attached serious importance to the contemptible discovery made at the milestone. After having examined and re-examined the fragment, he announced his intention of sending the clerk on a second errand—still without troubling himself to explain what his incomprehensible instructions meant.

'If I am not mistaken,' he began, 'the Reading Rooms, in our town, open as early as nine. Very well. Go to the Rooms this morning, on the stroke of the clock.' He stopped, and consulted the letter which lay open on his bed. 'Ask the librarian,' he continued, 'for the third volume of Gibbon's "Decline and Fall of the Roman Empire." Open the book at pages seventy-eight and seventy-nine. If you find a piece of paper between those two leaves, take possession of it when nobody is looking at you, and bring it to me. That's all, Dennis. And bear in mind that I shall not recover the use of my patience till I see you again.'

On ordinary occasions, the head clerk was not a man accustomed to insist on what was due to his dignity. At the same time he was a sensible human being, conscious of the consideration to which his responsible place in the office entitled him. Sir Giles's irritating reserve, not even excused by a word of apology, reached the limits of his endurance. He respectfully protested.

'I regret to find, sir,' he said, 'that I have lost my place in my

employer's estimation. The man to whom you confide the superintendence of your clerks and the transaction of your business has,
I venture to think, some claim (under the present circumstances)
to be trusted.'

The banker was now offended on his side.

' I readily admit your claim,' he answered, ' when you are sitting
at your desk in my office. But, even in these days of strikes, co-
operations, and bank holidays, an employer has one privilege left—
he has not ceased to be a Man, and he has not forfeited a man's
right to keep his own secrets. I fail to see anything in my conduct
which has given you just reason to complain.'

Dennis, rebuked, made his bow in silence, and withdrew.

Did these acts of humility mean that he submitted ? They
meant exactly the contrary. He had made up his mind that Sir
Giles Mountjoy's motives should, sooner or later, cease to be
mysteries to Sir Giles Mountjoy's clerk.

II

AREFULLY following his instructions, he consulted the third volume of Gibbon's great History, and found, between the seventy-eighth and seventy-ninth pages, something remarkable this time.

It was a sheet of delicately-made paper, pierced with a number of little holes, infinitely varied in size, and cut with the smoothest precision. Having secured this curious object, while the librarian's back was turned, Dennis Howmore reflected.

A page of paper, unintelligibly perforated for some purpose unknown, was in itself a suspicious thing. And what did suspicion suggest to the inquiring mind in South-Western Ireland, before the suppression of the Land League? Unquestionably—Police!

On the way back to his employer, the banker's clerk paid a visit to an old friend—a journalist by profession, and a man of varied learning and experience as well. Invited to inspect the remarkable morsel of paper, and to discover the object with which the perforations had been made, the authority consulted proved to be worthy of the trust reposed in him. Dennis left the newspaper office an enlightened man—with information at the disposal of Sir Giles, and with a sense of relief which expressed itself irreverently in these words: ' Now I have got him!'

The bewildered banker looked backwards and forwards from the paper to the clerk, and from the clerk to the paper. ' I don't understand it,' he said. ' Do you?'

Still preserving the appearance of humility, Dennis asked leave to venture on a guess. The perforated paper looked, as he thought, like a Puzzle. ' If we wait for a day or two,' he suggested, ' the Key to it may possibly reach us.'

On the next day, nothing happened. On the day after, a second letter made another audacious demand on the fast failing patience of Sir Giles Mountjoy.

Even the envelope proved to be a Puzzle on this occasion; the postmark was ' Ardoon.' In other words, the writer had used the postman as a messenger, while he or his accomplice was actually in the town, posting the letter within half-a-minute's walk of the bank! The contents presented an impenetrable mystery, the writing looked worthy of a madman. Sentences appeared in the wildest state of confusion, and words were so mutilated as to be unintelligible. This time the force of circumstances was more than Sir Giles could resist. He took the clerk into his confidence at last.

Lifting the perforated paper, he placed it delicately over the page which contained the unintelligible writing.

'Let us begin at the beginning,' he said. 'There is the letter you saw on my bed, when I first sent for you. I found it waiting on my table when I woke; and I don't know who put it there. Read it.'

Dennis read as follows:

'Sir Giles Mountjoy,—I have a disclosure to make, in which one of the members of your family is seriously interested. Before I can venture to explain myself, I must be assured that I can trust to your good faith. As a test of this, I require you to fulfil the two conditions that follow—and to do it without the slightest loss of time. I dare not trust you yet with my address, or my signature. Any act of carelessness, on my part, might end fatally for the true friend who writes these lines. If you neglect this warning, you will regret it to the end of your life.'

To the conditions on which the letter insisted there is no need to allude. They had been complied with when the discoveries were made at the back of the milestone, and between the pages of Gibson's History. Sir Giles had already arrived at the conclusion that a conspiracy was in progress to assassinate him, and perhaps to rob the bank. The wiser head clerk pointed to the perforated paper and the incomprehensible writing received that morning. 'If we can find out what these mean,' he said, 'you may be better able, sir, to form a correct opinion.'

'And who is to do that?' the banker asked.

'I can but try, sir, was the modest reply, 'if you see no objection to my making the attempt.'

Sir Giles approved of the proposed experiment, silently and satirically, by a bend of his head.

Too discreet a man to make a suspiciously ready use of the information which he had privately obtained, Dennis took care that his first attempt should not be successful. After modestly asking permission to try again, he ventured on the second occasion to arrive at a happy discovery. Lifting the perforated paper, he placed it delicately over the page which contained the unintelligible writing. Words and sentences now appeared (through the holes in the paper) in their right spelling and arrangement, and addressed Sir Giles in these terms:

'I beg to thank you, sir, for complying with my conditions. You have satisfied me of your good faith. At the same time, it is possible that you may hesitate to trust a man who is not yet able to admit you to his confidence. The perilous position in which I stand obliges me to ask for two or three days more of delay, before I can safely make an appointment with you. Pray be patient—and on no account apply for advice or protection to the police.'

'Those last words,' Sir Giles declared, 'are conclusive! The sooner I am under the care of the law the better. Take my card to the police-office.'

'May I say a word first, sir?'

'Do you mean that you don't agree with me?'

'I mean that.'

'You were always an obstinate man, Dennis : and it grows on you as you get older. Never mind! Let's have it out. Who do *you* say is the person pointed at in these rascally letters ? '

The head clerk took up the first letter of the two, and pointed to the opening sentence : ' Sir Giles Mountjoy, I have a disclosure to make in which one of the members of your family is seriously interested.' Dennis emphatically repeated the words : ' one of the members of your family.' His employer regarded him with a broad stare of astonishment.

' One of the members of my family ? ' Sir Giles repeated, on his side. ' Why, man alive, what are you thinking of ? I'm an old bachelor, and I haven't got a family.'

' There is your brother, sir.'

' My brother is in France—out of the way of the wretches who are threatening me. I wish I was with him ! '

' There are your brother's two sons, Sir Giles.'

' Well ? And what is there to be afraid of ? My nephew, Hugh, is in London—and, mind ! not on a political errand. I hope, before long, to hear that he is going to be married—if the strangest and nicest girl in England will have him. What's wrong now ? '

Dennis explained. ' I only wished to say, sir, that I was think-ing of your other nephew.'

Sir Giles laughed. ' Arthur in danger ! ' he exclaimed. ' As harmless a young man as ever lived. The worst one can say of him is that he is throwing away his money—farming in Kerry.'

' Excuse me, Sir Giles ; there's not much chance of his throwing away his money, where he is now. Nobody will venture to take his money. I met with one of Mr. Arthur's neighbours at the market yesterday. Your nephew is boycotted.'

' So much the better,' the obstinate banker declared. ' He will be cured of his craze for farming; and he will come back to the place I am keeping for him in the office.'

' God grant it ! ' the clerk said fervently.

For the moment, Sir Giles was staggered. ' Have you heard something that you haven't told me yet ? ' he asked.

' No, sir. I am only bearing in mind something which—with all respect—I think you have forgotten. The last tenant on that bit of land in Kerry refused to pay his rent. Mr. Arthur has taken what they call an evicted farm. It's my firm belief,' said the head clerk, rising and speaking earnestly, ' that the person who has addressed those letters to you knows Mr. Arthur, and knows he is in danger—and is trying to save your nephew (by means of your influence), at the risk of his own life.'

Sir Giles shook his head. ' I call that a far-fetched interpreta-tion, Dennis. If what you say is true, why didn't the writer of those anonymous letters address himself to Arthur, instead of to me ? '

' I gave it as my opinion just now, sir, that the writer of the letter knew Mr. Arthur.'

' So you did. And what of that ? '

Dennis stood to his guns.

'Anybody who is acquainted with Mr. Arthur,' he persisted, 'knows that (with all sorts of good qualities) the young gentleman is headstrong and rash. If a friend told him he was in danger on the farm, that would be enough of itself to make him stop where he is, and brave it out. Whereas you, sir, are known to be cautious and careful, and farseeing and discreet.' He might have added : And cowardly and obstinate, and narrow-minded and inflated by stupid self-esteem. But respect for his employer had blindfolded the clerk's observation for many a long year past. If one man may be born with the heart of a lion, another man may be born with the mind of a mule. Dennis's master was one of the other men.

' Very well put,' Sir Giles answered indulgently. ' Time will show, if such an entirely unimportant person as my nephew Arthur is likely to be assassinated. That allusion to one of the members of my family is a mere equivocation, designed to throw me off my guard. Rank, money, social influence, unswerving principles, mark ME out as a public character. Go to the police-office, and let the best man who happens to be off duty come here directly.'

Good Dennis Howmore approached the door very unwillingly. It was opened, from the outer side, before he had reached that end of the room. One of the bank porters announced a visitor.

' Miss Henley wishes to know, sir, if you can see her.'

Sir Giles looked agreeably surprised. He rose with alacrity to receive the lady.

III

HEN Iris Henley dies there will, in all probability, be friends left who remember her and talk of her—and there may be strangers present at the time (women for the most part), whose curiosity will put questions relating to her personal appearance. No replies will reward them with trustworthy information. Miss Henley's chief claim to admiration lay in a remarkable mobility of expression, which reflected every change of feeling peculiar to the nature of a sweet and sensitive woman. For this reason, probably, no descriptions of her will agree with each other. No existing likenesses will represent her. The one portrait that was painted of Iris is only recognisable by partial friends of the artist. In and out of London, photographic likenesses were taken of her. They have the honour of resembling the portraits of Shakespeare in this respect—compared with one another, it is not possible to discover that they present the same person. As for the evidence offered by the loving memory of her friends, it is sure to be contradictory in the last degree. She had a charming face, a commonplace face, an intelligent face—a poor complexion, a delicate complexion, no complexion at all—eyes that were expressive of a hot temper, of a bright intellect, of a firm character, of an affectionate disposition, of a truthful nature, of hysterical sensibility, of inveterate obstinacy—a figure too short; no, just the right height; no, neither one thing nor the other; elegant, if you like—dress shabby: oh, surely not; dress quiet and simple; no, something more than that; ostentatiously quiet, theatrically simple, worn with the object of looking unlike other people. In one last word, was this mass of contradictions generally popular, in the time when it was a living creature? Yes—among the men. No—not invariably. The man of all others who ought to have been fondest of her was the man who behaved cruelly to Iris—her own father. And, when the poor creature married (if she did marry), how many of you attended the wedding? Not one of us! And when she died, how many of you were sorry for her? All of us! What? no difference of opinion in that one particular? On the contrary, perfect concord, thank God.

Let the years roll back, and let Iris speak for herself, at the memorable time when she was in the prime of her life, and when a stormy career was before her.

IV

BEING Miss Henley's godfather, Sir Giles was a privileged person. He laid his hairy hands on her shoulders, and kissed her on either cheek. After that prefatory act of endearment, he made his inquiries. What extraordinary combination of events had led Iris to leave London, and had brought her to visit him in his banking-house at Ardoon?

' I wanted to get away from home,' she answered; ' and having nobody to go to but my godfather, I thought I should like to see You.'

' Alone ! ' cried Sir Giles.

' No—with my maid to keep me company.'

' Only your maid, Iris ? Surely you have acquaintances among young ladies like yourself ? '

' Acquaintances—yes. No friends.'

' Does your father approve of what you have done ? '

' Will you grant me a favour, godpapa ? '

' Yes—if I can.'

' Don't insist on my answering your last question.'

The faint colour that had risen in her face, when she entered the room, left it. At the same time, the expression of her mouth altered. The lips closed firmly; revealing that strongest of all resolutions which is founded on a keen sense of wrong. She looked older than her age : what she might be ten years hence, she was now. Sir Giles understood her. He got up, and took a turn in the room. An old habit, of which he had cured himself with infinite difficulty when he was made a Knight, showed itself again. He put his hands in his pockets.

' You and your father have had another quarrel,' he said, stopping opposite Iris.

' I don't deny it,' she replied.

' Who is to blame ? '

She smiled bitterly. ' The woman is always to blame.'

' Did your father tell you that ? '

My father reminded me that I was twenty-one years old, last birthday—and told me that I could do as I liked. I understood him, and I left the house.'

' You will go back again, I suppose ? '

' I don't know.'

Sir Giles began pacing the room once more. His rugged face,

telling its story of disaster and struggle in early life, showed· signs of disappointment and distress.

'Hugh promised to write to me,' he said, 'and he has not written. I know what that means; I know what you have done to offend your father. My nephew has asked you to marry him for the second time. And for the second time you have refused.'

Her face softened; its better and younger aspect revived. 'Yes,' she said, sadly and submissively; 'I have refused him again.'

Sir Giles lost his temper. 'What the devil is your objection to Hugh?' he burst out.

'My father said the same thing to me,' she replied, 'almost in the same words. I made him angry when I tried to give my reason. I don't want to make you angry, too.'

He took no notice of this. 'Isn't Hugh a good fellow?' he went on. 'Isn't he affectionate? and kindhearted? and honour· able?—aye, and a handsome man too, if you come to that.'

'Hugh is all that you say. I like him; I admire him; I owe to his kindness some of the happiest days of my sad life, and I am grateful—oh, with all my heart, I am grateful to Hugh!'

'If that's true, Iris——'

'Every word of it is true.'

'I say, if that's true—there's no excuse for you. I hate per· versity in a young woman! Why don't you marry him?'

'Try to feel for me,' she said gently; 'I can't love him.'

Her tone said more to the banker than her words had expressed. The secret sorrow of her life, which was known to her father, was known also to Sir Giles.

'Now we have come to it at last!' he said. 'You can't love my nephew Hugh. And you won't tell me the reason why, because your sweet temper shrinks from making me angry. Shall I men· tion the reason for you, my dear? I can do it in two words—Lord Harry.'

She made no reply; she showed no sign of feeling at what he had just said. Her head sank a little; her hands clasped themselves on her lap; the obstinate resignation which can submit to anything hardened her face, stiffened her figure—and that was all.

The banker was determined not to spare her.

'It's easy to see,' he resumed, 'that you have not got over your infatuation for that vagabond yet. Go where he may, into the vilest places and among the lowest people, he carries your heart along with him. I wonder you are not ashamed of such an attach· ment as that.'

He had stung her at last. She roused herself, and answered him.

'Harry has led a wild life,' she said; 'he has committed serious faults, and he may live to do worse than he has done yet. To what degradation, bad company, and a bad bringing-up may yet lead him, I leave his enemies to foresee. But I tell you this, he has redeeming qualities which you, and people like you, are not good Christians enough to discover. He has friends who can still appreciate him—your nephew, Arthur Mountjoy, is one of them. Oh, I know it by Arthur's letters to me! Blame Lord Harry as you may, I tell you he has the capacity for repentance in him, and one day—when it is too late, I dare say—he will show it. I can never be his wife. We are parted, never in all likelihood to meet again. Well, he is the only man whom I have ever loved; and he is the only man whom I ever shall love. If you think this state of mind proves that I am as bad as he is, I won't contradict you. Do we any of us know how bad we are——? Have you heard of Harry lately?'

The sudden transition, from an earnest and devoted defence of the man, to an easy and familiar inquiry about him, startled Sir Giles.

For the moment, he had nothing to say; Iris had made him think. She had shown a capacity for mastering her strongest feelings, at the moment when they threatened to overcome her, which is very rarely found in a young woman. How to manage her was a problem for patient resolution to solve. The banker's obstinacy, rather than his conviction, had encouraged him to hold to the hope of Hugh's marriage, even after his nephew had been refused for the second time. His headstrong goddaughter had come to visit him of her own accord. She had not forgotten the days of her childhood, when he had some influence over her—when she had found him kinder to her than her father had ever been. Sir Giles saw that he had taken the wrong tone with Iris. His anger had not alarmed her; his opinion had not influenced her. In Hugh's interests, he determined to try what consideration and indulgence would do towards cultivating the growth of her regard for him. Finding that she had left her maid and her luggage at the hotel, he hospitably insisted on their removal to his own house.

'While you are in Ardoon, Iris, you are my guest,' he said.

She pleased him by readily accepting the invitation—and then annoyed him by asking again if he had heard anything of Lord Harry.

He answered shortly and sharply: 'I have heard nothing. What is *your* last news of him?'

'News,' she said, 'which I sincerely hope is not true. An Irish paper has been sent to me, which reports that he has joined the secret society—nothing better than a society of assassins, I am afraid—which is known by the name of the Invincibles.'

As she mentioned that formidable brotherhood, Dennis Howmore returned from the police-office. He announced that a Sergeant was then waiting to receive instructions from Sir Giles.

V

IRIS rose to go.   Her godfather courteously stopped her.
'Wait here,' he said, 'until I have spoken to the
Sergeant, and I will escort you to my house.   My clerk
will do what is necessary at the hotel.   You don't look
quite satisfied.   Is the arrangement that I have proposed not agreeable to you ? '

Iris assured him that she gratefully acceded to the arrangement.
At the same time, she confessed to having been a little startled,
on discovering that he was in consultation with the police.   ' I
remember that we are in Ireland,' she explained, ' and I am foolish
enough to fear that you may be in some danger.   May I hope that
it is only a trifle ? '

Only a trifle !   Among other deficient sensibilities in the strange
nature of Iris, Sir Giles had observed an imperfect appreciation of
the dignity of his social position.   Here was a new proof of it !   The
temptation to inspire sentiments of alarm—not unmingled with
admiration—in the mind of his insensible goddaughter, by exhibiting himself as a public character threatened by a conspiracy, was
more than the banker's vanity could resist.   Before he left the room,
he instructed Dennis to tell Miss Henley what had happened, and
to let her judge for herself whether he had been needlessly
alarmed by, what she was pleased to call, ' a mere trifle.'

Dennis Howmore must have been more than mortal, if he could
have related his narrative of events without being influenced by his
own point of view.   On the first occasion when he mentioned
Arthur Mountjoy's name, Iris showed a sudden interest in his strange
which story took him by surprise.

' You know Mr. Arthur ? ' he said.

' Know him ! ' Iris repeated.   ' He was my playfellow when we
were both children.   He is as dear to me as if he was my brother.
Tell me at once—is he really in danger ? '

Dennis honestly repeated what he had already said, on that
subject, to his master.   Miss Henley, entirely agreeing with him,
was eager to warn Arthur of his position.   There was no tele-
graphic communication with the village which was near his farm.
She could only write to him, and she did write to him, by that
day's post—having reasons of her own for anxiety, which forbade
her to show her letter to Dennis.   Well aware of the devoted
friendship which united Lord Harry and Arthur Mountjoy—and
bearing in mind the newspaper report of the Irish lord's rash

association with the Invincibles—her fears now identified the noble vagabond as the writer of the anonymous letters, which had so seriously excited her godfather's doubts of his own safety.

When Sir Giles returned, and took her with him to his house, he spoke of his consultation with the Sergeant in terms which increased her dread of what might happen in the future. She was a dull and silent guest, during the interval that elapsed before it would be possible to receive Arthur's reply. The day arrived—and the post brought no relief to her anxieties. The next day passed without a letter. On the morning of the fourth day, Sir Giles rose later than usual. His correspondence was sent to him from the office, at breakfast-time. After opening one of the letters, he dispatched a messenger in hot haste to the police.

'Look at that,' he said, handing the letter to Iris. 'Does the assassin take me for a fool?'

She read the lines that follow :

'Unforeseen events force me, Sir Giles, to run a serious risk. I must speak to you, and it must not be by daylight. My one hope of safety is in darkness. Meet me at the first milestone, on the road to Garvan, when the moon sets at ten o'clock to-night. No need to mention your name. The password is : *Fidelity.*'

'Do you mean to go?' Iris asked.

'Do I mean to be murdered!' Sir Giles broke out. 'My dear child, do pray try to think before you speak. The Sergeant will represent me, of course.'

'And take the man prisoner?' Iris added.

'Certainly!'

'With that startling reply, the banker hurried away to receive the police in another room. Iris dropped into the nearest chair. The turn that the affair had now taken filled her with unutterable dismay.

Sir Giles came back, after no very long absence, composed and smiling. The course of proceeding had been settled to his complete satisfaction.

Dressed in private clothes, the Sergeant was to go to the milestone at the appointed time, representing the banker in the darkness, and giving the password. He was to be followed by two of his men who would wait in concealment, within hearing of his whistle, if their services were required. 'I want to see the ruffian when he is safely handcuffed,' Sir Giles explained; 'and I have arranged to wait for the police, to-night, at my office.'

There was but one desperate way that Iris could now discern of saving the man who had confided in her godfather's honour, and whose trust had already been betrayed. Never had she loved the outlawed Irish lord—the man whom she was forbidden, and rightly forbidden, to marry—as she loved him at that moment. Let the risk be what it might, this resolute woman had determined that the Sergeant should not be the only person who arrived at the milestone, and gave the password. There was one devoted friend to

Lord Harry, whom she could always trust—and that friend was herself.

Sir Giles withdrew, to look after his business at the bank. She waited until the clock had struck the servants' dinner hour, and then ascended the stairs to her godfather's dressing-room. Opening his wardrobe, she discovered in one part of it a large Spanish cloak, and, in another part, a high-crowned felt hat which he wore on his country excursions. In the dark, here was disguise enough for her purpose.

As she left the dressing-room, a measure of precaution occurred to her, which she put in action at once. Telling her maid that she had some purchases to make in the town, she went out, and asked her way to Garvan of the first respectable stranger whom she met in the street. Her object was to walk as far as the first milestone, in daylight, so as to be sure of finding it again by night. She had made herself familiar with the different objects on the road, when she returned to the banker's house.

As the time for the arrest drew nearer, Sir Giles became too restless to wait patiently at home. He went away to the police-office, eager to hear if any new counter-conspiracy had occurred to the authorities.

It was dark soon after eight o'clock, at that time of the year. At nine the servants assembled at the supper-table. They were all downstairs together, talking, and waiting for their meal.

Feeling the necessity of arriving at the place of meeting, in time to keep out of the Sergeant's way, Iris assumed her disguise as the clock struck nine. She left the house without a living creature to notice her, indoors or out. Clouds were gathering over the sky. The waning moon was only to be seen at intervals, as she set forth on her way to the milestone.

VI

THE wind rose a little, and the rifts in the clouds began to grow broader as Iris gained the high road.

For a while, the glimmer of the misty moonlight lit the way before her. As well as she could guess, she had passed over more than half of the distance between the town and the milestone before the sky darkened again. Objects by the wayside grew shadowy and dim. A few drops of rain began to fall. The milestone, as she knew —thanks to the discovery of it made by daylight—was on the right-hand side of the road. But the dull-grey colour of the stone was not easy to see in the dark.

A doubt troubled her whether she might not have passed the milestone. She stopped and looked at the sky.

The threatening of rain had passed away: signs showed themselves which seemed to promise another break in the clouds. She waited. Low and faint, the sinking moonlight looked its last at the dull earth. In front of her, there was nothing to be seen but the road. She looked back—and discovered the milestone.

A rough stone wall protected the land on either side of the road. Nearly behind the milestone there was a gap in this fence, partially closed by a hurdle. A half-ruined culvert, arching a ditch that had run dry, formed a bridge leading from the road to the field. Had the field been already chosen as a place of concealment by the police? Nothing was to be seen but a footpath, and the dusky line of a plantation beyond it. As she made these discoveries, the rain began to fall again; the clouds gathered once more; the moonlight vanished.

At the same moment an obstacle presented itself to her mind, which Iris had thus far failed to foresee.

Lord Harry might approach the milestone by three different ways : that is to say—by the road from the town, or by the road from the open country, or by way of the field and the culvert. How could she so place herself as to be sure of warning him, before he fell into the hands of the police ? To watch the three means of approach in the obscurity of the night, and at one and the same time, was impossible.

A man in this position, guided by reason, would in all probability have wasted precious time in trying to arrive at the right decision. A woman, aided by love, conquered the difficulty that confronted her in a moment.

Iris decided on returning to the milestone, and on waiting there to be discovered and taken prisoner by the police. Supposing Lord Harry to be punctual to his appointment, he would hear voices and movements, as a necessary consequence of the arrest, in time to make his escape. Supposing him on the other hand to be late, the police would be on the way back to the town with their prisoner : he would find no one at the milestone, and would leave it again in safety.

She was on the point of turning, to get back to the road, when something on the dark surface of the field, which looked like a darker shadow, became dimly visible. In another moment it seemed to be a shadow that moved. She ran towards it. It looked like a man as she drew nearer. The man stopped.

‘ The password,’ he said, in tones cautiously lowered.

‘ Fidelity,’ she answered in a whisper.

It was too dark for a recognition of his features ; but Iris knew him by his tall stature—knew him by the accent in which he had asked for the password. Erroneously judging of her, on his side, as a man, he drew back again. Sir Giles Mountjoy was above the middle height ; the stranger in a cloak, who had whispered to him, was below it. ‘ You are not the person I expected to meet,’ he said. ‘ Who are you ? ’

Her faithful heart was longing to tell him the truth. The temptation to reveal herself, and to make the sweet confession of her happiness at having saved him, would have overpowered her discretion, but for a sound that was audible on the road behind them. In the deep silence of the time and place mistake was impossible. It was the sound of footsteps.

There was just time to whisper to him : ‘ Sir Giles has betrayed you. Save yourself.’

‘ Thank you, whoever you are ! ’

With that reply, he suddenly and swiftly disappeared. Iris remembered the culvert, and turned towards it. There was a hiding-place under the arch, if she could only get down into the dry ditch in time. She was feeling her way to the slope of it with her feet, when a heavy hand seized her by the arm; and a resolute voice said : ' You are my prisoner.'

She was led back into the road. The man who had got her blew a whistle. Two other men joined him.

' Show a light,' he said; ' and let's see who the fellow is.'

The shade was slipped aside from a lantern: the light fell full on the prisoner's face. Amazement petrified the two attendant policemen. The pious Catholic Sergeant burst into speech : ' Holy Mary! it's a woman! '

Did the secret societies of Ireland enrol women? Was this a modern Judith, expressing herself by anonymous letters, and bent on assassinating a financial Holofernes who kept a bank? What account had she to give of herself? How came she to be alone in a desolate field on a rainy night? Instead of answering these questions, the inscrutable stranger preferred a bold and brief request. ' Take me to Sir Giles '—was all she said to the police.

The Sergeant had the handcuffs ready. After looking at the prisoner's delicate wrists by the lantern-light, he put his fetters back in his pocket. ' A lady—and no doubt about it,' he said to one of his assistants.

The two men waited, with a mischievous interest in seeing what he would do next. The list of their pious officer's virtues included a constitutional partiality for women, which exhibited the merciful side of justice when a criminal wore a petticoat. ' We will take you to Sir Giles, Miss,' he said—and offered his arm, instead of offering his handcuffs. Iris understood him, and took his arm.

She was silent—unaccountably silent as the men thought—on the way to the town. They heard her sigh : and, once, the sigh sounded more like a sob; little did they suspect what was in that silent woman's mind at the time.

The one object which had absorbed the attention of Iris had been the saving of Lord Harry. This accomplished, the free exercise of her memory had now reminded her of Arthur Mountjoy.

It was impossible to doubt that the object of the proposed meeting at the milestone had been to take measures for the preservation of the young man's life. A coward is always more or less cruel. The proceedings (equally treacherous and merciless) by which Sir Giles had provided for his own safety, had delayed—perhaps actually prevented—the execution of Lord Harry's humane design. It was possible, horribly possible, that a prompt employment of time might have been necessary to the rescue of Arthur from impending death by murder. In the agitation that overpowered her, Iris actually hurried the police on their return to the town.

Sir Giles had arranged to wait for news in his private room at the office—and there he was, with Dennis Howmore in attendance to receive visitors.

The Sergeant went into the banker's room alone, to make his report.   He left the door ajar; Iris could hear what passed.

'Have you got your prisoner? ' Sir Giles began.

'Yes, your honour.'

'Is the wretch securely handcuffed? '

'I beg your pardon, sir, it isn't a man.'

'Nonsense, Sergeant; it can't be a boy.'

The Sergeant confessed that it was not a boy.   'It's a woman,' he said.

'What!!!'

'A woman,' the patient officer repeated—'and a young one. She asked for You.'

'Bring her in.'

Iris was not the sort of person who waits to be brought in.   She walked in, of her own accord.

VII

'OOD Heavens!' cried Sir Giles. 'Iris! With my cloak on!! With my hat in her hand!!! Sergeant, there has been some dreadful mistake. This is my god-daughter—Miss Henley.'

'We found her at the milestone, your honour. The young lady and nobody else.'

Sir Giles appealed helplessly to his goddaughter. 'What does this mean?' Instead of answering, she looked at the Sergeant. The Sergeant, conscious of responsibility, stood his ground and looked at Sir Giles. His face confessed that the Irish sense of humour was tickled : but he showed no intention of leaving the room. Sir Giles saw that Iris would enter into no explanation in the man's presence. 'You needn't wait any longer,' he said.

'What am I to do, if you please, with the prisoner?' the Sergeant inquired.

Sir Giles waived that unnecessary question away with his hand. He was trebly responsible—as knight, banker, and magistrate into the bargain. 'I will be answerable,' he replied, 'for producing Miss Henley, if called upon. Good night.'

The Sergeant's sense of duty was satisfied. He made the military salute. His gallantry added homage to the young lady under the form of a bow. Then, and then only, he walked with dignity out of the room.

'Now,' Sir Giles resumed, 'I presume I may expect to receive an explanation. What does this impropriety mean? What were you doing at the milestone?'

'I was saving the person who made the appointment with you, Iris said; 'the poor fellow had no ill-will towards you—who had risked everything to save your nephew's life. Oh, sir, you committed a terrible mistake when you refused to trust that man!'

Sir Giles had anticipated the appearance of fear, and the reality of humble apologies. She had answered him indignantly, with a heightened colour, and with tears in her eyes. His sense of his own social importance was wounded to the quick. 'Who is the man you are speaking of?' he asked loftily. 'And what is your excuse for having gone to the milestone to save him—hidden under my cloak, disguised in my hat?'

'Don't waste precious time in asking questions!' was the desperate reply. 'Undo the harm that you have done already. Your help—oh, I mean what I say!—may yet preserve Arthur's life. Go to the farm, and save him.'

Sir Giles's anger assumed a new form, it indulged in an elaborate

mockery of respect. He took his watch from his pocket, and consulted it satirically. 'Must I make an excuse?' he asked with a
clumsy assumption of humility.

'No! you must go.'

'Permit me to inform you, Miss Henley, that the last train
started more than two hours since.'

'What does that matter? You are rich enough to hire a
train.'

Sir Giles, the actor, could endure it no longer; he dropped the
mask, and revealed Sir Giles, the man. His clerk was summoned
by a peremptory ring of the bell. 'Attend Miss Henley to the
house,' he said. 'You may come to your senses after a night's rest,'
he continued, turning sternly to Iris. 'I will receive your excuses
in the morning.'

In the morning, the breakfast was ready as usual at nine o'clock.
Sir Giles found himself alone at the table.

He sent an order to one of the women-servants to knock at Miss
Henley's door. There was a long delay. The housekeeper presented herself in a state of alarm; she had gone upstairs to make
the necessary investigation in her own person. Miss Henley was not
in her room; the maid was not in her room; the beds had not been
slept in; the heavy luggage was labelled—'To be called for from
the hotel.' And there was an end of the evidence which the absent
Iris had left behind her.

Inquiries were made at the hotel. The young lady had called
there, with her maid, early on that morning. They had their
travelling-bags with them; and Miss Henley had left directions
that the luggage was to be placed under care of the landlord until
her return. To what destination she had betaken herself nobody
knew.

Sir Giles was too angry to remember what she had said to him
on the previous night, or he might have guessed at the motive which
had led to her departure. 'Her father has done with her already,'
he said; 'and I have done with her now.' The servants received
orders not to admit Miss Henley, if her audacity contemplated a
return to her godfather's house.

VIII

N the afternoon of the same day, Iris arrived at the village situated in the near neighbourhood of Arthur Mountjoy's farm.

The infection of political excitement (otherwise the hatred of England) had spread even to this remote place. On the steps of his little chapel, the priest, a peasant himself, was haranguing his brethren of the soil. An Irishman who paid his landlord was a traitor to his country ; an Irishman who asserted his free birthright in the land that he walked on was an enlightened patriot. Such was the new law which the reverend gentleman expounded to his attentive audience. If his brethren there would like him to tell them how they might apply the law, this exemplary Christian would point to the faithless Irishman, Arthur Mountjoy. ' Buy not of him, sell not to him; avoid him if he approaches you; starve him out of the place. I might say more, boys—you know what I mean.'

To hear the latter part of this effort of oratory, without uttering a word of protest, was a trial of endurance under which Iris trembled. The secondary effect of the priest's address was to root the conviction of Arthur's danger with tenfold tenacity in her mind. After what she had just heard, even the slightest delay in securing his safety might be productive of deplorable results. She astonished a barefooted boy, on the outskirts of the crowd, by a gift of sixpence, and asked her way to the farm. The little Irishman ran on before her, eager to show the generous lady how useful he could be. In less than half an hour, Iris and her maid were at the door of the farm-house. No such civilised inventions appeared as a knocker or a bell. The boy used his knuckles instead—and ran away when he heard the lock of the door turned on the inner side. He was afraid to be seen speaking to any living creature who inhabited the ' evicted farm.'

A decent old woman appeared, and inquired suspiciously ' what the ladies wanted.' The accent in which she spoke was unmistakably English. When Iris asked for Mr. Arthur Mountjoy the reply was : ' Not at home.' The housekeeper inhospitably attempted to close the door. ' Wait one moment,' Iris said. ' Years have changed you; but there is something in your face which is not quite strange to me. Are you Mrs. Lewson ? '

The woman admitted that this was her name. ' But how is it that you are a stranger to me ? ' she asked distrustfully.

' If you have been long in Mr. Mountjoy's service,' Iris replied, ' you may perhaps have heard him speak of Miss Henley ? '

Mrs. Lewson's face brightened in an instant; she threw the door wide open with a glad cry of recognition.

' Come in, Miss, come in ! Who would have thought of seeing you in this horrible place ? Yes; I was the nurse who looked after you all three—when you and Mr. Arthur and Mr. Hugh were play-fellows together.' Her eyes rested longingly on her favourite of bygone days. The sensitive sympathies of Iris interpreted that look. She prettily touched her cheek, inviting the nurse to kiss her. At this act of kindness the poor old woman broke down ; she apologised quaintly for her tears : ' Think, Miss, how *I* must remember that happy time—when *you* have not forgotten it.'

Shown into the parlour, the first object which the visitor noticed was the letter that she had written to Arthur lying unopened on the table.

' Then he is really out of the house ? ' she said with a feeling of relief.

He had been away from the farm for a week or more. Had he received a warning from some other quarter ? and had he wisely sought refuge in flight ? The amazement in the housekeeper's face, when she heard these questions, pleaded for a word of explanation. Iris acknowledged without reserve the motives which had suggested her journey, and asked eagerly if she had been mistaken in assuming that Arthur was in danger of assassination.

Mrs. Lewson shook her head. Beyond all doubt the young master was in danger. But Miss Iris ought to have known his nature better than to suppose that he would beat a retreat, if all the land-leaguers in Ireland threatened him together. No ! It was his bold way to laugh at danger. He had left his farm to visit a friend in the next county ; and it was shrewdly guessed that a young lady who was staying in the house was the attraction which had kept him so long away. 'Anyhow, he means to come back to-morrow,' Mrs. Lewson said. ' I wish he would think better of it, and make his escape to England while he has the chance. If the savages in these parts must shoot somebody, I'm here—an old woman that can't last much longer. Let them shoot me.'

Iris asked if Arthur's safety was assured in the next county, and in the house of his friend.

' I can't say, Miss; I have never been to the house. He is in danger if he persists in coming back to the farm. There are chances of shooting him all along his road home. Oh, yes ; he knows it, poor dear, as well as I do. But, there !—men like him are such perverse creatures. He takes his rides just as usual. No ; he won't listen to an old woman like me ; and, as for friends to advise him, the only one of them that has darkened our doors is a scamp who had better have kept away. You may have heard tell of him. The old Earl, his wicked father, used to be called by a bad name. And the wild young lord is his father's true son.'

Mrs. Lewson's face brightened in an instant; she threw the door wide open with a glad cry of recognition.

' Not Lord Harry ? ' Iris exclaimed.

The outbreak of agitation in her tone and manner was silently noticed by her maid. The housekeeper did not attempt to conceal the impression that had been produced upon her. ' I hope you don't know such a vagabond as that ? ' she said very seriously. ' Perhaps you are thinking of his brother—the eldest son—a respectable man, as I have been told ? '

Miss Henley passed over these questions without notice. Urged by the interest in her lover, which was now more than ever an interest beyond her control, she said : ' Is Lord Harry in danger, on account of his friend ? '

' He has nothing to fear from the wretches who infest our part of the country,' Mrs. Lewson replied. ' Report says he's one of themselves. The police—there's what his young lordship has to be afraid of, if all's true that is said about him. Anyhow, when he paid his visit to my master, he came secretly like a thief in the night. And I heard Mr. Arthur, while they were together here in the parlour, loud in blaming him for something that he had done. No more, Miss, of Lord Harry ! I have something particular to say to you. Suppose I promise to make you comfortable—will you please wait here till to-morrow, and see Mr. Arthur and speak to him ? If there's a person living who can persuade him to take better care of himself, I do believe it will be you.'

Iris readily consented to wait for Arthur Mountjoy's return. Left together, while Mrs. Lewson was attending to her domestic duties, the mistress noticed an appearance of pre-occupation in the maid's face.

' Are you beginning to wish, Rhoda,' she said, ' that I had not brought you to this strange place, among these wild people ? '

The maid was a quiet amiable girl, evidently in delicate health. She smiled faintly. ' I was thinking, Miss, of another nobleman besides the one Mrs. Lewson mentioned just now, who seems to have led a reckless life. It was printed in a newspaper that I read before we left London.'

' Was his name mentioned ? ' Iris asked.

' No, Miss ; I suppose they were afraid of giving offence. He tried so many strange ways of getting a living—it was almost like reading a story-book.'

The suppression of the name suggested a suspicion from which Iris recoiled. Was it possible that her maid could be ignorantly alluding to Lord Harry.

' Do you remember this hero's adventures ? ' she said.

' I can try, Miss, if you wish to hear about him.'

The newspaper narrative appeared to have produced a vivid impression on Rhoda's mind. Making allowance for natural hesitations and mistakes, and difficulties in expressing herself correctly, she repeated with a singularly clear recollection the substance of what she had read.

IX

HE principal characters in the story were an old Irish nobleman, who was called the Earl, and the youngest of his two sons, mysteriously distinguished as 'the wild lord.'

It was said of the Earl that he had not been a good father; he had cruelly neglected both his sons. The younger one, badly treated at school, and left to himself in the holidays, began his adventurous career by running away. He got employment (under an assumed name) as a ship's boy. At the outset, he did well; learning his work, and being liked by the Captain and the crew. But the chief mate was a brutal man, and the young runaway's quick temper resented the disgraceful infliction of blows. He made up his mind to try his luck on shore, and attached himself to a company of strolling players. Being a handsome lad, with a good figure and a fine clear voice, he did very well for a while on the country stage. Hard times came; salaries were reduced; the adventurer wearied of the society of actors and actresses. His next change of life presented him in North Britain as a journalist, employed on a Scotch newspaper. An unfortunate love affair was the means of depriving him of this new occupation. He was recognised, soon afterwards, serving as assistant steward in one of the passenger steamers voyaging between Liverpool and New York. Arrived in this last city, he obtained notoriety, of no very respectable kind, as a 'medium' claiming powers of supernatural communication with the world of spirits. When the imposture was ultimately discovered, he had gained money by his unworthy appeal to the meanly prosaic superstition of modern times. A long interval had then elapsed, and nothing had been heard of him, when a starving man was discovered by a traveller, lost on a Western prairie. The ill-fated Irish lord had associated himself with an Indian tribe—had committed some offence against their laws—and had been deliberately deserted and left to die. On his recovery, he wrote to his elder brother (who had inherited the title and estates on the death of the old Earl) to say that he was ashamed of the life that he had led, and eager to make amendment by accepting any honest employment that could be offered to him. The traveller who had saved his life, and whose opinion was to be trusted, declared that the letter represented a sincerely penitent state of mind. There were good qualities in the vagabond, which only wanted a little merciful encouragement to assert themselves. The reply that he received

from England came from the lawyers employed by the new Earl.
They had arranged with their agents in New York to pay to the
younger brother a legacy of a thousand pounds, which represented
all that had been left to him by his father's will. If he wrote again
his letters would not be answered; his brother had done with him.
Treated in this inhuman manner, the wild lord became once more
worthy of his name. He tried a new life as a betting man at races
and trotting-matches. Fortune favoured him at the outset, and he
considerably increased his legacy. With the customary infatuation
of men who gain money by risking the loss of it, he presumed on
his good luck. One pecuniary disaster followed another, and left
him literally penniless. He was found again, in England, exhibiting
an open boat in which he and a companion had made one of those
foolhardy voyages across the Atlantic, which have now happily
ceased to interest the public. To a friend who remonstrated with
him, he answered that he reckoned on being lost at sea, and on so
committing a suicide worthy of the desperate life that he had led.
The last accounts of him, after this, were too vague and too contradictory to be depended on. At one time it was reported that he had
returned to the United States. Not long afterwards unaccountable
paragraphs appeared in newspapers declaring, at one and the same
time, that he was living among bad company in Paris, and that he
was hiding disreputably in an ill famed quarter of the city of
Dublin, called 'The Liberties.' In any case there was good reason
to fear that Irish-American desperadoes had entangled the wild lord
in the network of political conspiracy.

The maid noticed a change in the mistress which surprised her,
when she had reached the end of the newspaper story. Of Miss
Henley's customary good spirits not a trace remained. 'Few
people, Rhoda, remember what they read as well as you do.' She
said it kindly and sadly—and she said no more.

There was a reason for this.

Now at one time, and now at another, Iris had heard of Lord
Harry's faults and failings in fragments of family history. The
complete record of his degraded life, presented in an uninterrupted
succession of events, had now forced itself on her attention for the
first time. It naturally shocked her. She felt, as she had never
felt before, how entirely right her father had been in insisting on her
resistance to an attachment which was unworthy of her. So far,
but no farther, her conscience yielded to its own conviction of what
was just. But the one unassailable vital force in this world is the
force of love. It may submit to the hard necessities of life; it may
acknowledge the imperative claims of duty; it may be silent under
reproach, and submissive to privation—but, suffer what it may, it
is the master-passion still; subject to no artificial influences, owning
no supremacy but the law of its own being. Iris was above the
reach of self-reproach, when her memory recalled the daring action
which had saved Lord Harry at the milestone. Her better sense

acknowledged Hugh Mountjoy's superiority over the other man—but her heart, her perverse heart, remained true to its first choice in spite of her. She made an impatient excuse and went out alone to recover her composure in the farm-house garden.

The hours of the evening passed slowly.

There was a pack of cards in the house; the women tried to amuse themselves, and failed. Anxiety about Arthur preyed on the spirits of Miss Henley and Mrs. Lewson. Even the maid, who had only seen him during his last visit to London, said she wished to-morrow had come and gone. His sweet temper, his handsome face, his lively talk had made Arthur a favourite everywhere. Mrs. Lewson had left her comfortable English home to be his house-keeper, when he tried his rash experiment of farming in Ireland. And, more wonderful still, even wearisome Sir Giles became an agreeable person in his nephew's company.

Iris set the example of retiring at an early hour to her room.

There was something terrible in the pastoral silence of the place. It associated itself mysteriously with her fears for Arthur; it suggested armed treachery on tiptoe, taking its murderous stand in hiding; the whistling passage of bullets through the air; the piercing cry of a man mortally wounded, and that man, perhaps——? Iris shrank from her own horrid thought. A momentary faintness overcame her; she opened the window. As she put her head out to breathe the cool night-air, a man on horseback rode up to the house. Was it Arthur? No : the light-coloured groom's livery that he wore was just visible.

Before he could dismount to knock at the door, a tall man walked up to him out of the darkness.

Is that Miles?' the tall man asked.

The groom knew the voice. Iris was even better acquainted with it. She, too, recognised Lord Harry.

X

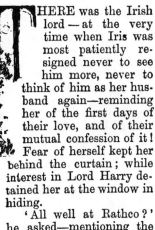

THERE was the Irish lord — at the very time when Iris was most patiently resigned never to see him more, never to think of him as her husband again—reminding her of the first days of their love, and of their mutual confession of it! Fear of herself kept her behind the curtain; while interest in Lord Harry detained her at the window in hiding.

'All well at Rathco?' he asked—mentioning the name of the house in which Arthur was one of the guests.

'Yes, my lord. Mr. Mountjoy leaves us to-morrow.'

'Does he mean to return to the farm?'

'Sorry I am to say it; he does mean that.'

'Has he fixed any time, Miles, for starting on his journey?'

Miles instituted a search through his pockets, and accompanied it by an explanation. Yes, indeed, Master Arthur had fixed a time; he had written a note to say so to Mistress Lewson, the house-keeper; he had said, 'Drop the note at the farm, on your way to the village.' And what might Miles want at the village, in the dark? Medicine, in a hurry, for one of his master's horses that was sick and sinking. And, speaking of that, here, thank God, was the note!

Iris, listening and watching alternately, saw to her surprise the note intended for Mrs. Lewson handed to Lord Harry. 'Am I expected,' he asked jocosely, 'to read writing without a light?' Miles produced a small lantern which was strapped to his groom's belt. 'There's parts of the road not over safe in the dark,' he said as he raised the shade which guarded the light. The wild lord coolly opened the letter, and read the few careless words which it contained. ' To Mrs. Lewson:—Dear old girl, expect me back to-morrow to dinner at three o'clock. Yours, ARTHUR.'

There was a pause.

' Are there any strangers at Rathco ? ' Lord Harry asked.

' Two new men,' Miles replied, ' at work in the grounds.'

There was another pause. ' How can I protect him ? ' the young lord said, partly to himself, partly to Miles. He suspected the two new men—spies probably who knew of Arthur's proposed journey home, and who had already reported to their employers the hour at which he would set out.

Miles ventured to say a word : ' I hope you won't be angry with me, my lord'——

' Stuff and nonsense ! Was I ever angry with you, when I was rich enough to keep a servant, and when you were the man ? '

The Irish groom answered in a voice that trembled with strong feeling. ' You were the best and kindest master that ever lived on this earth. I can't see you putting your precious life in peril'——

' My precious life ? ' Lord Harry repeated lightly. ' You're thinking of Mr. Mountjoy, when you say that. *His* life is worth saving. As for my life'—— He ended the sentence by a whistle, as the best way he could hit on of expressing his contempt for his own existence.

' My lord ! my lord ! ' Miles persisted ; ' the Invincibles are beginning to doubt you. If any of them find you hanging about Mr. Mountjoy's farm, they'll try a shot at you first, and ask afterwards whether it was right to kill you or not.'

To hear this said—and said seriously—after the saving of him at the milestone, was a trial of her firmness which Iris was unable to resist. Love got the better of prudence. She drew back the window-curtain. In another moment, she would have added her persuasion to the servant's warning, if Lord Harry himself had not accidentally checked her by a proceeding, on his part, for which she was not prepared.

' Show the light,' he said ; ' I'll write a line to Mr. Mountjoy.'

He tore off the blank page from the note to the housekeeper, and wrote to Arthur, entreating him to change the time of his departure from Rathco, and to tell no creature in the house, or out of the house, at what new hour he had arranged to go. ' Saddle your horse yourself,' the letter concluded. It was written in a feigned hand, without a signature.

' Give that to Mr. Mountjoy,' Lord Harry said. ' If he asks who wrote it, don't frighten him about me by telling the truth. Lie, Miles ! Say you don't know.' He next returned the note for Mrs. Lewson. ' If she notices that it has been opened,' he resumed, ' and asks who has done it, lie again. Good-night, Miles —and mind those dangerous places on your road home.'

The groom darkened his lantern; and the wild lord was lost to view, round the side of the house.

Left by himself, Miles rapped at the door with the handle of his whip. 'A letter from Mr. Arthur,' he called out. Mrs. Lewson at once took the note, and examined it by the light of the candle on the hall-table. 'Somebody has been reading this!' she exclaimed, stepping out to the groom, and showing him the torn envelope. Miles, promptly obeying his instructions, declared that he knew nothing about it, and rode away.

Iris descended the stairs, and joined Mrs. Lewson in the hall before she had closed the door. The housekeeper at once produced Arthur's letter.

'It's on my mind, Miss,' she said, 'to write an answer, and say something to Mr. Arthur which will persuade him to take care of himself, on his way back to the farm. The difficulty is, how am I to express it? You would be doing a kind thing if you would give me a word of advice.'

Iris willingly complied. A second note, from the anxious housekeeper, might help the effect of the few lines which Lord Harry had written.

Arthur's letter informed Iris that he had arranged to return at three o'clock. Lord Harry's question to the groom, and the man's reply, instantly recurred to her memory: 'Are there any strangers at Rathco?'—'Two new men at work in the grounds.' Arriving at the same conclusion which had already occurred to Lord Harry, Iris advised the housekeeper, in writing to Arthur, to entreat him to change the hour, secretly, at which he left his friend's house on the next day. Warmly approving of this idea, Mrs. Lewson hurried into the parlour to write her letter. 'Don't go to bed yet, Miss,' she said; 'I want you to read it before I send it away the first thing to-morrow morning.'

Left alone in the hall, with the door open before her, Iris looked out on the night, thinking.

The lives of the two men in whom she was interested—in widely different ways—were now both threatened; and the imminent danger, at that moment, was the danger of Lord Harry. He was an outlaw whose character would not bear investigation; but, to give him his due, there was no risk which he was not ready to confront for Arthur's sake. If he was still recklessly lingering, on the watch for assassins in the dangerous neighbourhood of the farm, who but herself possessed the influence which would prevail on him to leave the place? She had joined Mrs. Lewson at the door with that conviction in her mind. In another instant, she was out of the house, and beginning her search in the dark.

Iris made the round of the building; sometimes feeling her way in obscure places; sometimes calling to Lord Harry cautiously by his name. No living creature appeared; no sound of a movement disturbed the stillness of the night. The discovery of his absence, which she had not dared to hope for, was the cheering discovery which she had now made.

On her way back to the house, she became conscious of the rashness of the act into which her own generous impulse had betrayed her.

If she and Lord Harry had met, could she have denied the tender interest in him which her own conduct would then have revealed ?   Would he not have been justified in concluding that she had pardoned the errors and the vices of his life, and that he might without impropriety remind her of their engagement, and claim her hand in marriage ?   She trembled as she thought of the concessions which he might have wrung from her.   ' Never more,' she determined, ' shall my own folly be answerable for it, if he and I meet again.'

She had returned to Mrs. Lewson, and had read over the letter to Arthur, when the farm clock, striking the hour, reminded them that it was time to retire.   They slept badly that night.

At six in the morning, one of the two labourers who had remained faithful to Arthur was sent away on horseback with the housekeeper's reply, and with orders to wait for an answer.   Allowing time for giving the horse a rest, the man might be expected to return before noon.

XI

T was a fine sunshiny day; Mrs. Lewson's spirits began to improve. 'I have always held the belief,' the worthy old woman confessed, 'that bright weather brings good luck—of course provided the day is not a Friday. This is Wednesday. Cheer up, Miss.'

The messenger returned with good news. Mr. Arthur had been as merry as usual. He had made fun of another letter of good advice, received without a signature. 'But Mrs. Lewson must have her way,' he said. 'My love to the old dear—I'll start two hours later, and be back to dinner at five.'

'Where did Mr. Arthur give you that message?' Iris inquired.

'At the stables, Miss, while I was putting up the horse. The men about were all on the broad grin when they heard Mr. Arthur's message.'

Still in a morbid state of mind, Iris silently regretted that the message had not been written, instead of being delivered by word of mouth. Here, again, she (like the wild lord) had been afraid of listeners.

The hours wore slowly on until it was past four o'clock. Iris could endure the suspense no longer. 'It's a lovely afternoon,' she said to Mrs. Lewson. 'Let us take a walk along the road, and meet Arthur.' To this proposal the housekeeper readily agreed.

It was nearly five o'clock when they reached a place at which a by-road branched off, through a wood, from the highway which they had hitherto followed. Mrs. Lewson found a seat on a felled tree. 'We had better not go any farther,' she said.

Iris asked if there was any reason for this.

There was an excellent reason. A few yards farther on, the high road had been diverted from the straight line (in the interest of a large agricultural village), and was then directed again into its former course. The by-road through the wood served as a short cut, for horsemen and pedestrians, from one divergent point to the other. It was next to a certainty that Arthur would return by the short cut. But if accident or caprice led to his preferring the high-way, it was clearly necessary to wait for him within view of both the roads.

Too restless to submit to a state of passive expectation, Iris proposed to follow the bridle path through the wood for a little way, and to return if she failed to see anything of Arthur. 'You are tired,' she said kindly to her companion: 'pray don't move.'

Mrs. Lewson looked needlessly uneasy: 'You might lose your-self, Miss. Mind you keep to the path!'

Iris followed the pleasant windings of the woodland track. In the hope of meeting Arthur she considerably extended the length of her walk. The white line of the high road, as it passed the farther end of the wood, showed itself through the trees. She turned at once to rejoin Mrs. Lewson.

On her way back she made a discovery. A ruin which she had not previously noticed showed itself among the trees on her left hand. Her curiosity was excited; she strayed aside to examine it more closely. The crumbling walls, as she approached them, looked like the remains of an ordinary dwelling-house. Age is essential to the picturesque effect of decay: a modern ruin is an unnatural and depressing object—and here the horrid thing was.

As she turned to retrace her steps to the road, a man walked out of the inner space enclosed by all that was left of the dismantled house. A cry of alarm escaped her. Was she the victim of destiny, or the sport of chance? There was the wild lord whom she had vowed never to see again: the master of her heart—perhaps the master of her fate!

Any other man would have been amazed to see her, and would have asked how it had happened that the English lady presented herself to him in an Irish wood. This man enjoyed the delight of seeing her, and accepted it as a blessing that was not to be ques-tioned. 'My angel has dropped from Heaven,' he said. 'May Heaven be praised!'

He approached her; his arms closed round her. She struggled to free herself from his embrace. At that moment they both heard the crackle of breaking underwood among the trees behind them. Lord Harry looked round. 'This is a dangerous place,' he whispered; 'I'm waiting to see Arthur pass safely. Submit to be kissed, or I am a dead man.' His eyes told her that he was truly and fearfully in earnest. Her head sank on his bosom. As he bent down and kissed her, three men approached from their hiding-place among the trees. They had no doubt been watching him, under orders from the murderous brotherhood to which they belonged. Their pistols were ready in their hands—and what discovery had they made? There was the brother who had been denounced as having betrayed them, guilty of no worse treason than meeting his sweet-heart in a wood! 'We beg your pardon, my lord,' they cried, with a thoroughly Irish enjoyment of their own discomfiture—and burst into a roar of laughter—and left the lovers together. For the second time, Iris had saved Lord Harry at a crisis in his life.

'Let me go!' she pleaded faintly, trembling with superstitious fear for the first time in her experience of herself.

He held her to him as if he would never let her go again. 'Oh, my Sweet, give me a last chance. Help me to be a better man! You have only to will it, Iris, and to make me worthy of you.'

His arms suddenly trembled round her, and dropped. The

She drew out a silver travelling-flask.   One glance at the name engraved on it told him the terrible truth.

silence was broken by a distant sound, like the report of a shot. He looked towards the farther end of the wood. In a minute more, the thump of a horse's hoofs at a gallop was audible, where the bridle-path was hidden among the trees. It came nearer—nearer—the creature burst into view, wild with fright, and carrying an empty saddle. Lord Harry rushed into the path and seized the horse as it swerved at the sight of him. There was a leather pocket attached to the front of the saddle. 'Search it!' he cried to Iris, forcing the terrified animal back on its haunches. She drew out a silver travelling-flask. One glance at the name engraved on it told him the terrible truth. His trembling hands lost their hold. The horse escaped; the words burst from his lips:

'Oh, God, they've killed him!'

THE END OF THE PROLOGUE

THE STORY

FIRST PERIOD

CHAPTER I

THE SOUR FRENCH WINE

HILE the line to be taken by the new railway between Culm and Everill was still under discussion, the engineer caused some difference of opinion among the moneyed men who were the first Directors of the Company, by asking if they proposed to include among their Stations the little old town of Honeybuzzard.

For years past, commerce had declined, and population had decreased in this ancient and curious place. Painters knew it well, and prized its mediæval houses as a mine of valuable material for their art. Persons of cultivated tastes, who were interested in church architecture of the fourteenth century, sometimes pleased and flattered the Rector by subscribing to his fund for the restoration of the tower, and the removal of the accumulated rubbish of hundreds of years from the crypt. Small speculators, not otherwise in a state of insanity, settled themselves in the town, and tried the desperate experiment of opening a shop ; spent their little capital, put up the shutters, and disappeared. The old market-place still showed its list of market-laws, issued by the Mayor and Corporation in the prosperous bygone times ; and every week there were fewer and fewer people to obey the laws. The great empty enclosure looked more cheerful, when there was no market held, and when the boys of the town played in the deserted place. In the last warehouse left in a state of repair, the crane was generally idle ; the windows were mostly shut up ; and a solitary man represented languishing trade, idling at a half-opened door. The muddy river rose and fell with the distant tide. At rare intervals a collier discharged its cargo on the mouldering quay, or an empty barge took in a load of hay. One bold house advertised, in a dirty window, apartments to let. There was a lawyer in the town, who had no occasion to keep a clerk ; and there was a doctor who hoped to sell his practice for anything that it would fetch. The directors of the new railway, after a stormy meeting, decided on offering (by means of a Station) a last chance of revival to the dying town. The town had not vitality enough left to be grateful; the railway stimulant produced no effect. Of all his colleagues in Great Britain and Ireland, the station-master at Honeybuzzard was the idlest man—and this, as he said to the unemployed porter, through no want of energy on his own part.

Late on a rainy autumn afternoon, the slow train left one traveller at the Station. He got out of a first-class carriage; he carried an umbrella and a travelling-bag; and he asked his way to the best inn. The station-master and the porter compared notes. One of them said: 'Evidently a gentleman.' The other added: 'What can he possibly want here?'

The stranger twice lost his way in the tortuous old streets of the town before he reached the inn. On giving his orders, it appeared that he wanted three things: a private room, something to eat, and, while the dinner was being cooked, materials for writing a letter.

Answering her daughter's questions downstairs, the landlady described her guest as a nice-looking man dressed in deep mourning. 'Young, my dear, with beautiful dark brown hair, and a grand beard, and a sweet sorrowful look. Ah, his eyes would tell anybody that his black clothes are not a mere sham. Whether married or single, of course I can't say. But I noticed the name on his travelling-bag. A distinguished name in my opinion—Hugh Mountjoy. I wonder what he'll order to drink when he has his dinner? What a mercy it will be if we can get rid of another bottle of the sour French wine!'

The bell in the private room rang at that moment; and the landlady's daughter, it is needless to say, took the opportunity of forming her own opinion of Mr. Hugh Mountjoy.

She returned with a letter in her hand, consumed by a vain longing for the advantages of gentle birth. 'Ah, mother, if I was a young lady of the higher classes, I know whose wife I should like to be!' Not particularly interested in sentimental aspirations, the landlady asked to see Mr. Mountjoy's letter. The messenger who delivered it was to wait for an answer. It was addressed to: 'Miss Henley, care of Clarence Vimpany, Esquire, Honeybuzzard.' Urged by an excited imagination, the daughter longed to see Miss Henley. The mother was at a loss to understand why Mr. Mountjoy should have troubled himself to write the letter at all. 'If he knows the young lady who is staying at the doctor's house,' she said, 'why doesn't he call on Miss Henley?' She handed the letter back to her daughter. 'There! let the ostler take it; he's got nothing to do.'

'No, mother. The ostler's dirty hands mustn't touch it—I'll take the letter myself. Perhaps I may see Miss Henley.' Such was the impression which Mr. Hugh Mountjoy had innocently produced on a sensitive young person, condemned by destiny to the barren sphere of action afforded by a country inn!

The landlady herself took the dinner upstairs—a first course of mutton chops and potatoes, cooked to a degree of imperfection only attained in an English kitchen. The sour French wine was still on the good woman's mind. ' What would you choose to drink, sir ? ' she asked. Mr. Mountjoy seemed to feel no interest in what he might have to drink. ' We have some French wine, sir.' ' Thank you, ma'am ; that will do.'

When the bell rang again, and the time came to produce the second course of cheese and celery, the landlady allowed the waiter to take her place. Her experience of the farmers who frequented the inn, and who had in some few cases been induced to taste the wine, warned her to anticipate an outbreak of just anger from Mr. Mountjoy. He, like the others, would probably ask what she ' meant by poisoning him with such stuff as that.' On the return of the waiter, she put the question : ' Did the gentleman complain of the French wine ? '

' He wants to see you about it, ma'am.'

The landlady turned pale. The expression of Mr. Mountjoy's indignation was evidently reserved for the mistress of the house. ' Did he swear,' she asked, ' when he tasted it ? '

' Lord bless you, ma'am, no ! Drank it out of a tumbler, and— if you will believe me—actually seemed to like it.'

The landlady recovered her colour. Gratitude to Providence for having sent a customer to the inn, who could drink sour wine with-out discovering it, was the uppermost feeling in her ample bosom as she entered the private room. Mr. Mountjoy justified her antici-pations. He was simple enough—with his tumbler before him, and the wine as it were under his nose—to begin with an apology.

' I am sorry to trouble you, ma'am. May I ask where you got this wine ? '

' The wine, sir, was one of my late husband's bad debts. It was all he could get from a Frenchman who owed him money.'

' It's worth money, ma'am.'

' Indeed, sir ? '

' Yes, indeed. This is some of the finest and purest claret that I have tasted for many a long day past.'

An alarming suspicion disturbed the serenity of the landlady's mind. Was this extraordinary opinion of the wine sincere ? Or was it Mr. Mountjoy's wicked design to entrap her into praising her claret and then to imply that she was a cheat by declaring what he really thought of it ? She took refuge in a cautious reply : ' You are the first gentleman, sir, who has not found fault with it.'

' In that case, perhaps you would like to get rid of the wine ? ' Mr. Mountjoy suggested.

The landlady was still cautious. ' Who will buy it of me, sir ? '

' I will. How much do you charge for it by the bottle ? '

It was, by this time, clear that he was not mischievous—only a little crazy. The worldly-wise hostess took advantage of that circumstance to double the price. Without hesitation, she said : ' Five shillings a bottle, sir.'

Often, too often, the irony of circumstances brings together, on this earthly scene, the opposite types of vice and virtue. A lying landlady and a guest incapable of deceit were looking at each other across a narrow table; equally unconscious of the immeasurable moral gulf that lay between them. Influenced by honourable feeling, innocent Hugh Mountjoy lashed the landlady's greed for money to the full-gallop of human cupidity.

'I don't think you are aware of the value of your wine,' he said. 'I have claret in my cellar which is not so good as this, and which costs more than you have asked. It is only fair to offer you seven-and-sixpence a bottle.'

When an eccentric traveller is asked to pay a price, and deliberately raises that price against himself, where is the sensible woman —especially if she happens to be a widow conducting an unprofitable business—who would hesitate to improve the opportunity? The greedy landlady raised her terms.

'On reflection, sir, I think I ought to have ten shillings a bottle, if you please.'

'The wine may be worth it,' Mountjoy answered quietly; 'but it is more than I can afford to pay. No, ma'am; I will leave you to find some lover of good claret with a longer purse than mine.'

It was in this man's character, when he said No, to mean No. Mr. Mountjoy's hostess perceived that her crazy customer was not to be trifled with. She lowered her terms again with the headlong hurry of terror. 'You shall have it, Sir, at your own price,' said this entirely shameless and perfectly respectable woman.

The bargain having been closed under these circumstances, the landlady's daughter knocked at the door. 'I took your letter myself, sir,' she said modestly; 'and here is the answer.' (She had seen Miss Henley, and did not think much of her.) Mountjoy offered the expression of his thanks, in words never to be forgotten by a sensitive young person, and opened his letter. It was short enough to be read in a moment; but it was evidently a favourable reply. He took his hat in a hurry, and asked to be shown the way to Mr. Vimpany's house.

CHAPTER II

THE MAN SHE REFUSED

MOUNTJOY had decided on travelling to Honey-buzzard, as soon as he heard that Miss Henley was staying with strangers in that town. Having had no earlier opportunity of preparing her to see him, he had considerately written to her from the inn, in preference to presenting himself unexpectedly at the doctor's house. How would she receive the devoted friend, whose proposal of marriage she had refused for the second time, when they had last met in London?

The doctor's place of residence, situated in a solitary by-street, commanded a view, not perhaps encouraging to a gentleman who followed the medical profession: it was a view of the churchyard The door was opened by a woman-servant, who looked suspiciously at the stranger.

Without waiting to be questioned, she said her master was out.

Mountjoy mentioned his name, and asked for Miss Henley.

The servant's manner altered at once for the better; she showed him into a small drawing-room, scantily and cheaply furnished. Some poorly-framed prints on the walls (a little out of place perhaps in a doctor's house) represented portraits of famous actresses, who had been queens of the stage in the early part of the present

Impulsively she drew his head down.

century. The few books, too, collected on a little shelf above the chimney-piece, were in every case specimens of dramatic literature. 'Who reads these plays?' Mountjoy asked himself. 'And how did Iris find her way into this house?'

While he was thinking of her, Miss Henley entered the room.

Her face was pale and careworn; tears dimmed her eyes when Mountjoy advanced to meet her. In his presence, the horror of his brother's death by assassination shook Iris as it had not shaken her yet. Impulsively, she drew his head down to her, with the fond familiarity of a sister, and kissed his forehead. 'Oh, Hugh, I know how you and Arthur loved each other! No words of mine can say how I feel for you.'

'No words are wanted, my dear,' he answered tenderly. '*Your* sympathy speaks for itself.'

He led her to the sofa and seated himself by her side. 'Your father has shown me what you have written to him,' he resumed; 'your letter from Dublin and your second letter from this place. I know what you have so nobly risked and suffered in poor Arthur's interests. It will be some consolation to me if I can make a return—a very poor return, Iris—for all that Arthur's brother owes to the truest friend that ever man had. No,' he continued, gently interrupting the expression of her gratitude. 'Your father has not sent me here—but he knows that I have left London for the express purpose of seeing you, and he knows why. You have written to him dutifully and affectionately; you have pleaded for pardon and reconciliation, when he is to blame. Shall I venture to tell you how he answered me, when I asked if he had no faith left in his own child? "Hugh," he said, "you are wasting words on a man whose mind is made up. I will trust my daughter when that Irish lord is laid in his grave—not before." That is a reflection on you, Iris, which I cannot permit, even when your father casts it. He is hard, he is unforgiving; but he must, and shall, be conquered yet. I mean to make him do you justice; I have come here with that purpose, and that purpose only, in view. May I speak to you of Lord Harry?'

'How can you doubt it!'

'My dear, this is a delicate subject for me to enter on.'

'And a shameful subject for me!' Iris broke out bitterly. 'Hugh! you are an angel, by comparison with that man—how debased I must be to love him—how unworthy of your good opinion! Ask me anything you like; have no mercy on me. Oh,' she cried, with reckless contempt for herself, 'why don't you beat me? I deserve it!'

Mountjoy was well enough acquainted with the natures of women to pass over that passionate outbreak, instead of fanning the flame in her by reasoning and remonstrance.

'Your father will not listen to the expression of feeling,' he continued; 'but it is possible to rouse his sense of justice by the expression of facts. Help me to speak to him more plainly of Lord Harry than you could speak in your letters. I want to know what has happened, from the time when events at Ardoon brought you and the young lord together again, to the time when you left him in Ireland after my brother's death. If I seem to expect too much of you, Iris, pray remember that I am speaking with a true regard for your interests.'

In those words, he made his generous appeal to her. She proved herself to be worthy of it.

Stated briefly, the retrospect began with the mysterious anonymous letters which had been addressed to Sir Giles.

Lord Harry's explanation had been offered to Iris gratefully, but with some reserve, after she had told him who the stranger at the milestone really was. 'I entreat you to pardon me, if I shrink from entering into particulars,' he had said. 'Circumstances, at the time, amply justified me in the attempt to use the banker's political influence as a means of securing Arthur's safety. I knew enough of Sir Giles's mean nature to be careful in trusting him; but I did hope to try what my personal influence might do. If he had possessed a tenth part of your courage, Arthur might have been alive, and safe in England, at this moment. I can't say any more; I daren't say any more; it maddens me when I think of it!' He abruptly changed the subject, and interested Iris by speaking of other and later events. His association with the Invincibles—inexcusably rash and wicked as he himself confessed it to be—had enabled him to penetrate, and for a time to defeat secretly, the murderous designs of the brotherhood. His appearances, first at the farmhouse and afterwards at the ruin in the wood were referable to changes in the plans of the assassins which had come to his knowledge. When Iris had met with him he was on the watch, believing that his friend would take the short way back through the wood, and well aware that his own life might pay the penalty if he succeeded in warning Arthur. After the terrible discovery of the murder (committed on the high road), and the escape of the miscreant who had been guilty of the crime, the parting of Lord Harry and Miss Henley had been the next event. She had left him, on her return to England, and had refused to consent to any of the future meetings between them which he besought her to grant.

At this stage in the narrative, Mountjoy felt compelled to ask questions more searching than he had put to Iris yet. It was possible that she might be trusting her own impressions of Lord Harry, with the ill-placed confidence of a woman innocently self-deceived.

'Did he submit willingly to your leaving him?' Mountjoy said.

'Not at first,' she replied.

'Has he released you from that rash engagement, of some years since, which pledged you to marry him ? '

'No.'

'Did he allude to the engagement, on this occasion ? '

'He said he held to it as the one hope of his life.'

'And what did you say ? '

'I implored him not to distress me.'

'Did you say nothing more positive than that ? '

'I couldn't help thinking, Hugh, of all that he had tried to do to save Arthur. But I insisted on leaving him—and I have left him.'

'Do you remember what he said at parting ? '

'He said, "While I live, I love you." '

As she repeated the words, there was an involuntary change to tenderness in her voice which was not lost on Mountjoy.

'I must be sure,' he said to her gravely, 'of what I tell your father when I go back to him. Can I declare, with a safe conscience, that you will never see Lord Harry again ? '

'My mind is made up never to see him again.' She had answered firmly so far. Her next words were spoken with hesitation, in tones that faltered. 'But I am sometimes afraid,' she said, 'that the decision may not rest with me.'

'What do you mean ? '

'I would rather not tell you.'

'That is a strange answer, Iris.'

'I value your good opinion, Hugh, and I am afraid of losing it.'

'Nothing has ever altered my opinion of you,' he replied, 'and nothing ever will.'

She looked at him anxiously, with the closest attention. Little by little, the expression of doubt in her face disappeared; she knew how he loved her—she resolved to trust him.

'My friend,' she began abruptly, 'education has done nothing for me. Since I left Ireland, I have sunk (I don't know how or why) into a state of superstitious fear. Yes ! I believe in a fatality which is leading me back to Lord Harry, in spite of myself. Twice already, since I left home, I have met with him ; and each time I have been the means of saving him—once at the milestone, and once at the ruin in the wood. If my father still accuses me of being in love with an adventurer, you can say with perfect truth that I am afraid of him. I *am* afraid of the third meeting. I have done my best to escape from that man ; and, step by step, as I think I am getting away, Destiny is taking me back to him. I may be on my way to him here, hidden in this wretched little town. Oh, don't despise me ! Don't be ashamed of me ! '

'My dear, I am interested—deeply interested in you. That there may be some such influence as Destiny in our poor mortal lives, I dare not deny. But I don't agree with your conclusion. What Destiny has to do with you and with me, neither you nor I can pretend to know beforehand. In the presence of that great mystery, humanity must submit to be ignorant. Wait, Iris—wait!'

She answered him with the simplicity of a docile child: 'I will do anything you tell me.'

Mountjoy was too fond of her to say more of Lord Harry, for that day. He was careful to lead the talk to a topic which might be trusted to provoke no agitating thoughts. Finding Iris to all appearance established in the doctor's house, he was naturally anxious to know something of the person who must have invited her—the doctor's wife.

CHAPTER III

THE REGISTERED PACKET

OUNTJOY began by alluding to the second of Miss Henley's letters to her father, and to a passage in it which mentioned Mrs. Vimpany with expressions of the sincerest gratitude.

'I should like to know more,' he said, 'of a lady whose hospitality at home seems to equal her kindness as a fellow-traveller. Did you first meet with her on the railway?'

'She travelled by the same train to Dublin, with me and my maid, but not in the same carriage,' Iris answered; 'I was so fortunate as to meet with her on the voyage from Dublin to Holyhead. We had a rough crossing; and Rhoda suffered so dreadfully from sea-sickness that she frightened me. The stewardess was attending to ladies who were calling for her in all directions; I really don't know what misfortune might not have happened, if Mrs. Vimpany had not come forward in the kindest manner, and offered help. She knew so wonderfully well what was to be done, that she astonished me. "I am the wife of a doctor," she said; "and I am only imitating what I have seen my husband do, when his assistance has been required, at sea, in weather like this." In her poor state of health, Rhoda was too much exhausted to go on by the train, when we got to Holyhead. She is the best of good girls, and I am fond of her, as you know. If I had been by myself, I daresay I should have sent for medical help. What do you think dear Mrs. Vimpany offered to do? "Your maid is only faint," she said. "Give her rest and some iced wine, and she will be well enough to go on by the slow train. Don't be frightened about her; I will wait with you." And she did wait. Are there many strangers, Hugh, who are as unselfishly good to others as my chance-acquaintance in the steamboat?'

'Very few, I am afraid.'

Mountjoy made that reply with some little embarrassment; conscious of a doubt of Mrs. Vimpany's disinterested kindness, which seemed to be unworthy of a just man.

Iris went on.

'Rhoda was sufficiently recovered,' she said, 'to travel by the next train, and there seemed to be no reason for feeling any more anxiety. But, after a time, the fatigue of the journey proved to be too much for her. The poor girl turned pale—and fainted. Mrs.

Vimpany revived her, but as it turned out, only for a while. She fell into another fainting fit; and my travelling-companion began to look anxious. There was some difficulty in restoring Rhoda to her senses. In dread of another attack, I determined to stop at the next station. It looked such a poor place, when we got to it, that I hesitated. Mrs. Vimpany persuaded me to go on. The next station, she said, was *her* station. "Stop there," she suggested, "and let my husband look at the girl. I ought not perhaps to say it, but you will find no better medical man out of London." I took the good creature's advice gratefully. What else could I do?'

'What would you have done,' Mountjoy inquired, 'if Rhoda had been strong enough to get to the end of the journey?'

'I should have gone on to London, and taken refuge in a lodging—you were in town, as I believed, and my father might relent in time. As it was, I felt my lonely position keenly. To meet with kind people, like Mr. Vimpany and his wife, was a real blessing to such a friendless creature as I am—to say nothing of the advantage to Rhoda, who is getting better every day. I should like you to see Mrs. Vimpany, if she is at home. She is a little formal and old fashioned in her manner—but I am sure you will be pleased with her. Ah! you look round the room! They are poor, miserably poor for persons in their position, these worthy friends of mine. I have had the greatest difficulty in persuading them to let me contribute my share towards the household expenses. They only yielded when I threatened to go to the inn. You are looking very serious, Hugh. Is it possible that you see some objection to my staying in this house?'

The drawing-room door was softly opened, at the moment when Iris put that question. A lady appeared on the threshold. Seeing the stranger, she turned to Iris.

'I didn't know, dear Miss Henley, that you had a visitor. Pray pardon my intrusion.'

The voice was deep; the articulation was clear; the smile presented a certain modest dignity which gave it a value of its own. This was a woman who could make such a commonplace thing as an apology worth listening to. Iris stopped her as she was about to leave the room. 'I was just wishing for you,' she said. 'Let me introduce my old friend, Mr. Mountjoy. Hugh, this is the lady who has been so kind to me—Mrs. Vimpany.'

Hugh's impulse, under the circumstances, was to dispense with the formality of a bow, and to shake hands. Mrs. Vimpany met this friendly advance with a suavity of action, not often seen in these days of movement without ceremony. She was a tall slim woman, of a certain age. Art had so cleverly improved her complexion that it almost looked like nature. Her cheeks had lost the plumpness of youth, but her hair (thanks again perhaps to Art) showed no signs of turning grey. The expression of her large dark eyes—placed perhaps a little too near her high aquiline nose—

claimed admiration from any person who was so fortunate as to come within their range of view. Her hands, long, yellow, and pitiably thin, were used with a grace which checked to some extent their cruel betrayal of her age. Her dress had seen better days, but it was worn with an air which forbade it to look actually shabby. The faded lace that encircled her neck fell in scanty folds over her bosom. She sank into a chair by Hugh's side. ' It was a great pleasure to me, Mr. Mountjoy, to offer my poor services to Miss Henley; I can't tell you how happy her presence makes me in our little house.' The compliment was addressed to Iris with every advantage that smiles and tones could offer. Oddly artificial as it undoubtedly was, Mrs. Vimpany's manner produced nevertheless an agreeable impression. Disposed to doubt her at first, Mountjoy found that she was winning her way to a favourable change in his opinion. She so far interested him, that he began to wonder what her early life might have been, when she was young and handsome. He looked again at the portraits of actresses on the walls, and the plays on the bookshelf—and then (when she was speaking to Iris) he stole a sly glance at the doctor's wife. Was it possible that this remarkable woman had once been an actress ? He attempted to put the value of that guess to the test by means of a complimentary allusion to the prints.

' My memory as a playgoer doesn't extend over many years,' he began; ' but I can appreciate the historical interest of your beautiful prints.' Mrs. Vimpany bowed gracefully—and dumbly. Mountjoy tried again. ' One doesn't often see the famous actresses of past days,' he proceeded, ' so well represented on the walls of an English house.'

This time, he had spoken to better purpose. Mrs. Vimpany answered him in words.

' I have many pleasant associations with the theatre,' she said, ' first formed in the time of my girlhood.'

Mountjoy waited to hear something more. Nothing more was said. Perhaps this reticent lady disliked looking back through a long interval of years, or perhaps she had her reasons for leaving Mountjoy's guess at the truth still lost in doubt. In either case, she deliberately dropped the subject. Iris took it up. Sitting by the only table in the room, she was in a position which placed her exactly opposite to one of the prints—the magnificent portrait of Mrs. Siddons as The Tragic Muse.

' I wonder if Mrs. Siddons was really as beautiful as that ? ' she said, pointing to the print. ' Sir Joshua Reynolds is reported to have sometimes flattered his sitters.'

Mrs. Vimpany's solemn self-possessed eyes suddenly brightened; the name of the great actress seemed to interest her. On the point, apparently, of speaking, she dropped the subject of Mrs. Siddons as she had dropped the subject of the theatre. Mountjoy was left to answer Iris.

' We are none of us old enough,' he reminded her, ' to decide whether Sir Joshua's brush has been guilty of flattery or not.' He turned to Mrs. Vimpany, and attempted to look into her life from a new point of view. 'When Miss Henley was so fortunate as to make your acquaintance,' he said, ' you were travelling in Ireland. Was it your first visit to that unhappy country ? '

' I have been more than once in Ireland.'

Having again deliberately disappointed Mountjoy, she was assisted in keeping clear of the subject of Ireland by a fortunate interruption. It was the hour of delivery by the afternoon-post. The servant came in with a small sealed packet, and a slip of printed paper in her hand.

' It's registered, ma'am,' the woman announced. ' The postman says you are to please sign this. And he seems to be in a hurry.'

She placed the packet and the slip of paper on the table, near the inkstand. Having signed the receipt, Mrs. Vimpany took up the packet, and examined the address. She instantly looked at Iris, and looked away again. ' Will you excuse me for a moment ? ' saying this she left the room, without opening the packet.

The moment the door closed on her, Iris started up, and hurried to Mountjoy.

'Oh, Hugh,' she said, ' I saw the address on that packet when the servant put it on the table ! '

' My dear, what is there to excite you in the address ? '

' Don't speak so loud ! She may be listening outside the door.'

' Not only the words, but the tone in which they were spoken, amazed Mountjoy. ' Your friend, Mrs. Vimpany ! ' he exclaimed.

' Mrs. Vimpany was afraid to open the packet in our presence,' Iris went on : ' you must have seen that. The handwriting is familiar to me ; I am certain of the person who wrote the address.'

' Well ? And who is the person ? '

She whispered in his ear :

' Lord Harry.'

CHAPTER IV

THE GAME : MOUNTJOY LOSES

SURPRISE silenced Hugh for the moment. Iris understood the look that he fixed on her, and answered it. ' I am quite sure,' she told him, ' of what I say.'

Mountjoy's well-balanced mind hesitated at rushing to a conclusion.

' I am sure you are con-vinced of what you tell me,' he said. ' But mistakes do sometimes happen in form-ing a judgment of hand-writing.

In the state of excite-ment that now possessed her, Iris was easily irritated ; she was angry with Hugh for only supposing that she might have made a mistake. He had himself, as she re-minded him, seen Lord Harry's handwriting in past days. Was it possible to be mistaken in those bold thickly-written characters, with some of the letters so quaintly formed ? 'Oh, Hugh,' I am miserable enough as it is,' she broke out; ' don't distract me by disputing what I know ! Think of a woman so kind, so disinterested, so charming—the very opposite of a false creature —think of Mrs. Vimpany having deceived me !'

There was not the slightest reason, thus far, for placing that interpretation on what had happened. Mountjoy gently, very gently, remonstrated.

' My dear, we really don't know yet that Mrs. Vimpany has been acting under Lord Harry's instructions. Wait a little before you suspect your fellow-traveller of offering her services for the purpose of deceiving you.'

Iris was angry with him again : ' Why did Mrs. Vimpany never tell me she knew Lord Harry ? Isn't that suspicious ? '

Mountjoy smiled. ' Let me put a question on my side,' he said. ' Did *you* tell Mrs. Vimpany you knew Lord Harry ? ' Iris made no reply ; her face spoke for her. ' Well, then,' he urged, ' is *your* silence suspicious ? I am far, mind, from saying that this may not be a very unpleasant discovery. Only let us be sure first that we are right.'

With most of a woman's merits, Miss Henley had many of a woman's faults. Still holding to her own conclusion, she asked how they could expect to be sure of anything if they addressed their inquiries to a person who had already deceived them.

Mountjoy's inexhaustible indulgence still made allowances for her. ' When Mrs. Vimpany comes back,' he said, ' I will find an opportunity of mentioning Lord Harry's name. If she tells us that she knows him, there will be good reason in that one circumstance, as it seems to me, for continuing to trust her.'

' Suppose she shams ignorance,' Iris persisted, ' and looks as if she had never heard of his name before ? '

' In that case, I shall own that I was wrong, and shall ask you to forgive me.'

The finer and better nature of Iris recovered its influence at these words. ' It is I who ought to beg pardon,' she said. ' Oh, I wish I could think before I speak : how insolent and ill-tempered I have been! But suppose I turn out to be right, Hugh, what will you do then ? '

' Then, my dear, it will be my duty to take you and your maid away from this house, and to tell your father what serious reasons there are '—— He abruptly checked himself. Mrs. Vimpany had returned ; she was in perfect possession of her lofty courtesy, sweetened by the modest dignity of her smile.

' I have left you, Miss Henley, in such good company,' she said, with a gracious inclination of her head in the direction of Mountjoy, ' that I need hardly repeat my apologies—unless, indeed, I am interrupting a confidential conversation.'

It was possible that Iris might have betrayed herself, when the doctor's wife had looked at her after examining the address on the packet. In this case Mrs. Vimpany's allusion to ' a confidential conversation ' would have operated as a warning to a person of experience in the by-ways of deceit. Mountjoy's utmost exertion of cunning was not capable of protecting him on such conditions as these. The opportunity of trying his proposed experiment with Lord Harry's name seemed to have presented itself already. He rashly seized on it.

' You have interrupted nothing that was confidential,' he hastened to assure Mrs. Vimpany. ' We have been speaking of a reckless young gentleman, who is an acquaintance of ours. If what I hear is true, he has already become public property; his adventures have found their way into some of the newspapers.'

Here, if Mrs. Vimpany had answered Hugh's expectations, she ought to have asked who the young gentleman was. She merely listened in polite silence.

With a woman's quickness of perception, Iris saw that Mountjoy had not only pounced on his opportunity prematurely, but had spoken with a downright directness of allusion which must at once have put such a ready-witted person as Mrs. Vimpany on her guard. In trying to prevent him from pursuing his unfortunate experiment in social diplomacy, Iris innocently repeated Mountjoy's own mistake. She, too, seized her opportunity prematurely. That is to say, she was rash enough to change the subject.

'You were talking just now, Hugh, of our friend's adventures,' she said; 'I am afraid you will find yourself involved in an adventure of no very agreeable kind, if you engage a bed at the inn. I never saw a more wretched-looking place.'

It was one of Mrs. Vimpany's many merits that she seldom neglected an opportunity of setting her friends at their ease.

'No, no, dear Miss Henley,' she hastened to say; 'the inn is really a more clean and comfortable place than you suppose. A hard bed and a scarcity of furniture are the worst evils which your friend has to fear. Do you know,' she continued, addressing herself to Mountjoy, 'that I was reminded of a friend of mine, when you spoke just now of the young gentleman whose adventures are in the newspapers. Is it possible that you referred to the brother of the present Earl of Norland? A handsome young Irishman—with whom I first became acquainted many years since. Am I right in supposing that you and Miss Henley know Lord Harry?' she asked.

What more than this could an unprejudiced mind require? Mrs. Vimpany had set herself right with a simplicity that defied suspicion. Iris looked at Mountjoy. He appeared to know when he was beaten. Having acknowledged that Lord Harry was the young gentleman of whom he and Miss Henley had been speaking, he rose to take leave.

After what had passed, Iris felt the necessity of speaking privately to Hugh. The necessary excuse presented itself in the remote situation of the inn. 'You will never find your way back,' she said, 'through the labyrinth of crooked streets in this old town. Wait for me a minute, and I will be your guide.'

Mrs. Vimpany protested. 'My dear! let the servant show the way.'

Iris held gaily to her resolution, and ran away to her room. Mrs. Vimpany yielded with her best grace. Miss Henley's motive could hardly have been plainer to her, if Miss Henley had confessed it herself. 'What a charming girl!' the doctor's amiable wife said to Mountjoy, when they were alone. 'If I were a man, Miss Iris is just the young lady that I should fall in love with.' She looked

significantly at Mountjoy. Nothing came of it. She went on:
'Miss Henley must have had many opportunities of being married;
but the right man has, I fear, not yet presented himself.' Once
more her eloquent eyes consulted Mountjoy, and once more nothing
came of it. Some women are easily discouraged. Impenetrable
Mrs. Vimpany was one of the other women; she had not done with
Mountjoy yet—she invited him to dinner on the next day.

'Our early hour is three o'clock,' she said modestly. 'Pray
join us. I hope to have the pleasure of introducing my husband.'

Mountjoy had his reasons for wishing to see the husband. As
he accepted the invitation, Miss Henley returned to accompany him
to the inn.

Iris put the inevitable question to Hugh as soon as they were out
of the doctor's house—'What do you say of Mrs. Vimpany now?'

'I say that she must have been once an actress,' Mountjoy
answered; 'and that she carries her experience of the stage into
private life.'

'What do you propose to do next?'

'I propose to wait, and see Mrs. Vimpany's husband to-morrow.'

'Why?'

'Mrs. Vimpany, my dear, is too clever for me. If—observe,
please, that I do her the justice of putting it in that way—if she is
really Lord Harry's creature, employed to keep watch on you, and
to inform him of your next place of residence in England, I own
that she has completely deceived me. In that case, it is just
possible that the husband is not such a finished and perfect humbug
as the wife. I may be able to see through *him*. I can but try.'

Iris sighed. 'I almost hope you may not succeed,' she said.

Mountjoy was puzzled, and made no attempt to conceal it. 'I
thought you only wanted to get at the truth,' he answered.

'My mind might be easier, perhaps, if I was left in doubt,' she
suggested. 'A perverse way of thinking has set up my poor opinion
against yours. But I am getting back to my better sense. I
believe you were entirely right when you tried to prevent me from
rushing to conclusions; it is more than likely that I have done Mrs.
Vimpany an injustice. Oh, Hugh, I ought to keep a friend—I who
have so few friends—when I have got one! And there is another
feeling in me which I must not conceal from you. When I remember Lord Harry's noble conduct in trying to save poor Arthur,
I cannot believe him capable of such hateful deceit as consenting
to our separation, and then having me secretly watched by a spy.
What monstrous inconsistency! Can anybody believe it? Can
anybody account for it?'

'I think I can account for it, Iris, if you will let me make the
attempt. You are mistaken to begin with.'

'How am I mistaken?'

'You shall see. There is no such creature as a perfectly consistent human being on the face of the earth—and, strange as it may
seem to you, the human beings themselves are not aware of it.

The reason for this curious state of things is not far to seek. How can people who are ignorant—as we see every day—of their own characters be capable of correctly estimating the characters of others ? Even the influence of their religion fails to open their eyes to the truth. In the Prayer which is the most precious possession of Christendom, their lips repeat the entreaty that they may not be led into temptation—but their minds fail to draw the inference. If that pathetic petition means anything, it means that virtuous men and women are capable of becoming vicious men and women, if a powerful temptation puts them to the test. Every Sunday, devout members of the congregation in church—models of excellence in their own estimation, and in the estimation of their neighbours—declare that they have done those things which they ought not to have done, and that there is no health in them. Will you believe that they are encouraged by their Prayer-books to present this sad exposure of the frailty of their own admirable characters ? How inconsistent—and yet how entirely true ! Lord Harry, as you rightly say, behaved nobly in trying to save my dear. lost brother. He ought, as you think, and as other people think, to be consistently noble, after that, in all his thoughts and actions, to the end of his life. Suppose that temptation does try him—such temptation, Iris, as you innocently present—why doesn't he offer a superhuman resistance ? You might as well ask, Why is he a mortal man ? How inconsistent, how improbable, that he should have tendencies to evil in him, as well as tendencies to good ! Ah, I see you don't like this. It would be infinitely more agreeable (wouldn't it ?) if Lord Harry was one of the entirely consistent characters which are sometimes presented in works of fiction. Our good English readers are charmed with the man, the woman, or the child, who is introduced to them by the kind novelist as a being without faults. Do they stop to consider whether this is a true picture of humanity ? It would be a terrible day for the book if they ever did that. But the book is in no danger. The readers would even fail to discover the falseness of the picture, if they were presented to themselves as perfect characters. " We mustn't say so, but how wonderfully like us ! " There would be the only impression produced. I am not trying to dishearten you; I want to encourage you to look at humanity from a wider and truer point of view. Do not be too readily depressed, if you find your faith shaken in a person whom you have hitherto believed to be good. That person has been led into temptation. Wait till time shows you that the evil influence is not everlasting, and that the good influence will inconsistently renew your faith out of the very depths of your despair. Humanity, in general, is neither perfectly good nor perfectly wicked : take it as you find it. Is this a hard lesson to learn ? Well ! it's easy to do what other people do, under similar circumstances. Listen to the unwelcome truth to-day, my dear ; and forget it to-morrow.'

They parted at the door of the inn.

CHAPTER V

THE GAME : MOUNTJOY PLAYS A NEW CARD

MR. VIMPANY (of the College of Surgeons) was a burly man, heavily built from head to foot. His bold round eyes looked straight at his fellow-creatures with an expression of impudent good humour; his whiskers were bushy, his hands were big, his lips were thick, his legs were solid. Add to this a broad sunburnt face, and a grey coat with wide tails, a waistcoat with a check pattern, and leather riding-gaiters—and no stranger could have failed to mistake Mr. Vimpany for a farmer of the old school. He was proud of the false impression that he created. ' Nature built me to be a farmer,' he used to say. ' But my poor foolish old mother was a lady by birth, and she insisted on her son being a professional man. I hadn't brains for the Law, or money for the Army, or morals for the Church. And here I am a country doctor—the one representative of slavery left in the nineteenth century. You may not believe me, but I never see a labourer at the plough that I don't envy him.'

This was the husband of the elegant lady with the elaborate manners. This was the man who received Mountjoy with a ' Glad to see you, sir,' and a shake of the hand that hurt him.

' Coarse fare,' said Mr. Vimpany, carving a big joint of beef; ' but I can't afford anything better. Only a pudding to follow, and a glass of glorious old sherry. Miss Henley is good enough to excuse it—and my wife's used to it—and you will put up with it, Mr. Mountjoy, if you are half as amiable as you look. I'm an old-fashioned man. The pleasure of a glass of wine with you, sir.'

Hugh's first experience of the ' glorious old sherry ' led him to a discovery, which proved to be more important than he was disposed to consider it at the moment. He merely observed, with some amusement, that Mr. Vimpany smacked his lips in hearty approval of the worst sherry that his guest had ever tasted. Here, plainly self-betrayed, was a medical man who was an exception to a general rule in the profession—here was a doctor ignorant of the difference between good wine and bad !

Both the ladies were anxious to know how Mountjoy had passed the night at the inn. He had only time to say that there was nothing to complain of, when Mr. Vimpany burst into an explosion of laughter.

' Oh, but you must have had something to complain of ! ' said the big doctor. ' I would bet a hundred, if I could afford it, that the landlady tried to poison you with her sour French wine.'

' Do you speak of the claret at the inn, after having tasted it ? ' Mountjoy asked.

' What do you take me for ? ' cried Mr. Vimpany. ' After all I have heard of that claret, I am not fool enough to try it myself, I can tell you.' Mountjoy received this answer in silence. The doctor's ignorance and the doctor's prejudice, in the matter of wine, had started a new train of thought in Hugh's mind, which threatened serious consequences to Mr. Vimpany himself. There was a pause at the table ; nobody spoke. The doctor saw condemnation of his rudeness expressed in his wife's face. He made a rough apology to Mountjoy, who was still preoccupied. ' No offence, I hope ? It's in the nature of me, sir, to speak my mind. If I could fawn and flatter, I should have got on better in my profession. I'm what they call a rough diamond. No, offence, I say ? '

' None whatever, Mr. Vimpany.'

' That's right ! Try another glass of sherry.'

Mountjoy took the sherry.

Iris looked at him, lost in surprise. It was unlike Hugh to be interested in a stranger's opinion of wine. It was unlike him to drink wine which was evidently not to his taste. And it was especially unlike his customary courtesy to let himself fall into thought at dinner-time, when there were other persons at the table. Was he ill ? Impossible to look at him, and not see that he was in perfect health. What did it mean ?

Finding Mountjoy inattentive, Mr. Vimpany addressed himself to Iris.

' I had to ride hard, Miss Henley, to get home in time for dinner. There are patients, I must tell you, who send for the doctor, and then seem to think they know more about it than the very man whom they have called in to cure them. It isn't he who tells them what their illness is ; it's they who tell him. They dispute about the medical treatment that's best for them, and the one thing they are never tired of doing is talking about their symptoms. It was an old man's gabble that kept me late to-day. However, the Squire, as they call him in these parts, is a patient with a long purse ; I am obliged to submit.'

' A gentleman of the old school, dear Miss Henley,' Mrs. Vimpany explained. ' Immensely rich. Is he better ? ' she asked, turning to her husband.

' Better ? ' cried the outspoken doctor. ' Pooh ! there's nothing the matter with him but gluttony. He went to London, and consulted a great man, a humbug with a handle to his name. The famous physician got rid of him in no time—sent him abroad to boil himself in foreign baths. He came home again worse than ever, and consulted poor Me. I found him at dinner—a perfect feast, I give you my word of honour !—and the old fool gorging himself till he was black in the face. His wine, I should have said, was not up to the mark; wanted body and flavour, you know. Ah, Mr. Mountjoy, this seems to interest you; reminds you of the landlady's wine—eh? Well, sir, how do you think I treated the Squire? Emptied his infirm old inside with an emetic—and there he was on his legs again? Whenever he overeats himself he sends for me; and pays liberally. I ought to be grateful to him, and I am. Upon my soul, I believe I should be in the bankruptcy court but for the Squire's stomach. Look at my wife! She's shocked at me. We ought to keep up appearances, my dear? Not I! When I am poor, I say I am poor. When I cure a patient, I make no mystery of it; everybody's welcome to know how it's done. Don't be down-hearted, Arabella; nature never meant your husband for a doctor, and there's the long and the short of it. Another glass of sherry, Mr. Mountjoy?'

All social ceremonies—including the curious English custom which sends the ladies upstairs, after dinner, and leaves the gentlemen at the table—found a devoted adherent in Mrs. Vimpany. She rose as if she had been presiding at a banquet, and led Miss Henley affectionately to the drawing-room. Iris glanced at Hugh. No; his mind was not at ease yet; the preoccupied look had not left his face.

Jovial Mr. Vimpany pushed the bottle across the table to his guest, and held out a handful of big black cigars.

'Now for the juice of the grape,' he cried, 'and the best cigar in all England!'

He had just filled his glass, and struck a light for his cigar, when the servant came in with a note. Some men relieve their sense of indignation in one way, and some in another. The doctor's form of relief was an oath. 'Talk about slavery!' he shouted. 'Find me such a slave in all Africa as a man in my profession. There isn't an hour of the day or night that he can call his own. Here's a stupid old woman with an asthma, who has got another spasmodic attack—and I must leave my dinner-table and my friend, just as we are enjoying ourselves. I have half a mind not to go.'

The inattentive guest suddenly set himself right in his host's estimation. Hugh remonstrated with an appearance of interest in the case, which the doctor interpreted as a compliment to himself: 'Oh, Mr. Vimpany, humanity! humanity!'

'Oh, Mr. Mountjoy, money! money!' the facetious doctor answered. 'The old lady is our Mayor's mother, sir. You don't seem to be quick at taking a joke. Make your mind easy; I shall pocket my fee.'

As soon as he had closed the door, Hugh Mountjoy uttered a devout ejaculation. 'Thank God!' he said—and walked up and down the room, free to think without interruption at last.

The subject of his meditations was the influence of intoxication in disclosing the hidden weaknesses and vices of a man's character by exhibiting them just as they are, released from the restraint which he exercises over himself when he is sober. That there was a weak side, and probably a vicious side, in Mr. Vimpany's nature it was hardly possible to doubt. His blustering good humour, his audacious self-conceit, the tones of his voice, the expression in his eyes, all revealed him (to use one expressive word) as a humbug. Let drink subtly deprive him of his capacity for self-concealment, and the true nature of his wife's association with Lord Harry might sooner or later show itself—say, in after-dinner talk, under skilful management. The right method of entrapping him into a state of intoxication (which might have presented serious difficulties under other circumstances) was suggested, partly by his ignorance of the difference between good wine and bad, and partly by Mountjoy's knowledge of the excellent quality of the landlady's claret. He had recognised, as soon as he tasted it, that finest vintage of Bordeaux, which conceals its true strength—to a gross and ignorant taste— under the exquisite delicacy of its flavour. Encourage Mr. Vimpany by means of a dinner at the inn, to give his opinion as a man whose judgment in claret was to be seriously consulted—and permit him also to discover that Hugh was rich enough to have been able to buy the wine—and the attainment of the end in view would be simply a question of time. There was certainly the chance to be reckoned with, that his thick head might prove to be too strong for the success of the experiment. Mountjoy determined to try it, and did try it nevertheless.

Mr. Vimpany returned from his medical errand, thoroughly well satisfied with himself.

' The Mayor's mother has reason to thank you, sir,' he announced. ' If you hadn't hurried me away, the wretched old creature would have been choked. A regular stand-up fight, by Jupiter, between death and the doctor!—and the doctor has won! Give me the reward of merit. Pass the bottle.'

He took up the decanter, and looked at it.

' Why, what have you been about ? ' he asked. ' I made up my mind that I should want the key of the cellar when I came back, and I don't believe you have drunk a drop in my absence. What does it mean ? '

' It means that I am not worthy of your sherry,' Mountjoy answered. ' The Spanish wines are too strong for my weak diges-tion.'

Mr. Vimpany burst into one of his explosions of laughter. ' You miss the landlady's vinegar—eh ? '

' Yes, I do ! Wait a minute, doctor ; I have a word to say on my side—and, like you, I mean what I say. The landlady's vinegar is some of the finest Château Margaux I have ever met with— thrown away on ignorant people who are quite unworthy of it.'

The doctor's natural insolence showed itself. ' You have bought this wonderful wine, of course ? ' he said satirically.

' That,' Mountjoy answered, ' is just what I have done.'

For once in his life, Mr. Vimpany's self-sufficient readiness of speech failed him. He stared at his guest in dumb amazement.

On this occasion, Mountjoy improved the opportunity to good pur pose. Mr. Vimpany accepted with the utmost readiness an invita- tion to dine on the next day at the inn. But he made a condition. 'In case I don't agree with you about that Château—what-you- call-it,' he said, 'you won't mind my sending home for a bottle of sherry ? '

The next event of the day was a visit to the most interesting monument of antiquity in the town. In the absence of the doctor, caused by professional engagements, Miss Henley took Mountjoy to see the old church—and Mrs. Vimpany accompanied them, as a mark of respect to Miss Henley's friend.

When there was a chance of being able to speak confidentially, Iris was eager in praising the doctor's wife. ' You can't imagine, Hugh, how agreeable she has been, and how entirely she has con· vinced me that I was wrong, shamefully wrong, in thinking of her as I did. She sees that you dislike her, and yet she speaks so nicely of you. "Your clever friend enjoys your society," she said; "pray accompany me when I take him to see the church." How unselfish ! '

Mountjoy kept his own counsel. The generous impulses which sometimes led Iris astray were, as he well knew, beyond the reach of remonstrance. His own opinion of Mrs. Vimpany still pro- nounced steadily against her. Prepared for discoveries, on the next day, which might prove too serious to be trifled with, he now did his best to provide for future emergencies.

After first satisfying himself that there was nothing in the pre- sent state of the maid's health which need detain her mistress at Honeybuzzard, he next completed his preparations by returning to the inn, and writing to Mr. Henley. With strict regard to truth, his letter presented the daughter's claim on the father under a new point of view. Whatever the end of it might be, Mr. Henley was requested to communicate his intentions by telegraph. Will you receive Iris ? was the question submitted. The answer expected was : Yes or No.

CHAPTER VI

THE GAME: MOUNTJOY WINS

R. HENLEY'S telegram arrived at the inn the next morning.

He was willing to receive his daughter, but not unreservedly. The message was characteristic of the man: 'Yes—on trial.' Mountjoy was not shocked, was not even surprised. He knew that the successful speculations, by means of which Mr. Henley had accumulated his wealth, had raised against him enemies, who had spread scandalous reports which had never been completely refuted. The silent secession of friends, in whose fidelity he trusted, had hardened the man's heart and embittered his nature. Strangers in distress, who appealed to the rich retired merchant for help, found in their excellent references to character the worst form of persuasion that they could have adopted. Paupers without a rag of reputation left to cover them, were the objects of charity whom Mr. Henley relieved. When he was asked to justify his conduct, he said: 'I have a sympathy with bad characters—I am one of them myself.'

With the arrival of the dinner hour the doctor appeared, in no very amiable humour, at the inn.

'Another hard day's work,' he said; 'I should sink under it, if I hadn't a prospect of getting rid of my practice here. London— or the neighbourhood of London—there's the right place for a man like Me. Well? Where's the wonderful wine? Mind! I'm Tom-Tell-Truth; if I don't like your French tipple, I shall say so.'

The inn possessed no claret glasses; they drank the grand wine in tumblers as if it had been vin ordinaire.

Mr. Vimpany showed that he was acquainted with the formalities proper to the ceremony of tasting. He filled his makeshift glass, he held it up to the light, and looked at the wine severely; he moved the tumbler to and fro under his nose, and smelt at it again and again; he paused and reflected; he tasted the claret as cautiously as if he feared it might be poisoned; he smacked his lips, and emptied his glass at a draught; lastly, he showed some consideration for his host's anxiety, and pronounced sentence on the wine.

'Not so good as you think it, sir. But nice light claret; clean and wholesome. I hope you haven't given too much for it?'

Thus far, Hugh had played a losing game patiently. His

reward had come at last. After what the doctor had just said to him, he saw the winning card safe in his own hand.

The bad dinner was soon over. No soup, of course; fish, in the state of preservation usually presented by a decayed country town ; steak that rivalled the toughness of india-rubber; potatoes whose aspect said, ' Stranger, don't eat us '; pudding that would have produced a sense of discouragement, even in the mind of a child ; and the famous English cheese which comes to us, oddly enough, from the United States, and stings us vindictively when we put it into our mouths. But the wine, the glorious wine, would have made amends to anybody but Mr. Vimpany for the woeful deficien-cies of the food. Tumbler-full after tumbler-full of that noble vin-tage poured down his thirsty and ignorant throat; and still he persisted in declaring that it was nice light stuff, and still he unfor-givingly bore in mind the badness of the dinner.

' The feeding here,' said this candid man, ' is worse if possible than the feeding at sea, when I served as doctor on board a passenger-steamer. Shall I tell you how I lost my place ? Oh, say so plainly, if you don't think my little anecdote worth listening to ! '

' My dear sir, I am waiting to hear it.'

' Very good. No offence, I hope ? That's right ! Well, sir, the captain of the ship complained of me to the owners; I wouldn't go round, every morning, and knock at the ladies' cabin-doors, and ask how they felt after a sea-sick night. Who doesn't know what they feel, without knocking at their doors ? Let them send for the doctor when they want him. That was how I understood my duty; and there was the line of conduct that lost me my place. Pass the wine. Talking of ladies, what do you think of my wife ? Did you ever see such distinguished manners before ? My dear fellow, I have taken a fancy to you. Shake hands. I'll tell you another little anecdote. Where do you think my wife picked up her fashionable airs and graces ? Ho ! ho ! On the stage ! The highest branch of the profession, sir—a tragic actress. If you had seen her in Lady Macbeth, Mrs. Vimpany would have made your flesh creep. Look at me, and feast your eyes on a man who is above hypocritical objections to the theatre. Haven't I proved it by marrying an actress ? But we don't mention it here. The savages in this beastly place wouldn't employ me, if they knew I had married a stage-player. Hullo ! The bottle's empty again. Ha ! here's another bottle, full. I love a man who has always got a full bottle to offer his friend. Shake hands. I say, Mountjoy, tell me on your sacred word of honour, can you keep a secret ? My wife's secret, sir ! Stop ! let me look at you again. I thought I saw you smile. If a man smiles at me, when I am opening my whole heart to him, by the living jingo, I would knock that man down at his own table ! What ? you didn't smile ? I apologise. Your hand again; I drink your health in your own good wine. Where was I ? What was I talking about ? '

Mountjoy carefully humoured his interesting guest.

'You were about to honour me,' he said, ' by taking me into your confidence.' Mr. Vimpany stared in tipsy bewilderment. Mountjoy tried again in plainer language : ' You were going to tell me a secret.'

This time, the doctor grasped the idea. He looked round cunningly to the door. 'Any eavesdroppers ? ' he asked. 'Hush ! Whisper—this is serious—whisper ! What was it I was going to tell you ? What was the secret, old boy ? '

Mountjoy answered a little too readily : 'I think it related to Mrs. Vimpany.'

Mrs. Vimpany's husband threw himself back in his chair, snatched a dirty handkerchief out of his pocket, and began to cry.

'Here's a false friend ! ' the creature whimpered. ' Asks me to dinner, and takes advantage of my dependent situation to insult my wife. The loveliest of women, the sweetest of women, the innocentest of women. Oh, my wife ! my wife ! ' He suddenly threw his handkerchief to the other end of the room, and burst out laughing. 'Ho ! ho ! Mountjoy, what an infernal fool you must be to take me seriously. I can act, too. Do you think I care about my wife ? She was a fine woman once : she's a bundle of old rags now. But she has her merits. Hush ! I want to know something. Have you got a lord among your circle of acquaintance ? '

Experience made Mountjoy more careful ; perhaps a little too careful. He only said ' Yes.'

The doctor's dignity asserted itself. ' That's a short answer, sir, to a man in my position. If you want me to believe you, mention your friend's name.'

Here was a chance at last ! ' His name,' Mountjoy began, ' is Lord Harry——'

Mr. Vimpany lost his dignity in an instant. He struck his heavy fist on the table, with a blow that made the tumblers jump.

' Coincidence ! ' he cried. ' How wonderful—no ; that's not the word—providential is the word—how providential are coincidences ! I mean, of course, to a rightly constituted mind. Let nobody contradict me ! When I say a rightly constituted mind, I speak seriously ; and a young man like you will be all the better for it. Mountjoy ! dear Mountjoy ! jolly Mountjoy ! my wife's lord is your lord—Lord Harry. No ; none of your nonsense—I won't have any more wine. Yes, I will ; it might hurt your feelings if I didn't drink with you. Pass the bottle. Ha ! That's a nice ring you've got on your finger. Perhaps you think it valuable ? It's nothing, sir ; it's dross, it's dirt, compared to my wife's diamond pin ! There's a jewel, if you like ! It will be worth a fortune to us when we sell it. A gift, dear sir ! I'm afraid I've been too familiar with you. Speaking as a born gentleman, I beg to present my respects, and I call you " dear sir." Did I tell you the diamond pin was a gift ? It's nothing of the sort ; we are under no obligation ; my wife, my admirable wife, has earned that diamond pin. By regis-

tered post; and what I call a manly letter from Lord Harry. He
is deeply obliged (I give you the sense of it) by what my wife has
done for him; ready money is scarce with my lord; he sends a
family jewel, with his love. Oh, I'm not jealous. He's welcome to
love Mrs. Vimpany, in her old age, if he likes. Did you say that,
sir? Did you say that Lord Harry, or any man, was welcome to
love Mrs. Vimpany? I have a great mind to throw this bottle at
your head. No, I won't; it's wasting good wine! How kind
of you to give me good wine. Who are you? I don't like dining
with a stranger. Do you know any friend of mine? Do you
know a man named Mountjoy? Do you know two men named
Mountjoy? No: you don't. One of them is dead: killed by
those murdering scoundrels — what do you call them? Eh,
what?' The doctor's voice began to falter, his head dropped; he
slumbered suddenly and woke suddenly, and began talking again
suddenly. 'Would you like to be made acquainted with Lord
Harry? I'll give you a sketch of his character before I introduce
him. Between ourselves, he's a desperate wretch. Do you know
why he employed my wife, my admirable wife? You will agree
with me; he ought to have looked after his young woman himself.
We've got his young woman safe in our house. A nice girl. Not
my style; my medical knowledge certifies she's cold-blooded.
Lord Harry has only to come over here and find her. Why the
devil doesn't he come? What is it keeps him in Ireland? Do you
know? I seem to have forgotten. My own belief is I've got
softening of the brain. What's good for softening of the brain?
There isn't a doctor living who won't tell you the right remedy—
wine. Pass the wine. If this claret is worth a farthing, it's worth
a guinea a bottle. I ask you in confidence; did you ever hear of
such a fool as my wife's lord? His name escapes me. No matter;
he stops in Ireland—hunting. Hunting what? The fox? Nothing
so noble; hunting assassins. He's got some grudge against one of
them. Means to kill one of them. A word in your ear; they'll
kill *him*. Do you ever bet? Five to one, he's a dead man before
the end of the week. When is the end of the week? Tuesday,
Wednesday—no, Saturday—that's the beginning of the week—no,
it isn't—the beginning of the week isn't the Sabbath—Sunday, of
course—we are not Christians, we are Jews—I mean we are Jews,
we are not Christians—I mean——'

The claret got the better of his tongue, at last. He mumbled
and muttered; he sank back in his chair; he chuckled; he hic-
cupped; he fell asleep.

All and more than all that Mountjoy feared, he had now discovered. In a state of sobriety, the doctor was probably one of
those men who are always ready to lie. In a state of intoxication
the utterances of his drunken delirium might unconsciously betray
the truth. The reason which he had given for Lord Harry's continued absence in Ireland, could not be wisely rejected as unworthy
of belief. It was in the reckless nature of the wild lord to put his

Own life in peril, in the hope of revenging Arthur Mountjoy on the wretch who had killed him. Taking this bad news for granted, was there any need to distress Iris by communicating the motive which detained Lord Harry in his own country ? Surely not !

And, again, was there any immediate advantage to be gained by revealing the true character of Mrs. Vimpany, as a spy, and, worse still, a spy who was paid ? In her present state of feeling, Iris would, in all probability, refuse to believe it.

Arriving at these conclusions, Hugh looked at the doctor snoring and choking in an easy-chair. He had not wasted the time and patience devoted to the stratagem which had now successfully reached its end. After what he had just heard—thanks to the claret—he could not hesitate to accomplish the speedy removal of Iris from Mr. Vimpany's house; using her father's telegram as the only means of persuasion on which it was possible to rely. Mountjoy left the inn without ceremony, and hurried away to Iris in the hope of inducing her to return to London with him that night.

CHAPTER VII

DOCTORING THE DOCTOR

ASKING for Miss Henley at the doctor's door, Hugh was informed that she had gone out, with her invalid maid, for a walk. She had left word, if Mr. Mountjoy called in her absence, to beg that he would kindly wait for her return.

On his way up to the drawing-room, Mountjoy heard Mrs. Vimpany's sonorous voice occupied, as he supposed, in reading aloud. The door being opened for him, he surprised her, striding up and down the room with a book in her hand; grandly declaiming without anybody to applaud her. After what Hugh had already heard, he could only conclude that reminiscences of her theatrical career had tempted the solitary actress to make a private appearance, for her own pleasure, in one of those tragic characters to which her husband had alluded. She recovered her self-possession on Mountjoy's appearance, with the ease of a mistress of her art. 'Pardon me,' she said, holding up her book with one hand, and tapping it indicatively with the other : 'Shakespeare carries me out of myself. A spark of the poet's fire burns in the poet's humble servant. May I hope that I have made myself understood? You look as if you had a fellow-feeling for me.'

Mountjoy did his best to fill the sympathetic part assigned to him, and only succeeded in showing what a bad actor he would have been, if he had gone on the stage. Under the sedative influence thus administered, Mrs. Vimpany put away her book, and descended at once from the highest poetry to the lowest prose.

'Let us return to domestic events,' she said indulgently. 'Have the people at the inn given you a good dinner ? '

'The people did their best,' Mountjoy answered cautiously.

'Has my husband returned with you?' Mrs. Vimpany went on.

Mountjoy began to regret that he had not waited for Iris in the street. He was obliged to acknowledge that the doctor had not returned with him.

'Where is Mr. Vimpany?'

'At the inn.'

'What is he doing there?'

Mountjoy hesitated. Mrs. Vimpany rose again into the regions of tragic poetry. She stepped up to him, as if he had been Macbeth, and she was ready to use the daggers. 'I understand but too well,' she declared in terrible tones. 'My wretched husband's vices are known to me. Mr. Vimpany is intoxicated.'

Hugh tried to make the best of it. 'Only asleep,' he said. Mrs. Vimpany looked at him once more. This time, it was Queen Katharine looking at Cardinal Wolsey. She bowed with lofty courtesy, and opened the door. 'I have occasion,' she said, 'to go out'——and made an exit.

Five minutes later, Mountjoy (standing at the window, impatiently on the watch for the return of Iris) saw Mrs. Vimpany in the street. She entered a chemist's shop, on the opposite side of the way, and came out again with a bottle in her hand. It was enclosed in the customary medical wrapping of white paper. Majestically, she passed out of sight. If Hugh had followed her he would have traced the doctor's wife to the door of the inn.

The unemployed waiter was on the house-steps, looking about him—with nothing to see. He made his bow to Mrs. Vimpany, and informed her that the landlady had gone out.

'You will do as well,' was the reply. 'Is Mr. Vimpany here?'

The waiter smiled, and led the way through the passage to the foot of the stairs. 'You can hear him, ma'am.' It was quite true; Mr. Vimpany's snoring answered for Mr. Vimpany. His wife ascended the first two or three stairs, and stopped to speak again to the waiter. She asked what the two gentlemen had taken to drink with their dinner. They had taken 'the French wine.'

'And nothing else?'

The waiter ventured on a little joke. 'Nothing else,' he said—'and more than enough of it, too.'

'Not more than enough, I suppose, for the good of the house,' Mrs. Vimpany remarked.

'I beg your pardon, ma'am; the claret the two gentlemen drank is not charged for in the bill.'

'What do you mean?'

The waiter explained that Mr. Mountjoy had purchased the whole stock of the wine. Suspicion, as well as surprise, appeared in Mrs. Vimpany's face. She had hitherto thought it likely that Miss Henley's gentlemanlike friend might be secretly in love with the young lady. Her doubts of him, now, took a wider range of distrust. She went on up the stairs by herself, and banged the door of the private room as the easiest means of waking the sleeping man. To the utmost noise that she could make in this way, he was perfectly impenetrable. For a while she waited, looking at him across the table with unutterable contempt.

There was the man to whom the religion of the land and the law of the land, acting together in perfect harmony, had fettered her for life! Some women, in her position, might have wasted time in useless self-reproach. Mrs. Vimpany reviewed her miserable married life with the finest mockery of her own misfortune. 'Virtue,' she said to herself, ' is its own reward.'

Glancing with careless curiosity at the disorder of the dinner-table, she noticed some wine still left in the bottom of her husband's glass. Had artificial means been used to reduce him to his present condition? She tasted the claret. No; there was nothing in the flavour of it which betrayed that he had been drugged. If the waiter was to be believed, he had only drunk claret—and there he was, in a state of helpless stupefaction, nevertheless.

She looked again at the dinner-table, and discovered one, among the many empty bottles, with some wine still left in it. After a moment of reflection, she took a clean tumbler from the sideboard.

Here was the wine which had been an object of derision to Mr. Vimpany and his friends. They were gross feeders and drinkers; and it might not be amiss to put their opinions to the test. She was not searching for the taste of a drug now; her present experiment proposed to try the wine on its own merits.

At the time of her triumphs on the country stage—before the date of her unlucky marriage—rich admirers had entertained the handsome actress at suppers, which offered every luxury that the most perfect table could supply. Experience had made her acquainted with the flavour of the finest claret—and that experience was renewed by the claret which she was now tasting. It was easy to understand why Mr. Mountjoy had purchased the wine; and, after a little thinking, his motive for inviting Mr. Vimpany to dinner seemed to be equally plain. Foiled in their first attempt at discovery by her own prudence and tact, his suspicions had set their trap. Her gross husband had been tempted to drink, and to talk at random (for Mr. Mountjoy's benefit) in a state of intoxication! What secrets might the helpless wretch not have betrayed before the wine had completely stupefied him?

Urged by rage and fear, she shook him furiously. He woke; he glared at her with bloodshot eyes; he threatened her with his clenched fist. There was but one way of lifting his purblind stupidity to the light. She appealed to his experience of himself, on many a former occasion: 'You fool, you have been drinking again—and there's a patient waiting for you.' To that dilemma he was accustomed; the statement of it partially roused him. Mrs. Vimpany tore off the paper wrapping, and opened the medicine-bottle which she had brought with her.

He stared at it; he muttered to himself: ' Is she going to poison me?' She seized his head with one hand, and held the open bottle to his nose. 'Your own prescription,' she cried, 'for yourself and your hateful friends.'

His nose told him what words might have tried vainly to say : he swallowed the mixture. 'If I lose the patient,' he muttered oracularly, 'I lose the money.' His resolute wife dragged him out of his chair. The second door in the dining-room led into an empty bed-chamber. With her help, he got into the room, and dropped on the bed.

Mrs. Vimpany consulted her watch.

On many a former occasion she had learnt what interval of repose was required, before the sobering influence of the mixture could successfully assert itself. For the present, she had only to return to the other room. The waiter presented himself, asking if there was anything he could do for her. Familiar with the defective side of her husband's character, he understood what it meant when she pointed to the bedroom door. 'The old story, ma'am,' he said, with an air of respectful sympathy. 'Can I get you a cup of tea?'

Mrs. Vimpany accepted the tea, and enjoyed it thoughtfully.

She had two objects in view—to be revenged on Mountjoy, and to find a way of forcing him to leave the town before he could communicate his discoveries to Iris. How to reach these separate ends, by one and the same means, was still the problem which she was trying to solve, when the doctor's coarse voice was audible, calling for somebody to come to him.

If his head was only clear enough, by this time, to understand the questions which she meant to put, his answers might suggest the idea of which she was in search. Rising with alacrity, Mrs. Vimpany returned to the bed-chamber.

'You miserable creature,' she began, 'are you sober now?'

'I'm as sober as you are.'

'Do you know,' she went on, 'why Mr. Mountjoy asked you to dine with him?'

'Because he's my friend.'

'He is your worst enemy. Hold your tongue! I'll explain what I mean directly. Rouse your memory, if you have got a memory left. I want to know what you and Mr. Mountjoy talked about after dinner.'

He stared at her helplessly. She tried to find her way to his recollection by making suggestive inquiries. It was useless; he only complained of being thirsty. His wife lost her self-control. She was too furiously angry with him to be able to remain in the room. Recovering her composure when she was alone, she sent for soda-water and brandy. Her one chance of making him useful was to humour his vile temper ; she waited on him herself.

In some degree, the drink cleared his muddled head. Mrs. Vimpany tried his memory once more. Had he said this? Had he said that? Yes: he thought it likely. Had he, or had Mr. Mountjoy, mentioned Lord Harry's name? A glimmer of intelligence showed itself in his stupid eyes. Yes—and they had quarrelled about it: he rather thought he had thrown a bottle at Mr. Mountjoy's head. Had they, either of them, said anything about Miss Henley? Oh, of course! What was it? He was unable to remember. Had his wife done bothering him, now?

'Not quite,' she replied. 'Try to understand what I am going to say to you. If Lord Harry comes to us while Miss Henley is in our house——'

He interrupted her: 'That's your business.'

'Wait a little. It's my business, if I hear beforehand that his lordship is coming. But he is quite reckless enough to take us by surprise. In that case, I want you to make yourself useful. If you happen to be at home, keep him from seeing Miss Henley until I have seen her first.'

'Why?'

'I want an opportunity, my dear, of telling Miss Henley that I have been wicked enough to deceive her, before she finds it out for herself. I may hope she will forgive me, if I confess everything.'

The doctor laughed: 'What the devil does it matter whether she forgives you or not?'

'It matters a great deal.'

'Why, you talk as if you were fond of her!'

'I am.'

The doctor's clouded intelligence was beginning to clear; he made a smart reply: 'Fond of her, and deceiving her—aha!'

'Yes,' she said quietly, 'that's just what it is. It has grown on me, little by little; I can't help liking Miss Henley.'

'Well,' Mr. Vimpany remarked, 'you *are* a fool!' He looked at her cunningly. 'Suppose I do make myself useful, what am I to gain by it?'

'Let us get back,' she suggested, 'to the gentleman who invited you to dinner, and made you tipsy for his own purposes.'

'I'll break every bone in his skin!'

'Don't talk nonsense! Leave Mr. Mountjoy to me.'

'Do *you* take his part? I can tell you this. If I drank too much of that poisonous French stuff, Mountjoy set me the example. He was tipsy—as you call it—shamefully tipsy, I give you my word of honour. What's the matter now?'

His wife (so impenetrably cool, thus far) had suddenly become excited. There was not the smallest fragment of truth in what he had just said of Hugh, and Mrs. Vimpany was not for a moment deceived by it. But the lie had, accidentally, one merit—it suggested to her the idea which she had vainly tried to find over her cup of tea. 'Suppose I show you how you may be revenged on Mr. Mountjoy,' she said.

'Well?'

'Will you remember what I asked you to do for me, if Lord Harry takes us by surprise?'

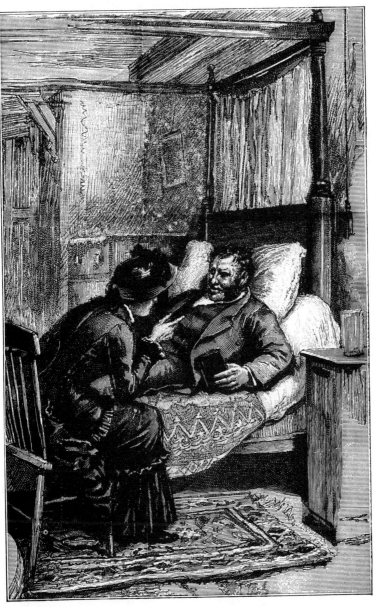

'Now,' she said, taking a chair by the bedside, 'you shall know what a clever wife you have got.'

He produced his pocket-diary, and told her to make a memorandum of it. She wrote as briefly as if she had been writing a telegram: 'Keep Lord Harry from seeing Miss Henley, till I have seen her first.'

'Now,' she said, taking a chair by the bedside, 'you shall know what a clever wife you have got. Listen to me.'

CHAPTER VIII

HER FATHER'S MESSAGE

LOOKING out of the drawing-room window, for the tenth time at least, Mountjoy at last saw Iris in the street, returning to the house.

She brought the maid with her into the drawing-room, in the gayest of good spirits, and presented Rhoda to Mountjoy.

'What a blessing a good long walk is, if we only knew it!' she exclaimed. 'Look at my little maid's colour! Who would suppose that she came here with heavy eyes and pale cheeks? Except that she loses her way in the town, whenever she goes out alone, we have every reason to congratulate ourselves on our residence at Honeybuzzard. The doctor is Rhoda's good genius, and the doctor's wife is her fairy godmother.'

Mountjoy's courtesy having offered the customary congratulations, the maid was permitted to retire; and Iris was free to express her astonishment at the friendly relations established (by means of the dinner-table) between the two most dissimilar men on the face of creation.

'There is something overwhelming,' she declared, 'in the bare idea of your having asked him to dine with you—on such a short acquaintance, and being such a man! I should like to have peeped in, and seen you entertaining your guest with the luxuries of the hotel larder. Seriously, Hugh, your social sympathies have taken a range for which I was not prepared. After the example that you have set me, I feel ashamed of having doubted whether Mr. Vimpany was worthy of his charming wife. Don't suppose that I am ungrateful to the doctor! He has found his way to my regard, after what he has done for Rhoda. I only fail to understand how he has possessed himself of *your* sympathies.'

So she ran on, enjoying the exercise of her own sense of humour in innocent ignorance of the serious interests which she was deriding.

Mountjoy tried to stop her, and tried in vain.

'No, no,' she persisted as mischievously as ever, 'the subject is too interesting to be dismissed. I am dying to know how you and your guest got through the dinner. Did he take more wine than was good for him? And, when he forgot his good manners, did he set it all right again by saying, "No offence," and passing the bottle?'

Hugh could endure it no longer. 'Pray control your high spirits for a moment,' he said. 'I have news for you from home.'

Those words put an end to her outbreak of gaiety, in an instant.

'News from my father?' she asked.

'Yes.'

'Is he coming here?'

'No; I have heard from him.'

'A letter?'

'A telegram,' Mountjoy explained, 'in answer to a letter from me. I did my best to press your claims on him, and I am glad to say I have not failed.'

'Hugh, dear Hugh! have you succeeded in reconciling us?'

Mountjoy produced the telegram. 'I asked Mr. Henley,' he said, 'to let me know at once whether he would receive you, and to answer plainly Yes or No. The message might have been more kindly expressed—but, at any rate, it is a favourable reply.'

Iris read the telegram. 'Is there another father in the world,' she said sadly, 'who would tell his daughter, when she asks to come home, that he will receive her on trial?'

'Surely, you are not offended with him, Iris?'

She shook her head. 'I am like you,' she said. 'I know him too well to be offended. He shall find me dutiful, he shall find me patient. I am afraid I must not expect you to wait for me in Honeybuzzard. Will you tell my father that I hope to return to him in a week's time?'

'Pardon me, Iris, I see no reason why you should waste a week in this town. On the contrary, the more eager you show yourself to return to your father, the more likely you are to recover your place in his estimation. I had planned to take you home by the next train.'

Iris looked at him in astonishment. 'Is it possible that you mean what you say?' she asked.

'My dear, I do most assuredly mean what I say. Why should you hesitate? What possible reason can there be for staying here any longer?'

'Oh, Hugh, how you disappoint me! What has become of your kind feeling, your sense of justice, your consideration for others? Poor Mrs. Vimpany!'

'What has Mrs. Vimpany to do with it?'

Iris was indignant.

'What has Mrs. Vimpany to do with it?' she repeated. 'After all that I owe to that good creature's kindness; after I have promised to accompany her—she has so few happy days, poor soul!—on excursions to places of interest in the neighbourhood, do you expect me to leave her—no! it's worse than that—do you expect me to throw her aside like an old dress that I have worn out? And this after I have so unjustly, so ungratefully suspected her in my own thoughts? Shameful! shameful!'

With some difficulty, Mountjoy controlled himself. After what she had just said, his lips were sealed on the subject of Mrs. Vimpany's true character. He could only persist in appealing to her duty to her father.

'You are allowing your quick temper to carry you to strange extremities,' he answered. 'If I think it of more importance to hasten a reconciliation with your father than to encourage you to make excursions with a lady whom you have only known for a week or two, what have I done to deserve such an outbreak of anger? Hush! Not a word more now! Here is the lady herself.'

As he spoke, Mrs. Vimpany joined them; returning from her interview with her husband at the inn. She looked first at Iris, and at once perceived signs of disturbance in the young lady's face.

Concealing her anxiety under that wonderful stage smile, which affords a refuge to so many secrets, Mrs. Vimpany said a few words excusing her absence. Miss Henley answered, without the slightest change in her friendly manner to the doctor's wife. The signs of disturbance were evidently attributable to some entirely unimportant cause, from Mrs. Vimpany's point of view. Mr. Mountjoy's discoveries had not been communicated yet.

In Hugh's state of mind, there was some irritating influence in the presence of the mistress of the house, which applied the spur to his wits. He mischievously proposed submitting to her the question in dispute between Iris and himself.

'It is a very simple matter,' he said to Mrs. Vimpany. 'Miss Henley's father is anxious that she should return to him, after an estrangement between them which is happily at an end. Do you think she ought to allow any accidental engagements to prevent her from going home at once? If she requests your indulgence, under the circumstances, has she any reason to anticipate a refusal?'

Mrs. Vimpany's expressive eyes looked up, with saintly resignation, at the dirty ceiling—and asked in dumb show what she had done to deserve the injury implied by a doubt!

'Mr. Mountjoy,' she said sternly, 'you insult me by asking the question. 'Dear Miss Henley,' she continued, turning to Iris, '*you* will do me justice, I am sure. Am I capable of allowing my own feelings to stand in the way, when your filial duty is concerned? Leave me, my sweet friend. Go! I entreat you, go home!'

She retired up the stage—no, no; she withdrew to the other end of the room—and burst into the most becoming of all human tears, theatrical tears. Impulsive Iris hastened to comfort the personification of self-sacrifice, the model of all that was most unselfish in female submission. 'For shame! for shame!' she whispered, as she passed Mountjoy.

Beaten again by Mrs. Vimpany—with no ties of relationship to justify resistance to Miss Henley; with two women against him, entrenched behind the privileges of their sex—the one last sacrifice of his own feelings, in the interests of Iris, that Hugh could make was to control the impulse which naturally urged him to leave the house. In the helpless position in which he had now placed himself, he could only wait to see what course Mrs. Vimpany might think it desirable to take. Would she request him, in her most politely malicious way, to bring his visit to an end? No: she looked at him—hesitated—directed a furtive glance towards the view of the street from the window—smiled mysteriously—and completed the sacrifice of her own feelings in these words:

'Dear Miss Henley, let me help you to pack up.'

Iris positively refused.

'No,' she said, 'I don't agree with Mr. Mountjoy. My father leaves it to me to name the day when we meet. I hold you, my dear, to our engagement—I don't leave an affectionate friend as I might leave a stranger.'

Even if Mr. Mountjoy communicated his discoveries to Miss Henley, on the way home, there would be no danger now of her believing him. Mrs. Vimpany put her powerful arm round the generous Iris, and, with infinite grace, thanked her by a kiss.

'Your kindness will make my lonely lot in life harder than ever to bear,' she murmured, 'when you are gone.'

'But we may hope to meet in London,' Iris reminded her; 'unless Mr. Vimpany alters his mind about leaving this place.'

'My husband will not do that, dear. He is determined to try his luck, as he says, in London. In the meantime you will give me your address, won't you? Perhaps you will even promise to write to me?'

Iris instantly gave her promise, and wrote down her address in London.

Mountjoy made no attempt to interfere: it was needless.

If the maid had not fallen ill on the journey, and if Mrs. Vimpany had followed Miss Henley to London, there would have been little to fear in the discovery of her address—and there was little to fear now. The danger to Iris was not in what might happen while she was living under her father's roof, but in what might happen if she was detained (by plans for excursions) in Mr. Vimpany's house, until Lord Harry might join her there.

Rather than permit this to happen, Hugh (in sheer desperation) meditated charging Mrs. Vimpany, to her face, with being the Irish lord's spy, and proving the accusation by challenging her to produce the registered letter and the diamond pin.

While he was still struggling with his own reluctance to inflict this degrading exposure on a woman, the talk between the two ladies came to an end. Mrs. Vimpany returned again to the window. On this occasion, she looked out into the street—with her handkerchief (was it used as a signal?) exhibited in her hand. Iris, on her side, advanced to Mountjoy. Easily moved to anger, her nature was incapable of sullen perseverance in a state of enmity. To see Hugh still patiently waiting—still risking the chances of insult—devoted to her, and forgiving her—was at once a reproach that punished Iris, and a mute appeal that no true woman's heart could resist.

With tears in her eyes she said to him: 'There must be no coolness between you and me. I lost my temper, and spoke shamefully to you. My dear, I am indeed sorry for it. You are never hard on me—you won't be hard on me now?'

She offered her hand to him. He had just raised it to his lips —when the drawing-room door was roughly opened. They both looked round.

The man of all others whom Hugh least desired to see was the man who now entered the room. The victim of 'light claret'— privately directed to lurk in the street, until he saw a handkerchief fluttering at the window—had returned to the house; primed with his clever wife's instructions; ready and eager to be even with Mountjoy for the dinner at the inn.

CHAPTER IX.

MR. VIMPANY ON INTOXICATION

HERE was no unsteadiness in the doctor's walk, and no flush on his face. He certainly did strut when he entered the room; and he held up his head with dignity, when he discovered Mountjoy. But he seemed to preserve his self-control. Was the man sober again already?

His wife approached him with her set smile; the appearance of her lord and master filled Mrs. Vimpany with perfectly-assumed emotions of agreeable surprise.

'This is an unexpected pleasure,' she said. 'You seldom favour us with your company, my dear, so early in the evening! Are there fewer patients in want of your advice than usual?'

'You are mistaken, Arabella. I am here in the performance of a painful duty.'

The doctor's language, and the doctor's manner, presented him to Iris in a character that was new to her. What effect had he produced on Mrs. Vimpany? That excellent friend to travellers in distress lowered her eyes to the floor, and modestly preserved silence. Mr. Vimpany proceeded to the performance of his duty; his painful responsibility seemed to strike him at first from a medical point of view.

'If there is a poison which undermines the sources of life,' he remarked, 'it is alcohol. If there is a vice that degrades humanity, it is intoxication. Mr. Mountjoy, are you aware that I am looking at you?'

'Impossible not to be aware of that,' Hugh answered. 'May I ask why you are looking at me?' It was not easy to listen gravely to Mr. Vimpany's denunciation of intemperance, after what had taken place at the dinner of that day. Hugh smiled. The moral majesty of the doctor entered its protest.

'This is really shameful,' he said. 'The least you can do is to take it seriously.'

'What is it?' Mountjoy asked. 'And why am I to take it seriously?'

Mr. Vimpany's reply was, to say the least of it, indirect. If such an expression may be permitted, it smelt of the stage. Viewed in connection with Mrs. Vimpany's persistent assumption of silent humility, it suggested to Mountjoy a secret understanding, of some kind, between husband and wife.

'What has become of your conscience, sir ?' Mr. Vimpany demanded. 'Is that silent monitor dead within you? After giving me a bad dinner, do you demand an explanation? Ha! you shall have it.'

Having delivered himself to this effect, he added action to words. Walking grandly to the door, he threw it open, and saluted Mountjoy with an ironical bow. Iris observed that act of insolence; her colour rose, her eyes glittered. 'Do you see what he has just done ?' she said to Mrs. Vimpany.

The doctor's wife answered softly: 'I don't understand it.' After a glance at her husband, she took Iris by the hand: 'Dear Miss Henley, shall we retire to my room ?'

Iris drew her hand away. 'Not unless Mr. Mountjoy wishes it,' she said.

'Certainly not!' Hugh declared. 'Pray remain here; your presence will help me to keep my temper.' He stepped up to Mr. Vimpany. 'Have you any particular reason for opening that door ?' he asked.

The doctor was a rascal; but, to do him justice, he was no coward. 'Yes,' he said, 'I have a reason.'

'What is it, if you please ?'

'Christian forbearance,' Mr. Vimpany answered.

'Forbearance towards me ?' Mountjoy continued.

The doctor's dignity suddenly deserted him.

'Aha, my boy, you have got it at last!' he cried. 'It's pleasant to understand each other, isn't it? You see, I'm a plain-spoken fellow; I don't wish to give offence. If there's one thing more than another I pride myself on, it's my indulgence for human frailty. But, in my position here, I'm obliged to be careful. Upon my soul, I can't continue my acquaintance with a man who—oh, come! come! don't look as if you didn't understand me. The circumstances are against you, sir. You have treated me infamously.'

'Under what circumstances have I treated you infamously ?' Hugh asked.

'Under pretence of giving me a dinner,' Mr. Vimpany shouted —'the worst dinner I ever sat down to!'

His wife signed to him to be silent. He took no notice of her. She insisted on being understood. 'Say no more!' she warned him, in a tone of command.

The brute side of his nature, roused by Mountjoy's contemptuous composure, was forcing its way outwards; he set his wife at defiance.

'Then don't let him look at me as if he thought I was in a state of intoxication!' cried the furious doctor. 'There's the man, Miss, who tried to make me tipsy,' he went on, actually addressing himself to Iris. 'Thanks to my habits of sobriety, he has been caught in his own trap. *He's* intoxicated. Ha, friend Mountjoy, have you got the right explanation at last? There's the door, sir!'

Mrs. Vimpany felt that this outrage was beyond endurance. If

something was not done to atone for it, Miss Henley would be
capable—her face, at that moment, answered for her—of leaving
the house with Mr. Mountjoy. Mrs. Vimpany seized her husband
indignantly by the arm.

'You brute, you have spoilt everything!' she said to him.
'Apologise directly to Mr. Mountjoy. You won't?'

'I won't!'

Experience had taught his wife how to break him to her will.
'Do you remember my diamond pin?' she whispered.

He looked startled. Perhaps he thought she had lost the pin.

'Where is it?' he asked eagerly.

'Gone to London to be valued. Beg Mr. Mountjoy's pardon, or
I will put the money in the bank—and not one shilling of it do
you get.'

In the meanwhile, Iris had justified Mrs. Vimpany's apprehensions. Her indignation noticed nothing but the insult offered
to Hugh. She was too seriously agitated to be able to speak to him.
Still admirably calm, his one anxiety was to compose her.

'Don't be afraid,' he said; 'it is impossible that I can degrade
myself by quarrelling with Mr. Vimpany. I only wait here to
know what you propose to do. You have Mrs. Vimpany to think of.'

'I have nobody to think of but You,' Iris replied. 'But for me,
you would never have been in this house. After the insult that has
been offered to you—oh, Hugh, I feel it too!—let us return to
London together. I have only to tell Rhoda we are going away,
and to make my preparations for travelling. Send for me from
the inn, and I will be ready in time for the next train.'

Mrs. Vimpany approached Mountjoy, leading her husband.

'Sorry I have offended you,' the doctor said. 'Beg your
pardon. It's only a joke. No offence, I hope?'

His servility was less endurable than his insolence. Telling
him that he need say no more, Mountjoy bowed to Mrs. Vimpany,
and left the room. She returned his bow mechanically, in silence.
Mr. Vimpany followed Hugh out—thinking of the diamond pin,
and eager to open the house door, as another act of submission
which might satisfy his wife.

Even a clever woman will occasionally make mistakes; especially
when her temper happens to have been roused. Mrs. Vimpany
found herself in a false position, due entirely to her own imprudence.

She had been guilty of three serious errors. In the first place
she had taken it for granted that Mr. Vimpany's restorative mixture
would completely revive the sober state of his brains. In the
second place, she had trusted him with her vengeance on the man
who had found his way to her secrets through her husband's
intemperance. In the third place, she had rashly assumed that
the doctor, in carrying out her instructions for insulting Mountjoy,
would keep within the limits which she had prescribed to him,
when she hit on the audacious idea of attributing his disgraceful
conduct to the temptation offered by his host's example. As a con-

sequence of these acts of imprudence, she had exposed herself to a misfortune that she honestly dreaded—the loss of the place which she had carefully maintained in Miss Henley's estimation. In the contradictory confusion of feelings, so often found in women, this deceitful and dangerous creature had been conquered—little by little, as she had herself described it—by that charm of sweetness and simplicity in Iris, of which her own depraved nature presented no trace. She now spoke with hesitation, almost with timidity, in addressing the woman whom she had so cleverly deceived, at the time when they first met.

'Must I give up all, Miss Henley, that I most value?' she asked.

'I hardly understand you, Mrs. Vimpany.'

'I will try to make it plainer. Do you really mean to leave me this evening?'

'I do.'

'May I own that I am grieved to hear it? Your departure will deprive me of some happy hours, in your company.'

'Your husband's conduct leaves me no alternative,' Iris replied.

'Pray do not humiliate me by speaking of my husband! I only want to know if there is a harder trial of my fortitude still to come. Must I lose the privilege of being your friend?'

'I hope I am not capable of such injustice as that,' Iris declared. 'It would be hard indeed to lay the blame of Mr. Vimpany's shameful behaviour on you. I don't forget that you made him offer an apology. Some women, married to such a man as that, might have been afraid of him. No, no; you have been a good friend to me—and I mean to remember it.'

Mrs. Vimpany's gratitude was too sincerely felt to be expressed with her customary readiness. She only said what the stupidest woman in existence could have said: 'Thank you.'

In the silence that followed, the rapid movement of carriage-wheels became audible in the street. The sound stopped at the door of the doctor's house.

CHAPTER X

THE MOCKERY OF DECEIT

HAD Mountjoy arrived to take Iris away, before her preparations for travelling were complete? Both the ladies hurried to the window, but they were too late. The rapid visitor, already hidden from them under the portico, was knocking smartly at the door. In another minute, a man's voice in the hall asked for 'Miss Henley.' The tones —clear, mellow, and pleasantly varied here and there by the Irish accent—were not to be mistaken by any one who had already hear them. The man in the hall was Lord Harry.

In that serious emergency, Mrs. Vimpany recovered her presence of mind.

She made for the door, with the object of speaking to Lord Harry before he could present himself in the drawing-room. But Iris had heard him ask for her in the hall; and that one circumstance instantly stripped of its concealments the character of the woman in whose integrity she had believed. Her first impression of Mrs. Vimpany—so sincerely repented, so eagerly atoned for— had been the right impression after all! Younger, lighter, and quicker than the doctor's wife, Iris reached the door first, and laid her hand on the lock.

'Wait a minute,' she said.

Mrs. Vimpany hesitated. For the first time in her life at a loss what to say, she could only sign to Iris to stand back. Iris refused to move. She put her terrible question in the plainest words:

'How does Lord Harry know that I am in this house?'

The wretched woman (listening intently for the sound of a step on the stairs) refused to submit to a shameful exposure, even now. To her perverted moral sense, any falsehood was acceptable, as a means of hiding herself from discovery by Iris. In the very face of detection, the skilled deceiver kept up the mockery of deceit.

'My dear,' she said, 'what has come to you? Why won't you let me go to my room?'

Iris eyed her with a look of scornful surprise. 'What next?' she said. 'Are you impudent enough to pretend that I have not found you out, yet?'

Sheer desperation still sustained Mrs. Vimpany's courage. She played her assumed character against the contemptuous incredulity of Iris, as she had sometimes played her theatrical characters against the hissing and hooting of a brutal audience.

' Miss Henley,' she said, ' you forget yourself ! '

' Do you think I didn't see in your face,' Iris rejoined, ' that *you* heard him, too ? Answer my question.'

' What question ? '

' You have just heard it.'

' No ! '

' You false woman ! '

' Don't forget, Miss Henley, that you are speaking to a lady.'

' I am speaking to Lord Harry's spy ! '

Their voices rose loud ; the excitement on either side had reached its climax ; neither the one nor the other was composed enough to notice the sound of the carriage-wheels, leaving the house again. In the meanwhile, nobody came to the drawing-room door. Mrs. Vimpany was too well acquainted with the hot-headed Irish lord not to conclude that he would have made himself heard, and would have found his way to Iris, but for some obstacle, below stairs, for which he was not prepared. The doctor's wife did justice to the doctor at last. Another person had, in all probability, heard Lord Harry's voice—and that person might have been her husband.

Was it possible that he remembered the service which she had asked of him ; and, even if he had succeeded in calling it to mind, was his discretion to be trusted ? As those questions occurred to her, the desire to obtain some positive information was more than she was able to resist. Mrs. Vimpany attempted to leave the drawing-room for the second time.

But the same motive had already urged Miss Henley to action. Again, the younger woman outstripped the elder. Iris descended the stairs, resolved to discover the cause of the sudden suspension of events in the lower part of the house.

CHAPTER XI

MRS. VIMPANY'S FAREWELL

THE doctor's wife followed Miss Henley out of the room, as far as the landing — and waited there.

She had her reasons for placing this restraint on herself. The position of the landing concealed her from the view of a person in the hall. If she only listened for the sound of voices she might safely discover whether Lord Harry was, or was not, still in the house. In the first event, it would be easy to interrupt his interview with Iris, before the talk could lead to disclosures which Mrs. Vimpany had every reason to dread. In the second event, there would be no need to show herself.

Meanwhile, Iris opened the dining-room door and looked in.

Nobody was there. The one other room on the ground floor, situated at the back of the building, was the doctor's consulting-room. She knocked at the door. Mr. Vimpany's voice answered: 'Come in.' There he was alone, drinking brandy and water, and smoking his big black cigar.

'Where is Lord Harry?' she said.

'In Ireland, I suppose,' Mr. Vimpany answered quietly.

Iris wasted no time in making useless inquiries. She closed the door again, and left him. He, too, was undoubtedly in the conspiracy to keep her deceived. How had it been done? Where was the wild lord, at that moment?

Whilst she was pursuing these reflections in the hall, Rhoda came up from the servants' tea-table in the kitchen. Her mistress gave her the necessary instructions for packing, and promised to help her before long. Mrs. Vimpany's audacious resolution to dispute the evidence of her own senses, still dwelt on Miss Henley's mind. Too angry to think of the embarrassment which an interview with Lord Harry would produce, after they had said their farewell words in Ireland, she was determined to prevent the doctor's wife from speaking to him first, and claiming him as an accomplice in her impudent denial of the truth. If he had been, by any chance, deluded into leaving the house, he would sooner or later discover the trick that had been played on him, and would certainly return. Iris took a chair in the hall.

.   .   .   .

It is due to the doctor to relate that he had indeed justified his wife's confidence in him.

The diamond pin, undergoing valuation in London, still represented a present terror in his mind. The money, the money—he was the most attentive husband in England when he thought of the money! At the time when Lord Harry's carriage stopped at his house-door, he was in the dining-room, taking a bottle of brandy from the cellaret in the sideboard. Looking instantly out of the window, he discovered who the visitor was, and decided on consulting his instructions in the pocket-diary. The attempt was rendered useless, as soon as he had opened the book, by the unlucky activity of the servant in answering the door. Her master stopped her in the hall. He was pleasantly conscious of the recovery of his cunning. But his memory (far from active under the most favourable circumstances) was slower than ever at helping him now. On the spur of the moment he could only call to mind that he had been ordered to prevent a meeting between Lord Harry and Iris. 'Show the gentleman into my consulting-room,' he said.

Lord Harry found the doctor enthroned on his professional chair, surprised and delighted to see his distinguished friend. The impetuous Irishman at once asked for Miss Henley.

'Gone,' Mr. Vimpany answered.

'Gone—where?' the wild lord wanted to know next.

'To London.'

'By herself?'

'No; with Mr. Hugh Mountjoy.'

Lord Harry seized the doctor by the shoulders, and shook him: 'You don't mean to tell me Mountjoy is going to marry her?'

Mr. Vimpany feared nothing but the loss of money. The weaker and the older man of the two, he nevertheless followed the young lord's example, and shook him with right good-will. 'Let's see how you like it in your turn,' he said. 'As for Mountjoy, I don't know whether he is married or single—and don't care.'

'The devil take your obstinacy! When did they start?'

'The devil take your questions! They started not long since.'

'Might I catch them at the station?'

'Yes; if you go at once.'

So the desperate doctor carried out his wife's instructions—without remembering the conditions which had accompanied them.

The way to the station took Lord Harry past the inn. He saw Hugh Mountjoy through the open house door paying his bill at the bar. In an instant the carriage was stopped, and the two men (never on friendly terms) were formally bowing to each other.

'I was told I should find you,' Lord Harry said, 'with Miss Henley, at the station.'

'Who gave you your information?'

'Vimpany—the doctor.'

'He ought to know that the train isn't due at the station for an hour yet.'

'Has the blackguard deceived me? One word more, Mr. Mountjoy. Is Miss Henley at the inn?'

'No.'

'Are you going with her to London?'

'I must leave Miss Henley to answer that.'

'Where is she, sir?'

'There is an end to everything, my lord, in the world we live in. You have reached the end of my readiness to answer questions.'

The Englishman and the Irishman looked at each other: the Anglo-Saxon was impenetrably cool; the Celt was flushed and angry. They might have been on the brink of a quarrel, but for Lord Harry's native quickness of perception, and his exercise of it at that moment. When he had called at Mr. Vimpany's house, and had asked for Iris, the doctor had got rid of him by means of a lie. After this discovery, at what conclusion could he arrive? The doctor was certainly keeping Iris out of his way. Reasoning in this rapid manner, Lord Harry let one offence pass, in his headlong eagerness to resent another. He instantly left Mountjoy. Again the carriage rattled back along the street; but it was stopped before it reached Mr. Vimpany's door.

Lord Harry knew the people whom he had to deal with, and took measures to approach the house silently, on foot. The coachman received orders to look out for a signal, which should tell him when he was wanted again.

Mr. Vimpany's ears, vigilantly on the watch for suspicious events, detected no sound of carriage wheels and no noisy use of the knocker. Still on his guard, however, a ring at the house-bell disturbed him in his consulting-room. Peeping into the hall, he saw Iris opening the door, and stole back to his room. 'The devil take her!' he said, alluding to Miss Henley, and thinking of the enviable proprietor of the diamond pin.

At the unexpected appearance of Iris, Lord Harry forgot every consideration which ought to have been present to his mind, at that critical moment.

He advanced to her with both hands held out in cordial greeting. She signed to him contemptuously to stand back—and spoke in tones cautiously lowered, after a glance at the door of the consulting-room.

'My only reason for consenting to see you,' she said, 'is to protect myself from further deception. Your disgraceful conduct is known to me. Go now,' she continued, pointing to the stairs, 'and consult with your spy, as soon as you like.' The Irish lord listened—guiltily conscious of having deserved what she had said to him—without attempting to utter a word in excuse.

Still posted at the head of the stairs, the doctor's wife heard Iris speaking; but the tone was not loud enough to make the words intelligible at that distance; neither was any other voice audible in reply. Vaguely suspicious of some act of domestic treachery, Mrs. Vimpany began to descend the stairs. At the turning which gave her a view of the hall, she stopped; thunderstruck by the discovery of Lord Harry and Miss Henley, together.

The presence of a third person seemed, in some degree, to relieve Lord Harry. He ran upstairs to salute Mrs. Vimpany, and was met again by a cold reception and a hostile look.

Strongly and strangely contrasted, the two confronted each other on the stairs. The faded woman, wan and ghastly under cruel stress of mental suffering, stood face to face with a fine, tall, lithe man, in the prime of his health and strength. Here were the bright blue eyes, the winning smile, and the natural grace of movement, which find their own way to favour in the estimation of the gentler sex. This irreclaimable wanderer among the perilous by-ways of the earth—christened 'Irish blackguard,' among respectable members of society, when they spoke of him behind his back—attracted attention, even among the men. Looking at his daring, finely-formed face, they noticed (as an exception to a general rule, in these days) the total suppression, by the razor, of whiskers, moustache, and beard. Strangers wondered whether Lord Harry was an actor or a Roman Catholic priest. Among chance acquaintances, those few favourites of Nature who are possessed of active brains, guessed that his life of adventure might well have rendered disguise necessary to his safety, in more than one part of the world. Sometimes they boldly put the question to him. The hot temper of an Irishman, in moments of excitement, is not infrequently a sweet temper in moments of calm. What they called Lord Harry's good-nature owned readily that he had been indebted, on certain occasions, to the protection of a false beard, and perhaps a colouring of his face and hair to match. The same easy disposition now asserted itself, under the merciless enmity of Mrs. Vimpany's eyes. 'If I have done anything to offend you,' he said, with an air of puzzled humility, 'I'm sure I am sorry for it. Don't be angry, Arabella, with an old friend. Why won't you shake hands?'

'I have kept your secret, and done your dirty work,' Mrs. Vimpany replied. 'And what is my reward? Miss Henley can tell you how your Irish blundering has ruined me in a lady's estimation. Shake hands, indeed! You will never shake hands with Me again as long as you live!'

She said those words without looking at him; her eyes were resting on Iris now. From the moment when she had seen the two together, she knew that it was all over; further denial in the face of plain proofs would be useless indeed! Submission was the one alternative left.

'Miss Henley,' she said, 'if you can feel pity for another woman's sorrow and shame, let me have a last word with you—out of this man's hearing.'

There was nothing artificial in her tones or her looks; no acting could have imitated the sad sincerity with which she spoke. Touched by that change, Iris accompanied her as she ascended the stairs. After a little hesitation, Lord Harry followed them. Mrs. Vimpany turned on him when they reached the drawing-room landing. 'Must I shut the door in your face?' she asked.

He was as pleasantly patient as ever:

'You needn't take the trouble to do that, my dear; I'll only ask your leave to sit down and wait on the stairs. When you have done with Miss Henley, just call me in. And, by the way, don't be alarmed in case of a little noise—say a heavy man tumbling downstairs. If the blackguard it's your misfortune to be married to happens to show himself, I shall be under the necessity of kicking him. That's all.'

Mrs. Vimpany closed the door. She spoke to Iris respectfully, as she might have addressed a stranger occupying a higher rank in life than herself.

'There is an end, madam, to our short acquaintance; and, as we both know, an end to it for ever. When we first met—let me tell the truth at last!—I felt a malicious pleasure in deceiving you. After that time, I was surprised to find that you grew on my liking, Can you understand the wickedness that tried to resist you? It was useless; your good influence has been too strong for me. Strange, isn't it? I have lived a life of deceit, among bad people. What could you expect of me, after that? I heaped lies on lies— I would have denied that the sun was in the heavens—rather than find myself degraded in your opinion. Well! that is all over-- useless, quite useless now. Pray don't mistake me. I am not attempting to excuse myself; a confession was due to you; the confession is made. It is too late to hope that you will forgive me. If you will permit it, I have only one favour to ask. Forget me.'

She turned away with a last hopeless look, which said as plainly as if in words: 'I am not worth a reply.'

Generous Iris insisted on speaking to her.

'I believe you are truly sorry for what you have done,' she said; 'I can never forget that—I can never forget You.' She held out her pitying hand. Mrs. Vimpany was too bitterly conscious of the past to touch it. Even a spy is not beneath the universal reach of the heartache. There were tears in the miserable woman's eyes when she had looked her last at Iris Henley.

CHAPTER XII

LORD HARRY'S DEFENCE

AFTER a short interval, the drawing-room door was opened again. Waiting on the threshold, the Irish lord asked if he might come in.

Iris replied coldly. 'This is not my house,' she said; 'I must leave you to decide for yourself.'

Lord Harry crossed the room to speak to her — and stopped. There was no sign of relenting towards him in that dearly-loved face. 'I wonder whether it would be a relief to you,' he suggested with piteous humility, 'if I went away?'

If she had been true to herself, she would have said, Yes. Where is the woman to be found, in her place, with a heart hard enough to have set her that example? She pointed to a chair. He felt her indulgence gratefully. Following the impulse of the moment, he attempted to excuse his conduct.

'There is only one thing I can say for myself,' he confessed, 'I didn't begin by deceiving you. While you had your eye on me, Iris, I was an honourable man.'

This extraordinary defence reduced her to silence. Was there another man in the world who would have pleaded for pardon in that way? 'I'm afraid I have not made myself understood,' he said. 'May I try again?'

'If you please.'

The vagabond nobleman made a resolute effort to explain himself intelligibly, this time:

'See now! We said good-bye, over there, in the poor old island. Well, indeed I meant it, when I owned that I was unworthy of you. I didn't contradict you, when you said you could never be my wife, after such a life as I have led. And, do remember, I submitted to your returning to England, without presuming to make a complaint. Ah, my sweet girl, it was easy to submit, while I could look at you, and hear the sound of your voice, and beg for that last kiss—and get it. Reverend gentlemen talk about the fall of Adam. What was that to the fall of Harry, when he was back in his own little cottage, without the hope of ever seeing you again? To the best of my recollection, the serpent that tempted Eve was up a tree. I found the serpent that tempted Me, sitting waiting in my own arm-chair, and bent on nothing worse than borrowing a trifle of money. Need I say who she was? I don't doubt that you think her a wicked woman.'

Never ready in speaking of acts of kindness, on her own part, Iris answered with some little reserve: 'I have learnt to think better of Mrs. Vimpany than you suppose.'

Lord Harry began to look like a happy man, for the first time since he had entered the room.

'I ought to have known it!' he burst out. 'Yours is the well-balanced mind, dear, that tempers justice with mercy. Mother Vimpany has had a hard life of it. Just change places with her for a minute or so—and you'll understand what she has had to go through. Find yourself, for instance, in Ireland, without the means to take you back to England. Add to that, a husband who sends you away to make money for him at the theatre, and a manager (not an Irishman, thank God!) who refuses to engage you—after your acting has filled his dirty pockets in past days—because your beauty has faded with time. Doesn't your bright imagination see it all now? My old friend Arabella, ready and anxious to serve me—and a sinking at this poor fellow's heart when he knew, if he once lost the trace of you, he might lose it for ever—there's the situation, as they call it on the stage. I wish I could say for myself what I may say for Mrs. Vimpany. It's such a pleasure to a clever woman to engage in a little deceit—we can't blame her, can we?'

Iris protested gently against a code of morality which included the right of deceit among the privileges of the sex. Lord Harry slipped through her fingers with the admirable Irish readiness; he agreed with Miss Henley that he was entirely wrong.

'And don't spare me while you're about it,' he suggested. 'Lay all the blame of that shameful stratagem on my shoulders. It was a despicable thing to do. When I had you watched, I acted in a manner—I won't say unworthy of a gentleman; have I been a gentleman since I first ran away from home? Why, it's even been said my way of speaking is no longer the way of a gentleman ; and small wonder, too, after the company I've kept. Ah, well! I'm off again, darling, on a sea voyage. Will you forgive me now ? or will you wait till I come back, if I do come back ? God knows! ' He dropped on his knees, and kissed her hand. 'Anyway,' he said, ' whether I live or whether I die, it will be some consolation to re-member that I asked your pardon—and perhaps got it.'

'Take it, Harry ; I can't help forgiving you!

She had done her best to resist him, and she had answered in those merciful words.

The effect was visible, perilously visible, as he rose from his knees. Her one chance of keeping the distance between them, on which she had been too weak to insist, was not to encourage him by silence. Abruptly, desperately, she made a commonplace inquiry about his proposed voyage. 'Tell me,' she resumed, 'where are you going when you leave England ? '

' Oh, to find money, dear, if I can—to pick up diamonds, or to hit on a mine of gold, and so forth.'

The fine observation of Iris detected something not quite easy in his manner, as he made that reply. He tried to change the subject : she deliberately returned to it. ' Your account of your travelling-plans is rather vague,' she told him. ' Do you know when you are likely to return ? '

He took her hand. One of the rings on her fingers happened to be turned the wrong way. He set it in the right position, and dis-covered an opal. 'Ah! the unlucky stone!' he cried, and turned it back again out of sight. She drew away her hand. 'I asked you,' she persisted, 'when you expect to return ? '

He laughed—not so gaily as usual.

' How do I know I shall ever get back ? ' he answered. ' Some-times the seas turn traitor, and sometimes the savages. I have had so many narrow escapes of my life, I can't expect my luck to last for ever.' He made a second attempt to change the subject. ' I wonder whether you're likely to pay another visit to Ireland ? My cottage is entirely at your disposal, Iris dear. Oh, when I'm out of the way, of course! The place seemed to please your fancy, when you saw it. You will find it well taken care of, I answer for that.'

Iris asked who was taking care of his cottage.

The wild lord's face saddened. He hesitated; rose from his chair restlessly, and walked away to the window; returned, and made up his mind to reply.

' My dear, you know her. She was the old housekeeper at——'

His voice failed him. He was unable, or unwilling, to pronounce the name of Arthur's farm.

Knowing, it is needless to say, that he had alluded to Mrs. Lew-son, Iris warmly commended him for taking care of her old nurse. At the same time, she remembered the unfriendly terms in which the housekeeper had alluded to Lord Harry, when they had talked of him.

'Did you find no difficulty,' she asked, 'in persuading Mrs. Lewson to enter your service?'

'Oh, yes, plenty of difficulty; I found my bad character in my way, as usual.' It was a relief to him, at that moment, to talk of Mrs. Lewson; the Irish humour and the Irish accent both asserted themselves in his reply. 'The curious old creature told me to my face I was a scamp. I took leave to remind her that it was the duty of a respectable person, like herself, to reform scamps; I also mentioned that I was going away, and she would be master and mistress too on my small property. That softened her heart towards me. You will mostly find old women amenable, if you get at them by way of their dignity. Besides, there was another lucky circumstance that helped me. The neighbourhood of my cottage has some attraction for Mrs. Lewson. She didn't say particularly what it was — and I never asked her to tell me.'

'Surely you might have guessed it, without being told,' Iris reminded him. 'Mrs. Lewson's faithful heart loves poor Arthur's memory—and Arthur's grave is not far from your cottage.'

'Don't speak of him!'

It was said loudly, peremptorily, passionately. He looked at her with angry astonishment in his face. 'You loved him too!' he said. 'Can you speak of him quietly? The noblest, truest, sweetest man that ever the Heavens looked on, foully assassinated. And the wretch who murdered him still living, free—oh, what is God's providence about?—is there no retribution that will follow him? no just hand that will revenge Arthur's death?'

As those fierce words escaped him, he was no longer the easy, gentle, joyous creature whom Iris had known and loved. The furious passions of the Celtic race glittered savagely in his eyes, and changed to a grey horrid pallor the healthy colour that was natural to his face. 'Oh, my temper, my temper!' he cried, as Iris shrank from him. 'She hates me now, and no wonder.' He staggered away from her, and burst into a convulsive fit of crying, dreadful to hear. Compassion, divine compassion, mastered the earthlier emotion of terror in the great heart of the woman who loved him. She followed him, and laid her hand caressingly on his shoulder. 'I don't hate you, my dear,' she said. 'I am sorry for Arthur—and, oh, so sorry for You!' He caught her in his arms. His gratitude, his repentance, his silent farewell were all expressed in a last kiss. It was a moment, never to be forgotten to the end of their lives. Before she could speak, before she could think, he had left her.

She called him back, through the open door. He never returned; he never even replied. She ran to the window, and threw it up—and was just in time to see him signal to the carriage and leap into it. Her horror of the fatal purpose that was but too plainly rooted in him—her conviction that he was on the track of the assassin, self devoted to exact the terrible penalty of blood for blood—

emboldened her to insist on being heard. ' Come back,' she cried.
' I must, I will, speak with you.'

He waved his hand to her with a gesture of despair. ' Start
your horses,' he shouted to the coachman. Alarmed by his voice
and his look, the man asked where he should drive to. Lord Harry
pointed furiously to the onward road. ' Drive,' he answered, ' to
the Devil ! '

THE END OF THE FIRST PERIOD

THE SECOND PERIOD

CHAPTER XIII

IRIS AT HOME

A LITTLE more than four months had passed, since the return of Iris to her father's house.

Among other events which occurred, during the earlier part of that interval, the course adopted by Hugh Mountjoy, when Miss Henley's suspicions of the Irish lord were first communicated to him, claims a foremost place.

It was impossible that the devoted friend of Iris could look at her, when they met again on their way to the station, without perceiving the signs of serious agitation. Only waiting until they were alone in the railway-carriage, she opened her heart unreservedly to the man in whose clear intellect and true sympathy she could repose implicit trust. He listened to what she could repeat of Lord Harry's language with but little appearance of surprise. Iris had only reminded him of one, among the disclosures which had escaped Mr. Vimpany at the inn. Under the irresistible influence of good wine, the doctor had revealed the Irish lord's motive for remaining in his own country, after the assassination of Arthur Mountjoy. Hugh met the only difficulty in his way, without shrinking from it. He resolved to clear his mind of its natural prejudice against the rival who had been preferred to him, before he assumed the responsibility of guiding Iris by his advice.

When he had in some degree recovered confidence in his own unbiassed judgment, he entered on the question of Lord Harry's purpose in leaving England.

Without attempting to dispute the conclusion at which Iris had arrived, he did his best to alleviate her distress. In his opinion, he was careful to tell her, a discovery of the destination to which Lord Harry proposed to betake himself, might be achieved. The Irish lord's allusion to a new adventure, which would occupy him in searching for diamonds or gold, might indicate a contemplated pursuit of the assassin, as well as a plausible excuse to satisfy Iris. It was at least possible that the murderer might have been warned of his danger if he remained in England, and that he might have contemplated directing his flight to a distant country, which would not only offer a safe refuge, but also hold out (in its mineral treasures) a hope of gain. Assuming that these circumstances had really happened, it was in Lord Harry's character to make sure of his revenge, by embarking in the steamship by which the assassin of Arthur Mountjoy was a passenger.

Wild as this guess at the truth undoubtedly was, it had one merit : it might easily be put to the test.

Hugh had bought the day's newspaper at the station. He proposed to consult the shipping advertisements relating, in the first place, to communication with the diamond-mines and the goldfields of South Africa.

This course of proceeding at once informed him that the first steamer, bound for that destination, would sail from London in two days' time. The obvious precaution to take was to have the Dock watched ; and Mountjoy's steady old servant, who knew Lord Harry by sight, was the man to employ.

Iris naturally inquired what good end could be attained, if the anticipated discovery actually took place.

To this Mountjoy answered, that the one hope—a faint hope, he must needs confess—of inducing Lord Harry to reconsider his desperate purpose, lay in the influence of Iris herself. She must address a letter to him, announcing that his secret had been betrayed by his own language and conduct, and declaring that she would never again see him, or hold any communication with him, if he persisted in his savage resolution of revenge. Such was the desperate experiment which Mountjoy's generous and unselfish devotion to Iris now proposed to try.

The servant (duly entrusted with Miss Henley's letter) was placed on the watch—and the event which had been regarded as little better than a forlorn hope, proved to be the event that really took place. Lord Harry was a passenger by the steamship.

Mountjoy's man presented the letter entrusted to him, and asked respectfully if there was any answer. The wild lord read it—looked (to use the messenger's own words) like a man cut to the heart—seemed at a loss what to say or do—and only gave a verbal answer : ' I sincerely thank Miss Henley, and I promise to write when the ship touches at Madeira.' The servant continued to watch him when he went on board the steamer ; saw him cast a look backwards, as if suspecting that he might have been followed ; and then lost sight of him in the cabin. The vessel sailed after a long interval of delay, but he never reappeared on the deck.

The ambiguous message sent to her aroused the resentment of Iris ; she thought it cruel. For some weeks perhaps to come, she was condemned to remain in doubt, and was left to endure the trial of her patience, without having Mountjoy at hand to encourage and console her. He had been called away to the south of France by the illness of his father.

But the fortunes of Miss Henley, at this period of her life, had their brighter side. She found reason to congratulate herself on the

The wild lord read it—looked (to use the messenger's own words) like a man cut to the heart, and seemed at a loss what to say or do.

reconciliation which had brought her back to her father. Mr. Henley had received her, not perhaps with affection, but certainly with kindness. ' If we don't get in each other's way, we shall do very well; I am glad to see you again.' That was all he had said to her, but it meant much from a soured and selfish man.

Her only domestic anxiety was caused by another failure in the health of her maid.

The Doctor declared that medical help would be of no avail, while Rhoda Bennet remained in London. In the country she had been born and bred, and to the country she must return. Mr. Henley's large landed property, on the north of London, happened to include a farm in the neighbourhood of Muswell Hill. Wisely waiting for a favourable opportunity, Iris alluded to the good qualities which had made Rhoda almost as much her friend as her servant, and asked leave to remove the invalid to the healthy air of the farm.

Her anxiety about the recovery of a servant so astonished Mr. Henley, that he was hurried (as he afterwards declared) into granting his daughter's request. After this concession, the necessary arrangements were easily made. The influence of Iris won the goodwill of the farmer and his wife; Rhoda, as an expert and willing needlewoman, being sure of a welcome, for her own sake, in a family which included a number of young children. Miss Henley had only to order her carriage, and to be within reach of the farm. A week seldom passed without a meeting between the mistress and the maid.

In the meantime, Mountjoy (absent in France) did not forget to write to Iris.

His letters offered little hope of a speedy return. The doctors had not concealed from him that his father's illness would end fatally; but there were reserves of vital power still left, which might prolong the struggle. Under these melancholy circumstances, he begged that Iris would write to him. The oftener she could tell him of the little events of her life at home, the more kindly she would brighten the days of a dreary life.

Eager to show, even in a trifling matter, how gratefully she appreciated Mountjoy's past kindness, Iris related the simple story of her life at home, in weekly letters addressed to her good friend. After telling Hugh (among other things) of Rhoda's establishment at the farm, she had some unexpected results to relate, which had followed the attempt to provide herself with a new maid.

Two young women had been successively engaged—each recommended, by the lady whom she had last served, with that utter disregard of moral obligation which appears to be shamelessly on the increase in the England of our day. The first of the two maids, described as 'rather excitable,' revealed infirmities of temper which suggested a lunatic asylum as the only fit place for her. The second young woman, detected in stealing eau-de-cologne, and using it (mixed with water) as an intoxicating drink, claimed merci-

ful construction of her misconduct, on the ground that she had been
misled by the example of her last mistress.

At the third attempt to provide herself with a servant, Iris was
able to report the discovery of a responsible person who told the
truth—an unmarried lady of middle age.

In this case, the young woman was described as a servant
thoroughly trained in the performance of her duties, honest, sober,
industrious, of an even temper, and unprovided with a 'follower'
in the shape of a sweetheart. Even her name sounded favourably
in the ear of a stranger—it was Fanny Mere. Iris asked how a
servant, apparently possessed of a faultless character, came to be
in want of a situation. At this question the lady sighed, and acknowledged that she had 'made a dreadful discovery,' relating to the
past life of her maid. It proved to be the old, the miserably old,
story of a broken promise of marriage, and of the penalty paid as
usual by the unhappy woman. 'I will say nothing of my own
feelings,' the maiden lady explained. 'In justice to the other female
servants, it was impossible for me to keep such a person in my
house; and, in justice to you, I must most unwillingly stand in the
way of Fanny Mere's prospects by mentioning my reason for parting
with her.'

'If I could see the young woman and speak to her,' Iris said, 'I
should like to decide the question of engaging her, for myself.'

The lady knew the address of her discharged servant, and—with
some appearance of wonder—communicated it. Miss Henley
wrote at once, telling Fanny Mere to come to her on the following
day.

When she woke on the next morning, later than usual, an event
occurred which Iris had been impatiently expecting for some time
past. She found a letter waiting on her bedside table, side by side
with her cup of tea. Lord Harry had written to her at last.

Whether he used his pen or his tongue, the Irish lord's conduct
was always more or less in need of an apology. Here were the guilty
one's new excuses, expressed in his customary medley of frank confession and flowery language :

'I am fearing, my angel, that I have offended you. You have
too surely said to yourself, This miserable Harry might have made
me happy by writing two lines—and what does he do ? He sends a
message in words which tell me nothing.

'My sweet girl, the reason why is that I was in two minds when
your man stopped me on my way to the ship.

'Whether it was best for you—I was not thinking of myself—to
confess the plain truth, or to take refuge in affectionate equivocation,
was more than I could decide at the time. When minutes are
enough for your intelligence, my stupidity wants days. Well! I saw
it at last. A man owes the truth to a true woman; and you are a
true woman. There you find a process of reasoning—I have been
five days getting hold of it.

'But tell me one thing first. Brutus killed a man; Charlotte

Corday killed a man. One of the two victims was a fine tyrant, and the other a mean tyrant. Nobody blames those two historical assassins. Why then blame me for wishing to make a third? Is a mere modern murderer beneath my vengeance, by comparison with two classical tyrants who did *their* murders by deputy? The man who killed Arthur Mountjoy is (next to Cain alone) the most atrocious homicide that ever trod the miry ways of this earth. There is my reply! I call it a crusher.

'So now my mind is easy. Darling, let me make your mind easy next.

'When I left you at the window of Vimpany's house, I was off to the other railroad to find the murderer in his hiding-place by the seaside. He had left it; but I got a trace, and went back to London —to the Docks. Some villain in Ireland, who knows my purpose, must have turned traitor. Anyhow, the wretch has escaped me.

'Yes; I searched the ship in every corner. He was not on board. Has he gone on before me, by an earlier vessel? Or has he directed his flight to some other part of the world? I shall find out in time. His day of reckoning will come, and he, too, shall know a violent death! Amen. So be it. Amen.

'Have I done now? Bear with me, gentle Iris—there is a word more to come.

'You will wonder why I went on by the steamship—all the way to South Africa—when I had failed to find the man I wanted, on board. What was my motive? You, you alone, are always my motive. Lucky men have found gold, lucky men have found diamonds. Why should I not be one of them? My sweet, let us suppose two possible things; my own elastic convictions would call them two likely things, but never mind that. Say, I come back a reformed character; there is your only objection to me, at once removed! And take it for granted that I return with a fortune of my own finding. In that case, what becomes of Mr. Henley's objection to me? It melts (as Shakespeare says somewhere) into thin air. Now do take my advice, for once. Show this part of my letter to your excellent father, with my love. I answer beforehand for the consequences. Be happy, my Lady Harry—as happy as I am—and look for my return on an earlier day than you may anticipate. Yours till death, and after.

'HARRY.'

Like the Irish lord, Miss Henley was 'in two minds,' while she rose, and dressed herself. There were parts of the letter for which she loved the writer, and parts of it for which she hated him.

What a prospect was before that reckless man—what misery, what horror, might not be lying in wait in the dreadful future! If he failed in the act of vengeance, that violent death of which he had written so heedlessly might overtake him from another hand. If he succeeded, the law might discover his crime, and the infamy of expiation on the scaffold might be his dreadful end. She turned, shuddering, from the contemplation of those hideous possibilities, and took refuge in the hope of his safe, his guiltless return. Even if his visions of success, even if his purposes of reform (how hopeless at his age!) were actually realised, could she consent to marry the man who had led his life, had written his letter, had contemplated (and still cherished) his merciless resolution of revenge? No woman in her senses could let the bare idea of being his wife enter her mind. Iris opened her writing-desk, to hide the letter from all eyes but her own. As she secured it with the key, her heart sank under the return of a terror remembered but too well. Once more, the superstitious belief in a destiny that was urging Lord Harry and herself nearer and nearer to each other, even when they seemed to be most widely and most surely separated, thrilled her under the chilling mystery of its presence. She dropped helplessly into a chair. Oh, for a friend who could feel for her, who could strengthen her, whose wise words could restore her to her better and calmer self! Hugh was far away; and Iris was left to suffer and to struggle alone.

Heartfelt aspirations for help and sympathy! Oh, irony of circumstances, how were they answered? The housemaid entered the room, to announce the arrival of a discharged servant, with a lost character.

'Let the young woman come in,' Iris said. Was Fanny Mere the friend whom she had been longing for? She looked at her troubled face in the glass—and laughed bitterly.

CHAPTER XIV

THE LADY'S MAID

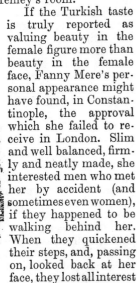

IT was not easy to form a positive opinion of the young woman who now presented herself in Miss Henley's room.

If the Turkish taste is truly reported as valuing beauty in the female figure more than beauty in the female face, Fanny Mere's personal appearance might have found, in Constantinople, the approval which she failed to receive in London. Slim and well balanced, firmly and neatly made, she interested men who met her by accident (and sometimes even women), if they happened to be walking behind her. When they quickened their steps, and, passing on, looked back at her face, they lost all interest in Fanny from that moment. Painters would have described the defect in her face as ' want of colour.' She was one of the whitest of fair female human beings. Light flaxen hair, faint blue eyes with no expression in them, and a complexion which looked as if it had never been stirred by a circulation of blood, produced an effect on her fellow-creatures in general which made them insensible to the beauty of her figure, and the grace of her movements. There was no betrayal of bad health in her strange pallor : on the contrary, she suggested the idea of rare physical strength. Her quietly respectful manner was, so to say, emphasised by an underlying self-possession, which looked capable of acting promptly and fearlessly in the critical emergencies of life. Otherwise, the expression of character in her face was essentially passive. Here was a steady, resolute young woman, possessed of qualities which failed to show themselves on the surface—whether good qualities or bad qualities experience alone could determine.

Finding it impossible, judging by a first impression, to arrive at any immediate decision favourable or adverse to the stranger, Iris opened the interview with her customary frankness; leaving the consequences to follow as they might.

'Take a seat, Fanny,' she said, 'and let us try if we can understand each other. I think you will agree with me that there must be no concealments between us. You ought to know that your mistress has told me why she parted with you. It was her duty to tell me the truth, and it is my duty not to be unjustly prejudiced against you after what I have heard. Pray believe me when I say that I don't know, and don't wish to know, what your temptation may have been——'

'I beg your pardon, Miss, for interrupting you. My temptation was vanity.'

Whether she did or did not suffer in making that confession, it was impossible to discover. Her tones were quiet; her manner was unobtrusively respectful; the pallor of her face was not disturbed by the slightest change of colour. Was the new maid an insensible person? Iris began to fear already that she might have made a mistake.

'I don't expect you to enter into particulars,' she said; 'I don't ask you here to humiliate yourself.'

'When I got your letter, Miss, I tried to consider how I might show myself worthy of your kindness,' Fanny answered. 'The one way I could see was not to let you think better of me than I deserve. When a person, like me, is told, for the first time, that her figure makes amends for her face, she is flattered by the only compliment that has been paid to her in all her life. My excuse, Miss (if I have an excuse) is a mean one—I couldn't resist a compliment. That is all I have to say.'

Iris began to alter her opinion. This was not a young woman of the ordinary type. It began to look possible, and more than possible, that she was worthy of a helping hand. The truth seemed to be in her.

'I understand you, and feel for you.' Having replied in those words, Iris wisely and delicately changed the subject. 'Let me hear how you are situated at the present time,' she continued. 'Are your parents living?'

'My father and mother are dead, Miss.'

'Have you any other relatives?'

'They are too poor to be able to do anything for me. I have lost my character—and I am left to help myself.'

'Suppose you fail to find another situation?' Iris suggested.

'Yes, Miss?'

'How can you help yourself?'

' I can do what other girls have done.'

' What do you mean ? '

' Some of us starve on needlework. Some take to the streets.
Some end it in the river. If there is no other chance for me, I
think I shall try that way,' said the poor creature, as quietly as if
she was speaking of some customary prospect that was open to her.
' There will be nobody to be sorry for me——and, as I have read,
drowning is not a very painful death.'

' You shock me, Fanny ! I, for one, should be sorry for you.'

' Thank you, Miss.'

' And try to remember,' Iris continued, ' that there may be chances
in the future which you don't see yet. You speak of what you have
read, and I have already noticed how clearly and correctly you express yourself. You must have been educated. Was it at home ?
or at school ? '

' I was once sent to school,' Fanny replied, not quite willingly.

' Was it a private school ? '

' Yes.'

That short answer warned Iris to be careful.

' Recollections of school,' she said good-humouredly, ' are not the
pleasantest recollections in some of our lives. Perhaps I have
touched on a subject which is disagreeable to you ? '

' You have touched on one of my disappointments, Miss. While
my mother lived, she was my teacher. After her death, my father
sent me to school. When he failed in business, I was obliged to
leave, just as I had begun to learn and like it. Besides, the girls
found out that I was going away, because there was no money at
home to pay the fees—and that mortified me. There is more that
I might tell you. I have a reason for hating my recollections of
the school—but I mustn't mention that time in my life which your
goodness to me tries to forget.'

All that appealed to her, so simply and so modestly, in that
reply, was not lost on Iris. After an interval of silence, she
said :

' Can you guess what I am thinking of, Fanny ? '

' No, Miss.'

' I am asking myself a question. If I try you in my service
shall I never regret it ? '

For the first time, strong emotion shook Fanny Mere. Her
voice failed her, in the effort to speak. Iris considerately
went on.

' You will take the place,' she said, ' of a maid who has been
with me for years—a good dear creature who has only left me
through ill-health. I must not expect too much of you ; I cannot
hope that you will be to me what Rhoda Bennet has been.'

Fanny succeeded in controlling herself. ' Is there any hope,'
she asked, ' of my seeing Rhoda Bennet ? '

' Why do you wish to see her ? '

' You are fond of her, Miss—that is one reason.'

'And the other ? '

' Rhoda Bennet might help me to serve you as I want to serve
you ; she might perhaps encourage me to try if I could follow her
example.' Fanny paused, and clasped her hands fervently. The
thought that was in her forced its way to expression. ' It's so
easy to feel grateful,' she said—' and, oh, so hard to show it ! '

' Come to me,' her new mistress answered, 'and show it to-
morrow.'

Moved by that compassionate impulse, Iris said the words which
restored to an unfortunate creature a lost character and a forfeited
place in the world.

CHAPTER XV

MR. HENLEY'S TEMPER

ROVIDED by nature with ironclad constitutional defences against illness, Mr. Henley was now and then troubled with groundless doubts of his own state of health. Acting under a delusion of this kind, he imagined symptoms which rendered a change of residence necessary from his town house to his country house, a few days only after his daughter had decided on the engagement of her new maid.

Iris gladly, even eagerly, adapted her own wishes to the furtherance of her father's plans. Sorely tried by anxiety and suspense, she needed all that rest and tranquillity could do for her. The first week in the country produced an improvement in her health. Enjoying the serene beauty of woodland and field, breathing the delicious purity of the air—sometimes cultivating her own corner in the garden, and sometimes helping the women in the lighter labours of the dairy—her nerves recovered their tone, and her spirits rose again to their higher level.

In the performance of her duties the new maid justified Miss Henley's confidence in her, during the residence of the household in the country.

She showed, in her own undemonstrative way, a grateful sense of her mistress's kindness. Her various occupations were intelligently and attentively pursued; her even temper never seemed to vary; she gave the servants no opportunities of complaining of her. But one peculiarity in her behaviour excited hostile remark, below-stairs. On the occasions when she was free to go out for the day, she always found some excuse for not joining any of the other female servants, who might happen to be similarly favoured. The one use she made of her holiday was to travel by railway to some place unknown; always returning at the right time in the evening. Iris knew enough of the sad circumstances to be able to respect her motives, and to appreciate the necessity for keeping the object of those solitary journeys a secret from her fellow-servants.

The pleasant life in the country house had lasted for nearly a month, when the announcement of Hugh's approaching return to England reached Iris. The fatal end of his father's long and lingering illness had arrived, and the funeral had taken place. Business, connected with his succession to the property, would detain him in London for a few days. Submitting to this necessity, he earnestly expressed the hope of seeing Iris again, the moment he was at liberty.

Hearing the good news, Mr. Henley obstinately returned to his plans—already twice thwarted—for promoting the marriage of Mountjoy and Iris.

He wrote to invite Hugh to his house in a tone of cordiality which astonished his daughter; and when the guest arrived, the genial welcome of the host had but one defect—Mr. Henley over-acted his part. He gave the two young people perpetual opportunities of speaking to each other privately; and, on the principle that none are so blind as those who won't see, he failed to discover that the relations between them continued to be relations of friendship, do what he might. Hugh's long attendance on his dying father had left him depressed in spirits; Iris understood him, and felt for him. He was not ready with his opinion of the new maid, after he had seen Fanny Mere. 'My inclination,' he said, 'is to trust the girl. And yet, I hesitate to follow my inclination—and I don't know why.'

When Hugh's visit came to an end, he continued his journey in a northerly direction. The property left to him by his father included a cottage, standing in its own grounds, on the Scotch shore of the Solway Firth. The place had been neglected during the long residence of the elder Mr. Mountjoy on the Continent. Hugh's present object was to judge, by his own investigation, of the necessity for repairs.

On the departure of his guest, Mr. Henley (still obstinately hopeful of the marriage on which he had set his mind) assumed a jocular manner towards Iris, and asked if the Scotch cottage was to be put in order for the honeymoon. Her reply, gently as it was expressed, threw him into a state of fury. His vindictive temper revelled, not only in harsh words, but in spiteful actions. He sold one of his dogs which had specially attached itself to Iris; and, seeing that she still enjoyed the country, he decided on returning to London.

She submitted in silence. But the events of that past time, when her father's merciless conduct had driven her out of his house, returned ominously to her memory. She said to herself: 'Is a day coming when I shall leave him again?' It was coming—and she little knew how.

CHAPTER XVI

THE DOCTOR IN FULL DRESS

M R. HENLEY'S household had been again established in London, when a servant appeared one morning with a visiting card, and announced that a gentleman had called who wished to see Miss Henley. She looked at the card. The gentleman was Mr. Vimpany.

On the point of directing the man to say that she was engaged, Iris checked herself.

Mrs. Vimpany's farewell words had produced a strong impression on her. There had been moments of doubt and gloom in her later life, when the remembrance of that unhappy woman was associated with a feeling (perhaps a morbid feeling) of self-reproach. It seemed to be hard on the poor penitent wretch not to have written to her. Was she still leading the same dreary life in the mouldering old town? Or had she made another attempt to return to the ungrateful stage? The gross husband, impudently presenting himself with his card and his message, could answer those questions if he could do nothing else. For that reason only Iris decided that she would receive Mr. Vimpany.

On entering the room, she found two discoveries awaiting her, for which she was entirely unprepared.

The doctor's personal appearance exhibited a striking change; he was dressed, in accordance with the strictest notions of professional propriety, entirely in black. More remarkable still, there happened to be a French novel among the books on the table—and that novel Mr. Vimpany, barbarous Mr. Vimpany, was actually reading with an appearance of understanding it!

'I seem to surprise you,' said the doctor. 'Is it this?' He held up the French novel as he put the question.

'I must own that I was not aware of the range of your accomplishments,' Iris answered.

'Oh, don't talk of accomplishments! I learnt my profession in Paris. For nigh on three years I lived among the French medical students. Noticing this book on the table, I thought I would try whether I had forgotten the language—in the time that has passed (you know) since those days. Well, my memory isn't a good one in most things, but strange to say (force of habit, I suppose), some of my French sticks by me still. I hope I see you well, Miss

Henley. Might I ask if you noticed the new address, when I sent up my card ? '

' I only noticed your name.'

The doctor produced his pocket-book, and took out a second card. With pride he pointed to the address : ' 5 Redburn Road, Hampstead Heath.' With pride he looked at his black clothes. ' Strictly professional, isn't it ? ' he said. ' I have bought a new practice ; and I have become a new man. It isn't easy at first. No, by jingo—I beg your pardon—I was about to say, my own respectability rather bothers me ; I shall get used to it in time. If you will allow me, I'll take a liberty. No offence, I hope ? '

He produced a handful of his cards, and laid them out in a neat little semicircle on the table.

' A word of recommendation, when you have the chance, would be a friendly act on your part,' he explained. ' Capital air in Red-burn Road, and a fine view of the Heath out of the garret windows —but it's rather an out-of-the-way situation. Not that I complain ; beggars mustn't be choosers. I should have preferred a practice in a fashionable part of London ; but our little windfall of money——'

He came to a full stop in the middle of a sentence. The sale of the superb diamond pin, by means of which Lord Harry had repaid Mrs. Vimpany's services, was, of all domestic events, the last which it might be wise to mention in the presence of Miss Henley. He was awkwardly silent. Taking advantage of that circumstance, Iris introduced the subject in which she felt interested.

' How is Mrs. Vimpany ? ' she asked.

' Oh, she's all right ! '

' Does she like your new house ? '

The doctor made a strange reply. ' I really can't tell you,' he said.

' Do you mean that Mrs. Vimpany declines to express an opinion ? '

He laughed. ' In all my experience,' he said, ' I never met with a woman who did that ! No, no ; the fact is, my wife and I have parted company. There's no need to look so serious about it ! In-compatibility of temper, as the saying is, has led us to a friendly separation. Equally a relief on both sides. She goes her way, I go mine.'

His tone disgusted Iris—and she let him see it. ' Is it of any use to ask you for Mrs. Vimpany's address ? ' she inquired.

His atrocious good-humour kept its balance as steadily as ever : ' Sorry to disappoint you. Mrs. Vimpany hasn't given me her address. Curious, isn't it ? The fact is, she moped a good deal, after you left us ; talked of her duty, and the care of her soul, and that sort of thing. When I hear where she is, I'll let you know with pleasure. To the best of my belief, she's doing nurse's work some-where.'

' Nurse's work ? What do you mean ? '

' Oh, the right thing—all in the fashion. She belongs to what they call a Sisterhood; goes about, you know, in a shabby black gown, with a poke bonnet. At least, so Lord Harry told me the other day.'

In spite of herself, Iris betrayed the agitation which those words instantly roused in her. 'Lord Harry!' she exclaimed. 'Where is he? In London?'

'Yes--at Parker's Hotel.'

'When did he return?'

'Oh, a few days ago; and—what do you think?—he's come back from the goldfields a lucky man. Damn it, I've let the cat out of the bag! I was to keep the thing a secret from everybody, and from you most particularly. He's got some surprise in store for you. Don't tell him what I've done! We had a little misunderstanding, in past days, at Honeybuzzard—and, now we are friends again, I don't want to lose his lordship's interest.'

Iris promised to be silent. But to know that the wild lord was in England again, and to remain in ignorance whether he had, or had not, returned with the stain of bloodshed on him, was more than she could endure.

'There is one question I must ask you,' she said. 'I have reason to fear that Lord Harry left this country, with a purpose of revenge——'

Mr. Vimpany wanted no further explanation. 'Yes, yes; I know. You may be easy about that. There's been no mischief done, either one way or the other. The man he was after, when he landed in South Africa (he told me so himself) has escaped him.'

With that reply, the doctor got up in a hurry to bring his visit to an end. He proposed to take to flight, he remarked facetiously, before Miss Henley wheedled him into saying anything more.

After opening the door, however, he suddenly returned to Iris, and added a last word in the strictest confidence.

'If you won't forget to recommend me to your friends,' he said, 'I'll trust you with another secret. You will see his lordship in a day or two, when he returns from the races. Good-bye.'

The races! What was Lord Harry doing at the races?

CHAPTER XVII

ON HAMPSTEAD HEATH

RIS had only to remember the manner in which she and Mountjoy had disappointed her father, to perceive the serious necessity of preventing Mountjoy's rival from paying a visit at Mr. Henley's house.

She wrote at once to Lord Harry, at the hotel which Mr. Vimpany had mentioned, entreating him not to think of calling on her. Being well aware that he would insist on a meeting, she engaged to write again and propose an appointment. In making this concession, Iris might have found it easier to persuade herself that she was yielding to sheer necessity, if she had not been guiltily conscious of a feeling of pleasure at the prospect of seeing Lord Harry again, returning to her an innocent man. There was some influence, in this train of thought, which led her mind back to Hugh. She regretted his absence—wondered whether he would have proposed throwing her letter to the Irish lord into the fire—sighed, closed the envelope, and sent the letter to the post.

On the next day, she had arranged to drive to Muswell Hill, and to pay the customary visit to Rhoda. Heavy rain obliged her to wait for a fitter opportunity. It was only on the third day that the sky cleared, and the weather was favourable again. On a sunshiny autumn morning, with a fine keen air blowing, she ordered the open carriage. Noticing, while Fanny Mere was helping her to dress, that the girl looked even paler than usual, she said, with her customary kindness to persons dependent on her, ' You look as if a drive in the fresh air would do you good—you shall go with me to the farm, and see Rhoda Bennet.'

When they stopped at the house, the farmer's wife appeared, attending a gentleman to the door. Iris at once recognised the local medical man. ' You're not in attendance, I hope, on Rhoda Bennet ? ' she said.

The doctor acknowledged that there had been some return of the nervous derangement from which the girl suffered. He depended mainly (he said) on the weather allowing her to be out as much as possible in the fresh air, and on keeping her free from all agitation. Rhoda was so far on the way to recovery, that she was now walking in the garden by his advice. He had no fear of her, provided she was not too readily encouraged, in her present state, to receive visitors. Her mistress would be, of course, an exception to this rule. But even Miss Henley would perhaps do well not to excite the girl by prolonging her visit. There was one other suggestion which he would venture to make, while he had the opportunity. Rhoda was not, as he thought, warmly enough clothed for the time of year; and a bad cold might be easily caught by a person in her condition.

Iris entered the farm-house; leaving Fanny Mere, after what the doctor had said on the subject of visitors, to wait for her in the carriage.

After an absence of barely ten minutes Miss Henley returned; personally changed, not at all to her own advantage, by the intro- duction of a novelty in her dress. She had gone into the farm- house, wearing a handsome mantle of sealskin. When she came out again, the mantle had vanished, and there appeared in its place a common cloak of drab-coloured cloth. Noticing the expres- sion of blank amazement in the maid's face, Iris burst out laughing.

' How do you think I look in my new cloak ? ' she asked.

Fanny saw nothing to laugh at in the sacrifice of a sealskin mantle. ' I must not presume, Miss, to give an opinion,' she said gravely.

' At any rate,' Iris continued, ' you must be more than mortal if my change of costume doesn't excite your curiosity. I found Rhoda Bennet in the garden, exposed to the cold wind in this ugly flimsy thing. After what the doctor had told me, it was high time to assert my authority. I insisted on changing cloaks with Rhoda. She made an attempt, poor dear, to resist; but she knows me of old—and I had my way. I am sorry you have been prevented from seeing her; you shall not miss the opportunity when she is well again. Do you admire a fine view? Very well; we will vary the drive on our return. Go back,' she said to the coachman, ' by Highgate and Hampstead.'

Fanny's eyes rested on the shabby cloak with a well-founded distrust of it as a protection against the autumn weather. She ventured to suggest that her mistress might feel the loss (in an open carriage) of the warm mantle which she had left on Rhoda's shoulders.

Iris made light of the doubt expressed by her maid. But by the time they had passed Highgate, and had approached the beginning of the straight road which crosses the high ridge of Hampstead Heath, she was obliged to acknowledge that she did indeed feel the cold. ' You ought to be a good walker,' she said, looking at her maid's firm well-knit figure. ' Exercise is all I want to warm me. What do you say to going home on foot ? ' Fanny was ready and willing to accompany her mistress. The carriage was dismissed, and they set forth on their walk.

As they passed the inn called ' The Spaniards,' two women who were standing at the garden gate stared at Iris, and smiled. A few paces further on, they were met by an errand-boy. He too looked at the young lady, and put his hand derisively to his head, with a shrill whistle expressive of malicious enjoyment. ' I appear to amuse these people,' Iris said. ' What do they see in me ? '

Fanny answered with an effort to preserve her gravity, which was not quite successfully disguised : ' I beg your pardon, Miss ; I think they notice the curious contrast between your beautiful bonnet and your shabby cloak.'

Persons of excitable temperament have a sense of ridicule, and a dread of it, unintelligible to their fellow-creatures who are made of coarser material. For the moment, Iris was angry. ' Why didn't you tell me of it,' she asked sharply, ' before I sent away the carriage ? How can I walk back, with everybody laughing at me ? '

She paused—reflected a little—and led the way off the high road, on the right, to the fine clump of fir-trees which commands the famous view in that part of the Heath.

' There's but one thing to be done,' she said, recovering her good temper ; ' we must make my grand bonnet suit itself to my miserable cloak. You will pull out the feather and rip off the lace (and keep them for yourself, if you like), and then I ought to look shabby enough from head to foot, I am sure ! No ; not here ; they may notice us from the road—and what may the fools not do when they see you tearing the ornaments off my bonnet ! Come down below the trees, where the ground will hide us.'

They had nearly descended the steep slope which leads to the valley, below the clump of firs, when they were stopped by a terrible discovery.

Close at their feet, in a hollow of the ground, was stretched the insensible body of a man. He lay on his side, with his face turned away from them. An open razor had dropped close by him. Iris stooped over the prostrate man, to examine his face. Blood flowing from a frightful wound in his throat, was the first thing that she saw. Her eyes closed instinctively, recoiling from that ghastly sight. The next instant she opened them again, and saw his face.

Dying or dead, it was the face of Lord Harry.

The shriek that burst from her, on making that horrible discovery, was heard by two men who were crossing the lower heath at some distance. They saw the women, and ran to them. One of the men was a labourer ; the other, better dressed, looked like a foreman of works. He was the first who arrived on the spot.

' Enough to frighten you out of your senses, ladies,' he said civilly. ' It's a case of suicide, I should say, by the look of it.'

' For God's sake, let us do something to help him ! ' Iris burst out. ' I know him ! I know him ! '

Fanny, equal to the emergency, asked Miss Henley for her handkerchief, joined her own handkerchief to it, and began to bandage the wound. ' Try if his pulse is beating,' she said quietly to her mistress. The foreman made himself useful by examining the suicide's pockets. Iris thought she could detect a faint fluttering in the pulse. 'Is there no doctor living near?' she cried. 'Is there no carriage to be found in this horrible place?'

The foreman had discovered two letters. Iris read her own name on one of them. The other was addressed 'To the person who may find my body.' She tore the envelope open. It contained one of Mr. Vimpany's cards, with these desperate words written on it in pencil: 'Take me to the doctor's address, and let him bury me, or dissect me, whichever he pleases.' Iris showed the card to the foreman. 'Is it near here?' she asked. 'Yes, Miss; we might get him to that place in no time, if there was a conveyance of any kind to be found.' Still preserving her presence of mind, Fanny pointed in the direction of 'The Spaniards' inn. 'We might get what we want there,' she said. 'Shall I go?'

Iris signed to her to attend to the wounded man, and ascended the sloping ground. She ran on towards the road. The men, directed by Fanny, raised the body and slowly followed her, diverging to an easier ascent. As Iris reached the road, a four-wheel cab passed her. Without an instant's hesitation, she called to the driver to stop. He pulled up his horse. She confronted a solitary gentleman, staring out of the window of the cab, and looking as if he thought that a lady had taken a liberty with him. Iris allowed the outraged stranger no opportunity of expressing his sentiments. Breathless as she was, she spoke first.

'Pray forgive me—you are alone in the cab—there is room for a gentleman, dangerously wounded—he will bleed to death if we don't find help for him—the place is close by—oh, don't refuse me!' She looked back, holding fast by the cab door, and saw Fanny and the men slowly approaching. 'Bring him here!' she cried.

'Do nothing of the sort!' shouted the gentleman in possession of the cab.

But Fanny obeyed her mistress; and the men obeyed Fanny. Iris turned indignantly to the merciless stranger. 'I ask you to do an act of Christian kindness,' she said. 'How can you, how dare you, hesitate?'

'Drive on!' cried the stranger.

'Drive on, at your peril,' Iris added, on her side.

The cabman sat, silent and stolid, on the box, waiting for events.

Slowly the men came in view, bearing Lord Harry, still insensible. The handkerchiefs on his throat were saturated with blood. At that sight, the cowardly instincts of the stranger completely mastered him. 'Let me out!' he clamoured; 'let me out!'

Finding the cab left at her disposal, Iris actually thanked him! He looked at her with an evil eye. 'I have my suspicions, I can tell you,' he muttered. 'If this comes to a trial in a court of law, I'm not going to be mixed up with it. Innocent people have been hanged before now, when appearances were against them.'

He walked off; and, by way of completing the revelation of his own meanness, forgot to pay his fare.

On the point of starting the horse to pursue him, the cabman was effectually stopped. Iris showed him a sovereign. Upon this hint (like Othello) he spoke.

'All right, Miss. I see your poor gentleman is a-bleeding. You'll take care—won't you?—that he doesn't spoil my cushions.' The driver was not a ill-conditioned man; he put the case of his property indulgently, with a persuasive smile. Iris turned to the two worthy fellows, who had so readily given her their help, and bade them good-bye, with a solid expression of her gratitude which they both remembered for many a long day to come. Fanny was already in the cab supporting Lord Harry's body. Iris joined her. The cabman drove carefully to Mr. Vimpany's new house.

CHAPTER XVIII

PROFESSIONAL ASSISTANCE

NUMBER Five was near the centre of the row of little suburban houses called Redburn Road. When the cab drew up at the door Mr. Vimpany himself was visible, looking out of the window on the ground floor—and yawning as he looked. Iris beckoned to him impatiently. 'Anything wrong?' he asked, as he approached the door of the cab. She drew back, and silently showed him what was wrong. The doctor received the shock with composure. When he happened to be sober and sad, looking for patients and failing to find them, Mr. Vimpany's capacity for feeling sympathy began and ended with himself.

'This is a new scrape, even for Lord Harry,' he remarked. 'Let's get him into the house.'

The insensible man was carried into the nearest room on the ground floor. Pale and trembling, Iris related what had happened, and asked if there was no hope of saving him.

'Patience!' Mr. Vimpany answered; 'I'll tell you directly.'

He removed the bandages, and examined the wound. 'There's been a deal of blood lost,' he said; 'I'll try and pull him through. While I am about it, Miss, go upstairs, if you please, and find your way to the drawing-room.' Iris hesitated. The doctor opened a neat mahogany box. 'The tools of my trade,' he continued; 'I'm going to sew up his lordship's throat.' Shuddering as she heard those words, Iris hurried out of the room. Fanny followed her mistress up the stairs. In her own very different way, the maid was as impenetrably composed as Mr. Vimpany himself. 'There was a second letter found in the gentleman's pocket, Miss,' she said. 'Will you excuse my reminding you that you have not read it yet.'

Iris read the lines that follow:

'Forgive me, my dear, for the last time. My letter is to say that I shall trouble you no more in this world—and, as for the other world, who knows? I brought some money back with me, from the goldfields. It was not enough to be called a fortune—I mean the sort of fortune which might persuade your father to let you marry me. Well! here in England, I had an opportunity of making ten times more of it on the turf; and, let me add, with private information of the horses which I might certainly count on to win. I don't stop to ask by what cruel roguery I was tempted to my ruin. My money is lost; and, with it, my last hope of a happy and harmless life with you comes to an end. I die, Iris dear, with the death of that hope. Something in me seems to shrink from suicide in the ugly gloom of great overgrown London. I prefer to make away with myself among the fields, where the green will remind me of dear old Ireland. When you think of me sometimes, say to yourself the poor wretch loved me—and perhaps the earth will lie lighter on Harry for those kind words, and the flowers (if you favour me by planting a few) may grow prettier on my grave.'

There it ended.

The heart of Iris sank as she read that melancholy farewell, expressed in language at once wild and childish. If he survived his desperate attempt at self-destruction, to what end would it lead? In silence, the woman who loved him put his letter back in her bosom. Watching her attentively—affected, it was impossible to say how, by that mute distress—Fanny Mere proposed to go downstairs, and ask once more what hope there might be for the wounded man. Iris knew the doctor too well to let the maid leave her on a useless errand.

'Some men might be kindly ready to relieve my suspense,' she said; 'the man downstairs is not one of them. I must wait till he comes to me, or sends for me. But there is something I wish to say to you, while we are alone. You have been but a short time in my service, Fanny. Is it too soon to ask if you feel some interest in me?'

'If I can comfort you or help you, Miss, be pleased to tell me how.' She made that reply respectfully, in her usual quiet manner; her pale cheeks showing no change of colour, her faint blue eyes resting steadily on her mistress's face. Iris went on:

'If I ask you to keep what has happened, on this dreadful day, a secret from everybody, may I trust you—little as you know of me—as I might have trusted Rhoda Bennet?'

'I promise it, Miss.' In saying those few words, the unde‧monstrative woman seemed to think that she had said enough.

Iris had no alternative but to ask another favour.

'And whatever curiosity you may feel, will you be content to do me a kindness—without wanting an explanation?'

'It is my duty to respect my mistress's secrets; I will do my duty.' No sentiment, no offer of respectful sympathy; a positive declaration of fidelity, left impenetrably to speak for itself. Was the girl's heart hardened by the disaster which had darkened her life? Or was she the submissive victim of that inbred reserve, which shrinks from the frank expression of feeling, and lives and dies self-imprisoned in its own secrecy? A third explanation, founded probably on a steadier basis, was suggested by Miss Henley's remembrance of their first interview. Fanny's nature had revealed a sensitive side, when she was first encouraged to hope for a refuge from ruin followed perhaps by starvation and death. Judging so far from experience, a sound conclusion seemed to follow. When circumstances strongly excited the girl, there was a dormant vitality in her that revived. At other times when events failed to agitate her by a direct appeal to personal interests, her constitutional reserve held the rule. She could be impenetrably honest, steadily industrious, truly grateful—but the intuitive expression of feeling, on ordinary occasions, was beyond her reach.

After an interval of nearly half an hour, Mr. Vimpany made his appearance. Pausing in the doorway, he consulted his watch, and entered on a calculation which presented him favourably from a professional point of view.

'Allow for time lost in reviving my lord when he fainted, and stringing him up with a drop of brandy, and washing my hands (look how clean they are!), I haven't been more than twenty minutes in mending his throat. Not bad surgery, Miss Henley.'

'Is his life safe, Mr. Vimpany?'

'Thanks to his luck—yes.'

'His luck?'

'To be sure! In the first place, he owes his life to your finding him when you did; a little later, and it would have been all over with Lord Harry. Second piece of luck: catching the doctor at home, just when he was most wanted. Third piece of luck: our friend didn't know how to cut his own throat properly. You needn't look black at me, Miss; I'm not joking. A suicide with a razor in his hand has generally one chance in his favour—he is ignorant of anatomy. That is my lord's case. He has only cut through the upper fleshy part of his throat, and has missed the larger blood vessels. Take my word for it, he will do well enough now; thanks to you, thanks to me, and thanks to his own ignorance. What do you say to that way of putting it? Ha! my brains

are in good working order to-day; I haven't been drinking any of
Mr. Mountjoy's claret—do you take the joke, Miss Henley?'

Chuckling over the recollection of his own drunken audacity,
he happened to notice Fanny Mere.

'Hullo! is this another injured person in want of me? You're
as white as a sheet, Miss. If you're going to faint, do me a favour
—wait till I can get the brandy-bottle. Oh! it's natural to you, is
it? I see. A thick skin and a slow circulation; you will live to
be an old woman. A friend of yours, Miss Henley?'

Fanny answered composedly for herself: 'I am Miss Henley's
maid, sir.'

'What's become of the other one?' Mr. Vimpany asked.
'Aye? aye? Staying at a farm-house for the benefit of her health,
is she? If I had been allowed time enough, I would have made
a cure of Rhoda Bennet. There isn't a medical man in England
who knows more than I do of the nervous maladies of women—
and what is my reward? Is my waiting-room crammed with rich
people coming to consult me? Do I live in a fashionable Square?
Have I even been made a Baronet? Damn it—I beg your pardon,
Miss Henley—but it *is* irritating, to a man of my capacity, to be
completely neglected. For the last three days not a creature has
darkened the doors of this house. Could I say a word to you?'

He led Iris mysteriously into a corner of the room. 'About
our friend downstairs?' he began.

'When may we hope that he will be well again, Mr. Vimpany?'

'Maybe in three weeks. In a month at most. I have nobody
here but a stupid servant girl. We ought to have a competent
nurse. I can get a thoroughly trained person from the hospital;
but there's a little difficulty. I am an outspoken man. When I
am poor, I own I am poor. My lord must be well fed; the nurse
must be well fed. Would you mind advancing a small loan, to
provide beforehand for the payment of expenses?'

Iris handed her purse to him, sick of the sight of Mr. Vimpany.
'Is that all?' she asked, making for the door.

'Much obliged. That's all.'

As they approached the room on the ground floor, Iris stopped:
her eyes rested on the doctor. Even to that coarse creature, the
eloquent look spoke for her. Fanny noticed it, and suddenly turned
her head aside. Over the maid's white face there passed darkly
an expression of unutterable contempt. Her mistress's weakness
had revealed itself—weakness for one of the betrayers of women;
weakness for a man! In the meantime, Mr. Vimpany (having got
the money) was ready to humour the enviable young lady with a
well-filled purse.

'Do you want to see my lord before you go?' he asked, amused
at the idea. 'Mind! you mustn't disturb him! No talking, and
no crying. Ready? Now look at him.'

There he lay on a shabby little sofa, in an ugly little room; his
eyes closed; one helpless hand hanging down; a stillness on his

ghastly face, horribly suggestive of the stillness of death—there he lay, the reckless victim of his love for the woman who had desperately renounced him again and again, who had now saved him for the third time. Ah, how her treacherous heart pleaded for him! Can you drive him away from you after this? You, who love him, what does your cold-blooded prudence say, when you look at him now?

She felt herself drawn, roughly and suddenly, back into the passage. The door was closed; the doctor was whispering to her. 'Hold up, Miss! I expected better things of you. Come! come! —no fainting. You'll find him a different man to-morrow. Pay us a visit, and judge for yourself.'

After what she had suffered, Iris hungered for sympathy. 'Isn't it pitiable?' she said to her maid as they left the house.

'I don't know, Miss.'

'You don't know? Good heavens, are you made of stone? Have you no such thing as a heart in you?'

'Not for the men,' Fanny answered. 'I keep my pity for the women.'

Iris knew what bitter remembrances made their confession in those words. How she missed Rhoda Bennet at that moment!

CHAPTER XIX

FOR a month, Mountjoy remained in his cottage on the shores of the Solway Firth, superintending the repairs.

His correspondence with Iris was regularly continued; and, for the first time in his experience of her, was a cause of disappointment to him.

Her replies revealed an incomprehensible change in her manner of writing, which became more and more marked in each succeeding instance. Notice it as he might in his own letters, no explanation followed on the part of his correspondent. She, who had so frankly confided her joys and sorrows to him in past days, now wrote with a reserve which seemed only to permit the most vague and guarded allusion to herself. The changes in the weather; the alternation of public news that was dull, and public news that was interesting; the absence of her father abroad, occasioned by doubt of the soundness of his investments in foreign securities; vague questions relating to Hugh's new place of abode, which could only have proceeded from a preoccupied mind—these were the topics on which Iris dwelt, in writing to her faithful old friend. It was hardly possible to doubt that something must have happened, which she had reasons—serious reasons, as it seemed only too natural to infer—for keeping concealed from Mountjoy. Try as he might to disguise it from himself, he now knew how dear, how hopelessly dear, she was to him by the anxiety that he suffered, and by the jealous sense of injury which defied his self-command. His immediate superintendence of the workmen at the cottage was no longer necessary. Leaving there a representative whom he could trust, he resolved to answer his last letter, received from Iris, in person.

The next day he was in London.

Calling at the house, he was informed that Miss Henley was not at home, and that it was impossible to say with certainty when she might return. While he was addressing his inquiries to the servant, Mr. Henley opened the library door. 'Is that you, Mountjoy?' he asked. 'Come in: I want to speak to you.'

Short and thick-set, with a thin-lipped mouth, a coarsely-florid complexion, and furtive greenish eyes; hard in his manner, and harsh in his voice; Mr. Henley was one of the few heartless men, who are innocent of deception on the surface: he was externally a person who inspired, at first sight, feelings of doubt and dislike. His manner failed to show even a pretence of being glad to see Hugh. What he had to say, he said walking up and down the room, and scratching his bristly iron-gray hair from time to time. These signs of restlessness indicated, to those who knew him well, that he had a selfish use to make of a fellow-creature, and failed to see immediately how to reach the end in view.

'I say, Mountjoy,' he began, 'have you any idea of what my daughter is about?'

'I don't even understand what you mean,' Hugh replied. 'For the last month I have been in Scotland.'

'You and she write to each other, don't you?'

'Yes.'

'Hasn't she told you——'

'Excuse me for interrupting you, Mr. Henley; she has told me nothing.'

Mr. Henley stared absently at the superbly-bound books on his library-shelves (never degraded by the familiar act of reading), and scratched his head more restlessly than ever.

'Look here, young man. When you were staying with me in the country, I rather hoped it might end in a marriage engagement. You and Iris disappointed me—not for the first time. But women do change their minds. Suppose she had changed *her* mind, after having twice refused you? Suppose she had given you an opportunity——'

Hugh interrupted him again. 'It's needless to suppose anything of the sort, sir; she would *not* have given me an opportunity.'

'Don't fence with me, Mountjoy! I'll put it in a milder way, if you prefer being humbugged. Do you feel any interest in that perverse girl of mine?'

Hugh answered readily and warmly: 'The truest interest!'

Even Mr. Henley was human; his ugly face looked uglier still. It assumed the self-satisfied expression of a man who had carried his point.

'Now I can go on, my friend, with what I had to say to you. I have been abroad on business, and only came back the other day. The moment I saw Iris I noticed something wrong about her. If I had been a stranger, I should have said: That young woman is not easy in her mind. Perfectly useless to speak to her about it. Quite happy and quite well—there was her own account of herself. I tried her maid next, a white-livered sulky creature, one of the steadiest liars I have ever met with. "I know of nothing amiss with my mistress, sir." There was the maid's way of keeping the secret, whatever it may be! I don't know whether you may have noticed it, in the course of your acquaintance with me—I hate to be beaten.'

'No, Mr. Henley, I have not noticed it.'

'Then you are informed of it now. Have you seen my housekeeper?'

'Once or twice, sir.'

'Come! you're improving; we shall make something of you in course of time. Well, the housekeeper was the next person I spoke to about my daughter. Had she seen anything strange in Miss Iris, while I was away from home? There's a dash of malice in my housekeeper's composition; I don't object to a dash of malice. When the old woman is pleased, she shows her yellow fangs. She *had* something to tell me: "The servants have been talking, sir, about Miss Iris." "Out with it, ma'am! what do they say?" "They notice, sir, that their young lady has taken to going out in the forenoon, regularly every day: always by herself, and always in the same direction. I don't encourage the servants, Mr. Henley: there was something insolent in the tone of suspicion that they adopted. I told them that Miss Iris was merely taking her walk. They reminded me that it must be a cruelly long walk; Miss Iris being away regularly for four or five hours together, before she came back to the house. After that" (says the housekeeper) "I thought it best to drop the subject." What do you think of it yourself, Mountjoy? Do you call my daughter's conduct suspicious?'

'I see nothing suspicious, Mr. Henley. When Iris goes out, she visits a friend.'

'And always goes in the same direction, and always visits the same friend,' Mr. Henley added. 'I felt a curiosity to know who that friend might be; and I made the discovery yesterday. When you were staying in my house in the country, do you remember the man who waited on you?'

Mountjoy began to feel alarmed for Iris; he answered as briefly as possible.

'Your valet,' he said.

'That's it! Well, I took my valet into my confidence—not for the first time, I can tell you: an invaluable fellow. When Iris went out yesterday, he tracked her to a wretched little suburban place near Hampstead Heath, called Redburn Road. She rang the bell at Number Five, and was at once let in—evidently well known there. My clever man made inquiries in the neighbourhood. The house belongs to a doctor, who has lately taken it. Name of Vimpany.'

Mountjoy was not only startled, but showed it plainly. Mr. Henley, still pacing backwards and forwards, happened by good fortune to have his back turned towards his visitor, at that moment.

'Now I ask you, as a man of the world,' Mr. Henley resumed, 'what does this mean? If you're too cautious to speak out—and I must say it looks like it—shall I set you the example?'

'Just as you please, sir.'

'Very well, then; I'll tell you what I suspect. When Iris is at home, and when there's something amiss in my family, I believe that scoundrel Lord Harry to be at the bottom of it. There's my experience, and there's my explanation. I was on the point of ordering my carriage, to go to the doctor myself, and insist on

'Does that mean, No?' Mr. Henley called after him.

knowing what the attraction is that takes my daughter to his house, when I heard your voice in the hall. You tell me you are interested in Iris. Very well; you are just the man to help me.'

'May I ask how, Mr. Henley?'

'Of course you may. You can find your way to her confidence, if you choose to try; she will trust you, when she won't trust her father. I don't care two straws about her other secrets; but I do want to know whether she is, or is not, plotting to marry the Irish blackguard. Satisfy me about that, and you needn't tell me anything more. May I count on you to find out how the land lies?'

Mountjoy listened, hardly able to credit the evidence of his own senses; he was actually expected to insinuate himself into the confidence of Iris, and then to betray her to her father! He rose, and took his hat—and, without even the formality of a bow, opened the door.

'Does that mean No?' Mr. Henley called after him.

'Most assuredly,' Mountjoy answered—and closed the door behind him.

CHAPTER XX

FIRST SUSPICIONS OF IRIS

FROM the last memorable day, on which Iris had declared to him that he might always count on her as his friend, but never as his wife, Hugh had resolved to subject his feelings to a rigorous control. As to conquering his hopeless love, he knew but too well that it would conquer him, on any future occasion when he and Iris happened to meet.

He had been true to his resolution, at what cost of suffering he, and he alone knew. Sincerely, unaffectedly, he had tried to remain her friend. But the nature of the truest and the firmest man has its weak place, where the subtle influence of a woman is concerned. Deeply latent, beyond the reach of his own power of sounding, there was jealousy of the Irish lord lurking in Mountjoy, and secretly leading his mind when he hesitated in those emergencies of his life which were connected with Iris. Ignorant of the influence which was really directing him, he viewed with contempt Mr. Henley's suspicions of a secret understanding between his daughter and the man who was, by her own acknowledgment, unworthy of the love with which it had been her misfortune to regard him. At the same time, Hugh's mind was reluctantly in search of an explanation, which might account (without degrading Iris) for her having been traced to the doctor's house. In his recollection of events at the old country town, he found a motive for her renewal of intercourse with such a man as Mr. Vimpany, in the compassionate feeling with which she regarded the doctor's unhappy wife. There might well be some humiliating circumstance, recently added to the other trials of Mrs. Vimpany's married life, which had appealed to all that was generous and forgiving in the nature of Iris. Knowing nothing of the resolution to live apart which had latterly separated the doctor and his wife, Mountjoy decided on putting his idea to the test by applying for information to Mrs. Vimpany at her husband's house.

In the nature of a sensitive man the bare idea of delay, under these circumstances, was unendurable. Hugh called the first cab that passed him, and drove to Hampstead.

Careful—morbidly careful, perhaps—not to attract attention needlessly to himself, he stopped the cab at the entrance to Redburn Road, and approached Number Five on foot. A servant-girl answered the door. Mountjoy asked if Mrs. Vimpany was at home.

The girl made no immediate reply. She seemed to be puzzled by Mountjoy's simple question. Her familiar manner, with its vulgar assumption of equality in the presence of a stranger, revealed the London-bred maid-servant of modern times. 'Did you say *Mrs.* Vimpany?' she inquired sharply.

'Yes.'

'There's no such person here.'

It was Mountjoy's turn to be puzzled. 'Is this Mr. Vimpany's house?' he said.

'Yes, to be sure it is.'

'And yet Mrs. Vimpany doesn't live here?'

'No Mrs. Vimpany has darkened these doors,' the girl declared positively.

'Are you sure you are not making a mistake?'

'Quite sure. I have been in the doctor's service since he first took the house.'

Determined to solve the mystery, if it could be done, Mountjoy asked if he could see the doctor. No: Mr. Vimpany had gone out.

'There's a young person comes to us,' the servant continued. 'I wonder whether you mean her, when you ask for Mrs. Vimpany? The name *she* gives is Henley.'

'Is Miss Henley here, now?'

'You can't see her—she's engaged.'

She was not engaged with Mrs. Vimpany, for no such person was known in the house. She was not engaged with the doctor, for the doctor had gone out. Mountjoy looked at the hat-stand in the passage, and discovered a man's hat and a man's greatcoat. To whom did they belong? Certainly not to Mr. Vimpany, who had gone out. Repellent as it was, Mr. Henley's idea that the explanation of his daughter's conduct was to be found in the renewed influence over her of the Irish lord, now presented itself to Hugh's mind under a new point of view. He tried in vain to resist the impression that had been produced on him. A sense of injury, which he was unable to justify to himself, took possession of him. Come what might of it, he determined to set at rest the doubts of which he was ashamed, by communicating with Iris. His card-case proved to be empty when he opened it; but there were letters in his pocket, addressed to him at his hotel in London. Removing the envelope from one of these, he handed it to the servant:

'Take that to Miss Henley, and ask when I can see her.'

The girl left him in the passage, and went upstairs to the drawing-room.

In the flimsily-built little house, he could hear the heavy step of a man, crossing the room above, and then the resonant tones of a man's voice raised as if in anger. Had she given him already the right to be angry with her? He thought of the time, when the betrayal of Lord Harry's vindictive purpose in leaving England had frightened her—when he had set aside his own sense of what was due to him, for her sake—and had helped her to communicate, by letter, with the man whose fatal ascendency over Iris had saddened his life. Was what he heard, now, the return that he had deserved?

After a short absence, the servant came back with a message.

'Miss Henley begs you will excuse her. She will write to you.'

Would this promised letter be like the other letters which he had received from her in Scotland? Mountjoy's gentler nature reminded him that he owed it to his remembrance of happier days, and truer friendship, to wait and see.

He was just getting into the cab, on his return to London, when a closed carriage, with one person in it, passed him on its way to Redburn Road. In that person he recognised Mr. Henley. As the cab-driver mounted to his seat, Hugh saw the carriage stop at Number Five.

CHAPTER XXI

THE PARTING SCENE

THE evening had advanced, and the candles had just been lit in Mountjoy's sitting-room at the hotel.

His anxiety to hear from Iris had been doubled and trebled, since he had made the discovery of her father's visit to the doctor's house, at a time when it was impossible to doubt that Lord Harry was with her. Hugh's jealous sense of wrong was now mastered by the nobler emotions which filled him with pity and alarm, when he thought of Iris placed between the contending claims of two such men as the heartless Mr. Henley and the reckless Irish lord. He had remained at the hotel, through the long afternoon, on the chance that she might write to him speedily by the hand of a messenger—and no letter had arrived. He was still in expectation of news which might reach him by the evening post, when the waiter knocked at the door.

'A letter?' Mountjoy asked.

'No, sir,' the man answered; 'a lady.'

Before she could raise her veil, Hugh had recognised Iris. Her manner was subdued; her face was haggard; her hand lay cold and passive in his hand, when he advanced to bid her welcome. He placed a chair for her by the fire. She thanked him and declined to take it. With the air of a woman conscious of committing an intrusion, she seated herself apart in a corner of the room.

'I have tried to write to you, and I have not been able to do it. She said that with a dogged resignation of tone and manner, so un-like herself that Mountjoy looked at her in dismay. 'My friend,' she went on, ' your pity is all I may hope for; I am no longer worthy of the interest you once felt in me.'

Hugh saw that it would be useless to remonstrate. He asked if it had been his misfortune to offend her.

'No,' she said, 'you have not offended me.'

· Then what in Heaven's name does this change in you mean ? '

: It means,' she said, as coldly as ever, 'that I have lost myself-respect ; it means that my father has renounced me, and that you will do well to follow his example. Have I not led you to believe that I could never be the wife of Lord Harry ? Well, I have de-ceived you—I am going to marry him.'

'I can't believe it, Iris ! I won't believe it ! '

She handed him the letter, in which the Irishman had declared his resolution to destroy himself. Hugh read it with contempt. 'Did my lord's heart fail him ? ' he asked scornfully.

'He would have died by his own hand, Mr. Mountjoy——'

'Oh, Iris—" *Mr !* " '

'I will say " Hugh," if you prefer it—but the days of our familiar friendship are none the less at an end. I found Lord Harry bleed-ing to death from a wound in his throat. It was in a lonely place on Hampstead Heath ; I was the one person who happened to pass by it. For the third time, you see, it has been my destiny to save him. How can I forget that ? My mind will dwell on it. I try to find happiness—oh, only happiness enough for me—in cheering my poor Irishman, on his way back to the life that I have preserved. There is my motive, if I have a motive. Day after day I have helped to nurse him. Day after day I have heard him say things to me—what is the use of repeating them ? After years of resist-ance I have given way ; let that be enough. My one act of discre-tion has been to prevent a quarrel between my father and Harry. I beg your pardon, I ought to have said Lord Harry. When my father came to the house, I insisted on speaking with him alone. I told him what I have just told you. He said : " Think again before you make your choice between that man and me. If you decide to marry him, you will live and die without one farthing of my money to help you." He put his watch on the table between us, and gave me five minutes to make up my mind. It was a long five minutes, but it ended at last. He asked me which he was to do—leave his will as it was, or go to his lawyer and make another. I said, " You will do as you please, sir." No ; it was not a hasty reply—you can't make that excuse for me. I knew what I was saying; and I saw the future I was preparing for myself, as plainly as you see it——'

Hugh could endure no longer the reckless expression of her despair.

'No ! ' he cried, 'you don't see your future as I see it. Will you hear what I have to say, before it is too late ? '

'It is too late already. But I will listen to you if you wish it.'

'And, while you listen,' Mountjoy added, 'you will acquit me of being influenced by a selfish motive. I have loved you dearly. Perhaps, in secret, I love you still. But, this I know: if you were to remain a single woman for the rest of your life, there would be no hope for Me. Do you believe that I am speaking the truth?'

'You always speak the truth.'

'I speak in your interest, at least. You think you see your future life plainly—you are blind to your future life. You talk as if you were resigned to suffer. Are you resigned to lose your sense of right and wrong? Are you resigned to lead the life of an outlaw, and—worse still—not to feel the disgrace of it?'

'Go on, Hugh.'

'You won't answer me?'

'I won't shock you.'

'You don't discourage me, my dear; I am still obstinate in the hope of restoring you to your calmer and truer self. Let me do every justice to Lord Harry. I believe, sincerely believe, that his miserable life has not utterly destroyed in him the virtues which distinguish an honourable man. But he has one terrible defect. In his nature, there is the fatal pliability which finds companionable qualities in bad friends. In this aspect of his character, he is a dangerous man—and he may be (forgive me!) a bad husband. It is a thankless task to warn you to any good purpose. A wife—and a loving wife more than another—feels the deteriorating influence of a husband who is not worthy of her. His ways of thinking are apt to become, little by little, her ways of thinking. She makes allowances for him, which he does not deserve; her sense of right and wrong becomes confused; and before she is aware of it herself, she has sunk to his level. Are you angry with me?'

'How can I be angry with you? Perhaps you are right.'

'Do you really mean that?'

'Oh, yes.'

'Then, for God's sake, reconsider your decision! Let me go to your father.'

'Mere waste of time,' Iris answered. 'Nothing that you can say will have the least effect on him.'

'At any rate,' Mountjoy persisted, 'I mean to try.'

Had he touched her? She smiled—how bitterly Hugh failed to perceive.

'Shall I tell you what happened to me when I went home to-day?' she said. 'I found my maid waiting in the hall—with everything that belongs to me, packed up for my departure. The girl explained that she had been forced to obey my father's positive orders. I knew what that meant—I had to leave the house, and find a place to live in.'

'Not by yourself, Iris?'

'No—with my maid. She is a strange creature; if she feels sympathy, she never expresses it. "I am your grateful servant,

Miss. Where you go, I go." That was all she said; I was not disappointed—I am getting used to Fanny Mere already. Mine is a lonely lot—isn't it? I have acquaintances among the few ladies who sometimes visit at my father's house, but no friends. My mother's family, as I have always been told, cast her off when she married a man in trade, with a doubtful reputation. I don't even know where my relations live. Isn't Lord Harry good enough for me, as I am now? When I look at my prospects, is it wonderful if I talk like a desperate woman? There is but one encouraging circumstance that I can see. This misplaced love of mine that everybody condemns has, oddly enough, a virtue that everybody must admire. It offers a refuge to a woman who is alone in the world.'

Mountjoy denied indignantly that she was alone in the world.

'Is there any protection that a man can offer to a woman,' he asked, 'which I am not ready and eager to offer to You? Oh, Iris, what have I done to deserve that you should speak of yourself as friendless in my hearing!'

He had touched her at last. Their tender charm showed itself once more in her eyes and in her smile. She rose and approached him.

'What exquisite kindness it must be,' she said, 'that blinds a clever man like you to obstacles which anyone else can see! Remember, dear Hugh, what the world would say to that protection which your true heart offers to me. Are you my near relation? are you my guardian? are you even an old man? Ah me! you are only an angel of goodness whom I must submit to lose. I shall still count on your kindness when we see each other no more. You will pity me, when you hear that I have fallen lower and lower; you will be sorry for me, when I end in disgracing myself.'

'Even then, Iris, we shall not be separated. The loving friend who is near you now, will be your loving friend still.'

For the first time in her life, she threw her arms round him. In the agony of that farewell, she held him to her bosom. ' Good-bye, dear,' she said faintly—and kissed him.

The next moment, a deadly pallor overspread her face. She staggered as she drew back, and dropped into the chair that she had just left. In the fear that she might faint, Mountjoy hurried out in search of a restorative. His bed-chamber was close by, at the end of the corridor; and there were smelling-salts in his dressing-case. As he raised the lid, he heard the door behind him, the one door in the room, locked from the outer side.

He rushed to the door, and called to her. From the farther end of the corridor, her voice reached him for the last time, repeating the last melancholy word: 'Good-bye.' No renewal of the miserable parting scene: no more of the heartache—Iris had ended it!

CHAPTER XXII

THE FATAL WORDS

HEN Mountjoy had rung for the servant, and the bed-room door had been unlocked, it was too late to follow the fugitive. Her cab was waiting for her outside; and the attention of the porter had been distracted, at the same time, by a new arrival of travellers at the hotel.

It is more or less in the nature of all men who are worthy of the name, to take refuge from distress in action. Hugh decided on writing to Iris, and on making his appeal to her father, that evening. He abstained from alluding, in his letter, to the manner in which she had left him; it was her right, it was even her duty to spare herself. All that he asked was to be informed of her present place of residence, so that he might communicate the result —in writing only if she preferred it—of his contemplated interview with her father. He addressed his letter to the care of Mr. Vimpany, to be forwarded, and posted it himself.

This done, he went on at once to Mr. Henley's house.

The servant who opened the door had evidently received his orders. Mr. Henley was 'not at home.' Mountjoy was in no humour to be trifled with. He pushed the man out of his way, and made straight for the dining-room. There, as his previous experience of the habits of the household had led him to anticipate, was the man whom he was determined to see. The table was laid for Mr. Henley's late dinner.

Hugh's well-meant attempt to plead the daughter's cause with the father ended as Iris had said it would end.

After hotly resenting the intrusion on him that had been committed, Mr. Henley declared that a codicil to his will, depriving his daughter absolutely of all interest in his property, had been legally executed that day. For a time, Mountjoy's self-control had resisted the most merciless provocation. All that it was possible to effect, by patient entreaty and respectful remonstrance, he had tried again and again, and invariably in vain. At last, Mr. Henley's unbridled insolence triumphed. Hugh lost his temper—and, in leaving the heartless old man, used language which he afterwards remembered with regret.

To feel that he had attempted to assert the interests of Iris, and that he had failed, was, in Hugh's heated state of mind, an irresistible stimulant to further exertion. It was perhaps not too late yet to make another attempt to delay (if not to prevent) the marriage.

In sheer desperation, Mountjoy resolved to inform Lord Harry that his union with Miss Henley would be followed by the utter ruin of her expectations from her father. Whether the wild lord only considered his own interests, or whether he was loyally devoted to the interests of the woman whom he loved, in either case the penalty to be paid for the marriage was formidable enough to make him hesitate.

The lights in the lower window, and in the passage, told Hugh that he had arrived in good time at Redburn Road.

He found Mr. Vimpany and the young Irishman sitting together, in the friendliest manner, under the composing influence of tobacco. Primed, as he would have said himself, with only a third glass of grog, the hospitable side of the doctor's character was displayed to view. He at once accepted Mountjoy's visit as offering a renewal of friendly relations between them.

'Forgive and forget,' he said, 'there's the way to settle that little misunderstanding, after our dinner at the inn. You know Mr. Mountjoy, my lord? That's right. Draw in your chair, Mountjoy. My professional prospects threaten me with ruin—but while I have a roof over my head, there's always a welcome for a friend. My dear fellow, I have every reason to believe that the doctor who sold me this practice was a swindler. The money is gone, and the patients don't come. Well! I am not quite bankrupt yet; I can offer you a glass of grog. Mix for yourself—we'll make a night of it.'

Hugh explained (with the necessary excuses) that his object was to say a few words to Lord Harry in private. The change visible in the doctor's manner, when he had been made acquainted with this circumstance, was not amiably expressed; he had the air of a man who suspected that an unfair advantage had been taken of him. Lord Harry, on his side, appeared to feel some hesitation in granting a private interview to Mr. Mountjoy.

'Is it about Miss Henley?' he asked.

Hugh admitted that it was. Lord Harry thereupon suggested that they might be acting wisely if they avoided the subject. Mountjoy answered that there were, on the contrary, reasons for approaching the subject sufficiently important to have induced him to leave London for Hampstead at a late hour of the night.

Hearing this, Lord Harry rose to lead the way to another room. Excluded from his visitor's confidence, Mr. Vimpany could at least remind Mountjoy that he exercised authority as master of the house. 'Oh, take him upstairs, my lord,' said the doctor; '*you* are at home under my humble roof!'

The two young men faced each other in the barely-furnished drawing-room; both sufficiently doubtful of the friendly result of the conference to abstain from seating themselves. Hugh came to the point, without wasting time in preparatory words. Admitting

that he had heard of Miss Henley's engagement, he asked if Lord
Harry was aware of the disastrous consequences to the young lady
which would follow her marriage. The reply to this was frankly
expressed. The Irish lord knew nothing of the consequences to
which Mr. Mountjoy had alluded. Hugh at once enlightened him,
and evidently took him completely by surprise.

'May I ask, sir,' he said, 'if you are speaking from your own
personal knowledge ? '

'I have just come, my lord, from Mr. Henley's house ; and what
I have told you, I heard from his own lips.'

There was a pause. Hugh was already inclined to think that
he had raised an obstacle to the immediate celebration of the marriage. A speedy disappointment was in store for him. Lord Harry
was too fond of Iris to be influenced, in his relations with her, by
mercenary considerations.

'You put it strongly,' he said. ' But let me tell you, Miss Henley
is far from being so dependent on her father—he ought to be
ashamed of himself, but that's neither here nor there—I say, she is
far from being so dependent on her father as you seem to think. I
am not, I beg to inform you, without resources which I shall offer
to her with all my heart and soul. Perhaps you wish me to descend
to particulars ? Oh, it's easily done ; I have sold my cottage in
Ireland.'

'For a large sum—in these times ? ' Hugh inquired.

'Never mind the sum, Mr. Mountjoy—let the fact be enough
for you. And, while we are on the question of money (a disgusting
question, with which I refuse to associate the most charming
woman in existence), don't forget that Miss Henley has an income
of her own ; derived, as I understand, from her mother's fortune.
You will do me the justice, sir, to believe that I shall not touch a
farthing of it.'

'Certainly ! But her mother's fortune,' Mountjoy continued,
obstinately presenting the subject on its darkest side, ' consists of
shares in a Company. Shares rise and fall—and Companies sometimes fail.'

'And a friend's anxiety about Miss Henley's affairs sometimes
takes a mighty disagreeable form,' the Irishman added, his temper
beginning to show itself without disguise. 'Let's suppose the
worst that can happen, and get all the sooner to the end of a conversation which is far from being agreeable to me. We'll say, if
you like, that Miss Henley's shares are waste paper, and her
pockets (God bless her !) as empty as pockets can be, does she run
any other risk that occurs to your ingenuity in becoming my wife ? '

'Yes, she does ! ' Hugh was provoked into saying. ' In the case
you have just supposed, she runs the risk of being left a destitute
widow—if you die.'

He was prepared for an angry reply—for another quarrel added,
on that disastrous night, to the quarrel with Mr. Henley. To his
astonishment, Lord Harry's brightly-expressive eyes rested on him

with a look of mingled distress and alarm. 'God forgive me!' he said to himself, 'I never thought of that! What am I to do? what am I to do?'

Mountjoy observed that deep discouragement, and failed to understand it.

Here was a desperate adventurer, whose wanderings had over and over again placed his life in jeopardy, now apparently overcome by merely having his thoughts directed to the subject of death! To place on the circumstances such a construction as this was impossible, after a moment's reflection. The other alternative was to assume that there must be some anxiety burdening Lord Harry's mind, which he had motives for keeping concealed—and here indeed the true explanation had been found. The Irish lord had reasons, known only to himself, for recoiling from the contemplation of his own future. After the murder of Arthur Mountjoy, he had severed his connection with the assassinating brotherhood of the Invincibles; and he had then been warned that he took this step at the peril of his life, if he remained in Great Britain after he had made himself an object of distrust to his colleagues. The discovery, by the secret tribunal, of his return from South Africa would be followed inevitably by the sentence of death. Such was the terrible position which Mountjoy's reply had ignorantly forced him to confront. His fate depended on the doubtful security of his refuge in the doctor's house.

While Hugh was still looking at him, in grave doubt, a new idea seemed to spring to life in Lord Harry's mind. He threw off the oppression that had weighed on his spirits in an instant. His manner towards Mountjoy changed, with the suddenness of a flash of light, from the extreme of coldness to the extreme of cordiality.

'I have got it at last!' he exclaimed. 'Let's shake hands. My dear sir, you're the best friend I have ever had!'

The cool Englishman asked: 'In what way?'

'In this way, to be sure! You have reminded me that I can provide for Miss Henley—and the sooner the better. There's our friend the doctor down-stairs, ready to be my reference. Don't you see it?'

Obstacles that might prevent the marriage Mountjoy was ready enough to see. Facilities that might hasten the marriage found his mind hard of access to new impressions.

'Are you speaking seriously?' he said.

The Irishman's irritable temper began to show itself again.

'Why do you doubt it?' he asked.

'I fail to understand you,' Mountjoy replied.

Never—as events were yet to prove—had words of such serious import fallen from Lord Harry's lips as the words that he spoke next.

'Clear your mind of jealousy,' he said, 'and you will understand me well enough. I agree with you that I am bound to provide for my widow—and I mean to do it by insuring my life.'

THE END OF THE SECOND PERIOD

THIRD PERIOD

CHAPTER XXIII

NEWS OF IRIS

AFTER his interview with the Irish lord, Mountjoy waited for two days, in the expectation of hearing from Iris. No reply arrived. Had Mr. Vimpany failed to forward the letter that had been entrusted to him?

On the third day, Hugh wrote to make inquiries.

The doctor returned the letter that had been confided to his care, and complained in his reply of the ungrateful manner in which he had been treated. Miss Henley had not trusted him with her new address in London; and Lord Harry had suddenly left Redburn Road; bidding his host goodbye in a few lines of commonplace apology, and nothing more. Mr. Vimpany did not deny that he had been paid for his medical services; but, he would ask, was nothing due to friendship? Was one man justified in enjoying another man's hospitality, and then treating him like a stranger? 'I have done with them both—and I recommend you, my dear sir, to follow my example.' In those terms the angry (and sober) doctor expressed his sentiments, and offered his advice.

Mountjoy laid down the letter in despair.

His last poor chance of preventing the marriage depended on his being still able to communicate with Iris—and she was as completely lost to him as if she had taken flight to the other end of the world. It might have been possible to discover her by following the movements of Lord Harry, but he too had disappeared without leaving a trace behind him. The precious hours and days were passing—and Hugh was absolutely helpless.

Tortured by anxiety and suspense, he still lingered at the hotel in London. More than once, he decided on giving up the struggle, and returning to his pretty cottage in Scotland. More than once, he deferred taking the journey. At one time, he dreaded to hear that Iris was married, if she wrote to him. At another time, he felt mortified and disappointed by the neglect which her silence implied. Was she near him, or far from him? In England, or out of England? Who could say!

After more weary days of waiting and suffering a letter arrived, addressed to Mountjoy in a strange handwriting, and bearing the post-mark of Paris. The signature revealed that his correspondent was Lord Harry.

His first impulse was to throw the letter into the fire, unread. There could be little doubt, after the time that had passed, of the information that it would contain. Could he endure to be told of the marriage of Iris, by the man who was her husband? Never! There was something humiliating in the very idea of it. He arrived at that conclusion—and what did he do in spite of it? He read the letter.

Lord Harry wrote with scrupulous politeness of expression. He regretted that circumstances had prevented him from calling on Mr. Mountjoy, before he left England. After the conversation that had taken place at Mr. Vimpany's house, he felt it his duty to inform Mr. Mountjoy that he had insured his life—and, he would add, for a sum of money amply, and more than amply, sufficient to provide for his wife in the event of her surviving him. Lady Harry desired her kind regards, and would write immediately to her old and valued friend. In the meantime, he would conclude by repeating the expression of his sense of obligation to Mr. Mountjoy.

Hugh looked back at the first page of the letter, in search of the writer's address. It was simply, 'Paris.' The intention to prevent any further correspondence, or any personal communication, could hardly have been more plainly implied. In another moment, the letter was in the fire.

In two days more, Hugh heard from Iris.

She, too, wrote regretfully of the sudden departure from England; adding, however, that it was her own doing. A slip of the tongue, on Lord Harry's part, in the course of conversation, had led her to fear that he was still in danger from political conspirators with whom he had imprudently connected himself. She had accordingly persuaded him to tell her the whole truth, and had thereupon insisted on an immediate departure for the Continent. She and her husband were now living in Paris; Lord Harry having friends in that city whose influence might prove to be of great importance to his pecuniary prospects. Some sentences followed, expressing the writer's grateful remembrance of all that she had owed to Hugh in past days, and her earnest desire that they might still hear of each other, from time to time, by correspondence. She could not venture to anticipate the pleasure of receiving a visit from him, under present circumstances. But, she hoped that he would not object to write to her, addressing his letters, for the present, to post-restante.

In a postscript a few words were added, alluding to Mr. Vimpany. Hugh was requested not to answer any inquiries which that bad man might venture to make, relating to her husband or to herself. In the bygone days, she had been thankful to the doctor for the care which he had taken, medically speaking, of Rhoda Bennet. But, since that time, his behaviour to his wife, and the opinions which he had expressed in familar conversation with Lord Harry, had convinced her that he was an unprincipled person. All further communication with him (if her influence could prevent it) must come to an end.

Still as far as ever from feeling reconciled to the marriage, Mountjoy read this letter with a feeling of resentment which dis-inclined him to answer it.

He believed (quite erroneously) that Iris had written to him under the superintendence of her husband. There were certain phrases which had been, as he chose to suspect, dictated by Lord Harry's distrust—jealous distrust, perhaps—of his wife's friend. Mountjoy would wait to reply, until, as he bitterly expressed it, Iris was able to write to him without the assistance of her master.

Again he thought of returning to Scotland—and, again, he hesitated.

On this occasion, he discovered objections to the cottage which had not occurred to him while Iris was a single woman. The situation was solitary; his nearest neighbours were fishermen. Here and there, at some little distance, there were only a few scattered houses inhabited by retired tradesmen. Further away yet, there was the country-seat of an absent person of distinction, whose health suffered in the climate of Scotland. The lonely life in prospect, on the shores of the Solway, now daunted Mountjoy for the first time.

He decided on trying what society in London would do to divert his mind from the burdens and anxieties that weighed on it. Acquaintances whom he had neglected were pleasantly surprised by visits from their rich and agreeable young friend. He attended dinner parties; he roused hope in mothers and daughters by accept-ing invitations to balls; he reappeared at his club. Was there any relief to his mind in this? was there even amusement? No; he was acting a part, and he found it a hard task to keep up appear-ances. After a brief and brilliant interval, society knew him no more.

Left by himself again, he enjoyed one happy evening in London. It was the evening on which he relented, in spite of himself, and wrote to Iris

CHAPTER XXIV

LORD HARRY'S HONEYMOON

THE next day, Hugh received a visit from the last person in the little world of his acquaintance whom he expected to see. The lost Mrs. Vimpany presented herself at the hotel.

She looked unnaturally older since Mountjoy had last seen her. Her artificial complexion was gone. The discarded rouge that had once overlaid her cheeks, through a long succession of years, had left the texture of the skin coarse, and had turned the colour of it to a dull yellowish tinge. Her hair, once so skilfully darkened, was now permitted to tell the truth, and revealed the sober colouring of age, in gray. The lower face had fallen away in substance; and even the penetrating brightness of her large dark eyes was a little dimmed. All that had been left in her of the attractions of past days, owed its vital preservation to her stage training. Her suave grace of movement, and the deep elocutionary melody of her voice, still identified Mrs. Vimpany—disguised as she was in a dress of dull brown, shorn without mercy of the milliner's hideous improvements to the figure. 'Will you shake hands with me, Mr. Mountjoy?' Those were the first words she said to him, in a sad subdued manner, on entering the room.

'Why not?' Hugh asked, giving her his hand.

'You can have no very favourable remembrance of me,' she answered. 'But I hope to produce a better impression—if you can spare me a little of your time. You may, or may not, have heard of my separation from my husband. Anyway, it is needless to trouble you on the subject; you know Mr. Vimpany; you can guess what I have suffered, and why I have left him. If he comes to you, I hope you will not tell him where Lady Harry is'——

Hugh interposed: 'Pray don't speak of her by that name! Call her "Iris," as I do.'

A faint reflection of the old stage-smile trembled on Mrs. Vimpany's worn and weary face.

'Ah, Mr. Mountjoy, I know whom she ought to have married! The worst enemy of women is their ignorance of men—and they only learn to know better, when it is too late. I try to be hopeful for Iris, in the time to come, but my fears conquer me.'

She paused, sighed, and pressed her open hand on her bosom;

unconsciously betraying in that action some of the ineradicable training of the theatre.

'I am almost afraid to say that I love Iris,' she resumed; 'but this I know; if I am not so bad as I once was, I owe it to that dearest and sweetest of women! But for the days that I passed in her company, I might never have tried to atone for my past life by works of mercy. When other people take the way of amendment, I wonder whether they find it as hard to follow, at first, as I did?'

'There is no doubt of it, Mrs. Vimpany—if people are sincere. Beware of the sinners who talk of sudden conversion and perfect happiness. May I ask how you began your new life?'

'I began unhappily, Mr. Mountjoy—I joined a nursing Sister-hood. Before long, a dispute broke out among them. Think of women who call themselves Christians, quarrelling about churches and church services—priest's vestments and attitudes, and candles and incense! I left them, and went to a hospital, and found the doctors better Christians than the Sisters. I am not talking about my own poor self (as you will soon see) without a reason. My experience in the hospital led to other things. I nursed a lady through a tedious illness, and was trusted to take her to some friends in the south of France. On my return, I thought of staying for a few days in Paris—it was an opportunity of seeing how the nurses did their work in the French hospitals. And, oh, it was far more than that! In Paris, I found Iris again.'

'By accident?' Hugh asked.

'I am not sure,' Mrs. Vimpany answered, 'that there are such things as meetings by accident. She and her husband were among the crowds of people on the Boulevards, who sit taking their coffee in view of the other crowds, passing along the street. I went by, without noticing them. *She* saw me, and sent Lord Harry to bring me back. I have been with them every day, at her invitation, from that time to this; and I have seen their life.'

She stopped, noticing that Hugh grew restless. 'I am in doubt,' she said, 'whether you wish to hear more of their life in Paris.'

Mountjoy at once controlled himself.

'Go on,' he said quietly.

'Even if I tell you that Iris is perfectly happy?'

'Go on,' Hugh repeated.

'May I confess,' she resumed, 'that her husband is irresistible —not only to his wife, but even to an old woman like me? After having known him for years at his worst, as well as at his best, I am still foolish enough to feel the charm of his high spirits and his delightful good-humour. Sober English people, if they saw him now, would almost think him a fit subject to be placed under restraint. One of his wild Irish ideas of expressing devotion to his wife is, that they shall forget they are married, and live the life of lovers. When they dine at a restaurant, he insists on having a private room. He takes her to public balls, and engages her to dance with him for the whole evening. When she stays at home and is a little fatigued, he sends me to the piano, and whirls her round the room in a waltz. "Nothing revives a woman," he says, "like dancing with the man she loves." When she is out of breath, and I shut up the piano, do you know what he does? He actually kisses Me—and says he is expressing his wife's feeling for me when she is not able to do it herself! He sometimes dines out with men, and comes back all on fire with the good wine, and more amiable than ever. On these occasions his pockets are full of sweetmeats, stolen for "his angel" from the dessert. "Am I a little tipsy?" he asks. "Oh, don't be angry; it's all for love of you. I have been in the highest society, my darling; proposing your health over and over and over again, and drinking to you deeper than all the rest of the company. You don't blame me? Ah, but I blame myself. I was wrong to leave you, and dine with men. What do I want with the society of men, when I have your society? Drinking your health is a lame excuse. I will refuse all invitations for the future that don't include my wife." And—mind!—he really means it, at the time. Two or three days later, he forgets his good resolutions, and dines with the men again, and comes home with more charming excuses, and stolen sweetmeats, and good resolutions. I am afraid I weary you, Mr. Mountjoy?'

'You surprise me,' Hugh replied. 'Why do I hear all this of Lord Harry?'

Mrs. Vimpany left her chair. The stage directions of other days had accustomed her to rise, when the character she played had anything serious to say. Her own character still felt the animating influence of dramatic habit: she rose now, and laid her hand impressively on Mountjoy's shoulder.

'I have not thoughtlessly tried your patience,' she said. 'Now that I am away from the influence of Lord Harry, I can recall my former experience of him: and I am afraid I can see the end that is coming. He will drift into bad company; he will listen to bad advice; and he will do things in the future which he might shrink from doing now. When that time comes, I fear him! I fear him!'

'When that time comes,' Hugh repeated, 'if I have any influence left over his wife, he shall find her capable of protecting herself. Will you give me her address in Paris?'

'Willingly—if you will promise not to go to her till she really needs you?'

'Who is to decide when she needs me?'

'I am to decide,' Mrs. Vimpany answered; 'Iris writes to me confidentially. If anything happens which she may be unwilling to trust to a letter, I believe I shall hear of it from her maid.'

'Are you sure the maid is to be relied on?' Mountjoy interposed.

'She is a silent creature, so far as I know anything of her,' Mrs. Vimpany admitted; 'and her manner doesn't invite confidence. But I have spoken with Fanny Mere; I am satisfied that she is true to her mistress and grateful to her mistress in her own strange way. If Iris is in any danger, I shall not be left in ignorance of it. Does this incline you to consult with me, before you decide on going to Paris ? Don't stand on ceremony ; say honestly, Yes or No.'

Honestly, Hugh said Yes.

He was at once trusted with the address of Iris. At the same time, Mrs. Vimpany undertook that he should know what news she received from Paris as soon as she knew it herself. On that understanding they parted, for the time being.

CHAPTER XXV

THE DOCTOR IN DIFFICULTIES

LOWLY the weeks passed. Strictly Mrs. Vimpany kept her promise.

When she heard from Iris the letter was always sent to Hugh, to be returned after he had read it. Events in the lives of the newly-married pair, many of which pointed to the end that Mrs. Vimpany saw and dreaded, were lightly, sometimes jestingly, related by the young wife. Her blind belief in her husband, sincerely asserted in the earlier part of the correspondence, began to betray, in her later letters, signs of self delusion. It was sad indeed to see that bright intelligence rendered incapable of conceiving suspicions, which might have occurred to the mind of a child.

When the latest news from Paris followed, in due course, Mountjoy was informed of it by a note from Mrs. Vimpany expressed in these terms:

' My last letter from Iris is really no letter at all. It simply encloses a circular, with her love, and asks me to send it on to you. If it is in your power to make inquiries in the right quarter, I am sure you will not hesitate to take the trouble. There can be little doubt, as I think, that Lord Harry is engaged in a hazardous speculation, more deeply than his wife is willing to acknowledge.'

The circular announced the contemplated publication of a weekly newspaper, printed partly in English, and partly in French, having its chief office in Paris, and being intended to dispute the advantages of a European circulation with the well-known Continental journal called ' Galignani's Messenger.' A first list of contributors included names of some notoriety in the literature of England and the literature of France. Speculators who wished to know, in the first place, on what security they might reckon, were referred to the managing committee, represented by persons of importance in the financial worlds of London and Paris.

Being in a position to make the inquiries which Mrs. Vimpany had suggested, Hugh received information which verified the statements contained in the circular, and vouched for the good faith of those persons who were concerned in directing the speculation. So far, so good.

But, when the question of success was next discussed, the authorities consulted shook their wise heads. It was impossible to say what losses might not be suffered, and what sums of money might not be required, before the circulation of the new journal would justify the hope of success. This opinion Hugh communicated to Mrs. Vimpany; Iris was informed of it by that day's post.

A longer time than usual elapsed before any further news of Lord Harry and his wife was received by Mountjoy. When he did at last hear again from Mrs. Vimpany, she forwarded a letter from Iris dated from a new address, in the suburb of Paris called Passy.

From motives of economy (Iris wrote) her husband had decided on a change of residence. They were just established in their new abode, with the advantages of a saving in rent, a pretty little garden to cultivate, and purer air to breathe than the air of Paris. There the letter ended, without the slightest allusion to the forthcoming newspaper, or to the opinion that had been pronounced on the prospects of success.

In forwarding this letter, Mrs. Vimpany wrote on the blank page as follows : ' I am sorry to add that some disquieting news of my husband has reached me. For the present, I will say no more. It is at least possible that the report may not be worthy of belief.'

A few days later the report was confirmed, under circumstances which had certainly not been foreseen. Mr. Vimpany himself arrived at the hotel, on a visit to Mountjoy.

Always more or less superior to the amiable weakness of modesty, the doctor seemed to have risen higher than ever in his own estimation, since Hugh had last seen him. He strutted ; he stared confidently at persons and things ; authority was in his voice when he spoke, and lofty indulgence distinguished his manner when he listened.

' How are you ? ' he cried with a grand gaiety, as he entered the room. ' Fine weather, isn't it, for the time of year ? You don't look well. I wonder whether you notice any change in me ? '

' You seem to be in good spirits,' Hugh replied, not very cordially.

' Do I carry my head high ? ' Mr. Vimpany went on. ' When calamity strikes at a man, don't let him cringe and cry for pity— let him hit back again ! Those are my principles. Look at me. Now do look at me. Here I am, a cultivated person, a member of an honourable profession, a man of art and accomplishment— stripped of every blessed thing belonging to me but the clothes I stand up in. Give me your hand, Mountjoy. It's the hand, sir, of a bankrupt.'

' You don't seem to mind it much,' Mountjoy remarked.

' Why should I mind it ? ' asked the doctor. ' There isn't a medical man in England who has less reason to reproach himself than I have. Have I wasted money in rash speculations ? Not a farthing. Have I been fool enough to bet at horse races ? My worst enemy daren't say it of me. What have I done then ?

I have toiled after virtue—that's what I have done. Oh, there's nothing to laugh at ! When a doctor tries to be the medical friend of humanity; when he only asks leave to cure disease, to soothe pain, to preserve life—isn't that virtue ? And what is my reward ? I sit at home, waiting for my suffering fellow-creatures ; and the only fellow-creatures who come to me are too poor to pay. I have gone my rounds, calling on the rich patients whom I bought when I bought the practice. Not one of them wanted me. Men, women, and children, were all inexcusably healthy—devil take them ! Is it wonderful if a man becomes bankrupt, in such a situation as mine ? By Jupiter, I go farther than that ! I say, a man owes it to himself (as a protest against undeserved neglect) to become a bankrupt. If you will allow me, I'll take a chair.'

He sat down with an air of impudent independence and looked round the room. A little cabinet, containing liqueurs, stood open on the sideboard. Mr. Vimpany got up again. ' May I take a friendly liberty ? ' he said—and helped himself, without waiting for per-mission.

Hugh bore with this, mindful of the mistake that he had com-mitted in consenting to receive the doctor. At the same time, he was sufficiently irritated to take a friendly liberty on his side. He crossed the room to the sideboard, and locked up the liqueurs. Mr. Vimpany's brazen face flushed deeply (not with shame) ; he opened his lips to say something worthy of himself, controlled the impulse, and burst into a boisterous laugh. He had evidently some favour still to ask.

' Devilish good ! ' he broke out cheerfully. ' Do you remember the landlady's claret ? Ha ! you don't want to tempt me this time. Well ! well ! to return to my bankruptcy.'

Hugh had heard enough of his visitor's bankruptcy. ' I am not one of your creditors,' he said.

Mr. Vimpany made a smart reply : ' Don't you be too sure ot that. Wait a little.'

' Do you mean,' Mountjoy asked, ' that you have come here to borrow money of me ? '

' Time—give me time,' the doctor pleaded : ' this is not a matter to be dispatched in a hurry ; this is a matter of business. You will hardly believe it,' he resumed, ' but I have actually been in my present position, once before.' He looked towards the cabinet of liqueurs. ' If I had the key,' he said, ' I should like to try a drop more of your good Curaçoa. You don't see it ? '

' I am waiting to hear what your business is,' Hugh replied.

Mr. Vimpany's pliable temper submitted with perfect amia-bility. ' Quite right,' he said ; ' let us return to business. I am a man who possesses great fertility of resource. On the last occa-sion when my creditors pounced on my property, do you think I was discouraged ? Nothing of the sort ! My regular medical prac-tice had broken down under me. Very well—I tried my luck as a quack. In plain English, I invented a patent medicine. The one thing wanting was money enough to advertise it. False friends buttoned up their pockets. You see ? '

' Oh, yes ; I see.'

' In that case,' Mr. Vimpany continued, ' you will not be surprised to hear that I draw on my resources again. You have no doubt noticed that we live in an age of amateurs. Amateurs write, paint, compose music, perform on the stage. I, too, am one of the accomplished persons who have taken possession of the field of Art. Did you observe the photographic portraits on the walls of my dining-room ? They are of my doing, sir—whether you observed them or not. I am one of the handy medical men, who can use the photograph. Not that I mention it generally ; the public have got a narrow-minded notion that a doctor ought to be nothing but a doctor. My name won't appear in a new work that I am contemplating. Of course, you want to know what my new work is. I'll tell you, in the strictest confidence. Imagine (if you can) a series of superb photographs of the most eminent doctors in England, with memoirs of their lives written by themselves ; published once a month, price half-a-crown. If there isn't money in that idea, there is no money in anything. Exert yourself, my good friend. Tell me what you think of it ? '

' I don't understand the subject,' Mountjoy replied. ' May I ask why you take *me* into your confidence ? '

' Because I look upon you as my best friend.'

' You are very good. But surely, Mr. Vimpany, you have older friends in your circle of acquaintance than I am.'

' Not one,' the doctor answered promptly, ' whom I trust as I trust you. Let me give you a proof of it.'

' Is the proof in any way connected with money ? ' Hugh inquired.

' I call that hard on me,' Mr. Vimpany protested. ' No unfriendly interruptions, Mountjoy ! I offer a proof of kindly feeling. Do you mean to hurt me ? '

' Certainly not. Go on.'

' Thank you ; a little encouragement goes a long way with me. I have found a bookseller, who will publish my contemplated work, on commission. Not a soul has yet seen the estimate of expenses. I propose to show it to You.'

' Quite needless, Mr. Vimpany.'

' Why quite needless ? '

' Because I decline lending you the money.'

' No, no, Mountjoy ! You can't really mean that ? '

' I do mean it.'

' No ! '

' Yes ! '

The doctor's face showed a sudden change of expression—a sinister and threatening change. ' Don't drive me into a corner,' he said. ' Think of it again.'

Hugh's capacity for controlling himself gave way at last.

'Do you presume to threaten me?' he said. 'Understand, if you please, that my mind is made up, and that nothing you can say or do will alter it.'

With that declaration he rose from his chair, and waited for Mr. Vimpany's departure.

The doctor put on his hat. His eyes rested on Hugh, with a look of diabolical malice: 'The time is not far off, Mr. Mountjoy, when you may be sorry you refused me.' He said those words deliberately—and took his leave.

Released from the man's presence, Hugh found himself strangely associating the interests of Iris with the language—otherwise beneath notice—which Mr. Vimpany had used on leaving the room.

In desperate straits for want of money, how would the audacious bankrupt next attempt to fill his empty purse? If he had, by any chance, renewed his relations with his Irish friend—and such an event was at least possible—his next experiment in the art of raising a loan might take him to Paris. Lord Harry had already ventured on a speculation which called for an immediate outlay of money, and which was only expected to put a profit into his pocket at some future period. In the meanwhile, his resources in money had their limits; and his current expenses would make imperative demands on an ill-filled purse. If the temptation to fail in his resolution to respect his wife's fortune was already trying his fortitude, what better excuse could be offered for yielding than the necessities of an old friend in a state of pecuniary distress?

Looking at the position of Iris, and at the complications which threatened it, from this point of view, Mountjoy left the hotel to consult with Mrs. Vimpany. It rested with her to decide whether the circumstances justified his departure for Paris.

CHAPTER XXVI

LONDON AND PARIS

INFORMED of all that Hugh could tell her relating to his interview with her husband, Mrs. Vimpany understood and appreciated his fears for the future. She failed, however, to agree with him that he would do well to take the journey to France, under present circumstances.

'Wait a little longer in London,' she said. 'If Iris doesn't write to me in the next few days there will be a reason for her silence ; and in that case (as I have already told you) I shall hear from Fanny Mere. You shall see me when I get a letter from Paris.'

On the last morning in the week, Mrs. Vimpany was announced. The letter that she brought with her had been written by Fanny Mere. With the pen in her hand, the maid's remarkable character expressed itself as strongly as ever :—

'Madam,—I said I would let you know what goes on here, when I thought there was need of it. There seems to be need now. Mr. Vimpany came to us yesterday. He has the spare bedroom. My mistress says nothing, and writes nothing. For that reason, I send you the present writing.—Your humble servant, F.'

Mountjoy was perplexed by this letter, plain as it was.

'It seems strange,' he said, 'that Iris herself has not written to you. She has never hitherto concealed her opinion of Mr. Vimpany.'

'She is concealing it now,' Mr. Vimpany's wife replied gravely.
'Do you know why?'

'I am afraid I do. Iris will not hesitate at any sacrifice of
herself to please Lord Harry. She will give him her money when
he wants it. If he tells her to alter her opinion of my husband,
she will obey him. He can shake her confidence in me, whenever
he pleases; and he has very likely done it already.'

'Surely it is time for me to go to her now?' Hugh said.

'Full time,' Mrs. Vimpany admitted—'if you can feel sure of
yourself. In the interests of Iris, can you undertake to be cool
and careful?'

'In the interests of Iris, I can undertake anything.'

'One word more,' Mrs. Vimpany continued, 'before you take
your departure. No matter whether appearances are for him, or
against him, be always on your guard with my husband. Let me
hear from you while you are away; and don't forget that there is
an obstacle between you and Iris, which will put even your
patience and devotion to a hard trial.'

'You mean her husband?'

'I do.'

There was no more to be said. Hugh set forth on his journey
to Paris.

.   .   .   .   .   .

On the morning after his arrival in the French capital, Mountjoy
had two alternatives to consider. He might either write to Iris,
and ask when it would be convenient to her to receive him—or he
might present himself unexpectedly in the cottage at Passy. Reflection convinced him that his best chance of placing an obstacle
in the way of deception would be to adopt the second alternative,
and to take Lord Harry and the doctor by surprise.

He went to Passy. The lively French taste had brightened
the cottage with colour: the fair white window curtains were tied
with rose-coloured ribbons, the blinds were gaily painted, the
chimneys were ornamental, the small garden was a paradise of
flowers. When Mountjoy rang the bell, the gate was opened by
Fanny Mere. She looked at him in grave astonishment.

'Do they expect you?' she asked.

'Never mind that,' Hugh answered. 'Are they at home?'

'They have just finished breakfast, sir.'

'Do you remember my name?'

'Yes, sir.'

'Then show me in.'

Fanny opened the door of a room on the ground floor, and
announced: 'Mr. Mountjoy.'

The two men were smoking; Iris was watering some flowers in
the window. Her colour instantly faded when Hugh entered the
room. In doubt and alarm, her eyes questioned Lord Harry. He
was in his sweetest state of good-humour. Urged by the genial
impulse of the moment, he set the example of a cordial reception.
'This is an agreeable surprise, indeed,' he said, shaking hands with

Mountjoy in his easy amiable way. 'It's kind of you to come and see us.' Relieved of anxiety (evidently when she had not expected it), Iris eagerly followed her husband's example: her face recovered its colour, and brightened with its prettiest smile. Mr. Vimpany stood in a corner; his cigar went out: his own wife would hardly have known him again—he actually presented an appearance of embarrassment! Lord Harry burst out laughing: 'Look at him Iris! The doctor is shy for the first time in his life.' The Irish good-humour was irresistible. The young wife merrily echoed her husband's laugh. Mr. Vimpany, observing the friendly reception offered to Hugh, felt the necessity of adapting himself to circumstances. He came out of his corner with an apology: 'Sorry I misbehaved myself, Mr. Mountjoy, when I called on you in London. Shake hands. No offence—eh?' Iris, in feverish high spirits, mimicked the doctor's coarse tones when he repeated his favourite form of excuse. Lord Harry clapped his hands, delighted with his wife's clever raillery: 'Ha! Mr. Mountjoy, you don't find that her married life has affected her spirits! May I hope that you have come here to breakfast? The table is ready as you see '—— 'And I have been taking lessons, Hugh, in French ways of cooking eggs,' Iris added; 'pray let me show you what I can do.' The doctor chimed in facetiously: 'I'm Lady Harry's medical referee'; you'll find her French delicacies half digested for you, sir, before you can open your mouth: signed, Clarence Vimpany, member of the College of Surgeons.' Remembering Mrs. Vimpany's caution, Hugh concealed his distrust of this outbreak of hospitable gaiety, and made his excuses. Lord Harry followed, with more excuses, on his part. He deplored it—but he was obliged to go out. Had Mr. Mountjoy met with the new paper which was to beat 'Galignani' out of the field? The 'Continental Herald '—there was the title. 'Forty thousand copies of the first number have just flown all over Europe; we have our agencies in every town of importance, at every point of the compass; and, one of the great proprietors, my dear sir, is the humble individual who now addresses you.' His bright eyes sparkled with boyish pleasure, as he made that announcement of his own importance. If Mr. Mountjoy would kindly excuse him, he had an appointment at the office that morning. 'Get your hat, Vimpany. The fact is our friend here carries a case of consumption in his pocket; consumption of the purse, you understand. I am going to enrol him among the contributors to the newspaper. A series of articles (between ourselves) exposing the humbug of physicians, and asserting with fine satirical emphasis the overstocked state of the medical profession. Ah, well! you'll be glad (won't you?) to talk over old times with Iris. My angel, show our good friend the " Continental Herald," and mind you keep him here till we get back. Doctor, look alive! Mr. Mountjoy, au revoir.' They shook hands again heartily. As Mrs. Vimpany had confessed, there was no resisting the Irish lord.

But Hugh's strange experience of that morning was not at an end, yet.

CHAPTER XXVII

THE BRIDE AT HOME

LEFT alone with the woman whose charm still held him to her, cruelly as she had tried his devotion by her marriage, Mountjoy found the fluent amiability of the husband imitated by the wife. She, too, when the door had hardly closed on Lord Harry, was bent on persuading Hugh that her marriage had been the happiest event of her life.

'Will you think the worse of me,' she began, 'if I own that I had little expectation of seeing you again?'

'Certainly not, Iris.'

'Consider my situation,' she went on. 'When I remember how you tried (oh, conscientiously tried!) to prevent my marriage—how you predicted the miserable results that would follow, if Harry's life and my life became one—could I venture to hope that you would come here, and judge for yourself? Dear and good friend, I have nothing to fear from the result; your presence was never more welcome to me than it is now!'

Whether it was attributable to prejudice on Mountjoy's part, or to keen and just observation, he detected something artificial in the ring of her enthusiasm; there was not the steady light of truth in her eyes, which he remembered in the past and better days of their companionship. He was a little—just a little—irritated. The temptation to remind her that his distrust of Lord Harry had once been her distrust too, proved to be more than his frailty could resist.

'Your memory is generally exact,' he said; 'but it hardly serves you now as well as usual.'

'What have I forgotten?'

'You have forgotten the time, my dear, when your opinion was almost as strongly against a marriage with Lord Harry as mine.'

Her answer was ready on the instant: 'Ah, I didn't know him then as well as I know him now!'

Some men, in Mountjoy's position, might have been provoked into hinting that there were sides to her husband's character which she had probably not discovered yet. But Hugh's gentle temper—ruffled for a moment only—had recovered its serenity. Her friend was her true friend still; he said no more on the subject of her marriage.

' Old habits are not easily set aside,' he reminded her. ' I have been so long accustomed to advise you and help you, that I find myself hoping there may be some need for my services still. Is there no way in which I might relieve you of the hateful presence of Mr. Vimpany ? '

' My dear Hugh, I wish you had not mentioned Mr. Vimpany.'

Mountjoy concluded that the subject was disagreeable to her. ' After the opinion of him which you expressed in your letter to me,' he said, ' I ought not to have spoken of the doctor. Pray for-give me.'

Iris looked distressed. ' Oh, you are quite mistaken ! The poor doctor has been sadly misjudged; and I '—she shook her head, and sighed penitently—' and, I,' she resumed, ' am one among other people who have ignorantly wronged him. Pray consult my hus-band. Hear what he can tell you—and you will pity Mr. Vimpany. The newspaper makes such large demands on our means that we can do little to help him. With your recommendation he might find some employment.'

' He has already asked me to assist him, Iris ; and I have refused. I can't agree with your change of opinion about Mr. Vimpany.'

' Why not ? Is it because he has separated from his wife ? '

' That is one reason, among many others,' Mountjoy replied.

' Indeed, indeed you are wrong ! Lord Harry has known Mrs. Vimpany for years, and he says—I am truly sorry to hear it—that the separation is her fault.'

Hugh changed the subject again. The purpose which had mainly induced him to leave England had not been mentioned yet.

Alluding to the newspaper, and to the heavy pecuniary demands made by the preliminary expenses of the new journal, he reminded Iris that their long and intimate friendship permitted him to feel some interest in her affairs. ' I won't venture to express an opinion,' he added ; ' let me only ask if Lord Harry's investments in this speculation have compelled him to make some use of your little fortune ? '

' My husband refused to touch my fortune,' Iris answered. ' But '— She paused, there. ' Do you know how honourably, how nobly, he has behaved ? ' she abruptly resumed. ' He has insured his life : he has burdened himself with the payment of a large sum of money every year. And all for me, if I am so unfortunate (which God forbid !) as to survive him. When a large share in the news-paper was for sale, do you think I could be ungrateful enough to let him lose the chance of making our fortune, when the profits begin to come in ? I insisted on advancing the money—we almost quarrelled about it—but, you know how sweet he is. I said : " Don't distress me " ; and the dearest of men let me have my own way.'

Mountjoy listened in silence. To have expressed what he felt would have been only to mortify and offend Iris. Old habit (as he had said) had made the idea of devoting himself to her interests the uppermost idea in his mind. He asked if the money had all been spent. Hearing that some of it was still left, he resolved on making the attempt to secure the remains of her fortune to herself.

'Tell me,' he said, 'have you ever heard of such a thing as buying an annuity?'

She knew nothing about it. He carefully explained the method by which a moderate sum of money might be made to purchase a sufficient income for life. She offered no objection, when he proposed to write to his lawyer in London for the necessary particulars. But when he asked her to tell him what the sum was of which she might be still able to dispose, Iris hesitated, and made no reply.

This time, Hugh arrived at the right conclusion.

It was only too plain to him that what remained of her money represented an amount so trifling that she was ashamed to mention it. Of the need for helping her, there could be no doubt now; and, as for the means, no difficulties presented themselves to Mountjoy—always excepting the one obstacle likely to be offered by the woman herself. Experience warned him to approach her delicately, by the indirect way.

'You know me well enough,' he said, 'to feel sure that I am incapable of saying anything which can embarrass you, or cause a moment's misunderstanding between two old friends. Won't you look at me, Iris, when I am speaking to you?'

She still looked away from him. 'I am afraid of what you are going to say to me,' she answered coldly.

'Then let me say it at once. In one of your letters, written long since—I don't suppose you remember it—you told me that I was an obstinate man when I once took a thing into my head. You were quite right. My dear, I have taken it into my head that you will be as ready as ever to accept my advice, and will leave me (as your man of business) to buy the annuity'——

She stopped him.

'No,' she cried, 'I won't hear a word more! Do you think I am insensible to years of kindness that I have never deserved? Do you think I forget how nobly you have forgiven me for those cruel refusals which have saddened your life? Is it possible that you expect me to borrow money of You?' She started wildly to her feet. 'I declare, as God hears me, I would rather die than take that base, that shameful advantage of all your goodness to me. The woman never lived who owed so much to a man, as I owe to you—but not money! Oh, my dear, not money! not money!'

He was too deeply touched to be able to speak to her—and she saw it. 'What a wretch I am,' she said to herself; 'I have made his heart ache!'

He heard those words. Still feeling for her—never, never for himself!—he tried to soothe her. In the passion of her self-reproach, she refused to hear him. Pacing the room from end to end, she fanned the fiery emotion that was consuming her. Now,

She burst into a passionate fit of weeping, broken down at last under the terrible strain laid on her.

she reviled herself in language that broke through the restraints by which good breeding sets its seal on a woman's social rank. And now, again, she lost herself more miserably still, and yielded with hysteric recklessness to a bitter outburst of gaiety.

'If you wish to be married happily,' she cried, 'never be as fond of any other woman as you have been of me. We are none of us worth it. Laugh at us, Hugh—do anything but believe in us. We all lie, my friend. And I have been lying—shamelessly! shamelessly!'

He tried to check her. 'Don't talk in that way, Iris,' he said sternly.

She laughed at him. 'Talk?' she repeated. 'It isn't that; it's a confession.'

'I don't desire to hear your confession.'

'You must hear it—you have drawn it out of me. Come! we'll enjoy my humiliation together. Contradict every word I said to you about that brute and blackguard, the doctor—and you will have the truth. What horrid inconsistency, isn't it? I can't help myself; I am a wretched, unreasonable creature; I don't know my own mind for two days together, and all through my husband —I am so fond of him; Harry is delightfully innocent; he's like a nice boy; he never seemed to think of Mr. Vimpany, till it was settled between them that the doctor was to come and stay here— and then he persuaded me—oh, I don't know how!—to see his friend in quite a new light. I believed him—and I believe him still—I mean I *would* believe him, but for you. Will you do me a favour? I wish you wouldn't look at me with those eyes that won't lie; I wish you wouldn't speak to me with that voice which finds things out. Oh, good Heavens, do you suppose I would let you think that my husband is a bad man, and my marriage an unhappy one? Never! If it turns my blood to sit and eat at the same table with Mr. Vimpany, I'm not cruel enough to blame the dear doctor. It's my wickedness that's to blame. We shall quarrel, if you tell me that Harry is capable of letting a rascal be his friend. I'm happy; I'm happy; I'm happy!—do you understand that? Oh, Hugh, I wish you had never come to see me!'

She burst into a passionate fit of weeping, broken down at last under the terrible strain laid on her. 'Let me hide myself!' was all that Iris could say to her old friend—before she ran out of the room, and left him.

CHAPTER XXVIII

THE MAID AND THE KEYHOLE

EEPLY as she had grieved him, keenly as he felt that his worst fears for her threatened already to be realised, it was characteristic of Mountjoy that he still refused to despair of Iris—even with the husband's influence against him.

The moral deterioration of her, revealed in the false words that she had spoken, and in the deceptions that she had attempted, would have justified the saddest misgivings, but for the voluntary confession which had followed, and the signs which it had shown of the better nature still struggling to assert itself. How could Hugh hope to encourage that effort of resistance to the evil influences that were threatening her—first and foremost, among them, being the arrival of Vimpany at the cottage? His presence kept her in a state of perpetual contention, between her own wise instincts which distrusted him, and her husband's authoritative assertions which recommended him to her confidence. No greater service could be rendered to Iris than the removal of this man—but how could it be accomplished, without giving offence to her husband? Mountjoy's mind was still in search of a means of overcoming the obstacle thus presented, when he heard the door open. Had Iris recovered herself? or had Lord Harry and his friend returned?

The person who now entered the room was the strange and silent maid, Fanny Mere.

'Can I speak to you, sir?'

'Certainly. What is it?'

'Please give me your address.'

'For your mistress?'

'Yes.'

'Does she wish to write to me?'

'Yes.'

Hugh gave the strange creature the address of his hotel in Paris. For a moment, her eyes rested on him with an expression of steady scrutiny. She opened the door to go out—stopped—considered—came back again.

'I want to speak for myself,' she said. 'Do you care to hear what a servant has to say?'

Mountjoy replied that he was ready to hear what she had to

say. She at once stepped up to him, and addressed him in these words :

' I think you are fond of my mistress ? '

An ordinary man might have resented the familiar manner in which she had expressed herself. Mountjoy waited for what was still to come. Fanny Mere abruptly went on, with a nearer approach to agitation in her manner than she had shown yet :

' My mistress took me into her service ; she trusted me when other ladies would have shown me the door. When she sent for me to see her, my character was lost ; I had nobody to feel for me, nobody to help me. She is the one friend who held out a hand to me. I hate the men ; I don't care for the women. Except one. Being a servant I mustn't say I love that one. If I was a lady, I don't know that I should say it. Love is cant ; love is rubbish. Tell me one thing. Is the doctor a friend of yours ? '

' The doctor is nothing of the kind.'

' Perhaps he is your enemy ? '

' I can hardly say that.'

She looked at Hugh discontentedly. ' I want to get at it,' she said. ' Why can't we understand each other ? Will you laugh at me, if I say the first thing that comes into my head ? Are you a good swimmer ? '

An extraordinary question, even from Fanny Mere. It was put seriously—and seriously Mountjoy answered it. He said that he was considered to be a good swimmer.

' Perhaps,' she continued, ' you have saved people's lives.'

' I have twice been so fortunate as to save lives,' he replied.

' If you saw the doctor drowning, would you save him ? *I* wouldn't ! '

' Do you hate him as bitterly as that ? ' Hugh asked.

She passed the question over without notice. ' I wish you would help me to get at it,' she persisted. ' Suppose you could rid my mistress of that man by giving him a kick, would you up with your foot and do it ? '

' Yes—with pleasure.'

' Thank you, sir. Now I've got it. Mr. Mountjoy, the doctor is the curse of my mistress's life. I can't bear to see it. If we are not relieved of him somehow, I shall do something wrong. When I wait at table, and see him using his knife, I want to snatch it out of his hand, and stick it into him. I had a hope that my lord might turn him out of the house when they quarrelled. My lord is too wicked himself to do it. For the love of God, sir, help my mistress —or show me the way how ! '

Mountjoy began to be interested. ' How do you know,' he asked, ' that Lord Harry and the doctor have quarrelled ? '

Without the slightest appearance of embarrassment, Fanny Mere informed him that she had listened at the door, while her master and his friend were talking of their secrets. She had also taken an opportunity of looking through the keyhole. ' I suppose, sir,' said this curious woman, still speaking quite respectfully, 'you have never tried that way yourself?'

'Certainly not!'

'Wouldn't you do it to serve my mistress?'

'No.'

'And yet, you're fond of her! You are a merciful one—the only merciful one, so far as I know—among men. Perhaps, if you were frightened about her, you might be more ready with your help. I wonder whether I can frighten you? Will you let me try?'

The woman's faithful attachment to Iris pleaded for her with Hugh. 'Try, if you like,' he said kindly.

Speaking as seriously as ever, Fanny proceeded to describe her experience at the keyhole. What she had seen was not worth relating. What she had heard proved to be more important.

The talk between my lord and the doctor had been about raising money. They had different notions of how to do that. My lord's plan was to borrow what was wanted, on his life-insurance. The doctor told him he couldn't do that, till his insurance had been going on for three or four years at least. 'I have something better and bolder to propose,' says Mr. Vimpany. It must have been also something wicked—for he whispered it in the master's ear. My lord didn't take to it kindly. 'How do you think I could face my wife,' he says, 'if she discovered me?' The doctor says: 'Don't be afraid of your wife; Lady Harry will get used to many things which she little thought of before she married you.' Says my lord to that: 'I have done my best, Vimpany, to improve my wife's opinion of you. If you say much more, I shall come round to her way of thinking. Drop it!'—'All right,' says the doctor, 'I'll drop it now, and wait to pick it up again till you come to your last bank note.' There the talk ended for that day—and Fanny would be glad to know what Mr. Mountjoy thought of it.

'I think you have done me a service,' Hugh replied.

'Tell me how, sir.'

'I can only tell you this, Fanny. You have shown me how to relieve your mistress of the doctor.'

For the first time, the maid's impenetrable composure completely failed her. The smouldering fire in Fanny Mere flamed up. She impulsively kissed Mountjoy's hand. The moment her lips touched it she shrank back: the natural pallor of her face became whiter than ever. Startled by the sudden change, Hugh asked if she was ill.

She shook her head.

'It isn't that. Yours is the first man's hand I have kissed, since——' She checked herself. 'I beg you won't ask me about it. I only meant to thank you, sir; I do thank you with all my heart—I mustn't stay here any longer.'

As she spoke the sound of a key was heard, opening the lock of the cottage-door. Lord Harry had returned.

CHAPTER XXIX

THE CONQUEST OF MR. VIMPANY

THE Irish lord came in—with his medical friend sulkily in attendance on him. He looked at Fanny, and asked where her mistress was.

'My lady is in her room, sir.

Hearing this, he turned sharply to Mountjoy. On the point of speaking, he seemed to think better of it, and went to his wife's room. The maid followed. 'Get rid of him now,' she whispered to Hugh, glancing at the doctor. Mr. Vimpany was in no very approachable humour—standing at the window, with his hands in his empty pockets, gloomily looking out. But Hugh was not disposed to neglect the opportunity; he ventured to say: 'You don't seem to be in such good spirits as usual.'

The doctor gruffly expressed his opinion that Mr. Mountjoy would not be particularly cheerful, in his place. My lord had taken

him to the office, on the distinct understanding that he was to earn a
little pocket-money by becoming one of the contributors to the news
paper.   And how had it ended?   The editor had declared that his
list of writers was full, and begged leave to suggest that Mr. Vimpany
should wait for the next vacancy.   A most impertinent proposal!
Had Lord Harry—a proprietor, remember—exerted his authority?
Not he!   His lordship had dropped the doctor 'like a hot potato,'
and had meanly submitted to his own servant.   What did Mr.
Mountjoy think of such conduct as that?

Hugh answered the question, with his own end in view.   Paving
the way for Mr. Vimpany's departure from the cottage at Passy, he
made a polite offer of his services.

'Can't I help you out of your difficulty?' he said.

'You!' cried the doctor.   'Have you forgotten how you received
me, sir, when I asked for a loan at your hotel in London?'

Hugh admitted that he might have spoken hastily.   'You took
me by surprise,' he said, 'and (perhaps I was mistaken, on my
side) I thought you were, to say the least of it, not particularly civil.
You did certainly use threatening language when you left me.   No
man likes to be treated in that way.'

Mr. Vimpany's big bold eyes stared at Mountjoy in a state
of bewilderment.   'Are you trying to make a fool of me?' he
asked.

'I am incapable, Mr. Vimpany, of an act of rudeness towards
anybody.'

'If you come to that,' the doctor stoutly declared, 'I am incapable too.   It's plain to me that we have been misunderstanding
each other.   Wait a bit; I want to go back for a moment to that
threatening language which you complained of just now.   I was
sorry for what I had said as soon as your door was shut on me.   On
my way downstairs I did think of turning back and making a
friendly apology before I gave you up.   Suppose I had done that?'
Mr. Vimpany asked, wondering internally whether Mountjoy was
foolish enough to believe him.

Hugh advanced a little nearer to the design that he had in view.

'You might have found me more kindly disposed towards you,'
he said, 'than you had anticipated.'

This encouraging reply cost him an effort.   He had stooped to
the unworthy practice of perverting what he had said and done on
a former occasion, to serve a present interest.   Remind himself as
he might of the end which, in the interests of Iris, did really appear
to justify the means, he still sank to a place in his own estimation
which he was honestly ashamed to occupy.

Under other circumstances his hesitation, slight as it was, might
have excited suspicion.   As things were, Mr. Vimpany could only
discover golden possibilities that dazzled his eyes.   'I wonder
whether you're in the humour,' he said, 'to be kindly disposed
towards me now?'

It was needless to be careful of the feelings of such a man as this. 'Suppose you had the money you want in your pocket,' Hugh suggested, 'what would you do with it?'

'Go back to London, to be sure, and publish the first number of that work of mine I told you of.'

'And leave your friend, Lord Harry?'

'What good is my friend to me? He's nearly as poor as I am —he sent for me to advise him—I put him up to a way of filling both our pockets, and he wouldn't hear of it. What sort of a friend do you call that?'

Pay him and get rid of him. There was the course of proceeding suggested by the private counsellor in Mountjoy's bosom.

'Have you got the publisher's estimate of expenses?' he asked.

The doctor instantly produced the document.

To a rich man the sum required was, after all, trifling enough. Mountjoy sat down at the writing-table. As he took up a pen, Mr. Vimpany's protuberant eyes looked as if they would fly out of his head.

'If I lend you the money——' Hugh began.

'Yes? Yes?' cried the doctor.

'I do so on condition that nobody is to know of the loan but ourselves.'

'Oh, sir, on my sacred word of honour——' An order on Mountjoy's bankers in Paris for the necessary amount, with something added for travelling expenses, checked Mr. Vimpany in full career of protestation. He tried to begin again: 'My friend! my benefactor——'

He was stopped once more. His friend and benefactor pointed to the clock.

'If you want the money to-day, you have just time to get to Paris before the bank closes.'

Mr. Vimpany did want the money—always wanted the money; his gratitude burst out for the third time: 'God bless you!'

The object of that highly original form of benediction pointed through the window in the direction of the railway station. Mr. Vimpany struggled no longer to express his feelings—he had made his last sacrifice to appearances—he caught the train.

The door of the room had been left open. A voice outside said: 'Has he gone?'

'Come in, Fanny,' said Mountjoy. 'He will return to London either to-night or to-morrow morning.'

The strange maid put her head in at the door. 'I'll be at the terminus,' she said, 'and make sure of him.'

Her head suddenly disappeared, before it was possible to speak to her again. Was there some other person outside? The other person entered the room; it was Lord Harry. He spoke without his customary smile.

'I want a word with you, Mr. Mountjoy.'

'About what, my lord?'

That direct question seemed to confuse the Irishman. He hesitated.

' About you,' he said, and stopped to consider. 'And another person,' he added mysteriously.

Hugh was constitutionally a hater of mysteries. He felt the need of a more definite reply, and asked for it plainly :

' Does your lordship associate that other person with me ?

' Yes, I do.'

' Who is the person ?

' My wife.'

CHAPTER XXX

SAXON AND CELT

HEN amicable relations between two men happen to be in jeopardy, there is least danger of an ensuing quarrel if the friendly intercourse has been of artificial growth, on either side. In this case, the promptings of self-interest, and the laws of politeness, have been animating influences throughout; acting under conditions which assist the effort of self-control. And for this reason: the man who has never really taken a high place in our regard is unprovided with those sharpest weapons of provocation, which make unendurable demands on human fortitude. In a true attachment, on the other hand, there is an innocent familiarity implied, which is forgetful of ceremony, and blind to consequences. The affectionate freedom which can speak kindly without effort is sensitive to offence, and can speak harshly without restraint. When the friend who wounds us has once been associated with the sacred memories of the heart, he strikes at a tender place, and no considerations of propriety are powerful enough to stifle our cry of rage and pain. The enemies who have once loved each other are the bitterest enemies of all.

Thus, the curt exchange of question and answer, which had taken place in the cottage at Passy, between two gentlemen artificially friendly to one another, led to no regrettable result. Lord Harry had been too readily angry: he remembered what was due to Mr. Mountjoy. Mr. Mountjoy had been too thoughtlessly abrupt: he remembered what was due to Lord Harry. The courteous Irishman bowed, and pointed to a chair. The well-bred Englishman returned the polite salute, and sat down. My lord broke the silence that followed.

'May I hope that you will excuse me,' he began, 'if I walk about the room? Movement seems to help me when I am puzzled how to put things nicely. Sometimes I go round and round the subject, before I get at it. I'm afraid I'm going round and round, now. Have you arranged to make a long stay in Paris?'

Circumstances, Mountjoy answered, would probably decide him.

'You have no doubt been many times in Paris before this,' Lord Harry continued. 'Do you find it at all dull, now?'

Wondering what he could possibly mean, Hugh said he never

found Paris dull—and waited for further enlightenment. The Irish lord persisted :

'People mostly think Paris isn't as gay as it used to be. Not such good plays and such good actors as they had at one time. The restaurants inferior, and society very much mixed. People don't stay there as long as they used. I'm told that Americans are getting disappointed, and are trying London for a change.'

Could he have any serious motive for this irrelevant way of talking ? Or was he, to judge by his own account of himself, going round and round the subject of his wife and his guest, before he could get at it ?

Suspecting him of jealousy from the first, Hugh failed—naturally perhaps in his position—to understand the regard for Iris, and the fear of offending her, by which her jealous husband was restrained. Lord Harry was attempting (awkwardly indeed !) to break off the relations between his wife and her friend, by means which might keep the true state of his feelings concealed from both of them. Ignorant of this claim on his forbearance, it was Mountjoy's impression that he was being trifled with. Once more, he waited for enlightenment, and waited in silence.

'You don't find my conversation interesting ? ' Lord Harry remarked, still with perfect good-humour.

'I fail to see the connection,' Mountjoy acknowledged, 'between what you have said so far, and the subject on which you expressed your intention of speaking to me. Pray forgive me if I appear to hurry you—or if you have any reasons for hesitation.'

Far from being offended, this incomprehensible man really appeared to be pleased. 'You read me like a book ! ' he exclaimed. 'It's hesitation that's the matter with me. I'm a variable man. If there's something disagreeable to say, there are times when I dash at it, and times when I hang back. Can I offer you any refreshment ? ' he asked, getting away from the subject again, without so much as an attempt at concealment.

Hugh thanked him, and declined.

'Not even a glass of wine ? Such white Burgundy, my dear sir, as you seldom taste.'

Hugh's British obstinacy was roused ; he repeated his reply. Lord Harry looked at him gravely, and made a nearer approach to an open confession of feeling than he had ventured on yet.

'With regard now to my wife. When I went away this morning with Vimpany—he's not such good company as he used to be ; soured by misfortune, poor devil ; I wish he would go back to London. As I was saying—I mean as I was about to say—I left you and Lady Harry together this morning ; two old friends, glad (as I supposed) to have a gossip about old times. When I come back, I find you left here alone, and I am told that Lady Harry is in her room. What do I see when I get there ? I see the finest pair of eyes in the world ; and the tale they tell me is, We have been crying. When I ask what may have happened to account for this

—" Nothing, dear," is all the answer I get. What's the impression naturally produced on my mind? There has been a quarrel perhaps between you and my wife.'

' I fail entirely, Lord Harry, to see it in that light.'

' Ah, likely enough! Mine's the Irish point of view. As an Englishman you fail to understand it. Let that be. One thing, Mr. Mountjoy, I'll take the freedom of saying at once. I'll thank you, next time, to quarrel with Me.'

' You force me to tell you, my lord, that you are under a complete delusion, if you suppose that there has been any quarrel, or approach to a quarrel, between Lady Harry and myself.'

' You tell me that, on your word of honour as a gentleman? '

' Most assuredly! '

' Sir! I deeply regret to hear it.'

' Which does your lordship deeply regret? That I have spoken to you on my word of honour, or that I have not quarrelled with Lady Harry? '

' Both, sir! By the piper that played before Moses, both! '

Hugh got up, and took his hat : ' We may have a better chance of understanding each other,' he suggested, ' if you will be so good as to write to me.'

' Put your hat down again, Mr. Mountjoy, and pray have a moment's patience. I've tried to like you, sir—and I'm bound in candour to own that I've failed to find a bond of union between us. Maybe, this frank confession annoys you.'

' Far from it! You are going straight to your subject at last, if I may venture to say so.'

The Irish lord's good-humour had completely disappeared by this time. His handsome face hardened, and his voice rose. The outbreak of jealous feeling, which motives honourable to himself had hitherto controlled, now seized on its freedom of expression. His language betrayed (as on some former occasions) that association with unworthy companions, which had been one of the evil results of his adventurous life.

' Maybe I'll go straighter than you bargain for,' he replied ; ' I'm in two humours about you. My common-sense tells me that you're my wife's friend. And the best of friends do sometimes quarrel, don't they? Well, sir, you deny it, on your own account. I find myself forced back on my other humour—and it's a black humour, I can tell you. You may be my wife's friend, my fine fellow, but you're something more than that. You have always been in love with her—and you're in love with her now. Thank you for your visit, but don't repeat it. Say! do we understand each other at last? '

' I have too sincere a respect for Lady Harry to answer you,' Mountjoy said. ' At the same time, let me acknowledge my obligations to your lordship. You have reminded me that I did a foolish thing when I called here without an invitation. I agree with you that the sooner my mistake is set right the better.'

He replied in those words, and left the cottage.

On the way back to his hotel, Hugh thought of what Mrs. Vimpany had said to him when they had last seen each other : ' Don't forget that there is an obstacle between you and Iris which will put even your patience and your devotion to a hard trial.' The obstacle of the husband had set itself up, and had stopped him already.

His own act (a necessary act after the language that had been addressed to him) had closed the doors of the cottage, and had put an end to future meetings between Iris and himself. If they attempted to communicate by letter, Lord Harry would have opportunities of discovering their correspondence, of which his jealousy would certainly avail itself. Through the wakeful night, Hugh's helpless situation was perpetually in his thoughts. There seemed to be no present alternative before him but resignation, and a return to England.

CHAPTER XXXI

THE SCHOOL FOR HUSBANDS

N the next day Mountjoy heard news of Iris, which was not of a nature to relieve his anxieties. He received a visit from Fanny Mere.

The leave-taking of Mr. Vimpany, on the previous evening, was the first event which the maid had to relate. She had been present when the doctor said good-bye to the master and mistress. Business in London was the reason he gave for going away. The master had taken the excuse as if he really believed in it, and seemed to be glad to get rid of his friend. The mistress expressed her opinion that Mr. Vimpany's return to London must have been brought about by an act of liberality on the part of the most generous of living men. '*Your* friend has, as I believe, got some money from *my* friend,' she said to her husband. My lord had looked at her very strangely when she spoke of Mr. Mountjoy in that way, and had walked out of the room. As soon as his back was turned, Fanny had obtained leave of absence. She had carried out her intention of watching the terminus, and had seen Mr. Vimpany take his place among the passengers to London by the mail train.

Returning to the cottage, it was Fanny's duty to ascertain if her services were required in her mistress's room.

On reaching the door, she had heard the voices of my lord and my lady, and (as Mr. Mountjoy would perhaps be pleased to know) had been too honourable to listen outside, on this occasion. She had at once gone away, and had waited until she should be sent for. After a long interval, the bell that summoned her had been rung. She had found the mistress in a state of agitation, partly angry, and partly distressed; and had ventured to ask if anything unpleasant had happened. No reply was made to that inquiry. Fanny had silently performed the customary duties of the night-toilet, in getting my lady ready for bed; they had said good-night to each other and had said no more.

In the morning (that present morning), being again in attendance as usual, the maid had found Lady Harry in a more indulgent frame of mind; still troubled by anxieties, but willing to speak of them now.

She had begun by talking of Mr. Mountjoy:

'I think you like him, Fanny: everybody likes him. You will

be sorry to hear that we have no prospect of seeing him again at the cottage.' There she had stopped; something that she had not said, yet, seemed to be in her mind, and to trouble her. She was near to crying, poor soul, but struggled against it. 'I have no sister,' she said, 'and no friend who might be like a sister to me. It isn't perhaps quite right to speak of my sorrow to my maid. Still, there is something hard to bear in having no kind heart near one—I mean, no other woman to speak to who knows what women feel. It is so lonely here—oh, so lonely! I wonder whether you understand me and pity me?' Never forgetting all that she owed to her mistress—if she might say so without seeming to praise herself—Fanny was truly sorry. It would have been a relief to her, if she could have freely expressed her opinion that my lord must be to blame, when my lady was in trouble. Being a man, he was by nature cruel to women; the wisest thing his poor wife could do would be to expect nothing from him. The maid was sorely tempted to offer a little good advice to this effect; but she was afraid of her own remembrances, if she encouraged them by speaking out boldly. It would be better to wait for what the mistress might say next.

Lord Harry's conduct was the first subject that presented itself when the conversation was resumed.

My lady mentioned that she had noticed how he looked, and how he left the room, when she had spoken in praise of Mr. Mountjoy. She had pressed him to explain himself—and she had made a discovery which proved to be the bitterest disappointment of her life. Her husband suspected her! Her husband was jealous of her! It was too cruel; it was an insult beyond endurance, an insult to Mr. Mountjoy as well as to herself. If that best and dearest of good friends was to be forbidden the house, if he was to go away and never to see her or speak to her again, of one thing she was determined—he should not leave her without a kind word of farewell; he should hear how truly she valued him; yes, and how she admired and felt for him! Would Fanny not do the same thing, in her place? And Fanny had remembered the time when she might have done it for such a man as Mr. Mountjoy. 'Mind you stay indoors this evening, sir,' the maid continued, looking and speaking so excitedly that Hugh hardly knew her again. 'My mistress is coming to see you, and I shall come with her.'

Such an act of imprudence was incredible. 'You must be out of your senses!' Mountjoy exclaimed.

'I'm out of myself, sir, if that's what you mean,' Fanny answered. 'I do so enjoy treating a man in that way! The master's going out to dinner—he'll know nothing about it—and,' cried the cool cold woman of other times, 'he richly deserves it.'

Hugh reasoned and remonstrated, and failed to produce the slightest effect.

His next effort was to write a few lines to Lady Harry, entreating her to remember that a jealous man is sometimes capable of acts of the meanest duplicity, and that she might be watched. When he gave the note to Fanny to deliver, she informed him respectfully that he had better not trust her. A person sometimes meant to do right (she reminded him), and sometimes ended in doing wrong. Rather than disappoint her mistress, she was quite capable of tearing up the letter, on her way home, and saying nothing about it. Hugh tried a threat next: 'Your mistress will not find me, if she comes here; I shall go out to-night.' The impenetrable maid looked at him with a pitying smile, and answered: 'Not you!'

It was a humiliating reflection—but Fanny Mere understood him better than he understood himself.

All that Mountjoy had said and done in the way of protest, had been really dictated by consideration for the young wife. If he questioned his conscience, selfish delight in the happy prospect of seeing Iris again asserted itself, as the only view with which he looked forward to the end of the day. When the evening approached, he took the precaution of having his own discreet and faithful servant in attendance, to receive Lady Harry at the door of the hotel, before the ringing of the bell could summon the porter from his lodge. On calm consideration, the chances seemed to be in favour of her escaping detection by Lord Harry. The jealous husband of the stage, who sooner (or later) discovers the innocent (or guilty) couple, as the case may be, is not always the husband of the world outside the theatre. With this fragment of experience present in his mind, Hugh saw the door of his sitting-room cautiously opened, at an earlier hour than he had anticipated. His trustworthy representative introduced a lady, closely veiled—and that lady was Iris.

CHAPTER XXXII

GOOD-BYE TO IRIS

ADY HARRY lifted her veil, and looked at Mountjoy with
sad entreaty in her eyes. 'Are you angry with me?'
she asked.

'I ought to be angry with you,' he said. 'This is
very imprudent, Iris.'

'It's worse than that,' she confessed. 'It's reckless and desperate. Don't say I ought to have controlled myself. I can't
control the shame I feel when I think of what has happened. Can
I let you go—oh, what a return for your kindness!—without taking
your hand at parting? Come and sit by me on the sofa. After my
poor husband's conduct, you and I are not likely to meet again. I
don't expect you to lament it as I do. Even your sweetness and
your patience—so often tried—must be weary of me now.'

'If you thought that possible, my dear, you would not have come
here to-night,' Hugh reminded her. 'While we live, we have the
hope of meeting again. Nothing in this world lasts, Iris—not even
jealousy. Lord Harry himself told me that he was a variable man.
Sooner or later he will come to his senses.'

Those words seemed to startle Iris. 'I hope you don't think
that my husband is brutal to me!' she exclaimed, still resenting
even the appearance of a reflection on her marriage, and still forgetting what she herself had said which justified a doubt of her
happiness. 'Have you formed a wrong impression?' she went on.
'Has Fanny Mere innocently——?'

Mountjoy noticed, for the first time, the absence of the maid.
It was a circumstance which justified him in interrupting Iris—for
it might seriously affect her if her visit to the hotel happened to be
discovered.

'I understood,' he said, 'that Fanny was to come here with
you.'

Yes! yes! She is waiting in the carriage. We are careful
not to excite attention at the door of the hotel; the coachman will
drive up and down the street till I want him again. Never mind
that! I have something to say to you about Fanny She thinks
of her own troubles, poor soul, when she talks to me, and exaggerates
a little without meaning it. I hope she has not misled you in speaking of her master. It is base and bad of him, unworthy of a gentleman, to be jealous—and he has wounded me deeply. But dear

Hugh, his jealousy is a gentle jealousy. I have heard of other men
who watch their wives—who have lost all confidence in them—
who would even have taken away from me such a trifle as this.'
She smiled, and showed to Mountjoy her duplicate key of the
cottage door. 'Ah, Harry is above such degrading distrust as that!
There are times when he is as heartily ashamed of his own weakness
as I could wish him to be. I have seen him on his knees before
me, shocked at his conduct. He is no hypocrite. Indeed, his repentance is sincere, while it lasts—only it doesn't last! His jealousy
rises and falls, like the wind. He said last night (when the wind
was high) : "If you wish to make me the happiest creature on the
face of the earth, don't encourage Mr. Mountjoy to remain in Paris!"
Try to make allowances for him!'

'I would rather make allowances, Iris, for you. Do *you*, too
wish me to leave Paris?'

Sitting very near to him—nearer than her husband might have
liked to see—Iris drew away a little. 'Did you mean to be cruel
in saying that?' she asked. 'I don't deserve it.'

'It was kindly meant,' Hugh assured her. 'If I can make your
position more endurable by going away, I will leave Paris to-
morrow.'

Iris moved back again to the place which she had already occupied. She was eager to thank him (for a reason not yet mentioned)
as she had never thanked him yet. Silently and softly she offered
her gratitude to Hugh, by offering her cheek. The irritating influence of Lord Harry's jealousy was felt by both of them at that
moment. He kissed her cheek—and lingered over it. She was
the first to recover herself.

'When you spoke just now of my position with my husband,'
she said, 'you reminded me of anxieties, Hugh, in which you once
shared, and of services which I can never forget.'

Preparing him in those words for the disclosure which she had
now to make, Iris alluded to the vagabond life of adventure which
Lord Harry had led. The restlessness in his nature which that life
implied, had latterly shown itself again; and his wife had traced
the cause to a letter from Ireland, communicating a report that the
assassin of Arthur Mountjoy had been seen in London, and was
supposed to be passing under the name of Carrigeen. Hugh would
understand that the desperate resolution to revenge the murder of
his friend, with which Lord Harry had left England in the past time,
had been urged into action once more. He had not concealed from
Iris that she must be resigned to his leaving her for awhile, if the
report which had reached him from Ireland proved to be true. It
would be useless, and worse than useless, to remind this reckless
man of the danger that threatened him from the Invincibles, if he
returned to England. In using her power of influencing the husband who still loved her, Iris could only hope to exercise a salutary
restraint in her own domestic interests, appealing to him for indulgence by careful submission to any exactions on which his capricious

jealousy might insist. Would sad necessity excuse her, if she accepted Mountjoy's offer to leave Paris, for the one reason that her husband had asked it of her as a favour?

Hugh at once understood her motive, and assured her of his sympathy.

'You may depend upon my returning to London to-morrow,' he said. 'In the meantime, is there no better way in which I can be of use to you? If your influence fails, do you see any other chance of keeping Lord Harry's desperate purpose under control?'

It had only that day occurred to Iris that there might be some prospect of an encouraging result, if she could obtain the assistance of Mrs. Vimpany.

The doctor's wife was well acquainted with Lord Harry's past life, when he happened to be in Ireland; and she had met many of his countrymen with whom he had associated. If one of those friends happened to be the officious person who had written to him, it was at least possible that Mrs. Vimpany's discreet interference might prevent his mischievous correspondent from writing again. Lord Harry, waiting for more news, would in this event wait in vain. He would not know where to go, or what to do next—and, with such a nature as his, the end of his patience and the end of his resolution were likely to come together.

Hugh handed his pocket-book to Iris. Of the poor chances in her favour, the last was to his mind the least hopeless of the two.

'If you have discovered the name of your husband's correspondent,' he said, 'write it down for me, and I will ask Mrs. Vimpany if she knows him. I will make your excuses for not having written to her lately; and, in any case, I answer for her being ready to help you.'

As Iris thanked him and wrote the name, the clock on the chimneypiece struck the hour.

She rose to say farewell. With a restless hand she half-lowered her veil, and raised it again. 'You won't mind my crying,' she said faintly, trying to smile through her tears. 'This is the saddest parting I have ever known. Dear, dear Hugh—good-bye!'

Great is the law of Duty; but the elder law of Love claims its higher right. Never, in all the years of their friendship, had they forgotten themselves as they forgot themselves now. For the first time her lips met his lips, in their farewell kiss. In a moment more, they remembered the restraints which honour imposed on them; they were only friends again. Silently she lowered her veil. Silently he took her arm and led her down to the carriage. It was moving away from them at a slow pace, towards the other end of the street. Instead of waiting for its return, they followed and overtook it.

'We shall meet again,' he whispered.

She answered sadly: 'Don't forget me.'

Mountjoy turned back. As he approached the hotel he noticed a tall man crossing from the opposite side of the street. Not two minutes after Iris was on her way home, her jealous husband and her old friend met at the hotel door.

Lord Harry spoke first. 'l have been dining out,' he said, 'and I came here to have a word with you, Mr. Mountjoy, on my road home.'

Hugh answered with formal politeness: 'Let me show your lordship the way to my rooms.'

'Oh, it's needless to trouble you,' Lord Harry declared. 'I have so little to say—do you mind walking on with me for a few minutes?'

Mountjoy silently complied. He was thinking of what might have happened if Iris had delayed her departure—or if the movement of the carriage had been towards, instead of away from the hotel. In either case it had been a narrow escape for the wife, from a dramatic discovery by the husband.

'We Irishmen,' Lord Harry resumed, 'are not famous for always obeying the laws; but it is in our natures to respect the law of hospitality. When you were at the cottage yesterday I was inhospitable to my guest. My rude behaviour has weighed on my mind since—and for that reason I have come here to speak to you. It was ill-bred on my part to reproach you with your visit, and to forbid you (oh, quite needlessly, I don't doubt!) to call on me again. If I own that I have no desire to propose a renewal of friendly intercourse between us, you will understand me, I am sure; with my way of thinking, the less we see of each other for the future, the better it may be. But, for what I said when my temper ran away with me, I ask you to accept my excuses, and the sincere expression of my regret.'

'Your excuses are accepted, my lord, as sincerely as you have offered them,' Mountjoy answered. 'So far as I am concerned, the incident is forgotten from this moment.'

Lord Harry expressed his courteous acknowledgments. 'Spoken as becomes a gentleman,' he said. 'I thank you.'

There it ended. They saluted each other; they wished each other good-night. 'A mere formality!' Hugh thought, when they had parted.

He had wronged the Irish lord in arriving at that conclusion. But time was to pass before events helped him to discover his error.

CHAPTER XXXIII

THE DECREE OF FATE

ON his arrival in London, Mountjoy went to the Nurses' Institute to inquire for Mrs. Vimpany.

She was again absent, in attendance on another patient. The address of the house (known only to the matron) was, on this occasion, not to be communicated to any friend who might make inquiries. A bad case of scarlet fever had been placed under the nurse's care, and the danger of contagion was too serious to be trifled with.

The events which had led to Mrs. Vimpany's present employment had not occurred in the customary course.

A nurse who had recently joined the Institute had been first engaged to undertake the case, at the express request of the suffering person—who was said to be distantly related to the young woman. On the morning when she was about to proceed to the scene of her labours, news had reached her of the dangerous illness of her mother. Mrs. Vimpany, who was free at the time, and who felt a friendly interest in her young colleague, volunteered to take her place. Upon this, a strange request had been addressed to the matron, on behalf of the sick man. He desired to be 'informed of it, if the new nurse was an Irishwoman.' Hearing that she was an Englishwoman, he at once accepted her services, being himself (as an additional element of mystery in the matter) an Irishman !

The matron's English prejudices at once assumed that there had been some discreditable event in the man's life, which might be made a subject of scandalous exposure if he was attended by one of his own countrypeople. She advised Mrs. Vimpany to have nothing to do with the afflicted stranger. The nurse answered that she had promised to attend on him—and she kept her promise.

Mountjoy left the Institute, after vainly attempting to obtain Mrs. Vimpany's address. The one concession which the matron offered to make was to direct his letter, and send it to the post, if he would be content with that form of communication.

On reflection, he decided to write the letter.

Prompt employment of time might be of importance, if it was possible to prevent any further communication with Lord Harry on the part of his Irish correspondent. Using the name with which Iris had provided him, Hugh wrote to inquire if it was familiar to Mrs. Vimpany, as the name of a person with whom she had been, at any time, acquainted. In this event, he assured her that an immediate consultation between them was absolutely necessary in the interests of Iris. He added, in a postscript, that he was in perfect health, and that he had no fear of infection—and sent his letter to the matron to be forwarded.

The reply reached him late in the evening. It was in the hand-writing of a stranger, and was to this effect :

'Dear Mr. Mountjoy,—It is impossible that I can allow you to run the risk of seeing me while I am in my present situation. So serious is the danger of contagion in scarlet fever, that I dare not even write to you with my own hand on note-paper which has been used in the sick room. This is no mere fancy of mine; the doctor in attendance here knows of a case in which a small piece of in-fected flannel communicated the disease after an interval of no less than a year. I must trust to your own good sense to see the necessity of waiting, until I can receive you without any fear of consequences to yourself. In the meantime, I may answer your inquiry relating to the name communicated in your letter. I first knew the gentleman you mention some years since ; we were intro-duced to each other by Lord Harry ; and I saw him afterwards on more than one occasion.'

Mountjoy read this wise and considerate reply to his letter with indignation.

Here was the good fortune for which he had not dared to hope, declaring itself in favour of Iris. Here (if Mrs. Vimpany could be persuaded to write to her friend) was the opportunity offered of keeping the hot-tempered Irish husband passive and harmless, by keeping him without further news of the assassin of Arthur Mount-joy. Under these encouraging circumstances the proposed consultation which might have produced such excellent results had been rejected; thanks to a contemptible fear of infection, excited by a story of a trumpery piece of flannel!

Hugh snatched up the unfortunate letter (cast away on the floor) to tear it in pieces and throw it into the waste-paper basket—and checked himself. His angry hand had seized on it with the blank leaf of the note-paper uppermost.

On that leaf he discovered two little lines of print, presenting, in the customary form, the address of the house at which the letter had been written! The writer, in taking the sheet of paper from the case, must have accidentally turned it wrong side uppermost on the desk, and had not cared to re-copy the letter, or had not discovered the mistake. Restored to his best good-humour, Hugh resolved to surprise Mrs. Vimpany by a visit, on the next day, which would set the theory of contagion at defiance, and render valuable service to Iris at a crisis in her life.

Having time before him for reflection, in the course of the evening, he was at no loss to discover a formidable obstacle in the way of his design.

Whether he gave his name or concealed his name, when he asked for Mrs. Vimpany at the house-door, she would in either case refuse to see him. The one accessible person whom he could consult in this difficulty was his faithful old servant.

That experienced man—formerly employed, at various times, in the army, in the police, and in service at a public school—obtained leave to make some preliminary investigations on the next morning.

He achieved two important discoveries. In the first place, Mrs. Vimpany was living in the house in which the letter to his master had been written. In the second place, there was a page attached to the domestic establishment (already under notice to leave his situation), who was accessible to corruption by means of a bribe. The boy would be on the watch for Mr. Mountjoy at two o'clock on that day, and would show him where to find Mrs. Vimpany, in the room near the sick man, in which she was accustomed to take her meals.

Hugh acted on his instructions, and found the page waiting to admit him secretly to the house. Leading the way upstairs, the boy pointed with one hand to a door on the second floor, and held out the other hand to receive his money. While he pocketed the bribe, and disappeared, Mountjoy opened the door.

Mrs. Vimpany was seated at a table waiting for her dinner. When Hugh showed himself she started to her feet with a cry of alarm.

'Are you mad?' she exclaimed. 'How did you get here? What do you want here? Don't come near me!'

She attempted to pass Hugh on her way out of the room. He caught her by the arm, led her back to her chair, and forced her to seat herself again. 'Iris is in trouble,' he pleaded, 'and you can help her.'

'The fever!' she cried, heedless of what he had said. 'Keep back from me—the fever!'

For the second time she tried to get out of the room. For the second time Hugh stopped her.

'Fever or no fever,' he persisted, 'I have something to say to you. In two minutes I shall have said it, and I will go.'

In the fewest possible words he described the situation of Iris with her jealous husband. Mrs. Vimpany indignantly interrupted him.

'Are you running this dreadful risk,' she asked, 'with nothing to say to me that I don't know already? Her husband jealous of her? Of course he is jealous of her! Leave me—or I will ring for the servant.'

'Ring, if you like,' Hugh answered; 'but hear this first. My letter to you alluded to a consultation between us, which might be necessary in the interests of Iris. Imagine her situation if you can! The assassin of Arthur Mountjoy is reported to be in London; and Lord Harry has heard of it.'

Mrs. Vimpany looked at him with horror in her eyes.

'Gracious God!' she cried, 'the man is here—under my care. Oh, I am not in the conspiracy to hide the wretch! I knew no more of him than you do when I offered to nurse him. The names that have escaped him, in his delirium, have told me the truth.'

As she spoke, a second door in the room was opened. An old woman showed herself for a moment, trembling with terror. 'He's breaking out again, nurse! Help me to hold him!'

Mrs. Vimpany instantly followed the woman into the bed-room. 'Wait and listen,' she said to Mountjoy—and left the door open.

The quick, fierce, muttering tones of a man in delirium were now fearfully audible. His maddened memory was travelling back over his own horrible life. He put questions to himself; he answered himself:

'Who drew the lot to kill the traitor? I did! I did! Who shot him on the road, before he could get to the wood? I did! I did! Arthur Mountjoy, traitor to Ireland. Set that on his tombstone, and disgrace him for ever. Listen, boys—listen! There is a patriot among you. I am the patriot—preserved by a merciful Providence. Ha, my Lord Harry, search the earth and search the sea, the patriot is out of your reach! Nurse! What's that the doctor said of me? The fever will kill him? Well, what does that matter, as long as Lord Harry doesn't kill me? Open the doors, and let everybody hear of it. I die the death of a saint—the greatest of all saints—the saint who shot Arthur Mountjoy. Oh, the heat, the heat, the burning raging heat!' The tortured creature burst into a dreadful cry of rage and pain. It was more than Hugh's resolution could support. He hurried out of the house.

. . . .

Ten days passed. A letter, in a strange handwriting, reached Iris at Passy.

The first part of the letter was devoted to the Irish desperado, whom Mrs. Vimpany had attended in his illness.

When she only knew him as a suffering fellow-creature she had promised to be his nurse. Did the discovery that he was an assassin justify desertion, or even excuse neglect? No! the nursing art, like the healing art, is an act of mercy—in itself too essentially noble to inquire whether the misery that it relieves merits help. All that experience, all that intelligence, all that care could offer, the nurse gave to the man whose hand she would have shrunk from touching in friendship, after she had saved his life.

A time had come when the fever threatened to take Lord Harry's vengeance out of his hands. The crisis of the disease declared itself. With the shadow of death on him, the wretch lived through it—saved by his strong constitution, and by the skilled and fearless woman who attended on him. At the period of his convalescence, friends from Ireland (accompanied by a medical man of their own choosing) presented themselves at the house, and asked for him by the name under which he passed—Carrigeen. With every possible care, he was removed; to what destination had never been discovered. From that time, all trace of him had been lost.

Terrible news followed on the next page.

The subtle power of infection had asserted itself against the poor mortal who had defied it. Hugh Mountjoy, stricken by the man who had murdered his brother, lay burning under the scarlet fire of the fever.

But the nurse watched by him, night and day.

CHAPTER XXXIV

MY LORD'S MIND

HERE, my old-vagabond-Vimpany, is an interesting case for you—the cry of a patient with a sick mind.

Look over it, and prescribe for your wild Irish friend, if you can.

You will perhaps remember that I have never thoroughly trusted you, in all the years since we have known each other. At this later date in our lives, when I ought to see more clearly than ever what an unfathomable man you are, am I rash enough to be capable of taking you into my confidence ?

I don't know what I am going to do; I feel like a man who has been stunned. To be told that the murderer of Arthur Mountjoy had been seen in London—to be prepared to trace him by his paltry assumed name of Carrigeen—to wait vainly for the next discovery which might bring him within reach of retribution at my hands— and then to be overwhelmed by the news of his illness, his recovery, and his disappearance : these are the blows which have stupefied me. Only think of it ! He has escaped me for the second time. Fever that kills thousands of harmless creatures has spared the assassin. He may yet die in his bed, and be buried, with the guiltless dead around him, in a quiet churchyard. I can't get over it; I shall never get over it.

Add to this, anxieties about my wife, and maddening letters from creditors—and don't expect me to write reasonably.

What I want to know is whether your art (or whatever you call it) can get at my diseased mind, through my healthy body. You have more than once told me that medicine can do this. The time has come for doing it. I am in a bad way, and a bad end may follow. My only medical friend, deliver me from myself.

In any case, let me beg you to keep your temper while you read what follows.

I have to confess that the devil whose name is Jealousy has entered into me, and is threatening the tranquillity of my married life. You dislike Iris, I know—and she returns your hostile feeling towards her. Try to do my wife justice, nevertheless, as I do. I don't believe my distrust of her has any excuse—and yet, I am jealous. More unreasonable still, I am as fond of her as I was in the first days of the honeymoon. Is she as fond as ever of me? You were a married man when I was a boy. Let me give you the means of forming an opinion by a narrative of her conduct, under (what I admit to have been) very trying circumstances.

When the first information reached Iris of Hugh Mountjoy's dangerous illness, we were at breakfast. It struck her dumb. She handed the letter to me, and left the table.

I hate a man who doesn't know what it is to want money; I hate a man who keeps his temper; I hate a man who pretends to be my wife's friend, and who is secretly in love with her all the time. What difference did it make to me whether Hugh Mountjoy ended in living or dying? If I had any interest in the matter, it ought by rights (seeing that I am jealous of him) to be an interest in his death. Well! I declare positively that the alarming news from London spoilt my breakfast! There is something about that friend of my wife—that smug, prosperous, well-behaved Englishman—which seems to plead for him (God knows how!) when my mind is least inclined in his favour. While I was reading about his illness, I found myself hoping that he would recover—and, I give you my sacred word of honour, I hated him all the time!

My Irish friend is mad—you will say. Your Irish friend, my dear fellow, does not dispute it.

Let us get back to my wife. She showed herself again after a long absence, having something (at last) to say to her husband.

'I am innocently to blame,' she began, 'for the dreadful mis- fortune that has fallen on Mr. Mountjoy. If I had not given him a message to Mrs. Vimpany, he would never have insisted on seeing her, and would never have caught the fever. It may help me to bear my misery of self-reproach and suspense, if I am kept informed of his illness. There is no fear of infection by my receiving letters. I am to write to a friend of Mrs. Vimpany, who lives in another house, and who will answer my inquiries. Do you object, dear Harry, to my getting news of Hugh Mountjoy every day, while he is in danger?'

I was perfectly willing that she should get that news, and she ought to have known it.

It seemed to me to be also a bad sign that she made her request with dry eyes. She must have cried, when she first heard that he was likely to sink under an attack of fever. Why were her tears kept hidden in her own room? When she came back to me, her face was pale and hard and tearless. Don't you think she might have for- gotten my jealousy, when I was so careful myself not to show it? My own belief is that she was longing to go to London, and help your wife to nurse the poor man, and catch the fever, and die with him if *he* died.

Is this bitter? Perhaps it is. Tear it off, and light your pipe with it.

Well, the correspondence relating to the sick man continued every day; and every day—oh, Vimpany, another concession to my jealousy!—she handed the letters to me to read. I made excuses (we Irish are good at that, if we are good at nothing else), and declined to read the medical reports. One morning, when she opened the letter of that day, there passed over her a change which is likely to remain in my memory as long as I live. Never have I seen such an ecstasy of happiness in any woman's face, as I saw when she read the lines which informed her that the fever was mastered. Iris is sweet and delicate and bright—essentially fascinating, in a word. But she was never a beautiful woman, until she knew that Mountjoy's life was safe ; and she will never be a beautiful woman again, unless the time comes when my death leaves her free to marry him. On her wedding-day, he will see the transformation that I saw—and he will be dazzled as I was.

She looked at me, as if she expected me to speak.

'I am glad indeed,' I said, 'that he is out of danger.'

She ran to me—she kissed me ; I wouldn't have believed it was in her to give such kisses. 'Now I have your sympathy,' she said, 'my happiness is complete!' Do you think I was indebted for those kisses to myself, or to that other man? No, no—here is an unworthy doubt. I discard it. Vile suspicion shall not wrong Iris this time.

And yet——

Shall I go on, and write the rest of it?

Poor, dear Arthur Mountjoy once told me of a foreign author, who was in great doubt of the right answer to some tough question that troubled him. He went into his garden and threw a stone at a tree. If he hit the tree, the answer would be—Yes. If he missed the tree, the answer would be—No. I am going into the garden to imitate the foreign author. You shall hear how it ends.

I have hit the tree. As a necessary consequence, I must go on and write the rest of it.

There is a growing estrangement between Iris and myself—and my jealousy doesn't altogether account for it. Sometimes, it occurs to me that we are thinking of what our future relations with Mountjoy are likely to be, and are ashamed to confess it to each other. Sometimes—and perhaps this second, and easiest, guess may be the right one—I am apt to conclude that we are only anxious about money matters. I am waiting for her to touch on the subject, and she is waiting for me ; and there we are at a deadlock.

I wish I had some reason for going to some other place. I wish I was lost among strangers. I should like to find myself in a state of danger, meeting the risks that I used to run in my vagabond days. Now I think of it, I might enjoy this last excitement by going back to England, and giving the Invincibles a chance of shooting me as a traitor to the cause. But my wife would object to that.

Suppose we change the subject.

You will be glad to hear that you know something of law, as well as of medicine. I sent instructions to my solicitor in London to raise a loan on my life-insurance. What you said to me turns

out to be right. I can't raise a farthing, for three years to come,
out of all the thousands of pounds which I shall leave behind me
when I die.

Are my prospects from the newspaper likely to cheer me after
such a disappointment as this ? The new journal, I have the pleasure of informing you, is much admired. When I inquire for my
profits, I hear that the expenses are heavy, and I am told that I
must wait for a rise in our circulation. How long ? Nobody knows.

I shall keep these pages open for a few days more, on the
chance of something happening which may alter my present position for the better.

My position has altered for the worse.

I have been obliged to fill my empty purse, for a little while,
by means of a bit of stamped paper. And how shall I meet my
liabilities when the note falls due ? Let time answer the question;
for the present the evil day is put off. In the meanwhile, if that
literary speculation of yours is answering no better than my newspaper, I can lend you a few pounds to get on with. What do you
say (on second thoughts) to coming back to your old quarters at
Passy, and giving me your valuable advice by word of mouth instead of by letter ?

Come, and feel my pulse, and look at my tongue—and tell me
how these various anxieties of mine are going to end, before we
are any of us a year older. Shall I, like you, be separated from
my wife—at her request; oh, not at mine ! Or shall I be locked
up in prison ? And what will become of You ? Do you take the
hint, doctor ?

CHAPTER XXXV

MY LADY S MIND

NTREAT Lady Harry not to write to me. She will be tempted to do so, when she hears that there is good hope of Mr. Mountjoy's recovery. But, even from that loving and generous heart, I must not accept expressions of gratitude which would only embarrass me. All that I have done, as a nurse, and all that I may yet hope to do, is no more than an effort to make amends for my past life. Iris has my heart's truest wishes for her happiness. Until I can myself write to her without danger, let this be enough.'

In those terms, dearest of women, your friend has sent your message to me. My love respects as well as admires you; your wishes are commands to me. At the same time, I may find some relief from the fears of the future that oppress me, if I can confide them to friendly ears. May I not harmlessly write to you, if I only write of my own poor self?

Try, dear, to remember those pleasant days when you were staying with us, in our honeymoon time, at Paris.

You warned me, one evening when we were alone, to be on my

guard against any circumstances which might excite my husband's jealousy. Since then, the trouble that you foresaw has fallen on me; mainly, I am afraid, through my own want of self-control. It is so hard for a woman, when she really loves a man, to understand a state of mind which can make him doubt her.

I have discovered that jealousy varies. Let me tell you what I mean.

Lord Harry was silent and sullen (ah, how well I knew what that meant!) while the life of our poor Hugh was in jeopardy. When I read the good news which told me that he was no longer in danger, I don't know whether there was any change worth remarking in myself—but, there was a change in my husband, delightful to see. His face showed such sweet sympathy when he looked at me, he spoke so kindly and nicely of Hugh, that I could only express my pleasure by kissing him. You will hardly believe me, when I tell you that his hateful jealousy appeared again, at that moment. He looked surprised, he looked suspicious—he looked, I declare, as if he doubted whether I meant it with all my heart when I kissed him! What incomprehensible creatures men are! We read in novels of women who are able to manage their masters. I wish I knew how to manage mine.

We have been getting into debt. For some weeks past, this sad state of things has been a burden on my mind. Day after day I have been expecting him to speak of our situation, and have found him obstinately silent. Is his mind entirely occupied with other things? Or is he unwilling to speak of our anxieties because the subject humiliates him? Yesterday, I could bear it no longer.

'Our debts are increasing,' I said. 'Have you thought of any way of paying them?'

I had feared that my question might irritate him. To my relief, he seemed to be diverted by it.

'The payment of debts,' he replied, 'is a problem that I am too poor to solve. Perhaps I got near to it the other day.'

I asked how.

'Well,' he said, 'I found myself wishing I had some rich friends. By-the-bye, how is *your* rich friend? What have you heard lately of Mr. Mountjoy?'

'I have heard that he is steadily advancing towards recovery.'

'Likely, I dare say, to return to France when he feels equal to it,' my husband remarked. 'He is a good-natured creature. If he finds himself in Paris again, I wonder whether he will pay us another visit?'

He said this quite seriously. On my side, I was too much astonished to utter a word. My bewilderment seemed to amuse him. In his own pleasant way he explained himself:

'I ought to have told you, my dear, that I was in Mr. Mountjoy's company the night before he returned to England. We had said some disagreeable things to each other here in the cottage, while you were away in your room. My tongue got the better of my judgment. In short, I spoke rudely to our guest. Thinking over it afterwards, I felt that I ought to make an apology. He received my sincere excuses with an amiability of manner, and a grace of language, which raised him greatly in my estimation.'

There you have Lord Harry's own words! Who would suppose that he had ever been jealous of the man whom he spoke of in this way?

I explain it to myself, partly by the charm in Hugh's look and manner, which everybody feels; partly by the readiness with which my husband's variable nature receives new impressions. I hope you agree with me. In any case, pray let Hugh see what I have written to you in this place, and ask him what he thinks of it.[1]

Encouraged, as you will easily understand, by the delightful prospect of a reconciliation between them, I was eager to take my first opportunity of speaking freely of Hugh. Up to that time, it had been a hard trial to keep to myself so much that was deeply interesting in my thoughts and hopes. But my hours of disappointment were not at an end yet. We were interrupted.

A letter was brought to us—one of many, already received!—insisting on immediate payment of a debt that had been too long unsettled. The detestable subject of our poverty insisted on claiming attention when there was a messenger outside, waiting for my poor Harry's last French bank note.

'What is to be done?' I said, when we were left by ourselves again.

My husband's composure was something wonderful. He laughed and lit a cigar.

'We have got to the crisis,' he said. 'The question of money has driven us into a corner at last. My darling, have you ever heard of such a thing as a promissory note?'

I was not quite so ignorant as he supposed me to be; I said I had heard my father speak of promissory notes.

This seemed to fail in convincing him. 'Your father,' he remarked, 'used to pay his notes when they fell due.'

I betrayed my ignorance, after all. 'Doesn't everybody do the same?' I asked.

He burst out laughing. 'We will send the maid to get a bit of stamped paper,' he said; 'I'll write the message for her, this time.'

Those last words alluded to Fanny's ignorance of the French language, which made it necessary to provide her with written instructions, when she was sent on an errand. In our domestic affairs, I was able to do this; but, in the present case, I only handed the message to her. When she returned with a slip of stamped paper, Harry called to me to come to the writing-table.

'Now, my sweet,' he said, 'see how easily money is to be got with a scratch of the pen.'

[1] *Note by Mrs. Vimpany.*—I shall certainly not be foolish enough to show what she has written to Mr. Mountjoy. Poor deluded Iris! Miserable fatal marriage!

I looked over his shoulder. In less than a minute it was done; and he had produced ten thousand francs on paper—in English money (as he told me), four hundred pounds. This seemed to be a large loan; I asked how he proposed to pay it back. He kindly reminded me that he was a newspaper proprietor, and, as such, possessed of the means of inspiring confidence in persons with money to spare. They could afford, it seems, to give him three months in which to arrange for repayment. In that time, as he thought, the profits of the new journal might come pouring in. He knew best, of course.

We took the next train to Paris, and turned our bit of paper into notes and gold. Never was there such a delightful companion as my husband, when he has got money in his pocket. After so much sorrow and anxiety, for weeks past, that memorable afternoon was like a glimpse of Paradise.

On the next morning, there was an end to my short-lived enjoyment of no more than the latter half of a day.

Watching her opportunity, Fanny Mere came to me while I was alone, carrying a thick letter in her hand. She held it before me with the address uppermost.

'Please to look at that,' she said.

The letter was directed (in Harry's handwriting) to Mr. Vimpany, at a publishing office in London. Fanny next turned the envelope the other way.

'Look at this side,' she resumed.

The envelope was specially protected by a seal; bearing a device of my husband's own invention; that is to say, the initials of his name (Harry Norland) surmounted by a star—his lucky star, as he paid me the compliment of calling it, on the day when he married me. I was thinking of that day now. Fanny saw me looking, with a sad heart, at the impression on the wax. She completely misinterpreted the direction taken by my thoughts.

'Tell me to do it, my lady,' she proceeded; 'and I'll open the letter.'

I looked at her. She showed no confusion. 'I can seal it up again,' she coolly explained, 'with a bit of fresh wax and my thimble. Perhaps Mr. Vimpany won't be sober enough to notice it.'

'Do you know, Fanny, that you are making a dishonourable proposal to me?' I said.

'I know there's nothing I can do to help you that I won't do,' she answered; 'and you know why. I have made a dishonourable proposal—have I? That comes quite naturally to a lost woman like me. Shall I tell you what Honour means? It means sticking at nothing, in your service. Please tell me to open the letter.'

'How did you come by the letter, Fanny?'

'My master gave it to me to put in the post.'

'Then, post it.'

The strange creature, so full of contraries—so sensitive at one time, so impenetrable at another—pointed again to the address.

'When the master writes to that man,' she went on—'a long letter (if you will notice), and a sealed letter—your ladyship ought to see what is inside it. I haven't a doubt myself that there's writing under this seal which bodes trouble to you. The spare bedroom is empty. Do you want to have the doctor for your visitor again? Don't tell me to post the letter, till I've opened it first.'

'I do tell you to post the letter.'

Fanny submitted, so far. But she had a new form of persuasion to try, before her reserves of resistance were exhausted. 'If the doctor comes back,' she continued, 'will your ladyship give me leave to go out, whenever I ask for it?'

This was surely presuming on my indulgence. 'Are you not expecting a little too much?' I suggested—not unkindly.

'If you say that, my lady,' she answered, 'I shall be obliged to ask you to suit yourself with another maid.'

There was a tone of dictation in this, which I found beyond endurance. In my anger, I said: 'Leave me whenever you like.'

'I shall leave you when I'm dead—not before,' was the reply that I received. 'But if you won't let me have my liberty without going away from you, for a time, I must go—for your sake.'

(For my sake! Pray observe that.)

She went on:

'Try to see it, my lady, as I do! If we have the doctor with us again, I must be able to watch him.'

'Why?'

'Because he is your enemy, as I believe.'

'How can he hurt me, Fanny?'

'Through your husband, my lady, if he can do it in no other way. Mr. Vimpany shall have a spy at his heels. Dishonourable! oh, dishonourable again! Never mind. I don't pretend to know what that villain means to do, if he and my lord get together again. But this I can tell you, if it's in woman's wit to circumvent him, here I am with my mind made up. With my mind made up!' she repeated fiercely—and recovered on a sudden her customary character as a quiet well-trained servant, devoted to her duties. 'I'll take my master's letter to the post now,' she said. 'Is there anything your ladyship wants in the town?'

What do you think of Fanny Mere? Ought I to have treated this last offer of her services, as I treated her proposal to open the letter? I was not able to do it.

The truth is, I was so touched by her devotion to me, that I could not prevail on myself to mortify her by a refusal. I believe there may be a good reason for the distrust of the doctor which possesses her so strongly; and I feel the importance of having this faithful and determined woman for an ally. Let me hope that Mr. Vimpany's return (if it is to take place) may be delayed until you can safely write, with your own hand, such a letter of wise advice as I sadly need.

In the meantime, give my love to Hugh, and say to this dear friend all that I might have said for myself, if I had been near him. But take care that his recovery is not retarded by anxiety for me. Pray keep him in ignorance of the doubts and fears with which I am now looking at the future. If I was not so fond of my husband, I should be easier in my mind. This sounds contradictory, but I believe you will understand it. For a while, my dear, good-bye.

CHAPTER XXXVI

THE DOCTOR MEANS MISCHIEF

N the day after Lord Harry's description of the state of his mind reached London, a gentleman presented himself at the publishing office of Messrs. Boldside Brothers, and asked for the senior partner, Mr. Peter Boldside. When he sent in his card, it bore the name of ' Mr. Vimpany.'

' To what fortunate circumstance am I indebted, sir, for the honour of your visit ? ' the senior partner inquired. His ingratiating manners, his genial smile, his roundly resonant voice, were personal advantages of which he made a merciless use. The literary customer who entered the office, hesitating before the question of publishing a work at his own expense, generally decided to pay the penalty when he encountered Mr. Peter Boldside.

' I want to inquire about the sale of my work,' Mr. Vimpany replied.

' Ah, doctor, you have come to the wrong man. You must go to my brother.'

Mr. Vimpany protested. ' You mentioned the terms when I first applied to you,' he said, ' and you signed the agreement.'

' That is in *my* department,' the senior partner gently explained. ' And I shall write the cheque when, as we both hope, your large profits shall fall due. But our sales of works are in the department of my brother, Mr. Paul Boldside.' He rang a bell; a clerk appeared, and received his instructions : ' Mr. Paul. Good-morning, doctor.'

Mr. Paul was, personally speaking, his brother repeated—without the deep voice, and without the genial smile. Conducted to the office of the junior partner, Mr. Vimpany found himself in the presence of a stranger, occupied in turning over the pages of a newspaper. When his name was announced, the publisher started, and handed his newspaper to the doctor.

' This is a coincidence,' he said. ' I was looking, sir, for your name in the pages which I have just put into your hand. Surely the editor can't have refused to publish your letter ? '

Mr. Vimpany was sober, and therefore sad, and therefore (again) not to be trifled with by a mystifying reception. ' I don't understand you,' he answered gruffly. ' What do you mean ? '

' Is it possible that you have not seen last week's number of the

paper ? ' Mr. Paul asked. 'And you a literary man !' He forth·
with produced the last week's number, and opened it at the right
place. 'Read that, sir,' he said, with something in his manner
which looked like virtuous indignation.

Mr. Vimpany found himself confronted by a letter addressed to
the editor. It was signed by an eminent physician, whose portrait
had appeared in the first serial part of the new work—accompanied
by a brief memoir of his life, which purported to be written by
himself. Not one line of the autobiography (this celebrated person
declared) had proceeded from his pen. Mr. Vimpany had impudently
published an imaginary memoir, full of false reports and scandalous
inventions—and this after he had been referred to a trustworthy
source for the necessary particulars. Stating these facts, the indig·
nant physician cautioned readers to beware of purchasing a work
which, so far as he was concerned, was nothing less than a fraud
on the public.

'If you can answer that letter, sir,' Mr. Paul Boldside resumed,
' the better it will be, I can tell you, for the sale of your publication.'

Mr. Vimpany made a reckless reply : 'I want to know how the
thing sells. Never mind the letter.'

'Never mind the letter?' the junior partner repeated. 'A
positive charge of fraud is advanced by a man at the head of his
profession against a work which *we* have published—and you say,
Never mind the letter.'

The rough customer of the Boldsides struck his fist on the
table. 'Bother the letter ! I insist on knowing what the sale is.'

Still preserving his dignity, Mr. Paul (like Mr. Peter) rang for
the clerk, and briefly gave an order. ' Mr. Vimpany's account,' he
said—and proceeded to admonish Mr. Vimpany himself.

' You appear, sir, to have no defence of your conduct to offer.
Our firm has a reputation to preserve. When I have consulted
with my brother, we shall be under the disagreeable necessity——'

Here (as he afterwards told his brother) the publisher was
brutally interrupted by the author :

'If you will have it,' said this rude man, 'here it is in two
words. The doctor's portrait is the likeness of an ass. As he
couldn't do it himself, I wanted materials for writing his life. He
referred me to the year of his birth, the year of his marriage, the
year of this, that, and the other. Who cares about dates ? The
public likes to be tickled by personal statements. Very well—I
tickled the public. There you have it in a nutshell.'

The clerk appeared at that auspicious moment, with the author's
account neatly exhibited under two sides : a Debtor side, which
represented the expenditure of Hugh Mountjoy's money ; and a
Creditor side, which represented (so far) Mr. Vimpany's profits.
Amount of these last : 3*l*. 14*s*. 10*d*.

Mr. Vimpany tore up the account, threw the pieces in the face
of Mr. Paul, and expressed his sentiments in one opprobrious word:
' Swindlers ! '

The publisher said: 'You shall hear of us, sir, through our lawyer.'

And the author answered: 'Go to the devil!'

Once out in the streets again, the first open door at which Mr. Vimpany stopped was the door of a tavern. He ordered a glass of brandy and water, and a cigar.

It was then the hour of the afternoon, between the time of luncheon and the time of dinner, when the business of a tavern is generally in a state of suspense. The dining-room was empty when Mr. Vimpany entered it: and the waiter's unoccupied attention was in want of an object. Having nothing else to notice, he looked at the person who had just come in. The deluded stranger was drinking fiery potato-brandy, and smoking (at the foreign price) an English cigar. Would his taste tell him the melancholy truth? No: it seemed to matter nothing to him what he was drinking or what he was smoking. Now he looked angry, and now he looked puzzled; and now he took a long letter from his pocket, and read it in places, and marked the places with a pencil. 'Up to some mischief,' was the waiter's interpretation of these signs. The stranger ordered a second glass of grog, and drank it in gulps, and fell into such deep thought that he let his cigar go out. Evidently, a man in search of an idea. And, to all appearance, he found what he wanted on a sudden. In a hurry he paid his reckoning, and left his small change and his unfinished cigar on the table, and was off before the waiter could say, 'Thank you.'

The next place at which he stopped was a fine house in a spacious square. A carriage was waiting at the door. The servant who opened the door knew him.

'Sir James is going out again, sir, in two minutes,' the man said. Mr. Vimpany answered: 'I won't keep him two minutes.'

A bell rang from the room on the ground floor; and a gentleman came out, as Mr. Vimpany was shown in. Sir James's stethoscope was still in his hand; his latest medical fee lay on the table. 'Some other day, Vimpany,' the great surgeon said; 'I have no time to give you now.'

'Will you give me a minute?' the humble doctor asked.

'Very well. What is it?'

'I am down in the world now, Sir James, as you know—and I am trying to pick myself up again.'

'Very creditable, my good fellow. How can I help you? Come, come—out with it. You want something?'

'I want your great name to do me a great service. I am going to France. A letter of introduction, from you, will open doors which might be closed to an unknown man like myself.'

'What doors do you mean?' Sir James asked.

'The doors of the hospitals in Paris.'

'Wait a minute, Vimpany. Have you any particular object in view?'

'A professional object, of course,' the ready doctor answered. 'I have got an idea for a new treatment of diseases of the lungs; and I want to see if the French have made any recent discoveries in that direction.'

Sir James took up his pen—and hesitated. His ill-starred medical colleague had been his fellow-student and his friend, in the days when they were both young men. They had seen but little of each other since they had gone their different ways—one of them, on the high road which leads to success, the other down the byways which end in failure. The famous surgeon felt a passing doubt of the use which his needy and vagabond inferior might make of his name. For a moment his pen was held suspended over the paper. But the man of great reputation was also a man of great heart. Old associations pleaded with him, and won their cause. His companion of former times left the house provided with a letter of introduction to the chief surgeon at the Hôtel Dieu, in Paris.

Mr. Vimpany's next, and last, proceeding for that day, was to stop at a telegraph-office, and to communicate economically with Lord Harry in three words:

'Expect me to-morrow.'

CHAPTER XXXVII

THE FIRST QUARREL

ARLY in the morning of the next day, Lord Harry received the doctor's telegram. Iris not having risen at the time, he sent for Fanny Mere, and ordered her to get the spare room ready for a guest. The maid's busy suspicion tempted her to put a venturesome question. She asked if the person expected was a lady or a gentleman.

'What business is it of yours who the visitor is?' her master asked sharply. Always easy and good-humoured with his inferiors in general, Lord Harry had taken a dislike to his wife's maid, from the moment when he had first seen her. His Irish feeling for beauty and brightness was especially offended by the unhealthy pallor of the woman's complexion, and the sullen self-suppression of her manner. All that his native ingenuity had been able to do was to make her a means of paying a compliment to his wife. 'Your maid has one merit in my eyes,' he said; 'she is a living proof of the sweetness of your temper.'

Iris joined her husband at the breakfast-table with an appearance of disturbance in her face, seldom seen, during the dull days of her life at Passy. 'I hear of somebody coming to stay with us,' she said. 'Not Mr. Vimpany again, I hope and trust?'

Lord Harry was careful to give his customary morning kiss, before he replied. 'Why shouldn't my faithful old friend come and see me again?' he asked, with his winning smile.

'Pray don't speak of that hateful man,' she answered, 'as your faithful old friend! He is nothing of the kind. What did you tell me when he took leave of us after his last visit, and I owned I was glad that he had gone? You said: "Faith, my dear, I'm as glad as you are."'

Her good-natured husband laughed at this little picture of himself. 'Ah, my darling, how many more times am I to make the same confession to my pretty priest? Try to remember, without more telling, that it's one of my misfortunes to be a man of many tempers. There are times when I get tired to death of Mr. Vimpany; and there are times when the cheery old devil exercises fascinations over me. I declare you're spoiling the eyebrows that I admire by letting them twist themselves into a frown! After the trouble I have taken to clear your mind of prejudice against an un-

fortunate man, it's disheartening to find you o hard on the poor
fellow's faults and so blind to his virtues.'

The time had been when this remonstrance might have influenced his wife's opinion. She passed it over without notice now.

'Does he come here by your invitation?' she asked.

'How else should he come here, my dear?'

She looked at her husband with doubt too plainly visible in her
eyes. 'I wonder what your motive is for sending for him,' she
said.

He was just lifting his teacup to his lips—he put it down again
when he heard those words.

'Are you ill this morning?' he asked.

'No.'

'Have I said anything that has offended you?'

'Certainly not.'

'Then I must tell you this, Iris; I don't approve of what you
have just said. It sounds, to my mind, unpleasantly like suspicion
of me and suspicion of my friend. I see your face confessing it,
my lady, at this moment.'

'You are half right, Harry, and no more. What you see in my
face is suspicion of your friend.'

'Founded on what, if you please?'

'Founded on what I have seen of him, and on what I know of
him. When you tried to alter my opinion of Mr. Vimpany some
time since, I did my best to make my view your view. I deceived
myself, for your sake; I put the best construction on what he said
and did, when he was staying here. It was well meant, but it was
of no use. In a thousand different ways, while he was doing his
best to win my favour, his true self was telling tales of him under
the fair surface. Mr. Vimpany is a bad man. He is the very worst
friend you could have about you at any time—and especially at a
time when your patience is tried by needy circumstances.'

'One word, Iris. The more eloquent you are, the more I
admire you. Only, don't mention my needy circumstances again.'

She passed over the interruption as she had already passed over
the remonstrance, without taking notice of it.

'Dearest, you are always good to me,' she continued gently.
'Am I wrong in thinking that love gives me some little influence
over you still? Women are vain—are they not?—and I am no
better than the rest of them. Flatter your wife's vanity, Harry, by
attaching some importance to her opinion. Is there time enough,
yet, to telegraph to Mr. Vimpany? Quite out of the question, is it?
Well, then, if he must come here, do—pray, pray do consider Me.
Don't let him stay in the house! I'll find a good excuse, and take
a bedroom for him in the neighbourhood. Anywhere else, so long
as he is not here. He turns me cold when I think of him, sleeping
under the same roof with ourselves. Not with *us*! oh, Harry, not
with *us*!'

Her eyes eagerly searched her husband's face; she looked there for indulgence, she looked for conviction. No! he was still admiring her.

'On my word of honour,' he burst out, ' you fascinate me. What an imagination you have got! One of these days, Iris, I shall be prouder of you than ever ; I shall find you a famous literary character. I don't mean writing a novel ; women who can't even hem a handkerchief can write a novel. It's poetry I'm thinking of. Irish melodies by Lady Harry that beat Tom Moore. What a gift! And there are fortunes made, as I have heard, by people who spoil fair white paper to some purpose. I wish I was one of them.'

'Have you no more to say to me?' she asked.

'What more should there be? You wouldn't have me take you seriously, in what you have just said of Vimpany?'

'Why not?'

'Oh, come, come, my darling! Just consider. With a bedroom empty and waiting, upstairs, is my old Vimpany to be sent to quarters for the night among strangers? I wouldn't speak harshly to you, Iris, for the whole world ; and I don't deny that the convivial doctor may be sometimes a little too fond of his drop of grog. You will tell me, maybe, that he hasn't got on nicely with his wife; and I grant it. There are not many people who set such a pretty example of matrimony as we do. Poor humanity—there's all that's to be said about it. But when you tell me that Vimpany is a bad man, and the worst friend I could possibly have, and so forth—what better can I do than set it down to your imagination? I've a pretty fancy, myself ; and I think I see my angel inventing poetical characters, up among congenial clouds. What's the matter? Surely, you haven't done breakfast yet?'

'Yes.'

'Are you going to leave me?'

'I am going to my room.'

'You're in a mighty hurry to get away. I never meant to vex you, Iris. Ah, well, if you must leave the table, I'll have the honour of opening the door for you, at any rate. I wonder what you're going to do?'

'To cultivate my imagination,' she answered, with the first outbreak of bitterness that had escaped her yet.

His face hardened. 'There seems to be something like bearing malice in this,' he said. 'Are you treating me, for the first time, to an exhibition of enmity? What am I to call it, if it's not that?'

'Call it disappointment,' she suggested quietly, and left him.

Lord Harry went back to his breakfast. His jealousy was up in arms again. 'She's comparing me with her absent friend,' he said to himself, 'and wishing she had married the amiable Mountjoy instead of me.'

So the first quarrel ended—and Mr. Vimpany had been the cause of it.

CHAPTER XXXVIII

ICI ON PARLE FRANÇAIS

THE doctor arrived in good time for dinner, and shook hands with the Irish lord in excellent spirits.

He looked round the room, and asked where my lady was. Lord Harry's reply suggested the presence of a cloud on the domestic horizon. He had been taking a long ride, and had only returned a few minutes since; Iris would (as he supposed) join them immediately.

The maid put the soup on the table, and delivered a message. Her mistress was suffering from a headache, and was not well enough to dine with the gentlemen.

As an old married man, Mr. Vimpany knew what this meant; he begged leave to send a comforting message to the suffering lady of the house. Would Fanny be good enough to say that he had made inquiries on the subject of Mr. Mountjoy's health, before he left London. The report was still favourable; there was nothing to complain of but the after-weakness which had followed the fever. On that account only, the attendance of the nurse was still a matter of necessity. 'With my respects to Lady Harry,' he called after Fanny, as she went out in dogged silence.

'I have begun by making myself agreeable to your wife,' the doctor remarked with a self-approving grin. 'Perhaps she will dine with us to-morrow. Pass the sherry.'

The remembrance of what had happened at the breakfast-table, that morning, seemed to be dwelling disagreeably on Lord Harry's mind. He said but little—and that little related to the subject on which he had already written, at full length, to his medical friend.

In an interval, when the service of the table required the attendance of Fanny in the kitchen, Mr. Vimpany took the opportunity of saying a few cheering words. He had come (he remarked) prepared with the right sort of remedy for an ailing state of mind, and he would explain himself at a fitter opportunity. Lord Harry impatiently asked why the explanation was deferred. If the presence of the maid was the obstacle which caused delay, it would be easy to tell her that she was not wanted to wait.

The wary doctor positively forbade this.

He had observed Fanny, during his previous visit, and had discovered that she seemed to distrust him. The woman was sly and suspicious. Since they had sat down to dinner, it was easy to see that she was lingering in the room to listen to the conversation, on one pretence or another. If she was told not to wait, there could be no doubt of her next proceeding: she would listen outside the door. 'Take my word for it,' the doctor concluded, 'there are all the materials for a spy in Fanny Mere.'

But Lord Harry was obstinate. Chafing under the sense of his helpless pecuniary position, he was determined to hear, at once, what remedy for it Vimpany had discovered.

'We can set that woman's curiosity at defiance,' he said.

'How?'

'When you were learning your profession, you lived in Paris for some years, didn't you?'

'All right!'

'Well, then, you can't have entirely forgotten your French?'

The doctor at once understood what this meant, and answered significantly by a wink. He had found an opportunity (he said) of testing his memory, not very long since. Time had undoubtedly deprived him of his early mastery over the French language; but he could still (allowing for a few mistakes) make a shift to understand it and speak it. There was one thing, however, that he wanted to know first. Could they be sure that my lady's maid had not picked up French enough to use her ears to some purpose? Lord Harry easily disposed of this doubt. So entirely ignorant was the maid of the language of the place in which she was living, that she was not able to ask the tradespeople for the simplest article of household use, unless it was written for her in French before she was sent on an errand.

This was conclusive. When Fanny returned to the dining-room, she found a surprise waiting for her. The two gentlemen had taken leave of their nationality, and were talking the language of foreigners.

An hour later, when the dinner-table had been cleared, the maid's domestic duties took her to Lady Harry's room to make tea. She noticed the sad careworn look on her mistress's face, and spoke of it at once in her own downright way.

'I thought it was only an excuse,' she said, 'when you gave me that message to the gentlemen, at dinner-time. Are you really ill, my lady?'

'I am a little out of spirits,' Iris replied.

Fanny made the tea. 'I can understand that,' she said to herself, as she moved away to leave the room; 'I'm out of spirits myself.'

Iris called her back: 'I heard you say just now, Fanny, that you were out of spirits yourself. If you were speaking of some troubles of your own, I am sorry for you, and I won't say any more. But if you know what my anxieties are, and share them——'

'Mine is the biggest share of the two,' Fanny broke out abruptly.

'It goes against the grain with me to distress you, my lady; but we are beginning badly, and you ought to know it. The doctor has beaten me already.'

'Beaten you already?' Iris repeated. 'Tell me plainly what you mean?'

'Here it is, if you please, as plainly as words can say it. Mr. Vimpany has something—something wicked, of course—to say to my master; and he won't let it pass his lips here, in the cottage.'

'Why not?'

'Because he suspects me of listening at the door, and looking through the keyhole. I don't know, my lady, that he doesn't even suspect You. "I've learnt something in the course of my life," he says to my master; "and it's a rule with me to be careful of what I talk about indoors, when there are women in the house. What are you going to do to-morrow?" he says. My lord told him there was to be a meeting at the newspaper office. The doctor says: "I'll go to Paris with you. The newspaper office isn't far from the Luxembourg Gardens. When you have done your business, you will find me waiting at the gate. What I have to tell you, you shall hear out of doors in the Gardens—and in an open part of them, too, where there are no lurking-places among the trees." My master seemed to get angry at being put off in this way. "What *is* it you have got to tell me?" he says. "Is it anything like the proposal you made, when you were on your last visit here?" The doctor laughed. "To-morrow won't be long in coming," he says. "Patience, my lord—patience." There was no getting him to say a word more. Now, what am I to do? How am I to get a chance of listening to him, out in an open garden, without being seen? There's what I mean when I say he has beaten me. It's you, my lady—it's you who will suffer in the end.'

'You don't *know* that, Fanny.'

'No, my lady—but I'm certain of it. And here I am, as help-less as yourself! My temper has been quiet, since my misfortune; it would be quiet still, but for this.' The one animating motive, the one exasperating influence, in that sad and secret life was still the mistress's welfare—still the safety of the generous woman who had befriended and forgiven her. She turned aside from the table, to hide her ghastly face.

'Pray try to control yourself.' As Iris spoke, she pointed kindly to a chair. 'There is something that I want to say when you are composed again. I won't hurry you; I won't look at you. Sit down, Fanny.'

She appeared to shrink from being seated in her mistress's presence. 'Please to let me go to the window,' she said; 'the air will help me.'

To the window she went, and struggled with the passionate self so steadily kept under at other times; so obstinately conquered now. 'What did you wish to say to me?' she asked.

'You have surprised—you have perplexed me,' Iris said. 'I

am at a loss to understand how you discovered what seems to have passed between your master and Mr. Vimpany. You don't surely mean to tell me that they talked of their private affairs while you were waiting at table ? '

' I don't tell lies, my lady,' Fanny declared impulsively. ' They talked of nothing else all through the dinner.'

' Before *you* ! ' Iris exclaimed.

There was a pause. Fear and shame confessed themselves furtively on the maid's colourless face. Silently, swiftly, she turned to the door. Had a slip of the tongue hurried her into the betrayal of something which it was her interest to conceal ? ' Don't be alarmed,' Iris said compassionately ; ' I have no wish to intrude on your secrets.'

With her hand on the door, Fanny Mere closed it again, and came back.

' I am not so ungrateful,' she said, ' as to have any secrets from You. It's hard to confess what may lower me in your good opinion, but it must be done. I have deceived your ladyship—and I am ashamed of it. I have deceived the doctor—and I glory in it. My master and Mr. Vimpany thought they were safe in speaking French, while I was waiting on them. I know French as well as they do.'

Iris could hardly believe what she heard. ' Do you really mean what you say ? ' she asked.

' There's that much good in me,' Fanny replied; ' I always mean what I say.'

' Why did you deceive me ? Why have you been acting the part of an ignorant woman ? '

' The deceit has been useful in your service,' the obstinate maid declared. ' Perhaps it may be useful again.'

' Was that what you were thinking of,' Iris said, ' when you allowed me to translate English into French for you, and never told me the truth ? '

' At any rate, I will tell you the truth, now. No : I was not thinking of you, when you wrote my errands for me in French—I was thinking again of some advice that was once given to me.'

' Was it advice given by a friend ? '

' Given by a man, my lady, who was the worst enemy I have ever had.'

Her considerate mistress understood the allusion, and forbade her to distress herself by saying more. But Fanny felt that atone-ment, as well as explanation, was due to her benefactress. Slowly, painfully she described the person to whom she had referred. He was a Frenchman, who had been her music-master during the brief period at which she had attended a school : he had promised her marriage ; he had persuaded her to elope with him. The little money that they had to live on was earned by her needle, and by his wages as accompanist at a music-hall. While she was still able to attract him, and to hope for the performance of his promise, he amused himself by teaching her his own language. When he deserted her, his letter of farewell contained, among other things the advice to which she had alluded.

'In your station of life,' this man had written, ' knowledge of French is still a rare accomplishment. Keep your knowledge to yourself. English people of rank have a way of talking French to each other, when they don't wish to be understood by their inferiors. In the course of your career, you may surprise secrets which will prove to be a little fortune, if you play your cards properly. Any-how, it is the only fortune I have to leave to you.' Such had been the villain's parting gift to the woman whom he had betrayed.

She had hated him too bitterly to be depraved by his advice.

On the contrary, when the kindness of a friend (now no longer in England) had helped her to obtain her first employment as a domestic servant, she had thought it might be to her interest to mention that she could read, write, and speak French. The result proved to be not only a disappointment, but a warning to her for the future. Such an accomplishment as a knowledge of a foreign language possessed by an Englishwoman, in her humble rank of life, was considered by her mistress to justify suspicion. Questions were asked, which it was impossible for her to answer truthfully. Small scandal drew its own conclusions—her life with the other servants became unendurable—she left her situation.

From that time, until the happy day when she met with Iris, concealment of her knowledge of French became a proceeding forced on her by her own poor interests. Her present mistress would undoubtedly have been taken into her confidence, if the opportunity had offered itself. But Iris had never encouraged her to speak of the one darkest scene in her life; and for that reason, she had kept her own counsel until the date of her mistress's marriage. Distrusting the husband, and the husband's confidential friend—for were they not both men?—she had thought of the vile Frenchman's advice, and had resolved to give it a trial; not with the degrading motive which he had suggested, but with the vague presentiment of making a discovery of wickedness, threatening mischief under a French disguise, which might be of service to her benefactress at some future time.

'And I may still turn it to your advantage, my lady,' Fanny ventured to add, ' if you will consent to say nothing to anybody of your having a servant who has learnt French.'

Iris looked at her coldly and gravely. ' Must I remind you,' she said, ' that you are asking my help in practising a deception on my husband ? '

' I shall be sent away,' Fanny answered, ' if you tell my master what I have told you.'

This was indisputably true. Iris hesitated. In her present situation, the maid was the one friend on whom she could rely. Before her marriage, she would have recoiled from availing herself, under any circumstances, of such services as Fanny's reckless gratitude had offered to her. But the moral atmosphere in which she was living had begun, as Mrs. Vimpany had foreseen, to exert its baneful influence. The mistress descended to bargaining with the servant.

'Deceive the doctor,' she said, 'and I well remember that it may be for my good.' She stopped, and considered for a moment. Her noble nature rallied its forces, and prompted her next words: 'But respect your master, if you wish me to keep your secret. I forbid you to listen to what my lord may say, when he speaks with Mr. Vimpany to-morrow.'

'I have already told your ladyship that I shall have no chance of listening to what they say to each other, out of doors,' Fanny rejoined. 'But I can watch the doctor at any rate. We don't know what he may not do when he is left by himself, while my master is at the meeting. I want to try if I can follow that rogue through the streets, without his finding me out. Please to send me on an errand to Paris to-morrow.'

'You will be running a terrible risk,' her mistress reminded her, 'if Mr. Vimpany discovers you.'

'I'll take my chance of that,' was the reckless reply.

Iris consented.

CHAPTER XXXIX

THE MYSTERY OF THE HOSPITAL

ON the next morning Lord Harry left the cottage, accompanied by the doctor.

After a long absence, he returned alone. His wife's worst apprehensions, roused by what Fanny had told her, were more than justified, by the change which she now perceived in him. His eyes were bloodshot, his face was haggard, his movements were feeble and slow. He looked like a man exhausted by some internal conflict, which had vibrated between the extremes of anger and alarm. 'I'm tired to death,' he said; 'get me a glass of wine.'

She waited on him with eager obedience, and watched anxiously for the reviving effect of the stimulant.

The little irritabilities which degrade humanity only prolong their mischievous existence, while the surface of life stagnates in calm. Their annihilation follows when strong emotion stirs in the depths, and raises the storm. The estrangement of the day before passed as completely from the minds of the husband and wife—both strongly agitated—as if it had never existed. All-mastering fear was busy at their hearts; fear, in the woman, of the unknown temptation which had tried the man; fear, in the man, of the tell-tale disturbance in him, which might excite the woman's suspicion. Without venturing to look at him, Iris said : ' I am afraid you have heard bad news ? ' Without venturing to look at her, Lord Harry answered : ' Yes, at the newspaper office.' She knew that he was deceiving her ; and he felt that she knew it. For awhile, they were both silent.

From time to time, she anxiously stole a look at him.

His mind remained absorbed in thought. There they were, in the same room—seated near each other ; united by the most intimate of human relationships—and yet how far, how cruelly far, apart ! The slowest of all laggard minutes, the minutes which are reckoned by suspense, followed each other tardily and more tardily, before there appeared the first sign of a change. He lifted his drooping head. Sadly, longingly, he looked at her. The unerring instinct of true love encouraged his wife to speak to him.

' I wish I could relieve your anxieties,' she said simply. ' Is there nothing I can do to help you ? '

' Come here, Iris.'

She rose and approached him. In the past days of the honeymoon and its sweet familiarities, he had sometimes taken her on his knee. He took her on his knee now, and put his arm round her. ' Kiss me,' he said.

With all her heart she kissed him. He sighed heavily ; his eyes rested on her with a trustful appealing look which she had never observed in them before.

' Why do you hesitate to confide in me ? ' she asked. ' Dear Harry, do you think I don't see that something troubles you ? '

' Yes,' he said, ' there is something that I regret.'

' What is it ? '

' Iris,' he answered, ' I am sorry I asked Vimpany to come back to us.'

At that unexpected confession, a bright flush of joy and pride overspread his wife's face. Again, the unerring instinct of love guided her to discovery of the truth. The opinion of his wicked friend must have been accidentally justified, at the secret interview of that day, by the friend himself ! In tempting her husband, Vimpany had said something which must have shocked and offended him. The result, as she could hardly doubt, had been the restoration of her domestic influence to its helpful freedom of control—whether for the time only it was not in her nature, at that moment of happiness, to inquire. ' After what you have just told me,' she ventured to say, ' I may own that I am glad to see you come home, alone.'

In that indirect manner, she confessed the hope that friendly intercourse between the two men had come to an end. His reply disappointed her.

' Vimpany only remains in Paris,' he said, ' to present a letter of introduction. He will follow me home.'

' Soon ? ' she asked, piteously.

' In time for dinner, I suppose.' She was still sitting on his

knee. His arm pressed her gently when he said his next words.
'I hope you will dine with us to-day, Iris?'

'Yes—if you wish it.'

'I wish it very much. Something in me recoils from being
alone with Vimpany. Besides, a dinner at home without you is no
dinner at all.'

She thanked him for that little compliment by a look. At the
same time, her grateful sense of her husband's kindness was
embittered by the prospect of the doctor's return. 'Is he likely to
dine with us often, now?' she was bold enough to say.

'I hope not.'

Perhaps he was conscious that he might have made a more
positive reply. He certainly took refuge in another subject—more
agreeable to himself.

'My dear, you have expressed the wish to relieve my anxieties,'
he said; 'and you can help me, I think, in that way. I have a
letter to write—of some importance, Iris, to your interests as well
as to mine—which must go to Ireland by to-day's post. You shall
read it, and say if you approve of what I have done. Don't let me
be disturbed. This letter, I can tell you, will make a hard demand
on my poor brains—I must go and write in my own room.'

Left alone with the thoughts that now crowded on her mind, Iris
found her attention claimed once more by passing events. Fanny
Mere arrived, to report herself on her return from Paris.

She had so managed her departure from Passy as to precede
Lord Harry and Mr. Vimpany, and to watch for their arrival in
Paris by a later train. They had driven from the railway to
the newspaper office—with the maid in attendance on them in
another cab. When they separated, the doctor proceeded on foot
to the Luxembourg Gardens. Wearing a plain black dress, and
protected from close observation by her veil, Fanny followed him,
cautiously keeping at a sufficient distance, now on one side of the
street and now on the other. When my lord joined his friend, she
just held them in view, and no more, as they walked up and down
in the barest and loneliest part of the Gardens that they could find.
Their talk having come to an end, they parted. Her master was
the first who came out into the street; walking at a great rate, and
looking most desperately upset. Mr. Vimpany next appeared,
sauntering along with his hands in his pockets, grinning as if his
own villainous thoughts were thoroughly amusing him. Fanny was
now more careful than ever not to lose sight of the doctor. The
course which he pursued led them to the famous hospital called
the Hôtel Dieu.

At the entrance she saw him take a letter out of his pocket, and
give it to the porter. Soon afterwards, a person appeared who
greeted him politely, and conducted him into the building. For
more than an hour, Fanny waited to see Mr. Vimpany come out
again, and waited in vain. What could he possibly want in a French
hospital? And why had he remained in that foreign institution

for so long a time? Baffled by these mysteries, and weary after much walking, Fanny made the best of her way home, and consulted her mistress.

Even if Iris had been capable of enlightening her, the opportunity was wanting. Lord Harry entered the room, with the letter which he had just written, open in his hand. As a matter of course, the maid retired.

CHAPTER XL

THE Irish lord had a word to say to his wife, before he submitted to her the letter which he had just written.

He had been summoned to a meeting of proprietors at the office of the newspaper, convened to settle the terms of a new subscription rendered necessary by unforeseen expenses incurred in the interests of the speculation. The vote that followed, after careful preliminary consultation, authorised a claim on the purses of subscribing proprietors, which sadly reduced the sum obtained by Lord Harry's promissory note. Nor was this inconvenience the only trial of endurance to which the Irish lord was compelled to submit. The hope which he had entertained of assistance from the profits of the new journal, when repayment of the loan that he had raised became due, was now plainly revealed as a delusion. Ruin stared him in the face, unless he could command the means of waiting for the pecuniary success of the newspaper, during an interval variously estimated at six months, or even at a year to come.

'Our case is desperate enough,' he said, 'to call for a desperate remedy. Keep up your spirits, Iris—I have written to my brother.'

Iris looked at him in dismay.

'Surely,' she said, 'you once told me you had written to your brother, and he answered you in the cruellest manner through his lawyers.'

'Quite true, my dear. But, this time, there is one circumstance in our favour—my brother is going to be married. The lady is said to be an heiress; a charming creature, admired and beloved wherever she goes. There must surely be something to soften the hardest heart in that happy prospect. Read what I have written, and tell me what you think of it.'

The opinion of the devoted wife encouraged the desperate husband: the letter was dispatched by the post of that day.

If boisterous good spirits can make a man agreeable at the dinner-table, then indeed Mr. Vimpany, on his return to the cottage, played the part of a welcome guest. He was inexhaustible in gallant attentions to his friend's wife; he told his most amusing stories in his happiest way; he gaily drank his host's fine white Burgundy, and praised with thorough knowledge of the sub-

ject the succulent French dishes; he tried Lord Harry with talk
on politics, talk on sport, and (wonderful to relate in these days)
talk on literature. The preoccupied Irishman was equally inac-
cessible on all three subjects. When the dessert was placed on the
table—still bent on making himself agreeable to Lady Harry—Mr.
Vimpany led the conversation to the subject of floriculture. In the
interests of her ladyship's pretty little garden, he advocated a complete change in the system of cultivation, and justified his revolu-
tionary views by misquoting the published work of a great authority
on gardening with such polite obstinacy that Iris (eager to confute
him) went away to fetch the book. The moment he had entrapped
her into leaving the room, the doctor turned to Lord Harry with a
sudden change to the imperative mood in look and manner.

'What have you been about,' he asked, 'since we had that talk
in the Gardens to-day? Have you looked at your empty purse,
and are you wise enough to take my way of filling it?'

'As long as there's the ghost of a chance left to me,' Lord
Harry replied, 'I'll take any way of filling my purse but yours.'

'Does that mean you have found a way?'

'Do me a favour, Vimpany. Defer all questions till the end of
the week.'

'And then I shall have your answer?'

'Without fail, I promise it. Hush!'

Iris returned to the dining-room with her book; and polite
Mr. Vimpany owned in the readiest manner that he had been mi-
taken.

The remaining days of the week followed each other wearily.
During the interval, Lord Harry's friend carefully preserved the
character of a model guest—he gave as little trouble as possible.
Every morning after breakfast the doctor went away by the train.
Every morning (with similar regularity) he was followed by the
resolute Fanny Mere. Pursuing his way through widely different
quarters of Paris, he invariably stopped at a public building, invariably presented a letter at the door, and was invariably asked to
walk in. Inquiries, patiently persisted in by the English maid,
led in each case to the same result. The different public buildings
were devoted to the same benevolent purpose. Like the Hôtel
Dieu, they were all hospitals; and Mr. Vimpany's object in visiting them remained as profound a mystery as ever.

Early on the last morning of the week the answer from Lord
Harry's brother arrived. Hearing of it, Iris ran eagerly into her
husband's room. The letter was already scattered in fragments on
the floor. What the tone of the Earl's inhuman answer had been
in the past time, that it was again now.

Iris put her arms round her husband's neck. 'Oh, my poor
love, what is to be done?'

He answered in one reckless word: 'Nothing!'

'Is there nobody else who can help us?' she asked.

'Ah, well, darling, there's perhaps one other person still left.'

'Who is the person?'

'Who should it be but your own dear self?'

She looked at him in undisguised bewilderment: 'Only tell me, Harry, what I can do?'

'Write to Mountjoy, and ask him to lend me the money.'

He said it. In those shameless words, he said it. She, who had sacrificed Mountjoy to the man whom she had married, was now asked by that man to use Mountjoy's devotion to her, as a means of paying his debts! Iris drew back from him with a cry of disgust.

'You refuse?' he said.

'Do you insult me by doubting it?' she answered.

He rang the bell furiously, and dashed out of the room. She heard him, on the stairs, ask where Mr. Vimpany was. The servant replied: 'In the garden, my lord.'

Smoking a cigar luxuriously in the fine morning air, the doctor saw his excitable Irish friend hastening out to meet him.

'Don't hurry,' he said, in full possession of his impudent good-humour; 'and don't lose your temper. Will you take my way out of your difficulties, or will you not? Which is it—Yes or No?'

'You infernal scoundrel—Yes!'

'My dear lord, I congratulate you.'

'On what, sir?'

'On being as great a scoundrel as I am.'

CHAPTER XLI

THE MAN IS FOUND.

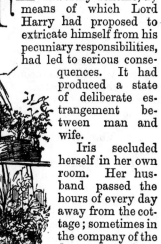

THE unworthy scheme, by means of which Lord Harry had proposed to extricate himself from his pecuniary responsibilities, had led to serious consequences. It had produced a state of deliberate estrangement between man and wife.

Iris secluded herself in her own room. Her husband passed the hours of every day away from the cottage; sometimes in the company of the doctor, sometimes among his friends in Paris. His wife suffered acutely under the self-imposed state of separation, to which wounded pride and keenly felt resentment compelled her to submit. No friend was near her, in whose compassionate advice she might have taken refuge. Not even the sympathy of her maid was offered to the lonely wife.

With the welfare of Iris as her one end in view, Fanny Mere

honestly believed that it would be better and safer for Lady Harry if she and her husband finally decided on living separate lives. The longer my lord persisted in keeping the doctor with him as his guest, the more perilously he was associated with a merciless wretch, who would be capable of plotting the ruin of anyone—man or woman, high person or low person—who might happen to be an obstacle in his way. So far as a person in her situation could venture on taking the liberty, the maid did her best to widen the breach between her master and her mistress.

While Fanny was making the attempt to influence Lady Harry, and only producing irritation as the result, Vimpany was exerting stronger powers of persuasion in the effort to prejudice the Irish lord against any proposal for reconciliation which might reach him through his wife.

'I find an unforgiving temper in your charming lady,' the doctor declared. 'It doesn't show itself on the surface, my dear fellow, but there it is. Take a wise advantage of circumstances—say you will raise no inconvenient objections, if she wants a separation by mutual consent. Now don't misunderstand me. I only recommend the sort of separation which will suit our convenience. You know as well as I do that you can whistle your wife back again——'

Mr. Vimpany's friend was rude enough to interrupt him, there.

'I call that a coarse way of putting it,' Lord Harry interposed.

'Put it how you like for yourself,' the doctor rejoined. 'Lady Harry may be persuaded to come back to you, when we want her for our grand project. In the meantime (for I am always a considerate man where women are concerned) we act delicately towards my lady, in sparing her the discovery of—what shall I call our coming enterprise?—venturesome villainy, which might ruin you in your wife's estimation. Do you see our situation now, as it really is? Very well. Pass the bottle, and drop the subject for the present.'

The next morning brought with it an event, which demolished the doctor's ingenious arrangement for the dismissal of Iris from the scene of action. Lord and Lady Harry encountered each other accidentally on the stairs.

Distrusting herself if she ventured to look at him, Iris turned her eyes away from her husband. He misinterpreted the action as an expression of contempt. Anger at once inclined him to follow Mr. Vimpany's advice.

He opened the door of the dining-room, empty at that moment, and told Iris that he wished to speak with her. What his villainous friend had suggested that he should say, on the subject of a separation, he now repeated with a repellent firmness which he was far from really feeling. The acting was bad, but the effect was produced. For the first time, his wife spoke to him.

'Do you really mean it?' she asked.

The tone in which she said those words, sadly and regretfully telling its tale of uncontrollable surprise; the tender remembrance of past happy days in her eyes; the quivering pain, expressive of wounded love, that parted her lips in the effort to breathe freely, touched his heart, try as he might in the wretched pride of the moment to conceal it. He was silent.

'If you are weary of our married life,' she continued, ' say so, and let us part. I will go away, without entreaties and without reproaches. Whatever pain I may feel, *you* shall not see it!' A passing flush crossed her face, and left it pale again. She trembled under the consciousness of returning love—the blind love that had so cruelly misled her! At a moment when she most needed firmness, her heart was sinking; she resisted, struggled, recovered herself. Quietly, and even firmly, she claimed his decision. 'Does your silence mean,' she asked, 'that you wish me to leave you?'

No man who had loved her as tenderly as her husband had loved her, could have resisted that touching self-control. He answered his wife without uttering a word—he held out his arms to her. The fatal reconciliation was accomplished in silence.

At dinner on that day Mr. Vimpany's bold eyes saw a new sight, and Mr. Vimpany's rascally lips indulged in an impudent smile. My lady appeared again in her place at the dinner-table. At the customary time, the two men were left alone over their wine. The reckless Irish lord, rejoicing in the recovery of his wife's tender regard, drank freely. Understanding and despising him, the doctor's devilish gaiety indulged in facetious reminiscences of his own married life.

'If I could claim a sovereign,' he said, 'for every quarrel between Mrs. Vimpany and myself, I put it at a low average when I declare that I should be worth a thousand pounds. How does your lordship stand in that matter? Shall we say a dozen breaches of the marriage agreement up to the present time?'

'Say two—and no more to come!' his friend answered cheerfully.

'No more to come!' the doctor repeated. ' My experience says plenty more to come; I never saw two people less likely to submit to a peaceable married life than you and my lady. Ha! you laugh at that? It's a habit of mine to back my opinion. I'll bet you a dozen of champagne there will be a quarrel which parts you two, for good and all, before the year is out. Do you take the bet?'

'Done!' cried Lord Harry. ' I propose my wife's good health, Vimpany, in a bumper. She shall drink confusion to all false prophets in the first glass of your champagne!'

The post of the next morning brought with it two letters.

One of them bore the postmark of London, and was addressed to Lady Harry Norland. It was written by Mrs. Vimpany, and it contained a few lines added by Hugh Mountjoy. ' My strength is slow in returning to me' (he wrote); 'but my kind and devoted nurse says that all danger of infection is at an end. You may write again to your old friend if Lord Harry sees no objection, as harmlessly as in the happy past time. My weak hand begins to tremble already. How glad I shall be to hear from you, it is, happily for me, quite needless to add.'

In her delight at receiving this good news Iris impulsively assumed that her husband would give it a kindly welcome on his side; she insisted on reading the letter to him. He said coldly, 'I am glad to hear of Mr. Mountjoy's recovery'—and took up the newspaper. Was this unworthy jealousy still strong enough to master him, even at that moment? His wife had forgotten it. Why had he not forgotten it too?

On the same day Iris replied to Hugh, with the confidence and affection of the bygone time before her marriage. After closing and addressing the envelope, she found that her small store of postage stamps was exhausted, and sent for her maid. Mr. Vimpany happened to pass the open door of her room, while she was asking for a stamp; he heard Fanny say that she was not able to accommodate her mistress. 'Allow me to make myself useful,' the polite doctor suggested. He produced a stamp, and fixed it himself on the envelope. When he had proceeded on his way downstairs, Fanny's distrust of him insisted on expressing itself. 'He wanted to find out what person you have written to,' she said. 'Let me make your letter safe in the post.' In five minutes more it was in the box at the office.

While these trifling events were in course of progress, Mr. Vimpany had gone into the garden to read the second of the two letters, delivered that morning, addressed to himself. On her return from the post-office, Fanny had opportunities of observing him while she was in the greenhouse, trying to revive the perishing flowers—neglected in the past days of domestic trouble.

Noticing her, after he had read his letter over for the second time, Mr. Vimpany sent the maid into the cottage to say that he wished to speak with her master. Lord Harry joined him in the garden—looked at the letter—and, handing it back, turned away. The doctor followed him, and said something which seemed to be received with objection. Mr. Vimpany persisted nevertheless, and apparently carried his point. The two gentlemen consulted the railway time-table, and hurried away together, to catch the train to Paris.

Fanny Mere returned to the conservatory, and absently resumed her employment among the flowers. On what evil errand had the doctor left the cottage? And, why, on this occasion, had he taken the master with him?

The time had been when Fanny might have tried to set these questions at rest by boldly following the two gentlemen to Paris; trusting to her veil, to her luck, and to the choice of a separate carriage in the train, to escape notice. But, although her ill-judged interference with the domestic affairs of Lady Harry had been forgiven, she had not been received again into favour unreservedly. Conditions were imposed, which forbade her to express any opinion on her master's conduct, and which imperatively ordered her to leave the protection of her mistress—if protection was really needed—in his lordship's competent hands. ' I gratefully appreciate your kind intentions,' Iris had said, with her customary tenderness of regard for the feelings of others; ' but I never wish to hear again of Mr. Vimpany, or of the strange suspicions which he seems to excite in your mind.' Still as gratefully devoted to Iris as ever, Fanny viewed the change in my lady's way of thinking as one of the deplorable results of her return to her husband, and waited resignedly for the coming time when her wise distrust of two unscrupulous men would be justified.

Condemned to inaction for the present, Lady Harry's maid walked irritably up and down the conservatory, forgetting the flowers. Through the open back door of the cottage the cheap clock in the hall poured its harsh little volume of sound, striking the hour. ' I wonder,' she said to herself, ' if those two wicked ones have found their way to a hospital yet ? ' That guess happened to have hit the mark. The two wicked ones were really approaching a hospital, well known to the doctor by more previous visits than one. At the door they were met by a French physician, attached to the institution—the writer of the letter which had reached Mr. Vimpany in the morning.

This gentleman led the way to the official department of the hospital, and introduced the two foreigners to the French authorities assembled for the transaction of business.

As a medical man, Mr. Vimpany's claims to general respect and confidence were carefully presented. He was a member of the English College of Surgeons; he was the friend, as well as the colleague of the famous President of that College, who had introduced him to the chief surgeon of the Hôtel Dieu. Other introductions to illustrious medical persons in Paris had naturally followed. Presented under these advantages, Mr. Vimpany announced his discovery of a new system of treatment in diseases of the lungs. Having received his medical education in Paris, he felt bound in gratitude to place himself under the protection of ' the princes of science,' resident in the brilliant capital of France. In that hospital, after much fruitless investigation in similar institutions, he had found a patient suffering from the form of lung disease, which offered to him the opportunity that he wanted. It was impossible that he could do justice to his new system, unless the circumstances were especially favourable. Air more pure than the air of a great city, and bed-room accommodation not shared by other sick persons, were among the conditions absolutely necessary to the success of the experiment. These, and other advantages, were freely offered to him by his noble friend, who would enter into any explanations which the authorities then present might think it necessary to demand.

The explanations having been offered and approved, there was a general move to the bed occupied by the invalid who was an object of professional interest to the English doctor.

The patient's name was Oxbye. He was a native of Denmark, and had followed in his own country the vocation of a schoolmaster. His knowledge of the English language and the French had offered him the opportunity of migrating to Paris, where he had obtained employment as translator and copyist. Earning his bread, poorly enough in this way, he had been prostrated by the malady which had obliged him to take refuge in the hospital. The French physician, under whose medical care he had been placed, having announced that he had communicated his notes enclosed in a letter to his English colleague, and having frankly acknowledged that the result of the treatment had not as yet sufficiently justified expectation, the officers of the institution spoke next. The Dane was informed of the nature of Mr. Vimpany's interest in him, and of the hospitable assistance offered by Mr. Vimpany's benevolent friend; and the question was then put, whether he preferred to remain where he was, or whether he desired to be removed under the conditions which had just been stated?

Tempted by the prospect of a change, which offered to him a bed-chamber of his own in the house of a person of distinction—with a garden to walk about in, and flowers to gladden his eyes, when he got better—Oxbye eagerly adopted the alternative of leaving the hospital. 'Pray let me go,' the poor fellow said: 'I am sure I shall be the better for it.' Without opposing this decision, the responsible directors reminded him that it had been adopted on impulse, and decided that it was their duty to give him a little time for consideration.

In the meanwhile, some of the gentlemen assembled at the bed-side, looking at Oxbye and then looking at Lord Harry, had observed a certain accidental likeness between the patient and ' Milord, the philanthropist,' who was willing to receive him. The restraints of politeness had only permitted them to speak of this curious discovery among themselves. At the later time, however, when the gentlemen had taken leave of each other, Mr. Vimpany—finding himself alone with Lord Harry—had no hesitation in introducing the subject, on which delicacy had prevented the Frenchmen from entering.

'Did you look at the Dane?' he began abruptly.

'Of course I did!'

'And you noticed the likeness?'

'Not I!'

The doctor's uproarious laughter startled the people who were walking near them in the street. 'Here's another proof,' he burst out, ' of the true saying that no man knows himself. You don't deny the likeness, I suppose?'

'Do you yourself see it?' Lord Harry asked.

Mr. Vimpany answered the question scornfully: 'Is it likely that I should have submitted to all the trouble I have taken to get possession of that man, if I had not seen a likeness between his face and yours?'

The Irish lord said no more. When his friend asked why he was silent, he gave his reason sharply enough: 'I don't like the subject.'

CHAPTER XLII

THE METTLESOME MAID

N the evening of that day Fanny Mere, entering the dining-room with the coffee, found Lord Harry and Mr. Vimpany alone, and discovered (as soon as she opened the door) that they changed the language in which they were talking from English to French.

She continued to linger in the room, apparently occupied in setting the various objects on the sideboard in order. Her master was speaking at the time; he asked if the doctor had succeeded in finding a bed-room for himself in the neighbourhood. To this Mr. Vimpany replied that he had got the bed-room. Also, that he had provided himself with something else, which it was equally important to have at his disposal. 'I mean,' he proceeded, in his bad French, 'that I have found a photographic apparatus on hire. We are ready now for the appearance of our interesting Danish guest.'

'And when the man comes,' Lord Harry added, 'what am I to say to my wife ? How am I to find an excuse, when she hears of a hospital patient who has taken possession of your bed-room at the cottage—and has done it with my permission, and with you to attend on him ? '

The doctor sipped his coffee. 'We have told a story that has satisfied the authorities,' he said coolly. 'Repeat the story to your wife.'

'She won't believe it,' Lord Harry replied.

Mr. Vimpany waited until he had lit another cigar, and had quite satisfied himself that it was worth smoking.

'You have yourself to thank for that obstacle,' he resumed. 'If you had taken my advice, your wife would have been out of our way by this time. I suppose I must manage it. If you fail, leave her ladyship to me. In the meanwhile, there's a matter of more importance to settle first. We shall want a nurse for our poor dear invalid. Where are we to find her ? '

As he stated that difficulty, he finished his coffee, and looked about him for the bottle of brandy which always stood on the dinner-table. In doing this, he happened to notice Fanny. Convinced that her mistress was in danger, after what she had already heard, the maid's anxiety and alarm had so completely absorbed her that she had forgotten to play her part. Instead of still busying herself at the sideboard, she stood with her back to it, palpably listening. Cunning Mr. Vimpany, possessing himself of the brandy, made a request too entirely appropriate to excite suspicion.

' Some fresh cold water, if you please,' was all that he said.

The moment that Fanny left the room, the doctor addressed his friend in English, with his eye on the door : 'News for you, my boy ! We are in a pretty pickle—Lady Harry's maid understands French.'

' Quite impossible,' Lord Harry declared.

' We will put that to the test,' Mr. Vimpany answered. ' Watch her when she comes in again.'

' What are you going to do.'

' I am going to insult her in French. Observe the result.'

In another minute Fanny returned with the fresh water. As she placed the glass jug before Mr. Vimpany he suddenly laid his hand on her arm and looked her straight in the face. 'Vous nous avez mis dedans, drôlesse!' [1] he said.

An uncontrollable look of mingled rage and fear made its plain confession in Fanny's face. She had been discovered; she had heard herself called ' drôlesse ; she stood before the two men self-condemned. Her angry master threatened her with instant dismissal from the house. The doctor interfered.

'No, no,' he said; 'you mustn't deprive Lady Harry, at a moment's notice, of her maid. Such a clever maid, too,' he added with his rascally smile. ' An accomplished person, who understands French, and is too modest to own it ! '

The doctor had led Fanny through many a weary and unrewarded walk when she had followed him to the hospitals; he had now inflicted a deliberate insult by calling her 'drôlesse'; and he had completed the sum of his offences by talking contemptuously of her modesty and her mastery of the French language. The woman's detestation of him, which under ordinary circumstances she might have attempted to conceal, was urged into audaciously asserting itself by the strong excitement that now possessed her. Driven to bay, Fanny had made up her mind to discover the conspiracy of which Mr. Vimpany was the animating spirit, by a method daring enough to be worthy of the doctor himself.

' My knowledge of French has told me something,' she said. ' I have just heard, Mr. Vimpany, that you want a nurse for your invalid gentleman. With my lord's permission, suppose you try Me ? '

Fanny's audacity was more than her master's patience could endure. He ordered her to leave the room.

The peace-making doctor interfered again : ' My dear lord, let me beg you will not be too hard on the young woman.' He turned to Fanny, with an effort to look indulgent, which ended in the

---

[1] In English : ' You have taken us in, you jade ! '

reappearance of his rascally smile. 'Thank you, my dear, for your proposal,' he said; 'I will let you know if we accept it, to-morrow.'

Fanny's unforgiving master pointed to the door; she thanked Mr. Vimpany, and went out. Lord Harry eyed his friend in angry amazement. 'Are you mad?' he asked.

'Tell me something first,' the doctor rejoined. 'Is there any English blood in your family?'

Lord Harry answered with a burst of patriotic feeling: 'I regret to say my family is adulterated in that manner. My grandmother was an Englishwoman.'

Mr. Vimpany received this extract from the page of family history with a coolness all his own.

'It's a relief to hear that,' he said. 'You may be capable (by the grandmother's side) of swallowing a dose of sound English sense. I can but try, at any rate. That woman is too bold and too clever to be treated like an ordinary servant—I incline to believe that she is a spy in the employment of your wife. Whether I am right or wrong in this latter case, the one way I can see of paring the cat's claws is to turn her into a nurse. Do you find me mad now?'

'Madder than ever!'

'Ah, you don't take after your grandmother! Now listen to me. Do we run the smallest risk, if Fanny finds it her interest to betray us? Suppose we ask ourselves what she has really found out. She knows we have got a sick man from a hospital coming here—does she know what we want him for? Not she! Neither you nor I said a word on that subject. But she also heard us agree that your wife was in our way. What does that matter? Did she hear us say what it is that we don't want your wife to dis-cover? Not she, I tell you again! Very well, then—if Fanny acts as Oxbye's nurse, sly as the young woman may be, she inno-cently associates herself with the end that we have to gain by the Danish gentleman's death! Oh, you needn't look alarmed! I mean his natural death by lung disease—no crime, my noble friend! no crime!'

The Irish lord, sitting near the doctor, drew his chair back in a hurry.

'If there's English blood in my family,' he declared, 'I'll tell you what, Vimpany, there's devil's blood in yours!'

'Anything you like but Irish blood,' the cool scoundrel re-joined.

As he made that insolent reply, Fanny came in again, with a sufficient excuse for her reappearance. She announced that a person from the hospital wished to speak to the English doctor.

The messenger proved to be a young man employed in the secretary's office. Oxbye still persisting in his desire to be placed under Mr. Vimpany's care, one last responsibility rested on the official gentlemen now in charge of him. They could implicitly trust the medical assistance and the gracious hospitality offered to the poor Danish patient; but, before he left them, they must also be satisfied that he would be attended by a competent nurse. If the person whom Mr. Vimpany proposed to employ in this capacity could be brought to the hospital, it would be esteemed a favour; and, if her account of herself satisfied the physician in charge of Oxbye's case, the Dane might be removed to his new quarters on the same day.

The next morning witnessed the first in a series of domestic incidents at the cottage, which no prophetic ingenuity could have foreseen. Mr. Vimpany and Fanny Mere actually left Passy together, on their way to Paris!

CHAPTER XLIII

FICTION: ATTEMPTED BY MY LORD

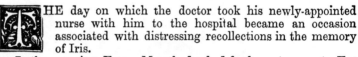HE day on which the doctor took his newly-appointed nurse with him to the hospital became an occasion associated with distressing recollections in the memory of Iris.

In the morning, Fanny Mere had asked for leave to go out. For some time past this request had been so frequently granted, with such poor results so far as the maid's own designs were concerned, that Lady Harry decided on administering a tacit reproof, by means of a refusal. Fanny made no attempt at remonstrance; she left the room in silence.

Half an hour later, Iris had occasion to ring for her attendant. The bell was answered by the cook—who announced, in explanation of her appearance, that Fanny Mere had gone out. More distressed than displeased by this reckless disregard of her authority, on the part of a woman who had hitherto expressed the most grateful sense of her kindness, Iris only said: 'Send Fanny to me as soon as she comes back.'

Two hours passed before the truant maid returned.

'I refused to let you go out this morning,' Lady Harry said; 'and you have taken the liberty of leaving the house for two hours. You might have made me understand, in a more becoming manner, that you intended to leave my service.'

Steadily respectful, Fanny answered: 'I don't wish to leave your ladyship's service.'

'Then what does your conduct mean?'

'It means, if you please, that I had a duty to do—and did it.'

'A duty to yourself?' Iris asked.

'No, my lady; a duty to you.'

As she made that strange reply the door was opened, and Lord Harry entered the room. When he saw Fanny Mere he turned away again, in a hurry, to go out. 'I didn't know your maid was with you,' he said. 'Another time will do.'

His permitting a servant to be an obstacle in his way, when he wished to speak to his wife, was a concession so entirely unbecoming in the master of the house, and so strangely contrary to his customary sense of what was due to himself, that Iris called him back in astonishment. She looked at her maid, who at once understood her, and withdrew. 'What can you possibly be thinking of?' she said to her husband, when they were alone. Putting that question, she noticed an embarrassment in his manner, and an appearance of confusion in his face, which alarmed her. 'Has something happened?' she asked; 'and is it so serious that you hesitate to mention it to me?'

He sat down by her and took her hand. The loving look in his eyes, which she knew so well, was not in them now; they expressed doubt, and something with it which suggested an effort at conciliation.

'I am fearing I shall surprise you,' he said.

'Don't keep me in suspense!' she returned. 'What is it?'

He smiled uneasily: 'It's something about Vimpany.'

Having got as far as that, he stopped. She drew her hand awɛy from him. 'I understand now,' she said; 'I must endeavour to control myself—you have something to tell me which will try my temper.'

He held up his hands in humorous protest: 'Ah, my darling, here's your vivid imagination again, making mountains out of molehills, as they say! It's nothing half so serious as you seem to think; I have only to tell you of a little change.'

'A little change?' she repeated. 'What change?'

'Well, my dear, you see ——' He hesitated and recovered himself. 'I mean, you must know that Vimpany's plans are altered. He won't any longer occupy his bedroom in the cottage here.'

Iris looked inexpressibly relieved. 'Going away, at last!' she exclaimed. 'Oh, Harry, if you have been mystifying me, I hope you will never do it again. It isn't like you; it's cruel to alarm me about nothing. Mr. Vimpany's empty bedroom will be the most interesting room in the house, when I look into it to-night.'

Lord Harry got up, and walked to the window. As a sign of trouble in his mind, and of an instinctive effort to relieve it, the object of this movement was well-known to Iris. She followed him and stood by his side. It was now plain to her that there was something more to be told—and that he was hesitating how to confide it to his wife.

'Go on,' she said resignedly.

He had expected her to take his arm, or perhaps to caress him, or at least to encourage him by her gentlest words and her prettiest smiles. The steady self-restraint which she now manifested was a sign, as he interpreted it, of suppressed resentment. Shrinking, honestly shrinking, from the bare possibility of another quarrel, he confronted the hard necessities of further confession.

'Well, now,' he said, 'it's only this—you mustn't look into the empty bedroom to-night.'

'Why not?'

'Ah, for the best of all good reasons! Because you might find somebody in there.'

This reply excited her curiosity : her eyes rested on him eagerly. 'Some friend of yours ? ' she asked.

He persisted in an assumption of good-humour, which betrayed itself as mere artifice in the clumsiest manner : ' I declare I feel as if I were in a court of justice, being cross-examined by a lawyer of skill and dexterity ! Well, my sweet counsellor, no—not exactly a friend of mine.'

She reflected for a moment. 'You don't surely mean one of Mr. Vimpany's friends ? ' she said.

He pretended not to have heard her, and pointed to the view of the garden from the window. 'Isn't it a lovely day ? Let's go and look at the flowers,' he suggested.

'Did you not hear what I said to you just now ? ' she persisted.

'I beg your pardon, dear ; I was thinking of something else. Suppose we go into the garden ? '

When women have a point to gain in which they are interested, how many of them are capable of deferring it to a better opportunity ? One in a thousand, perhaps. Iris kept her place at the window, resolved on getting an answer.

' I asked you, Harry, whether the person who is to occupy our spare bedroom, to-night, was one of Mr. Vimpany's friends ? '

' Say one of Mr. Vimpany's patients—and you will be nearer the truth,' he answered, with an outburst of impatience.

She could hardly believe him. ' Do you mean a person who is really ill ? ' she said.

'Of course I mean it,' he said ; irritated into speaking out, at last.

' A man ? or a woman ? '

' A man.'

' May I ask if he comes from England ? '

' He comes from one of the French hospitals. Anything more ? '

Iris left her husband to recover his good-humour, and went back to her chair. The extraordinary disclosure which she had extracted from him had produced a stupefying effect on her mind. Her customary sympathy with him, her subtle womanly observation of his character, her intimate knowledge of his merits and his defects, failed to find the rational motive which might have explained his conduct. She looked round at him with mingled feelings of perplexity and distrust.

He was still at the window, but he had turned his back on the view of the garden ; his eyes were fixed, in furtive expectation, on his wife. Was he waiting to hear her say something more ? She ran the risk and said it.

' I don't quite understand the sacrifice you seem to be making to Mr. Vimpany,' she confessed. ' Will you tell me, dear, what it means ? '

Here was the opportunity offered of following the doctor's advice, and putting his wife's credulity to the test. With her knowledge of Vimpany, would she really believe the story which had imposed on the strangers who managed the hospital? Lord Harry made up his mind to try the experiment. No matter what the result might be, it would bring the responsibilities that were crushing him to an end. He need say no more, if the deception succeeded. He could do no more, if it failed. Under the influence of this cheering reflection, he recovered his temper; his handsome face brightened again with its genial boyish smile.

'What a wonderful woman you are!' he cried. 'Isn't it just the thing that I am here for, to tell you what I mean—and my clever wife sees through and through me, and reminds me of what I must do! Pay my fee beforehand, Iris! Give me a kiss—and my poor meaning shall be offered in return. It will help me if you remember one thing. Vimpany and I are old friends, and there's nothing we won't do to accommodate each other. Mind that!'

Tried fairly on its own merits, the stupid fiction invented by the doctor produced an effect for which Lord Harry was not prepared. The longer Iris listened, the more strangely Iris looked at him. Not a word fell from her lips when he had done. He noticed that she had turned pale: it seemed to be almost possible that he had frightened her!

If his bird-witted brains could have coupled cause and effect, this was exactly the result which he might have anticipated.

She was asked to believe that a new system of medical practice had been invented by such a person as Mr. Vimpany. She was asked to believe that an invalid from a foreign hospital, who was a perfect stranger to Lord Harry, had been willingly made welcome to a bedroom at the cottage. She was asked to believe that this astounding concession had been offered to the doctor as a tribute of friendship, after her husband had himself told her that he regretted having invited Vimpany, for the second time, to become his guest. Here was one improbable circumstance accumulated on another, and a clever woman was expected to accept the monstrous excuses, thus produced, as a trustworthy statement of facts. Irresistibly, the dread of some evil deed in secret contemplation cast its darkening presence on the wife's mind. Lord Harry's observation had not misled him, when he saw Iris turn pale, and when the doubt was forced on him whether he might not have frightened her.

'If my explanation of this little matter has satisfied you,' he ventured to resume, 'we need say no more about it.'

'I agree with you,' she answered, 'let us say no more about it.' Conscious, in spite of the effort to resist it, of a feeling of oppression while she was in the same room with a man who had deliberately lied to her, and that man her husband, she reminded Lord Harry that he had proposed to take a walk in the garden. Out in the pure air, under the bright sky, she might breathe more freely. 'Come to the flowers,' she said.

They went to the garden together—the wife fearing the deceitful husband, the husband fearing the quick-witted wife.

Watching each other like two strangers, they walked silently side by side, and looked now and then at the collection of flowers and plants. Iris noticed a delicate fern which had fallen away from the support to which it had been attached. She stopped, and occupied herself in restoring it to its place. When she looked round again, after attending to the plant, her husband had disappeared, and Mr. Vimpany was waiting in his place.

CHAPTER XLIV

FICTION: IMPROVED BY THE DOCTOR

' HERE is Lord Harry ? ' Iris asked.

The reply startled her: 'Lord Harry leaves me to say to your ladyship, what he has not had resolution enough to say for himself.'

'I don't understand you, Mr. Vimpany.'

The doctor pointed to the fern which had just been the object of Lady Harry's care.

'You have been helping that sickly plant there to live and thrive,' he said, 'and I have felt some curiosity in watching you. There is another sickly plant, which I have undertaken to rear if the thing can be done. *My* gardening is of the medical kind—I can only carry it on indoors—and whatever else it may be, I tell you plainly, like the outspoken sort of fellow I am, it's not likely to prove agreeable to a lady. No offence, I hope ? Your humble servant is only trying to produce the right sort of impression—and takes leave to doubt his lordship in one particular.'

'In what particular, sir ? '

'I'll put it in the form of a question, ma'am. Has my friend persuaded you to make arrangements for leaving the cottage ? '

Iris looked at Lord Harry's friend without attempting to conceal her opinion of him.

'I call that an impertinent question,' she said. 'By what right do you presume to inquire into what my husband and I may, or may not, have said to each other ? '

'Will you do me a favour, my lady ? Or, if that is asking too much, perhaps you will not object to do justice to yourself. Suppose you try to exercise the virtue of self-control ? '

'Quite needless, Mr. Vimpany. Pray understand that you are not capable of making me angry.'

'Many thanks, Lady Harry : you encourage me to go on. When I was bold enough to speak of your leaving the cottage, my motive was to prevent you from being needlessly alarmed.'

Did this mean that he was about to take her into his confidence ? All her experience of him forbade her to believe it possible. But the doubts and fears occasioned by her interview with her husband had mastered her better sense ; and the effort to conceal from the doctor the anxiety under which she suffered was steadily weakening the influence of her self-respect. 'Why should I be alarmed?' she asked, in the vain hope of encouraging him to tell the truth.

The doctor arrived at a hasty conclusion, on his side. Believing that he had shaken her resolution, he no longer troubled himself to assume the forms of politeness which he had hitherto, with some difficulty, contrived to observe.

'In this curious little world of ours,' he resumed, 'we enjoy our lives on infernally hard terms. We live on condition that we die. The man I want to cure may die, in spite of the best I can do for him—he may sink slowly, by what we medical men call a hard death. For example, it wouldn't much surprise me if I found some difficulty in keeping him in his bed. He might roam all over your cottage when my back was turned. Or he might pay the debt of Nature—as somebody calls it—with screaming and swearing. If you were within hearing of him, I'm afraid you might be terrified, and, with the best wish to be useful, I couldn't guarantee (if the worst happened) to keep him quiet. In your place, if you will allow me to advise you——'

Iris interrupted him. Instead of confessing the truth, he was impudently attempting to frighten her. 'I don't allow a person in whom I have no confidence to advise me,' she said; 'I wish to hear no more.'

Mr. Vimpany found it desirable to resume the forms of politeness. Either he had failed to shake her resolution, or she was sufficiently in possession of herself to conceal what she felt.

'One last word!' he said. 'I won't presume to advise your ladyship; I will merely offer a suggestion. My lord tells me that Hugh Mountjoy is on the way to recovery. You are in communication with him by letter, as I happened to notice when I did you that trifling service of providing a postage-stamp. Why not go to London and cheer your convalescent friend? Harry won't mind it—I beg your pardon, I ought to have said Lord Harry. Come! come! my dear lady; I am a rough fellow, but I mean well. Take a holiday, and come back to us when my lord writes to say that he can have the pleasure of receiving you again.' He waited for a moment. 'Am I not to be favoured with an answer?' he asked.

'My husband shall answer you.'

With those parting words, Iris turned her back on him.

She entered the cottage. Now in one room, and now in another, she searched for Lord Harry; he was nowhere to be found. Had he purposely gone out to avoid her? Her own remembrance of Vimpany's language and Vimpany's manner told her that so it must be—the two men were in league together. Of all dangers, unknown danger is the most terrible to contemplate. Lady Harry's last resources of resolution failed her. She dropped helplessly into a chair.

After an interval—whether it was a long or a short lapse of time she was unable to decide—someone gently opened the door. Had her husband felt for her? Had he returned? 'Come in!' she cried eagerly—'come in!'

CHAPTER XLV

FACT: RELATED BY FANNY

THE person who now entered the room was Fanny Mere.

But one interest was stirring in the mind of Iris now. 'Do you know where your master is?' she asked.

'I saw him go out,' the maid replied. 'Which way I didn't particularly notice——' She was on the point of adding, 'and I didn't particularly care,' when she checked herself. 'Yesterday and to-day, my lady, things have come to my knowledge which I must not keep to myself,' the resolute woman continued. 'If a servant may say such a thing without offence, I have never been so truly my mistress's friend as I am now. I beg you to forgive my boldness; there is a reason for it.'

So she spoke, with no presumption in her looks, with no familiarity in her manner. The eyes of her friendless mistress filled with tears, the offered hand of her friendless mistress answered in silence. Fanny took that kind hand, and pressed it respectfully—a more demonstrative woman than herself might perhaps have kissed it. She only said, 'Thank you, my lady,' and went on with what she felt it her duty to relate.

As carefully as usual, as quietly as usual, she repeated the conversation, at Lord Harry's table; describing also the manner in which Mr. Vimpany had discovered her as a person who understood the French language, and who had cunningly kept it a secret. In this serious state of things, the doctor—yes, the doctor himself!—had interfered to protect her from the anger of her master, and, more wonderful still, for a reason which it seemed impossible to dispute. He wanted a nurse for the foreigner whose arrival was expected on that evening, and he had offered the place to Fanny. 'Your ladyship will, I hope, excuse me; I have taken the place.'

This amazing end to the strange events which had just been narrated proved to be more than Iris was immediately capable of understanding. 'I am in the dark,' she confessed. 'Is Mr. Vimpany a bolder villain even than I have supposed him to be?'

'That he most certainly is!' Fanny said with strong conviction. 'As to what he really had in his wicked head when he engaged me, I shall find that out in time. Anyway, I am the nurse who is to help him. When I disobeyed you this morning, my lady, it was to go to the hospital with Mr. Vimpany. I was taken to see the person whose nurse I am to be. A poor, feeble, polite creature, who looked as if he couldn't hurt a fly—and yet I promise you he startled me! I saw a likeness, the moment I looked at him.'

'A likeness to anybody whom I know ? ' Iris asked.

'To the person in all the world, my lady, whom you know most nearly—a likeness to my master.'

'What!'

'Oh, it's no fancy; I am sure of what I say. To my mind, that Danish man's likeness to my lord is (if you will excuse my language) a nasty circumstance. I don't know why or wherefore—all I can say is, I don't like it; and I sha'n't rest until I have found out what it means. Besides this, my lady, I must know the reason why they want to get you out of their way. Please to keep up your heart; I shall warn you in time, when I am sure of the danger.'

Iris refused to sanction the risk involved in this desperate design. ' It's *you* who will be in danger! ' she exclaimed.

In her coolest state of obstinacy, Fanny answered : 'That's in your ladyship's service—and that doesn't reckon.'

Feeling gratefully this simple and sincere expression of attachment, Iris held to her own opinion, nevertheless.

'You are in my service,' she said ; 'I won't let you go to Mr. Vimpany. Give it up, Fanny ! Give it up ! '

'I'll give it up, my lady, when I know what the doctor means to do—not before.'

The assertion of authority having failed, Iris tried persuasion next.

'As your mistress, it is my duty to set you an example,' she resumed. 'One of us must be considerate and gentle in a dispute— let me try to be that one. There can be no harm, and there may be some good, in consulting the opinion of a friend; some person in whose discretion we can trust.'

'Am I acquainted with the person your ladyship is thinking of ? ' Fanny inquired. ' In that case, a friend will know what we want of her by to-morrow morning. I have written to Mrs. Vimpany. '

'The very person I had in my mind, Fanny ! When may we expect to hear from her ? '

'If Mrs. Vimpany can put what she has to say to us into few words,' Fanny replied, ' we shall hear from her to-morrow by telegraph.'

As she answered her mistress in those cheering words, they were startled by a heavy knock at the door of the room. Under similar circumstances, Lord Harry's delicate hand would have been just loud enough to be heard, and no more. Iris called out suspiciously : 'Who's there ? '

The doctor's gross voice answered : 'Can I say a word, if you please, to Fanny Mere ? '

The maid opened the door. Mr. Vimpany's heavy hand laid hold of her arm, pulled her over the threshold, and closed the door behind her. After a brief absence, Fanny returned with news of my lord.

A commissioner had arrived with a message for the doctor; and Fanny was charged to repeat it or not, just as she thought right under the circumstances. Lord Harry was in Paris. He had been invited to go to the theatre with some friends, and to return with them to supper. If he was late in getting home, he was anxious that my lady should not be made uneasy. After having authorised Mr. Vimpany's interference in the garden, the husband evidently had his motives for avoiding another interview with the wife. Iris was left alone, to think over that discovery. Fanny had received orders to prepare the bedroom for the doctor's patient.

CHAPTER XLVI

MAN AND WIFE

TOWARDS evening, the Dane was brought to the cottage.

A feeling of pride which forbade any display of curiosity, strengthened perhaps by an irresistible horror of Vimpany, kept Iris in her room. Nothing but the sound of footsteps, outside, told her when the suffering man was taken to his bedchamber on the same floor. She was afterwards informed by Fanny that the doctor turned down the lamp in the corridor, before the patient was helped to ascend the stairs, as a means of preventing the mistress of the house from plainly seeing the stranger's face, and recognising the living likeness of her husband.

The hours advanced—the bustle of domestic life sank into silence —everybody but Iris rested quietly in bed.

Through the wakeful night the sense of her situation oppressed her sinking spirits. Mysteries that vaguely threatened danger made their presence felt, and took their dark way through her thoughts. The cottage, in which the first happy days of her marriage had been passed, might ere long be the scene of some evil deed, provoking the lifelong separation of her husband and herself! Were these the exaggerated fears of a woman in a state of hysterical suspicion? It was enough for Iris to remember that Lord Harry and Mr. Vimpany had been alike incapable of telling her the truth. The first had tried to deceive her; the second had done his best to frighten her. Why? If there was really nothing to be afraid of —why? The hours of the early morning came; and still she listened in vain for the sound of my lord's footstep on the stairs; still she failed to hear the cautious opening of his dressing-room door. Leaving her chair, Iris rested on the bed. As time advanced, exhaustion mastered her; she slept.

Awakening at a late hour, she rang for Fanny Mere. The master had just returned. He had missed the latest night-train to Passy; and, rather than waste money on hiring a carriage at that hour, he had accepted the offer of a bed at the house of his friends. He was then below stairs, hoping to see Lady Harry at breakfast.

His wife joined him.

Not even at the time of the honeymoon had the Irish lord been a more irresistibly agreeable man than he was on that memorable morning. His apologies for having failed to return at the right time were little masterpieces of grace and gaiety. The next best thing to having been present, at the theatrical performance of the previous night, was to hear his satirical summary of the story of the play, contrasting delightfully with his critical approval of the fine art of the actors. The time had been when Iris would have resented such merciless trifling with serious interests as this. In those earlier and better days, she would have reminded him affectionately of her claim to be received into his confidence—she would have tried all that tact and gentleness and patience could do to win his confession of the ascendency exercised over him by his vile friend—and she would have used the utmost influence of her love and her resolution to disunite the fatal fellowship which was leading him to his ruin.

But Iris Henley was Lady Harry now.

She was sinking—as Mrs. Vimpany had feared, as Mountjoy had foreseen—lower and lower on the descent to her husband's level. With a false appearance of interest in what he was saying she waited for her chance of matching him with his own weapons of audacious deceit. He ignorantly offered her the opportunity— setting the same snare to catch his wife, which she herself had it in contemplation to use for entrapping her husband into a confession of the truth.

'Ah, well—I have said more than enough of my last night's amusement,' he confessed. 'It's your turn now, my dear. Have you had a look at the poor fellow whom the doctor is going to cure?' he asked abruptly; eager to discover whether she had noticed the likeness between Oxbye and himself.

Her eyes rested on him attentively. 'I have not yet seen the person you allude to,' she answered. 'Is Mr. Vimpany hopeful of his recovery?'

He took out his case, and busied himself in choosing a cigar. In the course of his adventurous life, he had gained some knowledge

of the effect of his own impetuous temper on others, and of difficulties which he had experienced when circumstances rendered it
necessary to keep his face in a state of discipline.

'Oh, there's no reason for anxiety!' he said, with an over-acted
interest in examining his cigar. 'Mr. Oxbye is in good hands.'

'People do sometimes sink under an illness,' she quietly remarked.

Without making any reply he took out his matchbox. His
hand trembled a little; he failed at the first attempt to strike a
light.

'And doctors sometimes make mistakes,' Iris went on.

He was still silent. At the second attempt, he succeeded with
the match, and lit his cigar.

'Suppose Mr. Vimpany made a mistake, she persisted. 'In
the case of this stranger, it might lead to deplorable results.'

Lord Harry lost his temper, and with it his colour.

'What the devil do you mean?' he cried.

'I might ask, in my turn,' she said, 'what have I done to provoke an outbreak of temper? I only made a remark.'

At that critical moment, Fanny Mere entered the room with a
telegram in her hand.

'For you, my lady.'

Iris opened the telegram. The message was signed by Mrs.
Vimpany, and was expressed in these words: 'You may feel it your
duty to go to your father. He is dangerously ill.'

Lord Harry saw a sudden change in his wife's face that roused
his guilty suspicions. 'Is it anything about me?' he asked.

Iris handed the telegram to him in silence. Having looked
at it, he desired to hear what her wishes were.

'The telegram expresses my wishes,' she said. 'Have you any
objection to my leaving you?'

'None whatever,' he answered eagerly. 'Go, by all means.'

If it had still been possible for her to hesitate, that reply would
have put an end to all further doubt. She turned away to leave the
room. He followed her to the door.

'I hope you don't think there is any want of sympathy on my
part,' he said. 'You are quite right to go to your father. That
was all I meant.' He was agitated, honestly agitated, while he
spoke. Iris saw it, and felt it gratefully. She was on the point of
making a last appeal to his confidence, when he opened the door for
her. 'Don't let me detain you,' he said. His voice faltered; he
suddenly turned aside before she could look at him.

Fanny was waiting in the hall, eager to see the telegram. She
read it twice and reflected for a moment. 'How often do things
fit themselves to one's wishes in this convenient way?' she asked
herself. 'It's lucky,' she privately decided—'almost too lucky.
Let me pack up your things,' she continued, addressing her
mistress, 'while I have some time to myself. Mr. Oxbye is
asleep.'

*Fanny held her mistress for an instant in her arms. ' I know whom you are thinking of,'
she whispered.*

As the day wore on, the noble influences in the nature of Iris, failing fast, yet still at rare intervals struggling to assert themselves, inspired her with the resolution to make a last attempt to give her husband an opportunity of trusting her. He was not in his room, not in any other part of the house, not in the garden. The hours passed—she was left to eat her dinner in solitude. For the second time, he was avoiding her. For the second time, he distrusted the influence of his wife. With a heavy heart she prepared for her departure by the night-mail.

The duties of the new nurse kept her in the cottage. Filled with alarm for the faithful creature whom she was leaving—to what fate, who could say?—Iris kissed her at parting.

Fanny's faint blue eyes filled with tears. She dashed them away, and held her mistress for an instant in her arms. 'I know whom you are thinking of,' she whispered. 'He is not here to bid you good-bye. Let me see what I can find in his room.' Iris had already looked round the room, in the vain hope of finding a letter. Fanny rushed up the stairs, determined on a last search—and ran down again with a folded morsel of flimsy foreign notepaper in her hand. 'My ugly eyes are quicker than yours,' she said. 'The air must have come in at the window and blown it off the table.' Iris eagerly read the letter:

'I dare not deny that you will be better away from us, but only for a while. Forgive me, dearest; I cannot find the courage to say good-bye.' Those few words spoke for him—and no more.

Briefly on her side, but not unkindly, his wife answered him:

'You have spared me a bitter moment. May I hope to find the man whom I have trusted and honoured, when I come back? Good-bye.'

When were they to meet again? And how?

CHAPTER XLVII

THE PATIENT AND MY LORD

THERE now remained but one other person in Lord Harry's household whose presence on the scene was an obstacle to be removed.

This person was the cook. On condition of her immediate departure (excused by alleged motives of economy), she received a month's wages from her master, in advance of the sum due to her, and a written character which did ample justice to her many good qualities. The poor woman left her employment with the heartiest expressions of gratitude. To the end of her days, she declared the Irish lord to be a nobleman by nature. Republican principles, inherited from her excellent parents, disinclined her to recognise him as a nobleman by birth.

But another sweet and simple creature was still left to brighten the sinister gloom in the cottage.

The good Dane sorely tried the patience of Fanny Mere. This countryman of Hamlet, as he liked to call himself, was a living protest against the sentiments of inveterate contempt and hatred, with which his nurse was accustomed to regard the men. When pain spared him at intervals, Mr. Oxbye presented the bright blue eyes and the winning smile which suggested the resemblance to the Irish lord. His beardless face, thin towards the lower extremities, completed the likeness in some degree only. The daring expression

Fanny found herself in the presence of a male human being, who, in the painless intervals of his malady wrote little poems in her praise.

of Lord Harry, in certain emergencies, never appeared. Nursing
him carefully, on the severest principles of duty as distinguished
from inclination, Fanny found herself in the presence of a male
human being, who in the painless intervals of his malady, wrote
little poems in her praise; asked for a few flowers from the garden,
and made prettily arranged nosegays of them devoted to herself;
cried, when she told him he was a fool, and kissed her hand five
minutes afterwards, when she administered his medicine, and gave
him no pleasant sweet thing to take the disagreeable taste out of
his mouth. This gentle patient loved Lord Harry, loved Mr.
Vimpany, loved the furious Fanny, resist it as she might. On her
obstinate refusal to confide to him the story of her life—after he
had himself set her the example at great length—he persisted in
discovering for himself that ' this interesting woman was a victim
of sorrows of the heart.' In another state of existence, he was
offensively certain that she would be living with *him*. ' You are
frightfully pale, you will soon die; I shall break a blood-vessel, and
follow you; we shall sit side by side on clouds, and sing together
everlastingly to accompaniment of celestial harps. Oh, what a
treat!' Like a child, he screamed when he was in pain; and, like
a child, he laughed when the pain had gone away. When she was
angry enough with him to say, ' If I had known what sort of man
you were, I would never have undertaken to nurse you,' he only
answered, ' My dear, let us thank God together that you did *not*
know.' There was no temper in him to be roused; and, worse
still, on buoyant days, when his spirits were lively, there was no
persuading him that he might not live long enough to marry his
nurse, if he only put the question to her often enough. What was
to be done with such a man as this? Fanny believed that she
despised her feeble patient. At the same time, the food that
nourished him was prepared by her own hands—while the other
inhabitants of the cottag were left (in the absence of the cook) to
the tough mercies of a neighbouring restaurant. First and foremost among the many good deeds by which the conduct of women
claims the gratitude of the other sex, is surely the manner in which
they let an unfortunate man master them, without an unworthy
suspicion of that circumstance to trouble the charitable serenity of
their minds.

Carefully on the look-out for any discoveries which might
enlighten her, Fanny noticed with ever-increasing interest the effect
which the harmless Dane seemed to produce on my lord and the
doctor.

Every morning, after breakfast, Lord Harry presented himself
in the bedroom. Every morning, his courteous interest in his
guest expressed itself mechanically in the same form of words:

' Mr. Oxbye, how do you find yourself to-day? '

Sometimes the answer would be : ' Gracious lord, I am suffering
pain.' Sometimes it was : ' Dear and admirable patron, I feel as
if I might get well again.' On either occasion, Lord Harry listened

without looking at Mr. Oxbye—said he was sorry to hear a bad
account or glad to hear a good account, without looking at Mr.
Oxbye—made a remark on the weather, and took his leave, without
looking at Mr. Oxbye. Nothing could be more plain than that his
polite inquiries (once a day) were unwillingly made, and that it was
always a relief to him to get out of the room. So strongly was
Fanny's curiosity excited by this strange behaviour, that she ventured one day to speak to her master.

'I am afraid, my lord, you are not hopeful of Mr. Oxbye's recovering?'

'Mind your own business,' was the savage answer that she
received.

Fanny never again took the liberty of speaking to him; but she
watched him more closely than ever. He was perpetually restless.
Now he wandered from one room to another, and walked round and
round the garden, smoking incessantly. Now he went out riding,
or took the railway to Paris and disappeared for the day. On the
rare occasions when he was in a state of repose, he always appeared
to have taken refuge in his wife's room; Fanny's keyhole-observa-
tion discovered him, thinking miserably, seated in his wife's chair.
It seemed to be possible that he was fretting after Lady Harry.
But what did his conduct to Mr. Oxbye mean? What was the
motive which made him persist, without an attempt at concealment, in keeping out of Mr. Vimpany's way? And, treated in
this rude manner, how was it that his wicked friend seemed to be
always amused, never offended?

As for the doctor's behaviour to his patient, it was, in Fanny's
estimation, worthy of a savage.

He appeared to feel no sort of interest in the man who had
been sent to him from the hospital at his own request, and whose
malady it was supposed to be the height of his ambition to cure.
When Mr. Oxbye described his symptoms, Mr. Vimpany hardly
even made a pretence at listening. With a frowning face he applied the stethoscope, felt the pulse, looked at the tongue—and drew
his own conclusions in sullen silence. If the nurse had a favourable
report to make, he brutally turned his back on her. If discouraging
results of the medical treatment made their appearance at night,
and she felt it a duty to mention them, he sneered as if he doubted
whether she was speaking the truth. Mr. Oxbye's inexhaustible
patience and amiability made endless allowances for his medical
adviser. 'It is my misfortune to keep my devoted doctor in a state
of perpetual anxiety,' he used to say; 'and we all know what a
trial to the temper is the consequence of unrelieved suspense. I
believe in Mr. Vimpany.' Fanny was careful not to betray her own
opinion by making any reply; her doubts of the doctor had, by this
time, become terrifying doubts even to herself. Whenever an
opportunity favoured her, she vigilantly watched him. One of his
ways of finding amusement, in his leisure hours, was in the use of
a photographic apparatus. He took little pictures of the rooms in

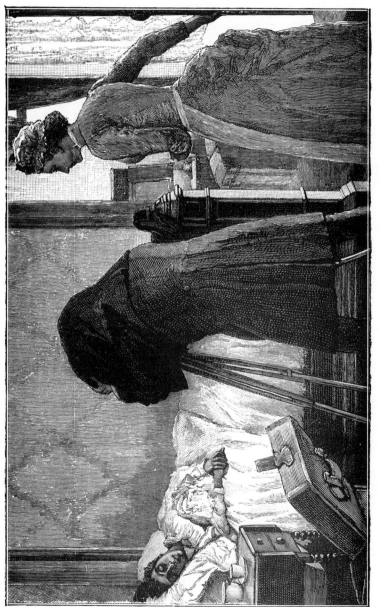

He completed the mystification of the nurse by producing a portrait of the Dane while he lay asleep one day.

the cottage, which were followed by views in the garden. These having come to an end, he completed the mystification of the nurse by producing a portrait of the Dane, while he lay asleep one day after he had been improving in health for some little time past. Fanny asked leave to look at the likeness when it had been 'printed' from the negative, in the garden. He first examined it himself— and then deliberately tore it up and let the fragments fly away in the wind. 'I am not satisfied with it,' was all the explanation he offered. One of the garden chairs happened to be near him ; he sat down, and looked like a man in a state of torment under his own angry thoughts.

If the patient's health had altered for the worse, and if the tendency to relapse had proved to be noticeable after medicine had been administered, Fanny's first suspicions might have taken a very serious turn. But the change in Oxbye—sleeping in purer air and sustained by better food than he could obtain at the hospital— pointed more and more visibly to a decided gain of vital strength. His hollow cheeks were filling out, and colour was beginning to appear again on the pallor of his skin. Strange as the conduct of Lord Harry and Mr. Vimpany might be, there was no possibility, thus far, of connecting it with the position occupied by the Danish guest. Nobody who had seen his face, when he was first brought to the cottage, could have looked at him again, after the lapse of a fortnight, and have failed to discover the signs which promise recovery of health.

CHAPTER XLVIII

'THE MISTRESS AND THE MAID'

IN the correspondence secretly carried on between the mistress in London and the maid at Passy, it was Fanny Mere's turn to write next. She decided on delaying her reply until she had once more given careful consideration to the first letter received from Lady Harry, announcing her arrival in England, and a strange discovery that had attended it.

Before leaving Paris, Iris had telegraphed instructions to Mrs. Vimpany to meet her at the terminus in London. Her first inquiries were for her father. The answer given, with an appearance of confusion and even of shame, was that there was no need to feel anxiety on the subject of Mr. Henley's illness. Relieved on hearing this good news, Iris naturally expressed some surprise at her father's rapid recovery. She asked if the doctors had misunderstood his malady when they believed him to be in danger. To this question Mrs. Vimpany had replied by making an unexpected confession.

She owned that Mr. Henley's illness had been at no time of any serious importance. A paragraph in a newspaper had informed her that he was suffering from nothing worse than an attack of gout. It was a wicked act to have exaggerated this report, and to have alarmed Lady Harry on the subject of her father's health. Mrs. Vimpany had but one excuse to offer. Fanny's letter had filled her with such unendurable doubts and forebodings that she had taken the one way of inducing Lady Harry to secure her own safety by at once leaving Passy—the way by a false alarm. Deceit, so sincerely repented, so resolutely resisted, had tried its power of temptation again, and had prevailed.

'When I thought of you at the mercy of my vile husband,' Mrs. Vimpany said, 'with *your* husband but too surely gained as an accomplice, my good resolutions failed me. Is it only in books that a true repentance never stumbles again? Or am I the one fallible mortal creature in the world? I am ashamed of myself. But, oh, Lady Harry, I was so frightened for you! Try to forgive me; I am so fond of you, and so glad to see you here in safety. Don't go back! For God's sake, don't go back!'

Iris had no intention of returning, while the doctor and his patient were still at Passy; and she found in Mrs. Vimpany's com-

passion good reason to forgive an offence committed through devotion to herself, and atoned for by sincere regret.

Fanny looked carefully over the next page of the letter, which
described Lady Harry's first interview with Mr. Mountjoy since his
illness. The expressions of happiness on renewing her relations
with her old and dear friend confirmed the maid in her first impression that there was no fear of a premature return to Passy, with
the wish to see Lord Harry again as the motive. She looked over
the later letters next—and still the good influence of Mr. Mountjoy
seemed to be in the ascendant. There was anxiety felt for Fanny's
safety, and curiosity expressed to hear what discoveries she might
have made ; but the only allusions to my lord contained ordinary
inquiries relating to the state of his health, and, on one occasion,
there was a wish expressed to know whether he was still on friendly
terms with Mr. Vimpany. There seemed to be no fear of tempting
her mistress to undervalue the danger of returning to the cottage, if
she mentioned the cheering improvement now visible in Mr. Oxbye.
And yet Fanny still hesitated to trust her first impressions,
even after they had been confirmed. Her own sad experience reminded her of the fatal influence which an unscrupulous man can
exercise over the woman who loves him. It was always possible
that Lady Harry might not choose to confide the state of her feelings towards her husband to a person who, after all, only occupied the position of her maid. The absence, in her letters, of any
expressions of affectionate regret was no proof that she was not
thinking of my lord. So far as he was personally concerned, the
Dane's prospects of recovery would appear to justify the action of
the doctor and his accomplice. Distrusting them both as resolutely
as ever, and determined to keep Lady Harry as long as possible
at the safe distance of London, Fanny Mere, in writing her reply,
preserved a discreet silence on the subject of Mr. Oxbye's health.

CHAPTER XLIX

THE NURSE IS SENT AWAY

'YOU have repented and changed your mind, Vimpany?'
said Lord Harry.

'I repented?' the doctor repeated, with a laugh.
'You think me capable of that, do you?'

'The man is growing stronger and better every day. You are
going to make him recover, after all. I was afraid'—he corrected
himself—'I thought'—the word was the truer—'that you were going to poison him.'

'You thought I was going—we were going, my lord—to commit
a stupid and a useless crime. And, with our clever nurse present,
all the time watching with the suspicions of a cat, and noting every
change in the symptoms? No—I confess his case has puzzled me
because I did not anticipate this favourable change. Well—it is
all for the best. Fanny sees him grow stronger every day—whatever happens she can testify to the care with which the man has
been treated. So far she thought she would have us in her power,
and we have her.'

'You are mighty clever, Vimpany; but sometimes you are too
clever for me, and, perhaps, too clever for yourself.'

'Let me make myself clearer'—conscious of the nurse's suspicions, he leaned forward and whispered: 'Fanny must go. Now
is the time. The man is recovering. The man must go: the
next patient will be your lordship himself. Now do you understand?'

'Partly.'

'Enough. If I am to act it is sufficient for you to understand
step by step. Our suspicious nurse is to go. That is the next step.
Leave me to act.'

Lord Harry walked away. He left the thing to the doctor. It
hardly seemed to concern him. A dying man; a conspiracy; a
fraud:—yet the guilty knowledge of all this gave him small uneasi-
ness. He carried with him his wife's last note: 'May I hope to
find on my return the man whom I have trusted and honoured?'
His conscience, callous as regards the doctor's scheme, filled him
with remorse whenever—which was fifty times a day—he took this
little rag of a note from his pocket-book and read it again. Yes:
she would always find the man, on her return—the man whom she

had trusted and honoured—the latter clause he passed over—it would be, of course the same man: whether she would still be able to trust and honour him—that question he did not put to himself. After all, the doctor was acting—not he, himself.

And he remembered Hugh Mountjoy. Iris would be with him —the man whose affection was only brought out in the stronger light by his respect, his devotion, and his delicacy. She would be in his society: she would understand the true meaning of this re-spect and delicacy: she would appreciate the depth of his devotion: she would contrast Hugh, the man she might have married, with himself, the man she did marry.

And the house was wretched without her; and he hated the sight of the doctor—desperate and reckless !

He resolved to write to Iris: he sat down and poured out his heart, but not his conscience, to her.

'As for our separation,' he said, 'I, and only I, am to blame. It is my own abominable conduct that has caused it. Give me your pardon, dearest Iris. If I have made it impossible for you to live with me, it is also impossible for me to live without you. So am I punished. The house is dull and lonely; the hours crawl, I know not how to kill the time; my life is a misery and a burden because you are not with me. Yet I have no right to complain; I ought to rejoice in thinking that you are happy in being relieved of my presence. My dear, I do not ask you to come at present '— he remembered, indeed, that her arrival at this juncture might be seriously awkward—'I cannot ask you to come back yet, but let me have a little hope—let me feel that in the sweetness of your nature you will believe in my repentance, and let me look forward to a speedy reunion in the future.'

When he had written this letter, which he would have done better to keep in his own hands for awhile, he directed it in a feigned hand to Lady Harry Norland, care of Hugh Mountjoy, at the latter's London hotel. Mountjoy would not know Iris's corres-pondent, and would certainly forward the letter. He calculated— with the knowledge of her affectionate and impulsive nature—that Iris would meet him half-way, and would return whenever he should be able to call her back. He did not calculate, as will be seen, on the step which she actually took.

The letter despatched, he came back to the cottage happier—he would get his wife again. He looked in at the sick-room. The patient was sitting up, chatting pleasantly; it was the best day he had known; the doctor was sitting in a chair placed beside the bed, and the nurse stood quiet, self-composed, but none the less watchful and suspicious.

'You are going on so well, my man,' Doctor Vimpany was say-ing, 'that we shall have you out and about again in a day or two. Not quite yet, though—not quite yet,' he pulled out his stethoscope and made an examination with an immense show of professional interest. 'My treatment has succeeded, you see'—he made a note or two in his pocket-book—'has succeeded,' he repeated. 'They will have to acknowledge that.'

'Gracious sir, I am grateful. I have given a great deal too much trouble.'

'A medical case can never give too much trouble—that is impossible. Remember, Oxbye, it is Science which watches at your bedside. You are not Oxbye; you are a case; it is not a man, it is a piece of machinery that is out of order. Science watches: she sees you through and through. Though you are made of solid flesh and bones, and clothed, to Science you are transparent. Her business is not only to read your symptoms, but to set the machinery right again.'

The Dane, overwhelmed, could only renew his thanks.

'Can he stand, do you think, nurse?' the doctor went on. 'Let us try—not to walk about much to-day, but to get out of bed, if only to prove to himself that he is so much better; to make him understand that he is really nearly well. Come, nurse, let us give him a hand.'

In the most paternal manner possible the doctor assisted his patient, weak, after so long a confinement to his bed, to get out of bed, and supported him while he walked to the open window, and looked out into the garden. 'There,' he said, 'that is enough. Not too much at first. To-morrow he will have to get up by himself. Well, Fanny, you agree at last, I suppose, that I have brought this poor man round? At last, eh?'

His look and his words showed what he meant. 'You thought that some devilry was intended.' That was what the look meant. 'You proposed to nurse this man in order to watch for and to discover this devilry. Very well, what have you got to say?'

All that Fanny had to say was, submissively, that the man was clearly much better; and, she added, he had been steadily improving ever since he came to the cottage.

That is what she said; but she said it without the light of confidence in her eyes—she was still doubtful and suspicious. Whatever power the doctor had of seeing the condition of lungs and hidden machinery, he certainly had the power of reading this woman's thoughts. He saw, as clearly as if upon a printed page, the bewilderment of her mind. She knew that something was intended—something not for her to know. That the man had been brought to the cottage to be made the subject of a scientific experiment she did not believe. She had looked to see him die, but he did not die. He was mending fast; in a little while he would be as well as ever he had been in his life. What had the doctor done it for? Was it really possible that nothing was ever intended beyond a scientific experiment, which had succeeded? In the case of any other man, the woman's doubts would have been entirely removed; in the case of Dr. Vimpany these doubts remained. There are some men of whom nothing good can be believed, whether of motive or of action; for if their acts seem good, their motive must be bad. Many women know, or fancy they know, such a man—one who seems to them wholly and hopelessly bad. Besides, what was the meaning of the secret conversation and the widespread colloquies of the doctor and my lord ? And why, at first, was the doctor so careless about his patient ?

'The time has come at last,' said the doctor that evening, when the two men were alone, 'for this woman to go. The man is get-, ting well rapidly, he no longer wants a nurse; there is no reason for keeping her. If she has suspicions there is no longer the least foundation for them ; she has assisted at the healing of a man desperately sick by a skilful physician. What more ? Nothing—positively nothing.'

'Can she tell my wife so much and no more ? ' asked Lord Harry. 'Will there be no more ? '

'She can tell her ladyship no more, because she will have no more to tell,' the doctor replied quietly. 'She would like to learn more ; she is horribly disappointed that there is no more to tell; but she shall hear no more. She hates me : but she hates your lordship more.'

'Why ? '

'Because her mistress loves you still. Such a woman as this would like to absorb the whole affection of her mistress in herself. You laugh. She is a servant, and a common person. How can such a person conceive an affection so strong as to become a passion for one so superior ? But it is true. It is perfectly well known, and there have been many recorded instances of such a woman, say a servant, greatly inferior in station, conceiving a desperate affection for her mistress, accompanied by the fiercest jealousy. Fanny Mere is jealous—and of you. She hates you; she wants your wife to hate you. She would like nothing better than to go back to her mistress with the proofs in her hand of such acts on your part— such acts, I say,' he chose his next words carefully, 'as would keep her from you for ever.'

'She's a devil, I dare say,' said Lord Harry, carelessly. 'What do I care ? What does it matter to me whether a lady's maid, more or less, hates me or loves me ? '

'There spoke the aristocrat. My lord, remember that a lady's maid is a woman. You have been brought up to believe, perhaps, that people in service are not men and women. That is a mistake —a great mistake. Fanny Mere is a woman—that is to say, an inferior form of man; and there is no man in the world so low or so base as not to be able to do mischief. The power of mischief is given to every one of us. It is the true, the only Equality of Man —we can all destroy. What ? a shot in the dark ; the striking or a lucifer match; the false accusation ; the false witness ; the defamation of character ;—upon my word, it is far more dangerous to be hated by a woman than by a man. And this excellent and faithful Fanny, devoted to her mistress, hates you, my lord, even more '—he paused and laughed—'even more than the charming

Mrs. Vimpany hates her husband. Never mind. To-morrow we see the last of Fanny Mere. She goes; she leaves her patient rapidly recovering. That is the fact that she carries away—not the fact she hoped and expected to carry away. She goes to-morrow and she will never come back again.'

The next morning the doctor paid a visit to his patient rather earlier than usual. He found the man going on admirably : fresh in colour, lively and cheerful, chatting pleasantly with his nurse.

'So,' said Dr. Vimpany, after the usual examination and ques-tions, ' this is better than I expected. You are now able to get up. You can do so by-and-by, after breakfast; you can dress yourself, you want no more help. Nurse,' he turned to Fanny, ' I think that we have done with you. I am satisfied with the careful watch you have kept over my patient. If ever you think of becoming a nurse by profession, rely on my recommendation. The experiment,' he added, thoughtfully, ' has fully succeeded. I cannot deny that it has been owing partly to the intelligence and patience with which you have carried out my instructions. But I think that your ser-vices may now be relinquished.'

'When am I to go, sir ? ' she asked, impassively.

'In any other case I should have said, " Stay a little longer, if you please. Use your own convenience." In your case I must say, " Go to your mistress." Her ladyship was reluctant to leave you behind. She will be glad to have you back again. How long will you take to get ready ? '

'I could be ready in ten minutes, if it were necessary.'

'That is not necessary. You can take the night mail *via* Dieppe and Newhaven. It leaves Paris at 9·50. Give yourself an hour to get from station to station. Any time, therefore, this evening before seven o'clock will do perfectly well. You will ask his lordship for any letters or messages he may have.'

'Yes, sir,' Fanny replied. ' With your permission, sir, I will go at once, so as to get a whole day in Paris.'

'As you please, as you please,' said the doctor, wondering why she wanted a day in Paris ; but it could have nothing to do with his sick man. He left the room, promising to see the Dane again in an hour or two, and took up a position at the garden gate through which the nurse must pass. In about half an hour she walked down the path carrying her box. The doctor opened the gate for her.

'Good-bye, Fanny,' he said. ' Again, many thanks for your care and your watchfulness—especially the latter. I am very glad,' he said, with what he meant for the sweetest smile, but it looked like a grin, ' that it has been rewarded in such a way as you hardly perhaps expected.'

'Thank you, sir,' said the girl. ' The man is nearly well now, and can do without me very well indeed.'

'The box is too heavy for you, Fanny. Nay, I insist upon it : I shall carry it to the station for you.'

It was not far to the station, and the box was not too heavy, but Fanny yielded it. 'He wants to see me safe out of the station,' she thought.

'I will see her safe out of the place,' he thought.

Ten minutes later the doors of the *salle d'attente* were thrown open, the train rolled in, and Fanny was carried away.

The doctor returned thoughtfully to the house. The time was come for the execution of his project. Everybody was out of the way.

'She is gone,' he said, when Lord Harry returned for breakfast at eleven. 'I saw her safely out of the station.'

'Gone!' his confederate echoed: 'and I am alone in the house with you and—and——'

'The sick man—henceforth, yourself, my lord, yourself.'

CHAPTER L

IN THE ALCOVE

THE doctor was wrong. Fanny Mere did return, though he did not discover the fact.

She went away in a state of mind which is dangerous when it possesses a woman of determination. The feminine mind loves to understand motives and intentions; it hates to be puzzled. Fanny was puzzled. Fanny could not understand what had been intended and what was now meant. For, first, a man, apparently dying, had been brought into the house—why? Then the man began slowly to recover, and the doctor, whose attentions had always been of the most slender character, grew more morose every day. Then he suddenly, on the very day when he sent her away, became cheerful, congratulated the patient on his prospect of recovery, and assisted in getting him out of bed for a change. The cook having been sent away, there was now no one in the house but the Dane, the doctor, and Lord Harry.

Man hunts wild creatures; woman hunts man. Fanny was impelled by the hunting instinct. She was sent out of the house to prevent her hunting; she began to consider next, how, without discovery, she could return and carry on the hunt.

Everything conspired to drive her back: the mystery of the thing; the desire to baffle, or at least to discover, a dark design; the wish to be of service to her mistress; and the hope of finding out something which would keep Iris from going back to her husband. Fanny was unable to comprehend the depth of her mistress's affection for Lord Harry; but that she was foolishly, weakly in love with him, and that she would certainly return to him unless plain proofs of real villainy were prepared—so much Fanny understood very well. When the omnibus set her down, she found a quiet hotel near the terminus for Dieppe. She spent the day walking about—to see the shops and streets, she would have explained; to consider the situation, she should have explained. She bought a new dress, a new hat, and a thick veil, so as to be disguised at a distance. As for escaping the doctor's acuteness by any disguise should he meet her face to face, that was impossible. But her mind was made up—she would run any risk, meet any danger, in order to discover the meaning of all this.

Next morning she returned by an omnibus service which would allow her to reach the cottage at about a quarter-past eleven. She chose this time for two reasons: first, because breakfast was sent in from the restaurant at eleven, and the two gentlemen would certainly be in the *salle à manger* over that meal; and, next, because the doctor always visited his patient after breakfast. She could, therefore, hope to get in unseen, which was the first thing.

The spare bedroom—that assigned to the patient—was on the ground-floor next to the dining-room; it communicated with the garden by French windows, and by a small flight of steps.

Fanny walked cautiously along the road past the garden-gate; a rapid glance assured her that no one was there; she hastily opened the gate and slipped in. She knew that the windows of the sick-room were closed on the inner side, and the blinds were still down. The patient, therefore, had not yet been disturbed or visited. The windows of the dining-room were on the other side of the house. The woman therefore slipped round to the back, where she found, as she expected, the door wide open. In the hall she heard the voices of the doctor and Lord Harry and the clicking of knives and forks. They were at breakfast.

One thing more—What should she say to Oxbye? What excuse should she make for coming back? How should she persuade him to keep silence about her presence? His passion suggested a plan and a reason. She had come back, she would tell him, for love of him, to watch over him, unseen by the doctor, to go away with him when he was strong enough to travel. He was a simple and a candid soul, and he would fall into such a little innocent conspiracy. Meantime, it would be quite easy for her to remain in the house perfectly undisturbed and unknown to either of the gentlemen.

She opened the door and looked in.

So far, no reason would be wanted. The patient was sleeping peacefully. But not in the bed. He was lying, partly dressed and covered with a blanket, on the sofa. With the restlessness of convalescence he had changed his couch in the morning after a wakeful night, and was now sleeping far into the morning.

The bed, as is common in French houses, stood in an alcove. A heavy curtain hung over a rod, also in the French manner. Part of this curtain lay over the head of the bed.

The woman perceived the possibility of using the curtain as a means of concealment. There was a space of a foot between the bed and the wall. She placed herself, therefore, behind the bed, in this space, at the head, where the curtain entirely concealed her. Nothing was more unlikely than that the doctor should look behind the bed in that corner. Then with her scissors she pierced a hole in the curtain large enough for her to see perfectly without the least danger of being seen, and she waited to see what would happen.

She waited for half an hour, during which the sleeping man slept on without movement, and the voices of the two men in the *salle à manger* rose and fell in conversation. Presently there was silence, broken only by an occasional remark. 'They have lit their cigars,' Fanny murmured; 'they will take their coffee, and in a few minutes they will be here.'

When they came in a few minutes later, they had their cigars, and Lord Harry's face was slightly flushed, perhaps with the wine he had taken at breakfast—perhaps with the glass of brandy after his coffee.

The doctor threw himself into a chair and crossed his legs, looking thoughtfully at his patient. Lord Harry stood over him.

'Every day,' he said, 'the man gets better.'

'He has got better every day, so far,' said the doctor.

'Every day his face gets fatter, and he grows less like me.'

'It is true,' said the doctor.

'Then—what the devil are we to do?'

'Wait a little longer,' said the doctor.

The woman in her hiding-place hardly dared to breathe.

'What?' asked Lord Harry. 'You mean that the man, after all——'

'Wait a little longer,' the doctor repeated quietly.

'Tell me'—Lord Harry bent over the sick man eagerly—'you think——'

'Look here,' the doctor said. 'Which of us two has had a medical education—you, or I?'

'You, of course.'

'Yes; I, of course. Then I tell you, as a medical man, that appearances are sometimes deceptive. This man, for instance—he looks better; he thinks he is recovering; he feels stronger. You observe that he is fatter in the face. His nurse, Fanny Mere, went away with the knowledge that he was much better, and the conviction that he was about to leave the house as much recovered as such a patient with such a disorder can expect.'

'Well?'

'Well, my lord, allow me to confide in you. Medical men mostly keep their knowledge in such matters to themselves. We know and recognise symptoms which to you are invisible. By these symptoms

—by these symptoms,' he repeated slowly and looking hard at the other man, 'I know that this man—no longer Oxbye, my patient, but—another—is in a highly dangerous condition. I have noted the symptoms in my book'—he tapped his pocket—'for future use.'

'And when—when——' Lord Harry was frightfully pale. His lips moved, but he could not finish the sentence. The Thing he had agreed to was terribly near, and it looked uglier than he had expected.

'Oh! when?' the doctor replied carelessly. 'Perhaps to-day—perhaps in a week. Here, you see, Science is sometimes baffled. I cannot say.'

Lord Harry breathed deeply. 'If the man is in so serious a condition,' he said, 'is it safe or prudent for us to be alone in the house without a servant and without a nurse?'

'I was not born yesterday, my lord, I assure you,' said the doctor in his jocular way. 'They have found me a nurse. She will come to-day. My patient's life is, humanly speaking'—Lord Harry shuddered—'perfectly safe until her arrival.'

'Well—but she is a stranger. She must know whom she is nursing.'

'Certainly. She will be told—I have already told her—that she is going to nurse Lord Harry Norland, a young Irish gentleman. She is a stranger. That is the most valuable quality she possesses. She is a complete stranger. As for you, what are you? Anything you please. An English gentleman staying with me under the melancholy circumstances of his lordship's illness. What more natural? The English doctor is staying with his patient, and the English friend is staying with the doctor. When the insurance officer makes inquiries, as he is very likely to do, the nurse will be invaluable for the evidence she will give.'

He rose, pulled up the blinds noiselessly, and opened the windows. Neither the fresh air nor the light awoke the sleeping man.

Vimpany looked at his watch. 'Time for the medicine,' he said. 'Wake him up while I get it ready.'

'Would you not—at least—suffer him to have his sleep out?' asked Lord Harry, again turning pale.

'Wake him up. Shake him by the shoulder. Do as I tell you,' said the doctor, roughly. 'He will go to sleep again. It is one of the finer qualities of my medicine that it sends people to sleep. It is a most soothing medicine. It causes a deep—a profound sleep. Wake him up, I say.' He went to the cupboard in which the medicines were kept. Lord Harry with some difficulty roused the sick man, who awoke dull and heavy, asking why he was disturbed.

'Time for your medicine, my good fellow,' said the doctor. 'Take it, and you shall not be disturbed again—I promise you that.'

The door of the cupboard prevented the spy from seeing what the doctor was doing; but he took longer than usual in filling the glass. Lord Harry seemed to observe this, for he left the Dane and looked over the doctor's shoulder. 'What are you doing?' he asked in a whisper.

'Better not inquire, my lord,' said the doctor. 'What do you know about the mysteries of medicine?'

'Why must I not inquire?'

Vimpany turned, closing the cupboard behind him. In his hand was a glass full of the stuff he was about to administer.

'If you look in the glass,' he said, 'you will understand why.'

Lord Harry obeyed. He saw a face ghastly in pallor: he shrank back and fell into a chair, saying no more.

'Now, my good friend,' said the doctor, 'drink this and you'll be better—ever so much better, ever so much better. Why—that is brave——' He looked at him strangely, 'How do you like the medicine?'

Oxbye shook his head as a man who has taken something nauseous. 'I don't like it at all,' he said. 'It doesn't taste like the other physic.'

'No; I have been changing it—improving it.'

The Dane shook his head again. 'There's a pain in my throat,' he said; 'it stings—it burns!'

'Patience—patience. It will pass away directly, and you will lie down again and fall asleep comfortably.'

Oxbye sank back upon the sofa. His eyes closed. Then he opened them again, looking about him strangely, as one who is suffering some new experience. Again he shook his head, again he closed his eyes, and he opened them no more. He was asleep.

The doctor stood at his head watching gravely. Lord Harry, in his chair, leaned forward, also watching, but with white face and trembling hands.

As they watched, the man's head rolled a little to the side, turning his face more towards the room. Then a curious and terrifying thing happened. His mouth began slowly to fall open.

'Is he—is he—is he fainting?' Lord Harry whispered.

'No; he is asleep. Did you never see a man sleep with his mouth wide open?'

They were silent for a space.

The doctor broke the silence.

'There's a good light this morning,' he said carelessly. 'I think I will try a photograph. Stop! Let me tie up his mouth with a handkerchief—so.' The patient was not disturbed by the operation, though the doctor tied up the handkerchief with vigour enough to awaken a sound sleeper. 'Now—we'll see if he looks like a post-mortem portrait.'

He went into the next room, and returned with his camera. In a few minutes he had taken the picture, and was holding the glass negative against the dark sleeve of his coat, so as to make it visible. 'We shall see how it looks,' he said, 'when it is printed. At present I don't think it is good enough as an imitation of you to be sent to the insurance offices. Nobody, I am afraid, who knew you, would

ever take this for a post-mortem portrait of Lord Harry. Well, we
shall see. Perhaps by-and-by—to-morrow—we may be able to take
a better photograph. Eh?' Lord Harry followed his movements,
watching him closely, but said nothing. His face remained pale
and his fingers still trembled. There was now no doubt at all in
his mind, not only as to Vimpany's intentions, but as to the crime
itself. He dared not speak or move.

A ring at the door pealed through the house. Lord Harry started
in his chair with a cry of terror.

'That,' said the doctor, quietly, 'is the nurse—the new nurse—
the stranger.' He took off the handkerchief from Oxbye's face,
looked about the room as if careful that everything should be in its
right place, and went out to admit the woman. Lord Harry sprang
to his feet and passed his hand over the sick man's face.

'Is it done?' he whispered. 'Can the man be poisoned? Is he
already dead?—already? Before my eyes?'

He laid his finger on the sick man's pulse. But the doctor's
step and voice stopped him. Then the nurse came in, following
Vimpany. She was an elderly, quiet-looking French woman.

Lord Harry remained standing at the side of the sofa, hoping to
see the man revive.

'Now,' said Vimpany, cheerfully, 'here is your patient, nurse.
He is asleep now. Let him have his sleep out—he has taken his
medicine and will want nothing more yet awhile. If you want anything let me know. We shall be in the next room or in the garden
—somewhere about the house. Come, my friend.' He drew away
Lord Harry gently by the arm, and they left the room.

Behind the curtain Fanny Mere began to wonder how she was
to get off unseen.

The nurse, left alone, looked at her patient, who lay with his
head turned partly round, his eyes closed, his mouth open. 'A
strange sleep,' she murmured; 'but the doctor knows, I suppose.
He is to have his sleep out.'

'A strange sleep, indeed!' thought the watcher. She was
tempted at this moment to disclose herself and to reveal what she
had seen; but the thought of Lord Harry's complicity stopped her.
With what face could she return to her mistress and tell her that
she herself was the means of her husband being charged with
murder? She stayed herself, therefore, and waited.

Chance helped her, at last, to escape.

The nurse took off her bonnet and shawl and began to look
about the room. She stepped to the bed and examined the sheets
and pillow-case as a good French housewife should. Would she
throw back the curtain? If so—what would happen next? Then
it would become necessary to take the new nurse into confidence,
otherwise—— Fanny did not put the remainder of this sentence
into words. It remained a terror: it meant that if Vimpany found
out where she had been and what she had seen and heard, there
would be two, instead of one, cast into a deep slumber.

The nurse turned from the bed, however, attracted by the half-open door of the cupboard. Here were the medicine bottles. She took them out one by one, looked at them with professional curiosity, pulled out the corks, smelt the contents, replaced the bottles. Then she went to the window, which stood open, she stepped out upon the stone steps which led into the garden, looking about her, to breathe the soft air of noon among the flowers.

She came back, and it again seemed as if she would examine the bed, but her attention was attracted by a small book-case. She began to pull down the books one after the other and to turn them over, as a half-educated person does, in the hope of finding something amusing. She found a book with pictures. Then she sat down in the armchair beside the sofa and began to turn over the leaves slowly. How long was this going to last?

It lasted about half an hour. The nurse laid down the volume with a yawn, stretched herself, yawned again, crossed her hands, and closed her eyes. She was going to sleep. If she would only fall so fast asleep that the woman behind the curtain could creep away!

But sometimes at the sleepiest moment sleep is driven away by an accident. The accident in this case was that the nurse before finally dropping off remembered that she was nursing a sick man, and sat up to look at him before she allowed herself to drop off.

Stung with sudden inspiration she sprang to her feet and bent over the man. 'Does he breathe?' she asked. She bent lower. 'His pulse! does it beat?' she caught his wrist.

'Doctor!' she shrieked, running into the garden. 'Doctor! Come—come quick! He is dead!'

Fanny Mere stepped from her hiding-place and ran out of the back door, and by the garden gate into the road.

She had escaped. She had seen the crime committed. She knew now at least what was intended and why she was sent away. The motive for the crime she could not guess.

CHAPTER LI

WHAT NEXT?

HAT should she do with the terrible secret?

She ought to inform the police. But there were two objections. First, the nurse may have been mistaken in supposing her patient to be dead. She herself had no choice but to escape as she did. Next, the dreadful thought occurred to her that she herself until the previous day had been the man's nurse—his only nurse, day and night. What was to prevent the doctor from fixing the guilt of poisoning upon herself? Nay; it would be his most obvious line of action. The man was left alone all the morning; the day before he had shown every sign of returning strength; she would have to confess that she was in hiding. How long had she been there? Why was she in hiding? Was it not after she had poisoned the man and when she heard the doctor's footstep? Naturally ignorant of poisons and their symptoms, it seemed to her as if these facts so put together would be conclusive against her. Therefore, she determined to keep quiet in Paris that day and to cross over by the night boat from Dieppe in the evening. She would at first disclose everything to Mrs. Vimpany and to Mountjoy. As to what she would tell her mistress she would be guided by the advice of the others.

She got to London in safety and drove straight to Mr. Mountjoy's hotel, proposing first to communicate the whole business to him. But she found in his sitting-room Mrs. Vimpany herself.

'We must not awake him,' she said, 'whatever news you bring. His perfect recovery depends entirely on rest and quiet. There'—she pointed to the chimneypiece—'is a letter in my lady's handwriting. I am afraid I know only too well what it tells him.'

'What does it tell?'

'This very morning,' Mrs. Vimpany went on, 'I called at her lodging. She has gone away.'

'Gone away? My lady gone away? Where is she gone?'

'Where do you think she is most likely to have gone?'

'Not?—oh!—not to her husband? Not to him!—oh! this is more terrible—far more terrible—than you can imagine.'

'You will tell me why it is now so much more terrible. Meantime, I find that the cabman was told to drive to Victoria. That is all I know. I have no doubt, however, but that she has gone back to her husband. She has been in a disturbed, despondent condition ever since she arrived in London. Mr. Mountjoy has been as kind as usual: but he has not been able to chase away her sadness. Whether she was fretting after her husband, or whether—but this I hardly think—she was comparing the man she had lost with the man she had taken—but I do not know. All I do know is that she has been uneasy ever since she came from France, and what I believe is that she has been reproaching herself with leaving her husband without good cause.'

'Good cause!' echoed Fanny. 'Oh! good gracious! If she only knew, there's cause enough to leave a hundred husbands.'

'Nothing seemed to rouse her,' Mrs. Vimpany continued, without regarding the interruption. 'I went with her to the farm to see her former maid, Rhoda. The girl's health is re-established; she is engaged to marry the farmer's brother. Lady Harry was kind, and said the most pleasant things; she even pulled off one of her prettiest rings and gave it to the girl. But I could see that it was an effort for her to appear interested—her thoughts were with her husband all the time. I was sure it would end in this way, and I am not in the least surprised. But what will Mr. Mountjoy say when he opens the letter?'

'Back to her husband!' Fanny repeated. 'Oh! what shall we do?

'Tell me what you mean. What has happened?'

'I must tell you. I thought I would tell Mr. Mountjoy first: but I must tell you, although——' She stopped.

'Although it concerns my husband. Never mind that consideration—go on.' Fanny told the story from the beginning.

When she had finished, Mrs. Vimpany looked towards the bedroom door. 'Thank God!' she said, 'that you told this story to me instead of to Mr. Mountjoy. At all events, it gives me time to warn you not to tell him what you have told me. We can do nothing. Meantime, there is one thing you must do—go away. Do not let Mr. Mountjoy find you here. He must not learn your story. If he hears what has happened and reads her letter, nothing will keep him from following her to Passy. He will see that there is every prospect of her being entangled in this vile conspiracy, and he will run any risk in the useless attempt to save her. He is too weak to bear the journey—far too weak for the violent emotions that will follow; and, oh! how much too weak to cope with my husband—as strong and as crafty as he is unprincipled!'

'Then, what, in Heaven's name, are we to do?'

'Anything—anything—rather than suffer Mr. Mountjoy, in his weak state, to interfere between man and wife.'

'Yes—yes—but such a man! Mrs. Vimpany, he was present when the Dane was poisoned. He *knew* that the man was poisoned. He sat in the chair, his face white, and he said nothing. Oh! It was as much as I could do not to rush out and dash the glass from his hands. Lord Harry said nothing.'

'My dear, do you not understand what you have got to do?'

Fanny made no reply.

'Consider—my husband—Lord Harry—neither of them knows that you were present. You can return with the greatest safety; and then whatever happens, you will be at hand to protect my lady. Consider, again, as her maid, you can be with her always—in hei own room; at night; everywhere and at all times; while Mr. Mountjoy could only be with her now and then, and at the price of not quarrelling with her husband.'

'Yes, said Fanny.

'And you are strong, and Mr. Mountjoy is weak and ill.'

'You think that I should go back to Passy?'

'At once, without the delay of an hour. Lady Harry started last night. Do you start this evening. She will thus have you with her twenty-four hours after her arrival.'

Fanny rose.

'I will go,' she said. 'It terrifies me even to think of going back to that awful cottage with that dreadful man. Yet I will go. Mrs. Vimpany, I know that it will be of no use. Whatever is going to happen now will happen without any power of mine to advance or to prevent. I am certain that my journey will prove useless. But I will go. Yes, I will go this evening.'

Then, with a final promise to write as soon as possible—as soon as there should be anything to communicate—Fanny went away.

Mrs. Vimpany, alone, listened. From the bedroom came no sound at all. Mr. Mountjoy slept still. When he should be strong enough it would be time to let him know what had been done. But she sat thinking—thinking—even when one has the worst husband in the world, and very well knows his character, it is disagreeable to hear such a story as Fanny had told that wife this morning.

CHAPTER LII

THE DEAD MAN'S PHOTOGRAPH

'HE is quite dead,' said the doctor, with one finger on the man's pulse and another lifting his eyelid. 'He is dead. I did not look for so speedy an end. It is not half an hour since I left him breathing peacefully. Did he show signs of consciousness?'

'No, sir; I found him dead.'

'This morning he was cheerful. It is not unusual in these complaints. I have observed it in many cases of my own experience. On the last morning of life, at the very moment when Death is standing on the threshold with uplifted dart, the patient is cheerful and even joyous : he is more hopeful than he has felt for many months : he thinks—nay, he is sure— that he is recovering : he says he shall be up and about before long : he has not felt so strong since the beginning of his illness. Then Death strikes him, and he falls.' He made this remark in a most impressive manner.

'Nothing remains,' he said, 'but to certify the cause of death and to satisfy the proper forms and authorities. I charge myself with this duty. The unfortunate young man belonged to a highly distinguished family. I will communicate with his friends and forward his papers. One last office I can do for him. For the sake of his family, nurse, I will take a last photograph of him as he lies upon his death-bed.' Lord Harry stood in the doorway, listening with an aching and a fearful heart. He dared not enter the chamber. It was the Chamber of Death. What was his own part in calling the Destroying Angel who is at the beck and summons of every man—even the meanest? Call him and he comes. Order him to strike—and he obeys. But under penalties.

The doctor's prophecy, then, had come true. But in what way and by what agency? The man was dead. What was his own share in the man's death? He knew when the Dane was brought into the house that he was brought there to die. As the man did not die, but began to recover fast, he had seen in the doctor's face that the man would have to die. He had heard the doctor prophesy out of his medical knowledge that the man would surely die; and then, after the nurse had been sent away because her patient required her services no longer, he had seen the doctor give the medicine which burned the patient's throat. What was that medicine? Not only had it burned his throat, but it caused him to fall into a deep sleep, in which his heart ceased to beat and his blood ceased to flow.

He turned away and walked out of the cottage. For an hour he walked along the road. Then he stopped and walked back. Ropes drew him; he could no longer keep away. He felt as if something must have happened. Possibly he would find the doctor arrested and the police waiting for himself, to be charged as an accomplice or a principal.

He found no such thing. The doctor was in the salon, with letters and official forms before him. He looked up cheerfully.

'My English friend,' he said, ' the unexpected end of this young Irish gentleman is a very melancholy affair. I have ascertained the name of the family solicitors and have written to them. I have also written to his brother as the head of the house. I find also, by examination of his papers, that his life is insured—the amount is not stated, but I have communicated the fact of the death. The authorities—they are, very properly, careful in such matters—have received the necessary notices and forms : to-morrow, all legal forms having been gone through, we bury the deceased.'

' So soon ? '

' So soon ? In these cases of advanced pulmonary disease the sooner the better. The French custom of speedy interment may be defended as more wholesome than our own. On the other hand, I admit that it has its weak points. Cremation is, perhaps, the best and only method of removing the dead which is open to no objections except one. I mean, of course, the chance that the deceased may have met with his death by means of poison. But such cases are rare, and, in most instances, would be detected by the medical man in attendance before or at the time of death. I think we need not—— My dear friend, you look ill. Are you upset by such a simple thing as the death of a sick man ? Let me prescribe for you. A glass of brandy neat. So,' he went into the *salle à manger* and returned with his medicine. ' Take that. Now let us talk.' The doctor continued his conversation in a cheerfully scientific strain, never alluding to the conspiracy or to the consequences which might follow. He told hospital stories bearing on deaths sudden and unexpected; some of them he treated in a jocular vein. The dead man in the next room was a Case: he knew of many similar and equally interesting Cases. When one has arrived at looking upon a dead man as a Case, there is little fear of the ordinary human weakness which makes us tremble in the awful presence of death.

Presently steps were heard outside. The doctor rose and left the room—but returned in a few minutes.

'The *croque-morts* have come,' he said. ' They are with the nurse engaged upon their business. It seems revolting to the outside world. To them it is nothing but the daily routine of work. By-the-way, I took a photograph of his lordship in the presence of the nurse. Unfortunately—but look at it——'

'It is the face of the dead man'—Lord Harry turned away. 'I don't want to see it. I cannot bear to see it. You forget—I was actually present when——'

'Not when he died. Come, don't be a fool. What I was going to say was this: The face is no longer in the least like you. Nobody who ever saw you once even would believe that this is your face. The creature—he has given us an unconscionable quantity of trouble—was a little like you when he first came. I was wrong in supposing that this likeness was permanent. Now he is dead, he is not in the least like you. I ought to have remembered that the resemblance would fade away and disappear in death. Come and look at him.'

'No, no.'

'Weakness! Death restores to every man his individuality. No two men are like in death, though they may be like in life. Well. It comes to this. We are going to bury Lord Harry Norland to-morrow, and we must have a photograph of him as he lay on his deathbed.'

'Well?'

'Well, my friend, go upstairs to your own room, and I will follow with the camera.'

In a quarter of an hour he was holding the glass against his sleeve.

'Admirable!' he said. 'The cheek a little sunken—that was the effect of the chalk and the adjustment of the shadows—the eyes closed, the face white, the hands composed. It is admirable! Who says that we cannot make the sun tell lies?'

As soon as he could get a print of the portrait, he gave it to Lord Harry.

'There,' he said, 'we shall get a better print to-morrow. This is the first copy.'

He had mounted it on a frame of card, and had written under it the name once borne by the dead man, with the date of his death. The picture seemed indeed that of a dead man. Lord Harry shuddered.

'There,' he said, 'everything else has been of no use to us—the presence of the sick man—the suspicions of the nurse—his death—even his death—has been of no use to us. We might have been spared the memory—the awful memory—of this death!'

'You forget, my English friend, that a dead body was necessary for us. We had to bury somebody. Why not the man Oxbye?'

CHAPTER LIII

THE WIFE'S RETURN

F course Mrs. Vimpany was quite right. Iris had gone back to her husband. She arrived, in fact, at the cottage in the evening just before dark—in the falling day, when some people are more than commonly sensitive to sights and sounds, and when the eyes are more apt than at other times to be deceived by strange appearances. Iris walked into the garden, finding no one there. She opened the door with her own key and let herself in. The house struck her as strangely empty and silent. She opened the dining-room door: no one was there. Like all French dining-rooms, it was used for no other purpose than for eating, and furnished with little more than the barest necessaries. She closed the door and opened that of the salon: that also was empty. She called her husband: there was no answer. She called the name of the cook: there was no answer. It was fortunate that she did not open the door of the spare room, for there lay the body of the dead man. She went upstairs to her husband's room. That too was empty. But there was something lying on the table—a photograph. She took it up. Her face became white suddenly and swiftly. She shrieked aloud, then dropped the picture and fell fainting to the ground. For the photograph was nothing less than that of her husband, dead in his white grave-clothes, his hands composed, his eyes closed, his cheek waxen.

The cry fell upon the ears of Lord Harry, who was in the garden below. He rushed into the house and lifted his wife upon the bed. The photograph showed him plainly what had happened.

She came to her senses again, but seeing her husband alive before her, and remembering what she had seen, she shrieked again, and fell into another swoon.

'What is to be done now?' asked the husband. 'What shall I tell her? How shall I make her understand? What can I do for her?'

As for help, there was none: the nurse was gone on some errand; the doctor was arranging for the funeral of Oxbye under the name of Lord Harry Norland; the cottage was empty.

Such a fainting fit does not last for ever. Iris came round, and sat up, looking wildly around.

'What is it?' she cried. 'What does it mean?'

'It means, my love, that you have returned to your husband.'
He laid an arm round her, and kissed her again and again.

'You are my Harry!—living!—my own Harry?'

'Your own Harry, my darling. What else should I be?'

'Tell me then, what does it mean—that picture—that horrid
photograph?'

'That means nothing—nothing—a freak—a joke of the doctor's.
What could it mean?' He took it up. 'Why, my dear, I am
living—living and well. What should this mean but a joke?'

He laid it on the table again, face downwards. But her eyes
showed that she was not satisfied. Men do not make jokes on death:
it is a sorry jest indeed to dress up a man in grave-clothes, and
make a photograph of him as of one dead.

'But you—you, my Iris; you are here—tell me how and why
—and when, and everything? Never mind that stupid picture:
tell me.'

'I got your letter, Harry,' she replied.

'My letter?' he repeated. 'Oh! my dear, you got my letter,
and you saw that your husband loved you still.'

'I could not keep away from you, Harry, whatever had happened. I stayed as long as I could. I thought about you day and
night. And at last I—I—I came back. Are you angry with me,
Harry?'

'Angry? Good God! my dearest, angry?' He kissed her
passionately—not the less passionately that she had returned at a
time so terrible. What was he to say to her? How was he to tell
her? While he showered kisses on her he was asking himself
these questions. When she found out—when he should confess to
her the whole truth—she would leave him again. Yet he did not
understand the nature of the woman who loves. He held her in
his arms; his kisses pleaded for him; they mastered her—she was
ready to believe, to accept, to surrender even her truth and honesty;
and she was ready, though she knew it not, to become the accomplice of a crime. Rather than leave her husband again, she would
do everything.

Yet, Lord Harry felt there was one reservation: he might
confess everything, except the murder of the Dane. No word of
confession had passed the doctor's lips, yet he knew too well that
the man had been murdered; and, so far as the man had been
chosen for his resemblance to himself, that was perfectly useless,
because the resemblance, though striking at the first, had been
gradually disappearing as the man Oxbye grew better; and was
now, as we have seen, wholly lost after death.

'I have a great deal—a great deal—to tell you, dear,' said the
husband, holding both her hands tenderly. 'You will have to be
very patient with me. You must make up your mind to be shocked
at first, though I shall be able to convince you that there was
really nothing else to be done—nothing else at all.'

'Oh! go on, Harry. Tell me all. Hide nothing.'

' I will tell you all,' he replied.

' First, where is that poor man whom the doctor brought here and Fanny nursed ? And where is Fanny ? '

' The poor man,' he replied carelessly, ' made so rapid a recovery that he has got on his legs and gone away—I believe, to report himself to the hospital whence he came. It is a great triumph for the doctor, whose new treatment is now proved to be successful. He will make a grand flourish of trumpets about it. I dare say, it all he claims for it is true, he has taken a great step in the treatment of lung diseases.'

Iris had no disease of the lungs, and consequently cared very little for the scientific aspect of the question.

' Where is my maid, then ? '

' Fanny ? She went away—let me see : to-day is Friday—on Wednesday morning. It was no use keeping her here. The man was well, and she was anxious to get back to you. So she started on Wednesday morning, proposing to take the night boat from Dieppe. She must have stopped somewhere on the way.'

' I suppose she will go to see Mrs. Vimpany. I will send her a line there.'

' Certainly. That will be sure to find her.'

' Well, Harry, is there anything else to tell me ? '

' A great deal,' he repeated. ' That photograph, Iris, which frightened you so much, has been very carefully taken by Vimpany for a certain reason.'

' What reason ? '

' There are occasions,' he replied, ' when the very best thing that can happen to a man is the belief that he is dead. Such a juncture of affairs has happened to myself—and to you—at this moment. It is convenient—even necessary—for me that the world should believe me dead. In point of fact, I must be dead henceforth. Not for anything that I have done, or that I am afraid of—don't think that. No ; it is for the simple reason that I have no longer any money or any resources whatever. That is why I must be dead. Had you not returned in this unexpected manner, my dear, you would have heard of my death from the doctor, and he would have left it to chance to find a convenient opportunity of letting you know the truth. I am, however, deeply grieved that I was so careless as to leave that photograph upon the table.'

' I do not understand,' she said. ' You pretend to be dead ? '

' Yes. I *must* have money. I have some left—a very little. I *must* have money ; and, in order to get it, I must be dead.'

' How will that help ? '

' Why, my dear, I am insured, and my insurances will be paid after my death ; but not before.'

' Oh ! must you get money—even by a——' She hesitated.

' Call it a conspiracy, my dear, if you please. As there is no other way whatever left, I must get money that way.'

' Oh, this is dreadful ! A conspiracy, Harry ? a—a—fraud ? '

'If you please. That is the name which lawyers give to it.'

'But oh, Harry!—it is a crime. It is a thing for which men are tried and found guilty and sentenced.'

'Certainly; if they are found out. Meantime, it is only the poor, ignorant, clumsy fool who gets found out. In the City these things are done every day. Quite as a matter of course,' he added carelessly. 'It is not usual for men to take their wives into confidence, but in this case I must take you into confidence: I have no choice, as you will understand directly.'

'Tell me, Harry, who first thought of this way?'

'Vimpany, of course. Oh! give him the credit where real cleverness is concerned. Vimpany suggested the thing. He found me well-nigh as desperately hard up as he is himself. He suggested it. At first, I confess, I did not like it. I refused to listen to any more talk about it. But, you see, when one meets destitution face to face, one will do anything—everything. Besides, as I will show you, this is not really a fraud. It is only an anticipation of a few years. However, there was another reason.'

'Was it to find the money to meet the promissory note?'

'My dear, you may forget—you may resolve never to throw the thing in my teeth; but my love for you will never suffer me to forget that I have lost your little fortune in a doubtful speculation. It is all gone, never to be recovered again; and this after I had sworn never to touch a farthing of it. Iris!'—he started to his feet and walked about the room as one who is agitated by emotion—'Iris! I could face imprisonment for debt, I could submit to pecuniary ruin, for that matter; the loss of money would not cause me the least trouble, but I cannot endure to have ruined you.'

'Oh! Harry, as if I mind. Everything that I have is yours. When I gave you myself I gave all. Take—use—lose it all. As you think, I should never *feel* reproach, far less utter a word of blame. Dearest Harry, if that is all——'

'No; it is the knowledge that you will not even feel reproach that is my constant accuser. At my death you will get all back again. But I am not old; I may live for many, many years to come. How can I wait for my own death when I can repair this wickedness by a single stroke?'

'But by another wickedness—and worse.'

'No—not another crime. Remember that this money is mine. It will come to my heirs some day, as surely as to-morrow's sun will rise. Sooner or later it will be mine; I will make it sooner, that is all. The Insurance Company will lose nothing but the paltry interest for the remainder of my life. My dear, if it is disgraceful to do this I will endure disgrace. It is easier to bear than the constant self-reproach which I feel when I think of you and of the losses I have inflicted upon you.'

Again he folded her in his arms; he knelt before her; he wept over her. Carried out of herself by this passion, Iris made no more resistance.

'Is it—is it,' she asked timidly, ' too late to draw back ? '

'It is too late,' he replied, thinking of the dead man below. 'It is too late. All is completed.'

' My poor Harry! What shall we do ? How shall we live ? How shall we contrive never to be found out ? '

She would not leave him, then. She accepted the situation. He was amazed at the readiness with which she fell; but he did not understand how she was ready to cling to him, for better for worse, through worse evils than this; nor could he understand how things formerly impossible to her had been rendered possible by the subtle deterioration of the moral nature, when a woman of lofty mind at the beginning loves and is united to a man of lower nature and coarser fibre than herself. Only a few months before, Iris would have swept aside these sophistries with swift and reso-lute hand. Now she accepted them.

' You have fallen into the doctor's hands, dear,' she said. ' Pray Heaven it brings us not into worse evils ! What can I say ? It is through love of your wife—through love of your wife—oh ! hus-band ! ' she threw herself into his arms, and forgave everything and accepted everything. Henceforth she would be—though this she knew not—the willing instrument of the two conspirators.

CHAPTER LIV

ANOTHER STEP

'HAVE left this terrible thing about once too often already,' and Lord Harry took it from the table. ' Let me put it in a place of safety.'

He unlocked a drawer and opened it. ' I will put it here,' he said. ' Why '—as if suddenly recollecting something— ' here is my will. I shall be leaving that about on the table next. Iris, my dear, I have left everything to you. All will be yours.' He took out the document. ' Keep it for me, Iris. It is yours. You may as well have it now, and then I know, in your careful hands, it will be quite safe. Not only is everything left to you, but you are the sole executrix.'

Iris took the will without a word. She understood, now, what it meant. If she was the sole executrix she would have to act. If everything was left to her she would have to receive the money. Thus, at a single step, she became not only cognisant of the con-spiracy, but the chief agent and instrument to carry it out.

This done, her husband had only to tell her what had to be done at once, in consequence of her premature arrival. He had planned, he told her, not to send for her—not to let her know or suspect anything of the truth until the money had been paid to the widow by the Insurance Company. As things had turned out, it would be best for both of them to leave Passy at once—that very evening—before her arrival was known by anybody, and to let Vimpany carry out the rest of the business. He was quite to be trusted—he would do everything that was wanted. ' Already,' he said, ' the Office will have received from the doctor a notification of my death. Yesterday evening he wrote to everybody—to my brother—confound him !—and to the family solicitor. Every moment that I stay here increases the danger of my being seen and recognised—after the Office has been informed that I am dead.'

' Where are we to go ? '

' I have thought of that. There is a little quiet town in Belgium where no English people ever come at all. We will go there, then we will take another name ; we will be buried to the outer world, and will live, for the rest of our lives, for ourselves alone. Do you agree ? '

' I will do, Harry, whatever you think best.'

' It will be for a time only. When all is ready, you will have to step to the front—the will in your hand to be proved—to receive what is due to you as the widow of Lord Harry Norland. You will go back to Belgium, after awhile, so as to disarm suspicion, to become once more the wife of William Linville.'

Iris sighed heavily, Then she caught her husband's eyes gathering with doubt, and she smiled again.

'In everything, Harry,' she said, 'I am your servant. When shall we start ? '

'Immediately. I have only to write a letter to the doctor. Where is your bag ? Is this all ? Let me go first to see that no one is about. Have you got the will ? Oh ! it is here—yes—in the bag. I will bring along the bag.'

He ran downstairs, and came up quickly.

'The nurse has returned,' he said. 'She is in the spare room.'

'What nurse ? '

'The nurse who came after Fanny left. The man was better, but the doctor thought it wisest to have a nurse to the end,' he explained hurriedly, and she suspected nothing till afterwards. 'Come down quietly—go out by the back-door—she will not see you.' So Iris obeyed. She went out of her own house like a thief, or like her own maid Fanny, had she known. She passed through the garden, and out of the garden into the road. There she waited for her husband.

Lord Harry sat down and wrote a letter.

' Dear Doctor,' he said, ' while you are arranging things outside an unexpected event has happened inside. Nothing happens but the unexpected. My wife has come back. It is the most unexpected event of any. Anything else might have happened. Most fortunately she has not seen the spare bedroom, and has no idea of its contents.

' At this point reassure yourself.

' My wife has gone.

' She found on the table your first print of the negative. The sight of this before she saw me threw her into some kind of swoon, from which, however, she recovered.

' I have explained things to a certain point. She understands that Lord Harry Norland is deceased. She does not understand that it was necessary to have a funeral ; there is no necessity to tell her of that. I think she understands that she must not seem to have been here. Therefore she goes away immediately.

' The nurse has not seen her. No one has seen her.

' She understands, further, that as the widow, heir, and executrix of Lord Harry she will have to prove his will, and to receive the money due to him by the Insurance Company. She will do this out of love for her husband. I think that the persuasive powers of a certain person have never yet been estimated at their true value.

' Considering the vital importance of getting her out of the place before she can learn anything of the spare bedroom, and of getting me out of the place before any messenger can arrive from the London office, I think you will agree with me that I am right in leaving Passy—and Paris—with Lady Harry this very afternoon.

'You may write to William Linville, Poste-Restante, Louvain, Belgium. I am sure I can trust you to destroy this letter.

'Louvain is a quiet, out-of-the-way place, where one can live quite separated from all old friends, and very cheaply.

'Considering the small amount of money that I have left, I rely upon you to exercise the greatest economy. I do not know how long it may be before just claims are paid up—perhaps in two months—perhaps in six—but until things are settled there will be tightness.

'At the same time it will not be difficult, as soon as Lady Harry goes to London, to obtain some kind of advance from the family solicitor on the strength of the insurance due to her from her late husband.

'I am sorry, dear doctor, to leave you alone over the obsequies of this unfortunate gentleman. You will also have, I hear, a good deal of correspondence with his family. You may, possibly, have to see them in England. All this you will do, and do very well. Your bill for medical attendance you will do well to send in to the widow.

'One word more. Fanny Mere, the maid, has gone to London; but she has not seen Lady Harry. As soon as she hears that her mistress has left London she will be back to Passy. She may come at any moment. I think if I were you I would meet her at the garden gate and send her on. It would be inconvenient if she were to arrive before the funeral.

'My dear doctor, I rely on your sense, your prudence, and your capability.—Yours very sincerely,

'Your English Friend.'

He read this letter very carefully. Nothing in it he thought the least dangerous, and yet something suggested danger. However, he left it; he was obliged to caution and warn the doctor, and he was obliged to get his wife away as quietly as possible.

This done, he packed up his things and hurried off to the station, and Passy saw him no more.

The next day the mortal remains of Lord Harry Norland were lowered into the grave.

CHAPTER LV

THE ADVENTURES OF A FAITHFUL MAID

T was about five o'clock on Saturday afternoon. The funeral was over. The unfortunate young Irish gentleman was now lying in the cemetery of Auteuil in a grave purchased in perpetuity. His name, age, and rank were duly inscribed in the registers, and the cause of his death was vouched for by the English physician who had attended him at the request of his family. He was accompanied, in going through the formalities, by the respectable woman who had nursed the sick man during his last seizure. Everything was perfectly in order. The physician was the only mourner at the funeral. No one was curious about the little procession. A funeral, more or less, excites no attention.

The funeral completed, the doctor gave orders for a simple monument to be put in memory of Lord Harry Norland, thus prematurely cut off. He then returned to the cottage, paid and dismissed the nurse, taking her address in case he should find an opportunity, as he hoped, to recommend her among his numerous and distinguished *clientèle*, and proceeded to occupy himself in setting everything in order before giving over the key to the landlord. First of all he removed the medicine bottles from the cupboard with great care, leaving nothing. Most of the bottles he threw outside into the dust-hole ; one or two he placed in a fire which he made for the purpose in the kitchen: they were shortly reduced to two or three lumps of molten glass. These contained, no doubt, the mysteries and secrets of Science. Then he went into every room and searched in every possible place for any letters or papers which might have been left about. Letters left about are always indiscreet, and the consequences of an indiscretion may be far-reaching and incalculable. Satisfied at last that the place was perfectly cleared, he sat down in the salon and continued his business correspondence with the noble family and the solicitors. Thus engaged, he heard footsteps outside, footsteps on the gravel, footsteps on the doorstep. He got up, not without the slightest show of nervousness, and opened the door. Lord Harry was right. There stood the woman who had been his first nurse—the woman who overheard and watched —the woman who suspected. The suspicion and the intention of watching were legible in her eyes still. She had come back to renew her watch.

In her hand she carried her box, which she had lugged along from the place where the omnibus had deposited her. She made as if she were stepping in; but the big form of the doctor barred the way.

'Oh!' he said carelessly, 'it is you. Who told you to come back?'

'Is my mistress at home?'

'No; she is not.' He made no movement to let her pass.

'I will come in, please, and wait for her.'

He still stood in the way.

'What time will she return?'

'Have you heard from her?'

'No.'

'Did she leave orders that you were to follow her?'

'No; none that I received. I thought——'

'Servants should never think. They should obey.'

'I know my duty, Dr. Vimpany, without learning it from you. Will you let me pass?'

He withdrew, and she entered.

'Come in, by all means,' he said, 'if you desire my society for a short time. But you will not find your mistress here.'

'Not here! Where is she, then?'

'Had you waited in London for a day or two you would, I dare say, have been informed. As it is, you have had your journey for nothing.'

'Has she not been here?'

'She has not been here.'

'Dr. Vimpany,' said the woman, driven to desperation, 'I don't believe you! I am certain she has been here. What have you done with her?'

'Don't you believe me? That is sad, indeed. But one cannot always help these wanderings. You do not believe me? Melancholy, truly!'

'You may mock as much as you like. Where is she?'

'Where, indeed?'

'She left London to join his lordship. Where is he?'

'I do not know. He who would answer that question would be a wise man indeed.'

'Can I see him?'

'Certainly not. He has gone away. On a long journey. By himself.'

'Then I shall wait for him. Here!' she added with decision. 'In this house!'

'By all means.'

She hesitated. There was an easy look about the doctor which she did not like.

'I believe,' she said, 'that my mistress is in the house. She must be in the house. What are you going to do with her? I believe you have put her somewhere.'

'Indeed!'

'You would do anything! I will go to the police.'

'If you please.'

'Oh! doctor, tell me where she is!'

'You are a faithful servant: it is good, in these days, to find a woman so zealous on account of her mistress. Come in, good and faithful. Search the house all over. Come in—what are you afraid of? Put down your box, and go and look for your mistress.' Fanny obeyed. She ran into the house, opened the doors of the salon and the dining-room one after the other: no one was there. She ran up the stairs and looked into her mistress's room: nothing was there, not even a ribbon or a hair-pin, to show the recent presence of a woman. She looked into Lord Harry's room. Nothing was there. If a woman leaves hair-pins about, a man leaves his toothbrush: nothing at all was there. Then she threw open the armoire in each room: nothing behind the doors. She came downstairs slowly, wondering what it all meant.

'May I look in the spare room?' she asked, expecting to be roughly refused.

'By all means—by all means,' said the doctor, blandly. 'You know your way about. If there is anything left belonging to your mistress or to you, pray take it.'

She tried one more question.

'How is my patient? How is Mr. Oxbye?'

'He is gone.'

'Gone? Where has he gone to? Gone?'

'He went away yesterday—Friday. He was a grateful creature. I wish we had more such grateful creatures as well as more such faithful servants. He said something about finding his way to London in order to thank you properly. A good soul, indeed!'

'Gone?' she repeated. 'Why, on Thursday morning I saw him——' She checked herself in time.

'It was on Wednesday morning that you saw him, and he was then recovering rapidly.'

'But he was far too weak to travel.'

'You may be quite certain that I should not have allowed him to go away unless he was strong enough.'

Fanny made no reply. She had seen with her own eyes the man lying still and white, as if in death; she had seen the new nurse rushing off, crying that he was dead. Now she was told that he was quite well, and that he had gone away! But it was no time for thought.

She was on the point of asking where the new nurse was, but she remembered in time that it was best for her to know nothing, and to awaken no suspicions. She opened the door of the spare room and looked in. Yes; the man was gone—dead or alive—and there were no traces left of his presence. The place was cleared up; the cupboard stood with open doors, empty; the bed was made; the curtain pushed back; the sofa was in its place against the wall;

the window stood open. Nothing in the room at all to show that there had been an occupant only two days before. She stared blankly. The dead man was gone, then. Had her senses altogether deceived her ? Was he not dead, but only sleeping ? Was her horror only a thing of imagination ? Behind her, in the hall, stood the doctor, smiling, cheerful.

She remembered that her first business was to find her mistress. She was not connected with the Dane. She closed the door and returned to the hall.

'Well,' asked the doctor, 'have you made any discoveries ? You see that the house is deserted. You will perhaps learn before long why. Now what will you do ? Will you go back to London ? '

' I must find her ladyship.'

The doctor smiled.

' Had you come here in a different spirit,' he said, ' I would have spared you all this trouble. You come, however, with suspicion written on your face. You have always been suspecting and watching. It may be in a spirit of fidelity to your mistress; but such a spirit is not pleasing to other people, especially when there is not a single person who bears any resentment towards that mistress. Therefore, I have allowed you to run over the empty house, and to satisfy your suspicious soul. Lady Harry is not hidden here. As for Lord Harry—but you will hear in due time—no doubt. And now I don't mind telling you that I have her lady, ship's present address.'

' Oh ! What is it ? '

' She appears to have passed through Paris on her way to Switzerland two days ago, and has sent here her address for the next fortnight. She has now, I suppose, arrived there. The place is Berne ; the Hôtel —— But how do I know that she wants you ? '

' Of course she wants me.'

' Or of course you want her ? Very good. Yours is the responsibility, not mine. Her address is the Hôtel d'Angleterre. Shall I write it down for you ? There it is. " Hôtel d'Angleterre, Berne." Now you will not forget. She will remain there for one fortnight only. After that, I cannot say whither she may go. And, as all her things have been sent away, and as I am going away, I am not likely to hear.'

' Oh ! I must go to her. I must find her ! ' cried the woman earnestly ; 'if it is only to make sure that no evil is intended for her.'

' That is your business. For my own part, I know of no one who can wish her ladyship any evil.'

' Is my lord with her ? '

' I don't know whether that is your business. I have already told you that he is gone. If you join your mistress in Berne, you will very soon find out if he is there as well.' Something in his tone made Fanny look up quickly. But his face revealed nothing. ' What shall you do then ? ' asked the doctor. ' You must make up your mind quickly whether you will go back to England or whether you will go on to Switzerland. You cannot stay here, because I am putting together the last things, and I shall give the landlord the key of the house this evening. All the bills are paid, and I am going to leave the place.'

'I do not understand. There is the patient,' she murmured vaguely. 'What does it mean? I cannot understand.'

'My good creature,' he replied roughly, 'what the devil does it matter to me whether you understand or whether you do not understand? Her ladyship is, as I have told you, at Berne. If you please to follow her there, do so. It is your own affair, not mine. If you prefer to go back to London, do so. Still—your own affair. Is there anything else to say?'

Nothing. Fanny took up her box—this time the doctor did not offer to carry it for her.

'Where are you going?' he asked. 'What have you decided?'

'I can get round by the Chemin de Fer de Ceinture to the Lyons station. I shall take the first cheap train which will take me to Berne.'

'Bon voyage!' said the doctor, cheerfully, and shut the door.

It is a long journey from Paris to Berne even for those who can travel first class and express—that is, if sixteen hours can be called a long journey. For those who have to jog along by third class, stopping at all the little country stations, it is a long and tedious journey indeed. The longest journey ends at last. The train rolled slowly into the station of Berne, and Fanny descended with her box. Her wanderings were over for the present. She would find her mistress and be at rest.

She asked to be directed to the Hôtel d'Angleterre. The Swiss guardian of the peace with the cocked hat stared at her. She repeated the question.

'Hôtel d'Angleterre?' he echoed. 'There is no Hôtel d'Angleterre in Berne.'

'Yes, yes; there is. I am the maid of a lady who is staying at that hotel.'

'No; there is no Hôtel d'Angleterre,' he reported. 'There is the Hôtel Bernehof.'

'No.' She took out the paper and showed it to him—'Lady Harry Norland, Hôtel d'Angleterre, Berne.'

'There is the Hôtel de Belle Vue, the Hôtel du Faucon, the Hôtel Victoria, the Hôtel Schweizerhof. There is the Hôtel Schrödel, the Hôtel Schneider, the Pension Simkin.'

Fanny as yet had no other suspicion than that the doctor had accidentally written a wrong name. Her mistress was at Berne: she would be in one of the hotels. Berne is not a large place. Very good; she would go round to the hotels and inquire. She did so. There are not, in fact, more than half a dozen hotels in Berne where an English lady could possibly stay. Fanny went to every one of these. No one had heard of any such lady: they showed her the lists of their visitors. She inquired at the post-office. No lady of that name had asked for letters. She asked if there were any pensions, and went round them all—uselessly.

No other conclusion was possible. The doctor had deceived her wilfully. To get her out of the way he sent her to Berne. He would have sent her to Jericho if her purse had been long enough to pay the fare. She was tricked.

She counted her money. There was exactly twenty-eight shillings and tenpence in her purse.

She went back to the cheapest (and dirtiest) of the pensions she had visited. She stated her case—she had missed milady her mistress—she must stay until she should receive orders to go on, and money—would they take her in until one or the other arrived? Certainly. They would take her in, at five francs a day, payable every morning in advance.

·She made a little calculation—she had twenty-eight and tenpence; exactly thirty-five francs—enough for seven days. If she wrote to Mrs. Vimpany at once she could get an answer in five days.

She accepted the offer, paid her five shillings, was shown into a room, and was informed that the dinner was served at six o'clock.

Very good. Here she could rest, at any rate, and think what was to be done. And first she wrote two letters—one to Mrs. Vimpany and one to Mr. Mountjoy.

In both of these letters she told exactly what she had found: neither Lord Harry nor his wife at the cottage, the place vacated, and the doctor on the point of going away. In both letters she told how she had been sent all the way into Switzerland on a fool's errand, and now found herself planted there without the means of getting home. In the letter to Mrs. Vimpany she added the remarkable detail that the man whom she had seen on the Thursday morning apparently dead, whose actual poisoning she thought she had witnessed, was reported on the Saturday to have walked out of the cottage, carrying his things, if he had any, and proposing to make his way to London in order to find out his old nurse. ' Make what you can out of that,' she said. ' For my own part, I understand nothing.'

In the letter which she wrote to Mr. Mountjoy she added a petition that he would send her money to bring her home. This, she said, her mistress she knew would willingly defray.

She posted these letters on Tuesday, and waited for the answers. Mrs. Vimpany wrote back by return post.

' My dear Fanny,' she said, ' I have read your letter with the greatest interest. I am not only afraid that some villainy is afloat, but I am perfectly sure of it. One can only hope and pray that her ladyship may be kept out of its influence. You will be pleased to hear that Mr. Mountjoy is better. As soon as he was sufficiently recovered to stand the shock of violent emotion, I put Lady Harry's

She counted her money.   There was exactly twenty-eight shillings and tenpence in her purse.

letter into his hands. It was well that I had kept it from him, for he fell into such a violence of grief and indignation that I thought he would have had a serious relapse. "Can any woman," he cried, "be justified in going back to an utterly unworthy husband until he has proved a complete change? What if she had received a thousand letters of penitence? Penitence should be shown by acts, not words : she should have waited." He wrote her a letter, which he showed me. "Is there," he asked, "anything in the letter which could justly offend her?" I could find nothing. He told her, but I fear too late, that she risks degradation—perhaps worse, if there is anything worse—if she persists in returning to her unworthy husband. If she refuses to be guided by his advice, on the last occasion on which he would presume to offer any device, he begged that she would not answer. Let her silence say—No. That was the substance of his letter. Up to the present moment no answer has been received from Lady Harry. Nor has he received so much as an acknowledgment of the letter. What can be understood by this silence? Clearly, refusal.

'You must return by way of Paris, though it is longer than by Basle and Laon. Mr. Mountjoy, I know, will send you the money you want. He has told me as much. "I have done with Lady Harry," he said. "Her movements no longer concern me, though I can never want interest in what she does. But since the girl is right to stick to her mistress, I will send her the money—not as a loan to be paid back by Iris, but as a gift from myself."

'Therefore, my dear Fanny, stop in Paris for one night at least, and learn what has been done if you can. Find out the nurse, and ask her what really happened. With the knowledge that you already possess, it will be hard, indeed, if we cannot arrive at the truth. There must be people who supplied things to the cottage—the restaurant, the *pharmacien*, the laundress. See them all—you know them already, and we will put the facts together. As for finding her ladyship, that will depend entirely upon herself. I shall expect you back in about a week. If anything happens here I shall be able to tell you when you arrive.

'Yours affectionately,

'L. VIMPANY.'

This letter exactly coincided with Fanny's own views. The doctor was now gone. She was pretty certain that he was not going to remain alone in the cottage; and the suburb of Passy, though charming in many ways, is not exactly the place for a man of Dr. Vimpany's temperament. She would stay a day, or even two days or more, if necessary, at Passy. She would make those inquiries.

The second letter, which reached her the same day, was from Mr. Mountjoy. He told her what he had told Mrs. Vimpany: he would give her the money, because he recognised the spirit of fidelity which caused Fanny to go first to Paris and then to Berne.

But he could not pretend to any right to interference in the affairs of Lord and Lady Harry Norland. He enclosed a *mandat postal* for a hundred and twenty-five francs, which he hoped would be sufficient for her immediate wants.

She started on her return-journey on the same day—namely, Saturday. On Sunday evening she was in a pension at Passy, ready to make those inquiries. The first person whom she sought out was the *rentier*—the landlord of the cottage. He was a retired tradesman—one who had made his modest fortune in a *charcuterie* and had invested it in house property. Fanny told him that she had been lady's-maid to Lady Harry Norland, in the recent occupancy of the cottage, and that she was anxious to know her present address.

' Merci, mon Dieu ! que sais-je ? What do I know about it ? ' he replied. ' The wife of the English milord is so much attached to her husband that she leaves him in his long illness——'

' His long illness ? '

' Certainly—Mademoiselle is not, perhaps, acquainted with the circumstances—his long illness ; and does not come even to see his dead body after he is dead. There is a wife for you—a wife of the English fashion ! '

Fanny gasped.

' After he is dead ! Is Lord Harry dead ? When did he die ? '

' But, assuredly, Mademoiselle has not heard ? The English milord died on Thursday morning, a week and more ago, of consumption, and was buried in the cemetery of Auteuil last Saturday. Mademoiselle appears astonished.'

' En effet, Monsieur, I am astonished.'

' Already the tombstone is erected to the memory of the unhappy young man, who is said to belong to a most distinguished family of Ireland. Mademoiselle can see it with her own eyes in the cemetery.'

' One word more, Monsieur. If Monsieur would have the kindness to tell her who was the nurse of milord in his last seizure ? '

' But certainly. All the world knows the widow La Chaise. It was the widow La Chaise who was called in by the doctor. Ah ! there is a man—what a man ! What a miracle of science ! What devotion to his friend ! What admirable sentiments ! Truly, the English are great in sentiments when their insular coldness allows them to speak. This widow can be found—easily found.'

He gave Fanny, in fact, the nurse's address. Armed with this, and having got out of the landlord the cardinal fact of Lord Harry's alleged death, the lady's-maid went in search of this respectable widow.

She found her, in her own apartments, a respectable woman indeed, perfectly ready to tell everything that she knew, and evidently quite unsuspicious of anything wrong. She was invited to take charge of a sick man on the morning of Thursday : she was told that he was a young Irish lord, dangerously ill of a pulmonary

disorder; the doctor, in fact, informed her that his life hung by a
thread, and might drop at any moment, though on the other hand
he had known such cases linger on for many months. She arrived
as she had been ordered, at midday: she was taken into the sick-
room by the doctor, who showed her the patient placidly sleeping on
a sofa: the bed had been slept in, and was not yet made. After
explaining the medicines which she was to administer, and the times
when they were to be given, and telling her something about his diet,
the doctor left her alone with the patient.

'He was still sleeping profoundly,' said the nurse.

'You are sure that he was sleeping, and not dead?' asked
Fanny, sharply.

'Mademoiselle, I have been a nurse for many years. I know
my duties. The moment the doctor left me I verified his statements. I proved that the patient was sleeping by feeling his pulse
and observing his breath.'

Fanny made no reply. She could hardly remind this respectable person that after the doctor left her she employed herself first
in examining the cupboards, drawers, *armoire*, and other things;
that she then found a book with pictures, in which she read for a
quarter of an hour or so; that she then grew sleepy and dropped
the book——

'I then,' continued the widow, 'made arrangements against his
waking—that is to say, I drew back the curtains and turned over
the sheet to air the bed'—O Madame! Madame! Surely this was
needless!—'shook up the pillows, and occupied myself in the cares
of a conscientious nurse until the time came to administer the first
dose of medicine. Then I proceeded to awaken my patient.
Figure to yourself! He whom I had left tranquilly breathing, with
the regularity of a convalescent rather than a dying man, was
dead! He was dead!'

'You are sure he was dead?'

'As if I had never seen a dead body before! I called the doctor,
but it was for duty only, for I knew that he was dead.'

'And then?'

'Then the doctor—who must also have known that he was
dead—felt his pulse and his heart, and looked at his eyes, and
declared that he was dead.'

'And then?'

'What then? If a man is dead he is dead. You cannot
restore him to life. Yet one thing the doctor did. He brought a
camera and took a photograph of the dead man for the sake of his
friends.'

'Oh! he took a photograph of—of Lord Harry Norland. What
did he do that for?'

'I tell you: for the sake of his friends.'

Fanny was more bewildered than ever. Why on earth should
the doctor want a photograph of the Dane Oxbye to show the
friends of Lord Harry? Could he have made a blunder as stupid

as it was uncalled for? No one could possibly mistake the dead face of that poor Dane for the dead face of Lord Harry.

She had got all the information she wanted—all, in fact, that was of any use to her. One thing remained. She would see the grave.

The cemetery of Auteuil is not so large as that of Père-la-Chaise, nor does it contain so many celebrated persons as the latter—perhaps the greatest cemetery, as regards its illustrious dead, in the whole world. It is the cemetery of the better class. The tombs are not those of Immortals but of Respectables.

Among them Fanny easily found, following the directions given to her, the tomb she was searching after.

On it was written in English, 'Sacred to the Memory of Lord Harry Norland, second son of the Marquis of Malven.' Then followed the date and the age, and nothing more.

Fanny sat down on a bench and contemplated this mendacious stone.

'The Dane Oxbye,' she said, 'was growing better fast when I went away. That was the reason why I was sent away. The very next day the doctor, thinking me far away, poisoned him. I saw him do it. The nurse was told that he was asleep, and being left alone presently discovered that he was dead. She has been told that the sick man is a young Irish gentleman. He is buried under the name of Lord Harry. That is the reason I found the doctor alone. And my lady? Where is she?'

CHAPTER LVI

FANNY'S NARRATIVE

ANNY returned to London. Partly, the slenderness of her resources gave her no choice; partly, she had learned all there was to learn, and would do no good by staying longer at Passy.

She arrived with thirty shillings left out of Mr. Mountjoy's timely gift. She sought a cheap lodging, and found a room, among people who seemed respectable, which she could have for four-and-sixpence a week, with board at a shilling a day. This settled, she hastened to Mr. Mountjoy's hotel brimful of her news for Mrs. Vimpany.

Everyone knows the disappointment when the one person in the world whom you want at the moment to see and to talk with proves to be out. Then the news has to be suppressed; the conclusions, the suspicions, the guesses have to be postponed; the active brain falls back upon itself.

This disappointment—almost as great as that at Berne—was experienced by Fanny Mere at the hotel.

Mr. Mountjoy was no longer there.

The landlady of the hotel, who knew Fanny, came out herself and told her what had happened.

'He was better,' she said, 'but still weak. They sent him down to Scotland in Mrs. Vimpany's care. He was to travel by quick or slow stages, just as he felt able. And I've got the address for you. Here it is. Oh! and Mrs. Vimpany left a message. Will you, she says, when you write, send the letter to her and not to him? She says, you know why.'

Fanny returned to her lodging profoundly discouraged. She was filled with this terrible secret that she had discovered. The only man who could advise at this juncture was Mr. Mountjoy, and he was gone. And she knew not what had become of her mistress. What could she do? The responsibility was more than she could bear.

The conversation with the French nurse firmly established one thing in her mind. The man who was buried in the cemetery of Auteuil with the name of Lord Harry Norland on a headstone, the man who had lingered so long with pulmonary disease, was the man whose death she had witnessed. It was Oxbye the Dane. Of that there could be no doubt. Equally there was no doubt in her

own mind that he had been poisoned by the doctor—by Mrs. Vim
pany's husband—in the presence and, to all appearance, with the
consent and full knowledge of Lord Harry himself. Then her mis·
tress was in the power of these two men—villains who had now
added murder to their other crimes. As for herself, she was alone,
almost friendless; in a week or two she would be penniless. If she
told her tale, what mischief might she not do? If she was silent,
what mischief might not follow?

She sat down to write to the only friend she had. But her
trouble froze her brain. She had not been able to put the case
plainly. Words failed her.

She was not at any time fluent with her pen. She now found
herself really unable to convey any intelligible account of what had
happened. To state clearly all that she knew so that the conclusion
should be obvious and patent to the reader would have been at all
times difficult, and was now impossible. She could only confine
herself to a simple vague statement. 'I can only say that from all
I have seen and heard I have reasons for believing that Lord Harry
is not dead at all.' She felt that this was a feeble way of summing
up, but she was not at the moment equal to more. 'When I write
again, after I have heard from you, I will tell you more. To-day I
cannot. I am too much weighed down. I am afraid of saying too
much. Besides, I have no money, and must look for work. I am
not anxious, however, about my own future, because my lady will
not forsake me. I am sure of that. It is my anxiety about her
and the dreadful secrets I have learned which give me no rest.'

Several days passed before the answer came. And then it was
an answer which gave her little help. 'I have no good news for
you,' she said. 'Mr. Mountjoy continues weak. Whatever your
secret, I cannot ask you to communicate it to him in his present
condition. He has been grieved and angry beyond all belief by
Lady Harry's decision to rejoin her husband. It is hard to under·
stand that a man should be so true a friend and so constant a lover.
Yet he has brought himself to declare that he has broken off all
friendly relations with her. He could no longer endure London.
It was associated with thoughts and memories of her. In spite of
his weak condition, he insisted on coming down here to his Scotch
villa. Ill as he was, he would brook no delay. We came down by
very easy stages, stopping at Peterborough, York, Durham, New·
castle, and Berwick—at some places for one night, and others for
more. In spite of all my precautions, when we arrived at the villa
he was dangerously exhausted. I sent for the local doctor, who
seems to know something. At all events, he is wise enough to
understand that this is not a case for drugs. Complete rest and
absence from all agitating thoughts must be aimed at. Above all,
he is not to see the newspapers. That is fortunate, because, I suppose, Lord Harry's death has been announced in them, and the
thought that his former mistress is a widow might excite him very
dangerously. You will now understand why I left that message at

the hotel for you, and why I have not shown him your letter. I told him, it is true, that you had returned without finding your mistress. "Speak no more to me of Lady Harry," he replied irritably. So I have said no more. As for money, I have a few pounds by me, which are at your service. You can repay me at some future time. I have thought of one thing—that new Continental paper started by Lord Harry. Wherever she may be, Lady Harry is almost sure to see that. Put an advertisement in it addressed to her, stating that you have not heard of her address, but that you yourself will receive any letter sent to some post-office which you can find. I think that such an advertisement will draw a reply from her, unless she desires to remain in seclusion.'

Fanny thought the suggestion worth adopting. After careful consideration, she drew up an advertisement :—

' Fanny M. to L—— H——. I have not been able to ascertain your address. Please write to me, at the Post Office, Hunter Street, London, W.C.'

She paid for the insertion of this advertisement three times on alternate Saturdays. They told her that this would be a more likely way than to take three successive Saturdays. Then, encouraged by the feeling that something, however little, had been done, she resolved to sit down to write out a narrative in which she would set down in order everything that had happened—exactly as it had happened. Her intense hatred and suspicion of Dr. Vimpany aided her, strange to say, to keep to the strictest fidelity as regards the facts. For it was not her desire to make up charges and accusations. She wanted to find out the exact truth, and so to set it down that anybody who read her statement would arrive at the same conclusion as she herself had done. In the case of an eye-witness there are thousands of things which cannot be produced in evidence which yet are most important in directing and confirming suspicions. The attitude, the voice, the look of a speaker, the things which he conceals as well as the things which he reveals—all these are evidence. But these Fanny was unable to set down. Therefore it behoved her to be strictly careful.

First, she stated how she became aware that there was some secret scheme under consideration between Lord Harry and the doctor. Next, she set down the fact that they began to talk French to each other, thinking that she could not understand them ; that they spoke of deceiving Lady Harry by some statement which had already deceived the authorities ; that the doctor undertook to get the lady out of the house ; that they engaged herself as nurse to a sick man ; that she suspected from the beginning that their design was to profit in some way by the death of this sick man, who bore a slight resemblance to Lord Harry himself. And so on, following the story as closely as she could remember, to the death of the Dane and her own subsequent conversation with the nurse. She was careful to put in the dates, day after day. When she had done all this—it took a good deal of time—she bought a manuscript book and copied it all out. This enabled her to remember two or three facts which had escaped her at the beginning. Then she made another copy—this time without names of people or place. The second copy she forwarded as a registered letter to Mrs. Vimpany, with a letter of which this was the conclusion: 'Considering, therefore, that on Wednesday morning I left Lord Harry in perfect health; considering that on the Thursday morning I saw the man who had been ill so long actually die—how, I have told you in the packet enclosed; considering that the nurse was called in purposely to attend a patient who was stated to have long been ill—there can be no doubt whatever that the body in the cemetery is that of the unfortunate Dane, Oxbye; and that, somewhere or other, Lord Harry is alive and well.

'What have they done it for? First of all, I suppose, to get money. If it were not for the purpose of getting money the doctor would have had nothing to do with the conspiracy, which was his own invention. That is very certain. Your idea was they would try to get money out of the Insurance Offices. I suppose that is their design. But Lord Harry may have many other secret reasons of his own for wishing to be thought dead. They say his life has been full of wicked things, and he may well wish to be considered dead and gone. Lots of wicked men would like above all things, I should think, to be considered dead and buried. But the money matter is at the bottom of all, I am convinced. What are we to do?'

What could they do? These two women had got hold of a terrible secret. Neither of them could move. It was too big a thing. One cannot expect a woman to bring her own husband—however wicked a husband he may be—to the awful shame and horror of the gallows if murder should be proved—or to a lifelong imprisonment if the conspiracy alone should be brought home to him. Therefore Mrs. Vimpany could do nothing. As for Fanny, the mere thought of the pain she would inflict upon her mistress, were Lord Harry, through her interference, to be brought to justice and an infamous sentence, kept her quiet.

Meantime, the announcement of Lord Harry's death had been made. Those who knew the family history spoke cheerfully of the event. 'Best thing he had ever done. Very good thing for his people. One more bad lot out of the way. Dead, Sir, and a very good thing, too. Married, I believe. One of the men who have done everything. Pity they can't write a life of him.' These were the comments made upon the decease of this young gentleman. Such is fame. Next day he was clean forgotten; just as if he had never existed. Such is life.

He stayed indoors all day, only venturing out after dark.

CHAPTER LVII

AT LOUVAIN

NOT many English tourists go out of their way to visit Louvain, even though it has a Hôtel de Ville surpassing even that of Brussels itself, and though one can get there in an hour from that city of youth and pleasure. And there are no English residents at all in the place—at least, none in evidence, though perhaps there may be some who have gone there for the same reasons which led Mr. William Linville and his wife to choose this spot—in order to be private and secluded. There are many more people than we know of who desire, above all things, seclusion and retirement, and dread nothing so much as a chance meeting with an old friend.

Mr. William Linville took a small house, furnished, like the cottage at Passy, and, also like that little villa, standing in its own garden. Here, with a cook and a maid, Iris set up her modest *ménage*. To ask whether she was happy would be absurd. At no time since her marriage had she been happy; to live under the condition of perpetual concealment is not in itself likely to make a woman any the happier. Fortunately she had no time to experience the full bitterness of the plan proposed by her husband.

Consider. Had their scheme actually been carried out quite successfully, this pair, still young, would have found themselves condemned to transportation for life. That was the first thing. Next, they could never make any friends among their own countrymen or countrywomen for fear of discovery. Iris could never again speak to an English lady. If they had children the risk would appear ten times more terrible, the consequences ten times more awful. The children themselves would have to grow up without family and without friends. The husband, cut off from intercourse with other men, would be thrown back upon himself. Husband and wife, with this horrible load laid upon them, would inevitably grow to loathe and hate the sight of each other. The man would almost certainly take to drink : the woman—but we must not follow this line any further. The situation lasted only so long as to give the wife a glimpse of what it might become in the future.

They took their house, and sat down in it. They were very silent. Lord Harry, his great *coup* successfully carried so far, sat taciturn and glum. He stayed indoors all day, only venturing out after dark. For a man whose whole idea of life was motion, society, and action, this promised ill.

The monotony was first broken by the arrival of Hugh's letter, which was sent in with other documents from Passy. Iris read it; she read it again, trying to understand exactly what it meant. Then she tore it up. 'If he only knew,' she said, ' he would not have taken the trouble even to write this letter. There is no answer, Hugh. There can be none—now. Act by your advice? Henceforth, I must act by order. I am a conspirator.'

Two days afterwards came a letter from the doctor. He did not think it necessary to say anything about Fanny's appearance or her journey to Berne. 'Everything,' he wrote, 'has so far gone well. The world knows, through the papers, that Lord Harry is dead. There will be now only the business of claiming the money. For this purpose, as his widow is the sole heiress and executrix, it will be necessary for her to place the will and the policies of insurance in the hands of her husband's lawyers, so that the will may be proved and the claims duly made. Forms will have to be signed. The medical certificate of death and the forms attesting the burial are already in the lawyers' hands. The sooner the widow goes to London the better. She should write to announce her arrival, and she should write from Paris as if she had been staying there after her husband's death.

'I have only to remind you, my dear Linville, that you are indebted to me in a good round sum. Of course, I shall be very pleased to receive a cheque for this sum in full as soon as you have touched the amount due to you. I shall be in Paris, at the Hôtel Continental, where you may address me. Naturally, there is no desire for concealment, and if the Insurance Companies desire any information from me I am always ready and willing to afford it.'

Lord Harry gave this letter to his wife.

She read it, and laid it open in her lap.

' Must it be, Harry ? Oh ! must it be ? '

' There is no other way possible, dear. But really, it is nothing. You were not at Passy when your husband died. You had been in London—you were in Brussels—anywhere; when you arrived it was all over; you have seen his headstone. Dr. Vimpany had him in his care; you knew he was ill, but you thought it was a trifling matter which time would cure ; you go to the lawyers and present the will. They have the policies, and will do everything else ; you will not even have to sign anything. The only thing that you must do is to get a complete rig-out of widow's weeds. Mind—there will not be the slightest doubt or question raised. Considering everything, you will be more than justified in seeing no one and going nowhere.'

Hugh's letter breaking in upon her fool's paradise had awakened the poor woman to her better self; she had gone so far with the fraud as to acquiesce in it; but she recoiled with horror and shame when this active part was forced upon her.

'Oh, Harry!'—she burst into tears. 'I cannot—I cannot. You ask me to be a liar and a thief—oh! heavens!—a vile thief!'

'It is too late, Iris! We are all vile thieves. It is too late to begin crying now.'

'Harry'—she threw herself upon her knees—'spare me! Let some other woman go, and call herself your widow. Then I will go away and hide myself.'

'Don't talk nonsense, Iris,' he replied roughly. 'I tell you it is far too late. You should have thought of this before. It is now all arranged.'

'I cannot go,' she said.

'You must go; otherwise, all our trouble may prove useless.

'Then I will not go!' she declared, springing to her feet. 'I will not degrade myself any further. I will not go!'

Harry rose too. He faced her for a moment. His eyes dropped. Even he remembered, at that moment, how great must be the fall of a woman who would consent to play such a part!

'You shall not go,' he said, 'unless you like. You can leave me to the consequences of my own acts—to my own degradation. Go back to England. In one thing only spare me. Do not tell what you know. As for me, I will forge a letter from you——'

'Forge a letter!'

'It is the only way left open, giving the lawyers authority to act, and inclosing the will. What will happen next? By whose hands the money is to reach me I know not yet. But you can leave me, Iris. Better that you should leave me—I shall only drag you lower.'

'Why must you forge the letter? Why not come with me somewhere—the world is large!—to some place where you are not known, and there let us begin a new life? We have not much money, but I can sell my watches and chains and rings, and we shall have enough. O Harry! for once be guided—listen to me! We shall find some humble manner of living, and we may be happy yet. There is no harm done if you have only pretended to be dead; nobody has been injured or defrauded——'

'Iris, you talk wildly! Do you imagine, for one moment, that the doctor will release me from my bargain?'

'What bargain?'

'Why—of course he was to be paid for the part he has taken in the business. Without him it could never have been done at all.'

'Yes—yes—it was in the letter that you gave me,' she said, conscious that such agreements belonged to works of fiction and to police courts.

'Certainly I have to pay him a good large slice out of the money.'

'It is fifteen thousand pounds, is it not? How much is to be paid to the—to the doctor?'

'We agreed that he was to have the half,' said Lord Harry, laughing lightly. 'But as I thought that seven thousand five hundred pounds was a sum of money which would probably turn his head and bring him to starvation in a year or two, I told him that the whole amount was four thousand pounds. Therefore he is to have two thousand pounds for his share. And quite enough too.'

'Treachery on treachery!' said his wife. 'Fraud on fraud! Would to GOD,' she added with a sigh, 'that you had never met this man!'

'I dare say it would have been better for me, on the whole,' he replied. 'But then, my dear, a man like myself is always meeting people whom it would have been better not to have met. Like will to like, I suppose. Given the active villain and the passive consenter, and they are sure to meet. Not that I throw stones at the worthy doctor. Not at all.'

'We cannot, Harry,' said his wife.

'We cannot, my dear. *Bien entendu!* Well, Iris, there is no more to be said. You know the situation completely. You can back out of it if you please, and leave me. Then I shall have to begin all over again a new conspiracy far more dangerous than the last. Well, I shall not drag you down with me. That is my resolution. If it comes to public degradation——but it shall not. Iris, I promise you one thing.' For once he looked as if he meant it. 'Death before dishonour. Death without your name being mixed up at all, save with pity for being the wife of such a man.'

Again he conquered her.

'Harry,' she said, 'I will go.'

A hansom cab drove to the offices of the very respectable firm of solicitors.

CHAPTER LVIII

OF COURSE THEY WILL PAY

HREE days afterwards a hansom cab drove to the offices of the very respectable firm of solicitors who managed the affairs of the Norland family. They had one or two other families as well, and in spite of agricultural depression, they made a very good thing indeed out of a very comfortable business. The cab contained a lady in deep widow's weeds.

Lady Harry Norland expected to be received with coldness and suspicion. Her husband, she knew, had not led the life expected in these days of a younger son. Nor had his record been such as to endear him to his elder brother. Then, as may be imagined, there were other tremors, caused by a guilty knowledge of certain facts which might by some accident ' come out.' Everybody has tremors for whom something may come out. Also, Iris had had no experience of solicitors, and was afraid of them.

Instead of being received, however, by a gentleman as solemn as the Court of Chancery and as terrible as the Court of Assize, she found an elderly gentleman, of quiet, paternal manners, who held both her hands, and looked as if he was weeping over her bereavement. By long practice this worthy person could always, at a moment's notice, assume the appearance of one who was weeping with his client.

' My dear lady! ' he murmured. ' My dear lady ! This is a terrible time for you.'

She started. She feared that something had come out.

' In the moment of bereavement, too, to think of business.'

' I have brought you,' she replied curtly, ' my husband's—my late husband's—will.'

' Thank you. With your permission—though it may detain your ladyship—I will read it. Humph ! it is short and to the point. This will certainly give us little trouble. I fear, however, that, besides the insurances, your ladyship will not receive much.'

' Nothing. My husband was always a poor man, as you know. At the time of his death he left a small sum of money only. I am, as a matter of fact, greatly inconvenienced.'

' Your ladyship shall be inconvenienced no longer. You must draw upon us. As regards Lord Harry's death, we are informed by Dr. Vimpany, who seems to have been his friend as well as his medical adviser——'

'Dr. Vimpany had been living with him for some time.'

—'that he had a somewhat protracted illness?'

'I was away from my husband. I was staying here in London —on business—for some time before his death. I was not even aware that he was in any danger. When I hurried back to Passy I was too late. My husband was—was already buried.'

'It was most unfortunate. And the fact that his lordship was not on speaking terms with the members of his own family—pray understand that I am not expressing any opinion on the case—but this fact seems to render his end more unhappy.'

'He had Dr. Vimpany,' said Iris, in a tone which suggested to the lawyer jealousy or dislike of the doctor.

'Well,' he said, 'it remains to prove the will and to make our claims against the Insurance Office. I have the policy here. His lordship was insured in the Royal Unicorn Life Insurance Company for the sum of 15,000*l.* We must not expect to have this large claim satisfied quite immediately. Perhaps the office will take three months to settle. But, as I said before, your ladyship can draw upon us.'

'You are certain that the Company will pay?'

'Assuredly. Why not? They must pay.'

'Oh! I thought that perhaps so large a sum——'

'My dear Madam'—the man who administered so much real and personal property smiled—'fifteen thousand pounds is not what we call a very large sum. Why, if an Insurance Company refused to pay a lawful claim it would cut its own throat—absolutely. Its very existence depends upon its meeting all just and lawful claims. The death being proved it remains for the Company to pay the insurance into the hands of the person entitled to receive it. That is, in this case, to me, acting for you.'

'Yes—I see—but I thought that, perhaps, my husband having died abroad there might be difficulty——'

'There might, if he had died in Central Africa. But he died in a suburb of Paris, under French law, which, in such matters, is even more careful and exacting than our own. We have the official papers, and the doctor's certificate. We have, besides, a photograph of the unfortunate gentleman lying on his death-bed—this was well thought of: it is an admirable likeness—the sun cannot lie—we have also a photograph of the newly erected tombstone. Doubt? Dear me, Madam, they could no more raise a doubt as to your husband's death than if he were buried in the family vault. If anything should remove any ground for doubt, it is the fact that the only person who benefits by his death is yourself. If, on the other hand, he had been in the hands of persons who had reason to wish for his death, there might have been suspicions of foul play, which would have been matter for the police—but not for an insurance company.'

'Oh! I am glad to learn, at least, that there will be no trouble. I have no knowledge of business, and I thought that——'

'No—no—your ladyship need have no such ideas. In fact, I have already anticipated your arrival, and have sent to the manager of the company. He certainly went so far as to express a doubt as to the cause of death. Consumption in any form was not supposed to be in your husband's family. But Lord Harry—ahem !—tried his constitution—tried his constitution, as I put it.'

He had put it a little differently. What he said was to the following effect—'Lord Harry Norland, sir, was a devil. There was nothing he did not do. I only wonder that he has lived so long. Had I been told that he died of everything all together, I should not have been surprised. Ordinary rapid consumption was too simple for such a man.'

Iris gave the lawyer her London address, obeyed him by drawing a hundred pounds, half of which she sent to Mr. William Linville, at Louvain, and went home to wait. She must now stay in London until the claim was discharged.

She waited six weeks. At the end of that time she learned from her solicitors that the company had settled, and that they, the lawyers, had paid to her bankers the sum of 15,000*l.*, being the whole of the insurance.

Acting, then, on her husband's instructions, she sought another bank and opened an account for one William Linville, gentleman, residing abroad. She gave herself as a reference, left the usual signature of William Linville, and paid to his account a cheque for 8,000*l.* She saw the manager of her own bank, explained that this large cheque was for an investment, and asked him to let her have 2,000*l.* in bank notes. This sum, she added, was for a special purpose. The manager imagined that she was about to perform some act of charity, perhaps an expiatory work on behalf of her late husband.

She then wrote to Dr. Vimpany, who was in Paris, making an appointment with him. Her work of fraud and falsehood was complete.

'There has been no trouble at all,' she wrote to her husband; 'and there will not be any. The insurance company has already settled the claim. I have paid 8,000*l.* to the account of William Linville. My own banker—who knows my father—believes that the money is an investment. My dear Harry, I believe that, unless the doctor begins to worry us—which he will do as soon as his money is all gone—a clear course lies before us. Let us, as I have already begged you to do, go straight away to some part of America, where you are certain not to be known. You can dye your hair and grow a beard to make sure. Let us go away from every place and person that may remind us of the past. Perhaps, in time, we may recover something of the old peace and—can it ever be ?—the old self-respect.'

There was going to be trouble, however, and that of a kind little expected, impossible to be guarded against. And it would be trouble caused by her own act and deed.

CHAPTER LIX

THE CONSEQUENCES OF AN ADVERTISEMENT

THE trouble was made by Iris herself.

In this way—

She saw Fanny's advertisement. Her first impulse was to take her back into her service. But she remembered the necessity for concealment. She must not place herself—she realised already the fact that she had done a thing which would draw upon her the vengeance of the law—and her husband in the power of this woman, whose fidelity might not stand the shock of some fit of jealousy, rage, or revenge for fancied slight. She must henceforth be cut off altogether from all her old friends.

She therefore answered the letter by one which contained no address, and which she posted with her own hand at the General Post Office. She considered her words carefully. She must not say too much or too little.

'I enclose,' she said, 'a bank note for ten pounds to assist you. I am about to travel abroad, but must, under existing circumstances, dispense with the services of a maid. In the course of my travels I expect to be in Brussels. If, therefore, you have anything to tell me or to ask of me, write to me at the Poste Restante of that city, and in the course of six months or so I am tolerably sure to send for the letter. In fact, I shall expect to find a letter from you. Do not think that I have forgotten you or your faithful services, though for a moment I am not able to call you to my side. Be patient.'

There was no address given in the letter. This alone was mysterious. If Lady Harry was in London—and the letter was posted at the General Post Office—why should she not give her address? If she was abroad, why should she hide her address? In any case, why should she do without a maid—she who had never been without a maid—to whom a maid was as necessary as one of her hands? Oh! she could never get along at all without a maid. As for Iris's business in London and her part in the conspiracy, of course Fanny neither knew nor suspected.

She had recourse again to her only friend—Mrs. Vimpany—to whom she sent Lady Harry's letter, and imploring her to lay the whole before Mr. Mountjoy.

'He is getting so much stronger,' Mrs. Vimpany wrote back, 'that I shall be able to tell him everything before long. Do not be in a hurry. Let us do nothing that may bring trouble upon her.

But I am sure that something is going on—something wicked. I have read your account of what has happened over and over again. I am as convinced as you could possibly be that my husband and Lord Harry are trading on the supposed death of the latter. We can do nothing. Let us wait.'

Three days afterwards she wrote again.

'The opportunity for which I have been waiting has come at last. Mr. Mountjoy is, I believe, fully recovered. This morning, seeing him so well and strong, I asked him if I might venture to place in his hands a paper containing a narrative.

'"Is it concerning Iris?" he asked.

'"It has to do with Lady Harry—indirectly."

'For a while he made no reply. Then he asked me if it had also to do with her husband.

'"With her husband and with mine," I told him.

'Again he was silent.

'After a bit he looked up and said, "I had promised myself never again to interfere in Lady Harry Norland's affairs. You wish me to read this document, Mrs. Vimpany?"

'"Certainly; I am most anxious that you should read it and should advise upon it."

'"Who wrote it?"

'"Fanny Mere, Lady Harry's maid."

'"If it is only to tell me that her husband is a villain," he said, "I will not read it."

'"If you were enabled by reading it to keep Lady Harry from a dreadful misfortune?" I suggested.

'"Give me the document," he said.

'Before I gave it to him—it was in my pocket—I showed him a newspaper containing a certain announcement.

'"Lord Harry dead?" he cried. "Impossible! Then Iris is free."

'"Perhaps you will first read the document." I drew it out of my pocket, gave it to him, and retired. He should be alone while he read it.

'Half an hour afterwards I returned. I found him in a state of the most violent agitation, without, however, any of the weakness which he betrayed on previous occasions.

'"Mrs. Vimpany," he cried, "this is terrible! There is no doubt —not the least doubt—in my mind that the man Oxbye is the man buried under the name of Lord Harry, and that he was murdered— murdered in cold blood—by that worst of villains——"

'"My husband," I said.

'"Your husband—most unfortunate of wives! As for Lord Harry's share in the murder. it is equally plain that he knew of it, even if he did not consent to it. Good heavens! Do you under-stand? Do you realise what they have done? Your husband and Iris's husband may be tried—actually tried—for murder and put to a shameful death. Think of it!"

' " I do think of it, Heaven knows ! I think of it every day—1 think of it all day long. But, remember, I will say nothing that will bring this fate upon them. And Fanny will say nothing. Without Fanny's evidence there cannot be even a suspicion of the truth."

' " What does Iris know about it ? "

' " I think that she cannot know anything of the murder. Consider the dates. On Wednesday Fanny was dismissed ; on Thursday she returned secretly and witnessed the murder. It was on Thursday morning that Lady Harry drove to Victoria on her return to Passy, as we all supposed, and as I still suppose. On Saturday Fanny was back again. The cottage was deserted. She was told that the man Oxbye had got up and walked away ; that her mistress had not been at the house at all, but was travelling in Switzerland ; and that Lord Harry was gone on a long journey. And she was sent into Switzerland to get her out of the way. I gather from all this that Lady Harry was taken away by her husband directly she arrived—most likely by night—and that of the murder she knew nothing."

' " No—no—she could know nothing ! That, at least, they dared not tell her. But about the rest ? How much does she know ? How far has she lent herself to the conspiracy ? Mrs. Vimpany, I shall go back to London to-night. We will travel by the night train. I feel quite strong enough."

' I began this letter in Scotland ; I finish it in London.

' We are back again in town. Come to the hotel at once, and see us.'

So, there was now a Man to advise. For once, Fanny was thankful for the creation of Man. To the most misanthropic female there sometimes comes a time when she must own that Man has his uses. These two women had now got a Man with whom to take counsel.

' I do not ask you,' said Mr. Mountjoy, with grave face, ' how far this statement of yours is true : I can see plainly that it is true in every particular.'

' It is quite true, sir ; every word of it is true. I have been tempted to make out a worse case against the doctor, but I have kept myself to the bare truth.'

' You could not make out a worse case against any man. It is the blackest case that I ever heard of or read. It is the foulest murder. I do not understand the exact presence of Lord Harry when the medicine was given. Did he see the doctor administer it ? Did he say anything ? '

' He turned white when the doctor told him that the man was going to die—that day, perhaps, or next day. When the doctor was pouring out the medicine he turned pale again and trembled. While the doctor was taking the photograph he trembled again. I think, sir—I really think—that he knew all along that the man was going to die, but when it came to the moment, he was afraid. If it had depended on him, Oxbye would be alive still.'

'He was a consenting party. Well; for the moment both of you keep perfect silence. Don't discuss the thing with each other lest you should be overheard: bury the thing. I am going to make some inquiries.'

The first thing was to find out what steps had been taken, if any, with insurance companies. For Iris's sake his inquiry had to be conducted quite openly. His object must seem none other than the discovery of Lady Harry Norland's present address. When bankers, insurance companies, and solicitors altogether have to conduct a piece of business it is not difficult to ascertain such a simple matter.

He found out the name of the family solicitor. He went to the office, sent in his card, and stated his object. As a very old friend of Lady Harry's, he wanted to learn her address. He had just come up from Scotland, where he had been ill, and had only just learned her terrible bereavement.

The lawyer made no difficulty at all. There was no reason why he should. Lady Harry had been in London; she was kept in town for nearly two months by business connected with the unfortunate event; but she had now gone—she was travelling in Switzerland or elsewhere. As for her address, a letter addressed to his care should be forwarded on hearing from her ladyship.

'Her business, I take it, was the proving of the will and the arrangement of the property.'

'That was the business which kept her in town.'

'Lady Harry,' Mr. Mountjoy went on, 'had a little property of her own apart from what she may ultimately get from her father. About five thousand pounds—not more.'

'Indeed? She did not ask my assistance in respect of her own property.'

'I suppose it is invested and in the hands of trustees. But, indeed, I do not know. Lord Harry himself, I have heard, was generally in a penniless condition. Were there any insurances?'

'Yes; happily there was insurance paid for him by the family. Otherwise there would have been nothing for the widow.'

'And this has been paid up, I suppose?'

'Yes; it has been paid into her private account.'

'Thank you,' said Mr. Mountjoy. 'With your permission, I will address a letter to Lady Harry here. Will you kindly order it to be forwarded at the very earliest opportunity?'

'Iris,' he thought, 'will not come to London any more. She has been persuaded by her husband to join in the plot. Good heavens! She has become a swindler—a conspirator—a fraudulent woman! Iris!—it is incredible—it is horrible! What shall we do?'

He first wrote a letter, to the care of the lawyers. He informed her that he had made a discovery of the highest importance to herself—he refrained from anything that might give rise to suspicion; he implored her to give him an interview anywhere, in any part of the world—alone. He told her that the consequences of refusal might be fatal—absolutely fatal—to her future happiness: he conjured her to believe that he was anxious for nothing but her happiness : that he was still, as always, her most faithful friend.

Well ; he could do no more. He had not the least expectation that his letter would do any good ; he did not even believe that it would reach Iris. The money was received and paid over to her own account. There was really no reason at all why she should place herself again in communication with these lawyers. What would she do, then ? One thing only remained. With her guilty husband, this guilty woman must remain in concealment for the rest of their days, or until death released her of the man who was pretending to be dead. At the best, they might find some place where there would be no chance of anybody ever finding them who knew either of them before this wicked thing was done.

But could she know of the murder ?

He remembered the instruction given to Fanny. She was to write to Brussels. Let her therefore write at once. He would arrange what she was to say. Under his dictation, therefore, Fanny wrote as follows :—

' My Lady,—I have received your ladyship's letter, and your kind gift of ten pounds. I note your directions to write to you at Brussels, and I obey them.

' Mr. Mountjoy, who has been ill and in Scotland, has come back to London. He begs me to tell you that he has had an interview with your lawyers, and has learned that you have been in town on business, the nature of which he has also learned. He has left an important letter for you at their office. They will for-ward it as soon as they learn your address.

' Since I came back from Passy I have thought it prudent to set down in writing an exact account of everything that happened there under my own observation. Mr. Mountjoy has read my story, and thinks that I ought without delay to send a copy of it to you. I therefore send you one, in which I have left out all the names, and put in A, B, and C instead, by his directions. He says that you will have no difficulty in filling up the names.

' I remain, my dear Lady,

' Your ladyship's most obedient and humble servant,

' FANNY MERE.'

This letter, with the document, was dispatched to Brussels that night. And this is the trouble which Iris brought upon herself by answering Fanny's advertisement.

CHAPTER LX

ON THE EVE OF A CHANGE

IRIS returned to Louvain by way of Paris. She had to settle up with the doctor.

He obeyed her summons and called upon her at the hotel.

'Well, my lady,' he began in his gross voice, rubbing his hands and laughing, 'it has come off, after all; hasn't it?'

'I do not desire, Dr. Vimpany, to discuss anything with you. We will proceed to settle what business we have together.'

'To think that your ladyship should actually fall in!' he replied. 'Now I confess that this was to me the really difficult part of the job. It is quite easy to pretend that a man is dead, but not so easy to touch his money. I really do not see how we could have managed at all without your co-operation. Well, you've had no difficulty, of course?'

'None at all.'

'I am to have half.'

'I am instructed to give you two thousand pounds. I have the money here for you.'

'I hope you consider that I deserve this share?'

'I think, Dr. Vimpany, that whatever you get in the future or the present you will richly deserve. You have dragged a man down to your own level——'

'And a woman too.'

'A woman too. Your reward will come, I doubt not.'

'If it always takes the form of bank-notes I care not how great the reward may be. You will doubtless, as a good Christian, expect your own reward—for him and for you?'

'I have mine already,' she replied sadly. 'Now, Dr. Vimpany, let me pay you, and get rid of your company.'

He counted the money carefully and put it in the banker's bag in his coat-pocket. 'Thank you, my lady. We have exchanged compliments enough over this job.'

'I hope—I pray—that we may never set eyes on you again.'

'I cannot say. People run up against each other in the strangest manner, especially people who've done shady things and have got to keep in the background.'

'Enough!—enough!'

'The background of the world is a very odd place, I assure you.

It is full of interesting people. The society has a piquancy which
you will find, I hope, quite charming. You will be known by
another name, of course ? '

'I shall not tell you by what name——'

'Tut—tut! I shall soon find out. The background gets
narrower when you fall into misery.'

'What do you mean ? '

'I mean, Lady Harry, that your husband has no idea whatever
as to the value of money. The two thousand that you are taking
him will vanish in a year or two. What will you do then ? As for
myself, I know the value of money so well that I am always buying
the most precious and delightful things with it. I enjoy them immensely. Never any man enjoyed good things so much as I do.
But the delightful things cost money. Let us be under no illusions.
Your ladyship and your noble husband and I all belong to the background ; and in a year or two we shall belong to the needy background. I daresay that very soon after that the world will learn
that we all belong to the criminal background. I wish your ladyship a joyful reunion with your husband ! '

He withdrew, and Iris set eyes on him no more. But the
prophecy with which he departed remained with her, and it was
with a heart foreboding fresh sorrrows that she left Paris and
started for Louvain.

Here began the new life—that of concealment and false pretence.
Iris put off her weeds, but she never ventured abroad without a
thick veil. Her husband, discovering that English visitors sometimes ran over from Brussels to see the Hôtel de Ville, never ventured out at all till evening. They had no friends and no society of
any kind.

The house, which stood secluded behind a high wall in its
garden, was in the quietest part of this quiet old city ; no sound of
life and work reached it ; the pair who lived there seldom spoke to
each other. Except at the midday breakfast and the dinner they
did not meet. Iris sat in her own room, silent ; Lord Harry sat in
his, or paced the garden walks for hours.

Thus the days went on monotonously. The clock ticked ; the
hours struck ; they took meals ; they slept ; they rose and dressed ;
they took meals again—this was all their life. This was all that
they could expect for the future.

The weeks went on. For three months Iris endured this life.
No news came to her from the outer world ; her husband had even
forgotten the first necessary of modern life—the newspaper. It
was not the ideal life of love, apart from the world, where the two
make for themselves a Garden of Eden ; it was a prison, in which
two were confined together who were kept apart by their guilty
secret.

They ceased altogether to speak ; their very meals were taken
in silence. The husband saw continual reproach in his wife's eyes ;

her sad and heavy look spoke more plainly than any words, ' It is to this that you have brought me.'

One morning Iris was idly turning over the papers in her desk. There were old letters, old photographs, all kinds of trifling treasures that reminded her of the past—a woman keeps everything; the little mementoes of her childhood, her first governess, her first school, her school friendships—everything. As Iris turned over these things her mind wandered back to the old days. She became again a young girl—innocent, fancy free; she grew up—she was a woman innocent still. Then her mind jumped at one leap to the present, and she saw herself as she was—innocent no longer, degraded and guilty, the vile accomplice of a vile conspiracy.

Then, as one who has been wearing coloured glasses puts them off and sees things in their own true colours, she saw how she had been pulled down by a blind infatuation to the level of the man who had held her in his fascination; she saw him as he was—reckless, unstable, careless of name and honour. Then for the first time she realised the depths into which she was plunged and the life which she was henceforth doomed to lead. The blind love fell from her —it was dead at last; but it left her bound to the man by a chain which nothing could break; she was in her right senses; she saw things as they were; but the knowledge came too late.

Her husband made no attempt to bridge over the estrangement which had thus grown up between them : it became wider every day; he lived apart and alone; he sat in his own room, smoking more cigars, drinking more brandy-and-water than was good for him ; sometimes he paced the gravel walks in the garden; in the evening, after dinner, he went out and walked about the empty streets of the quiet city. Once or twice he ventured into a café, sitting in a corner, his hat drawn over his eyes; but that was dangerous. For the most part he kept in the streets, and he spoke to no one.

Meantime the autumn had given place to winter, which began in wet and dreary fashion. Day and night the rain fell, making the gravel walks too wet and the streets impossible. Then Lord Harry sat in his room and smoked all day long. And still the melancholy of the one increased, and the boredom of the other.

He spoke at last. It was after breakfast.

' Iris,' he said, ' how long is this to continue ? '

' This—what ? '

' This life—this miserable solitude and silence.'

' Till we die,' she replied. ' What else do you expect ? You have sold our freedom, and we must pay the price.'

' No ; it shall end. I will end it. I can endure it no longer.'

' You are still young. You will perhaps have forty years more to live—all like this—as dull and empty. It is the price we must pay.'

' No,' he repeated, ' it shall end. I swear that I will go on like this no longer.'

'You had better go to London and walk in Piccadilly to get a little society.'

'What do you care what I do or where I go ? '

'We will not reproach each other, Harry.'

'Why—what else do you do all day long but reproach me with your gloomy looks and your silence ? '

'Well—end it if you can. Find some change in the life.'

'Be gracious for a little, and listen to my plan. I have made a plan. Listen, Iris. I can no longer endure this life. It drives me mad.'

'And me too. That is one reason why we should not desire to change it. Mad people forget. They think they are somewhere else. For us to believe that we were somewhere else would be in itself happiness.'

'I am resolved to change it—to change it, I say—at any risk. We will leave Louvain.'

'We can, I dare say,' Iris replied coldly, 'find another town, French or Belgian, where we can get another cottage, behind high walls in a garden, and hide there.'

'No. I will hide no longer. I am sick of hiding.'

'Go on. What is your plan ? Am I to pretend to be some one else's widow ? '

'We will go to America. There are heaps of places in the States where no English people ever go—neither tourists nor settlers —places where they have certainly never heard of us. We will find some quiet village, buy a small farm, and settle among the people. I know something about farming. We need not trouble to make the thing pay. And we will go back to mankind again. Perhaps, Iris—when we have gone back to the world—you will—' he hesitated—' you will be able to forgive me, and to regard me again with your old thoughts. It was done for your sake.'

'It was not done for my sake. Do not repeat that falsehood. The old thoughts will never come back, Harry. They are dead and gone. I have ceased to respect you or myself. Love cannot survive the loss of self-respect. Who am I that I should give love to anybody ? Who are you that you should expect love ? '

'Will you go with me to America—love or no love ? I cannot stay here—I will not stay here.'

'I will go with you wherever you please. I should like not to run risks. There are still people whom it would pain to see Iris Henley tried and found guilty with two others on a charge of fraudulent conspiracy.'

'I wouldn't accustom myself, if I were you, Iris, to speak of things too plainly. Leave the thing to me and I will arrange it. See now, we will travel by a night train from Brussels to Calais. We will take the cross-country line from Amiens to Havre; there we will take boat for New York—no English people ever travel by the Havre line. Once in America we will push up country—to Kentucky or somewhere—and find that quiet country place : after that I ask no more. I will settle down for the rest of my life, and have no more adventures. Do you agree, Iris ? '

' I will do anything that you wish,' she replied coldly.

' Very well. Let us lose no time. I feel choked here. Will you go into Brussels and buy a Continental Bradshaw or a Baedeker, or something that will tell us the times of sailing, the cost of passage, and all the rest of it ?   We will take with us money to start us with : you will have to write to your bankers. We can easily arrange to have the money sent to New York, and it can be invested there—except your own fortune—in my new name. We shall want no outfit for a fortnight at sea. I have arranged it all beautifully. Child, look like your old self.' He took an unresisting hand. ' I want to see you smile and look happy again.'

' You never will.'

' Yes—when we have got ourselves out of this damnable, unwholesome way of life ; when we are with our fellow-creatures again. You will forget this—this little business—which was, you know, after all, an unhappy necessity.'

' Oh ! how can I ever forget ? '

' New interests will arise ; new friendships will be formed——'

' Harry, it is myself that I cannot forgive. Teach me to forgive myself, and I will forget everything.'

He pressed her no longer.

' Well, then,' he said, ' go to Brussels and get this information. If you will not try to conquer this absurd moral sensitiveness—which comes too late—you will at least enable me to place you in a healthier atmosphere.'

' I will go at once,' she said, ' I will go by the next train.'

' There is a train at a quarter to two. You can do all you have to do and catch the train at five. Iris '—the chance of a change made him impatient—' let us go to-morrow. Let us go by the night express. There will be English travellers, but they shall not recognise me. We shall be in Calais at one in the morning. We will go on by an early train before the English steamer comes in. Will you be ready ? '

' Yes ; there is nothing to delay me. I suppose we can leave the house by paying the rent ?   I will go and do what you want.'

' Let us go this very night.'

' If you please ; I am always ready.'

' No : there will be no time ; it will look like running away. We will go to-morrow night. Besides, you would be too tired after going to Brussels and back. Iris, we are going to be happy again—I am sure we are.' He, for one, looked as if there was nothing to prevent a return of happiness. He laughed and waved his hands. ' A new sky—new scenes—new work—you will be happy again, Iris. You shall go, dear. Get me the things I want.'

She put on her thick veil and started on her short journey. The husband's sudden return to his former good spirits gave her a gleam of hope. The change would be welcome indeed if it permitted him to go about among other men, and to her if it gave her occupation. As to forgetting—how could she forget the past, so long as they were reaping the fruit of their wickedness in the shape of solid dividends? She easily found what she wanted. The steamer of the Compagnie Générale Transatlantique left Havre every eighth day. They would go by that line. The more she considered the plan the more it commended itself. They would at any rate go out of prison. There would be a change in their life. Miserable condition! To have no other choice of life but that of banishment and concealment: no other prospect than that of continual fraud renewed by every post that brought them money.

When she had got all the information that was wanted she had still an hour or two before her. She thought she would spend the time wandering about the streets of Brussels. The animation and life of the cheerful city—where all the people except the market-women are young—pleased her. It was long since she had seen any of the cheerfulness that belongs to a busy street. She walked slowly along, up one street and down another, looking into the shops. She made two or three little purchases. She looked into a place filled with Tauchnitz Editions, and bought two or three books. She was beginning to think that she was tired and had better make her way back to the station, when suddenly she remembered the post-office and her instructions to Fanny Mere.

'I wonder,' she said, 'if Fanny has written to me.'

She asked the way to the post-office. There was time if she walked quickly.

At the Poste Restante there was a letter for her—more than a letter, a parcel, apparently a book.

She received it and hurried back to the station.

In the train she amused herself with looking through the leaves of her new books. Fanny Mere's letter she would read after dinner.

At dinner they actually talked. Lord Harry was excited with the prospect of going back to the world. He had enjoyed his hermitage, he said, quite long enough. Give him the society of his fellow-creatures. 'Put me among cannibals,' he said, 'and I should make friends with them. But to live alone—it is the devil! To-morrow we begin our new flight.'

After dinner he lit his cigar, and went on chattering about the future. Iris remembered the packet she had got at the post-office, and opened it. It contained a small manuscript book filled with writing and a brief letter. She read the letter, laid it down, and opened the book.

CHAPTER LXI

THE LAST DISCOVERY

'I SHALL like to turn farmer,' Lord Harry went on talking while Iris opened and began to read Fanny s manuscript. 'After all my adventures, to settle down in a quiet place and cultivate the soil. On market-day we will drive into town together'—he talked as if Kentucky were Warwickshire—' side by side in a spring cart. I shall have samples of grain in bags, and you will have a basket of butter and cream. It will be an ideal life. We shall dine at the ordinary, and, after dinner, over a pipe and a glass of grog, I shall discuss the weather and the crops. And while we live in this retreat of ours, over here the very name of Harry Norland will have been forgotten. Queer, that! We shall go on living long after we are dead and buried and forgotten. In the novels the man turns up after he is supposed to be cast away—wrecked—drowned—dead long ago. But he never turns up when he is forgotten—unless he is Rip Van Winkle. By Gad, Iris! when we are old people we will go home and see the old places together. It will be something to look forward to—something to live for—eh?'

'I feel quite happy this evening, Iris; happier than I have been for months. The fact is, this infernal place has hipped us both confoundedly. I didn't like to grumble, but I've felt the monotony more than a bit. And so have you. It's made you brood over things. Now, for my part, I like to look at the bright side. Here we are comfortably cut off from the past. That's all done with. Nothing in the world can revive the memory of disagreeable things if we are only true to ourselves and agree to forget them. What has been done can never be discovered. Not a soul knows except the doctor, and between him and ourselves we are going to put a few thousand—— What's the matter, Iris? What the devil is the matter?'

For Iris, who had been steadily reading while her husband chattered on, suddenly dropped the book, and turned upon him a white face and eyes struck with horror.

'What is it?' Lord Harry repeated.

'Oh! Is this true?'

'What?'

'I cannot say it. Oh, my God! can this be true?'

'What? Speak, Iris.' He sprang to his feet. 'Is it—is it discovered?'

'Discovered? Yes, all—all—all—is discovered!'

'Where? How? Give me the thing, Iris. Quick! Who knows? What is known?'

He snatched the book from her hands. She shrank from his touch, and pushed back her chair, standing in an attitude of self-defence—watching him as one would watch a dangerous creature.

He swiftly read page after page, eager to know the worst. Then he threw the book upon the table.

'Well?' he said, not lifting his eyes.

'The man was murdered—murdered!' she whispered.

He made no reply.

'You looked on while he was murdered! You looked on consenting! You are a murderer!'

'I had no share or part in it. I did not know he was being poisoned.'

'You knew when I was with you. Oh! the dead man—the murdered man—was in the house at the very moment! Your hands were red with blood when you took me away—to get me out of the way—so that I should not know——' She stopped, she could not go on.

'I did not know, Iris—not with certainty. I thought he was dying when he came into the house. He did not die; he began to recover. When the doctor gave him his medicine—after that woman went away—I suspected. When he died, my suspicions were stronger. I challenged him. He did not deny it. Believe me, Iris, I neither counselled it nor knew of it.'

'You acquiesced in it. You consented. You should have warned the—the other murderer that you would denounce him if the man died. You took advantage of it. His death enabled you to carry out your fraud with me as your accomplice. With ME! I am an accomplice in a murder!'

'No, no, Iris; you knew nothing of it. No one can ever accuse you——'

'You do not understand. It is part of the accusation which I make against myself.'

'As for what this woman writes,' her husband went on, 'it is true. I suppose it is useless to deny a single word of it. She was hidden behind the curtain, then! She heard and saw all! If Vimpany had found her! He was right. No one so dangerous as a woman. Yes; she has told you exactly what happened. She suspected all along. We should have sent her away and changed our plans. This comes of being too clever. Nothing would do for the doctor but the man's death. I hoped—we both hoped—that he would die a natural death. He did not. Without a dead man we were powerless. We had to get a dead man. Iris, I will hide nothing more from you, whatever happens. I confess everything. I knew that he was going to die. When he began to get well I was filled with forebodings, because I knew that he would never be allowed to go away. How else could we find a dead body? You can't steal a body; you can't make one up. You must have one for proof of death. I say '—his voice was harsh and hoarse—' I say that I knew he must die. I saw his death in the doctor's face. And there was no more money left for a new experiment if Oxbye should get well and go away. When it came to the point I was seized with mortal terror. I would have given up everything—everything—to see the man get up from his bed and go away. But it was too late. I saw the doctor prepare the final dose, and when he had it to his lips I saw by his eyes that it was the drink of death. I have told you all,' he concluded.

'You have told me all,' she repeated. 'All! Good Heavens! All!'

'I have hidden nothing from you. Now there is nothing more to tell.'

She stood perfectly still—her hands clasped, her eyes set, her face white and stern.

'What I have to do now,' she said, 'lies plain before me.'

'Iris! I implore you, make no change in our plans. Let us go away as we proposed. Let the past be forgotten. Come with me——'

'Go with you? With you? With you? Oh!' she shuddered.

'Iris! I have told you all. Let us go on as if you had heard nothing. We cannot be more separated than we have been for the last three months. Let us remain as we are until the time when you will be able to feel for me—to pity my weakness—and to forgive me.'

'You do not understand. Forgive you? It is no longer a question of forgiveness. Who am I that my forgiveness should be of the least value to you—or to any?'

'What is the question, then?'

'I don't know. A horrible crime has been committed—a horrible, ghastly, dreadful crime—such a thing as one reads of in the papers and wonders, reading it, what manner of wild beasts must be those who do such things. Perhaps one wonders, besides, what manner of women must be those who associate with those wild beasts. My husband is one of those wild beasts!—my husband!—my husband! —and—I—I am one of the women who are the fit companions of these wild creatures.'

'You can say what you please, Iris; what you please.'

'I have known—only since I came here have I really known and understood—that I have wrecked my life in a blind passion. I have loved you, Harry; it has been my curse. I followed you against the warnings of everybody: I have been rewarded—by this. We are in hiding. If we are found we shall be sent to a convict prison for conspiracy. We shall be lucky if we are not tried for murder and hanged by the neck until we are dead. This is my reward!'

'I have never played the hypocrite with you, Iris. I have never pretended to virtues which I do not possess. So far——'

'Hush! Do not speak to me. I have something more to say, and then I shall never speak to you any more. Hush! Let me collect my thoughts. I cannot find the words. I cannot . . . Wait—wait! Oh!' She sat down and burst into sobbings and moanings. But only for a minute. Then she sprang to her feet again and dashed back the tears. 'Time for crying,' she said, 'when all is done. Harry, listen carefully; these are my last words. You will never hear from me any more. You must manage your own life in your own way, to save it or to spoil it; I will never more bear any part in it. I am going back to England—alone. I shall give up your name, and I shall take my maiden name again—or some other. I shall live somewhere quietly where you will not discover me. But perhaps you will not look for me?'

'I will not,' he said. 'I owe you so much. I will not look for you.'

'As regards this money which I have obtained for you under false pretences, out of the fifteen thousand pounds for which you were insured, five thousand have been paid to my private account. I shall restore to the Company all that money.'

'Good Heavens! Iris, you will be prosecuted on a criminal charge.'

'Shall I? That will matter little, provided I make reparation. Alas! who shall make reparation—who shall atone—for the blood-spilling? For all things else in this world we may make what we call atonement; but not for the spilling of blood.'

'You mean this? You will deliberately do this?'

'I mean every word. I will do nothing and say nothing that will betray you. But the money that I can restore, I will restore— So HELP ME, GOD!' With streaming eyes she raised her hand and pointed upwards.

Her husband bowed his head.

'You have said all you wished to say?' he asked humbly.

'I have said all.'

'Let me look in your face once more—so—full—with the light upon it. Yes; I have loved you, Iris—I have always loved you. Better, far better, for you had you fallen dead at my feet on the day when you became my wife. Then I should have been spared— I should have been spared a great deal. You are right, Iris. Your duty lies plainly before you. As for me, I must think of mine. Farewell! The lips of a murderer are not fit to touch even the hem of your garments. Farewell!'

He left her. She heard the hall door open and shut. She would see her husband no more.

She went to her own room and packed a single box with necessary things. Then she called the housemaid and informed her that she had been summoned to return suddenly to England; she must reach Brussels at least that evening. The woman brought a porter who carried her box to the station; and Iris left Louvain—and her husband—for ever.

CHAPTER LXII

THE BOARD OF DIRECTORS

T a Board Meeting of the Royal Unicorn Life Insurance Company, specially convened, the Chairman had to make a communication of a very remarkable character.

'Gentlemen,' he said, 'I call upon the Secretary, without further introduction, to read a letter, to consider which you are called together this day.'

'The letter,' the Secretary began, 'is simply headed "Paris," dated two days ago.'

'Only two days ago,' said the Chairman, mysteriously. 'But, of course, that means nothing. There has been plenty of time for him to change his residence. I dare say he may be in London at our very elbow. Go on, if you please.'

'Gentlemen'—the Secretary proceeded to read the letter. 'It is now three months since a claim was sent in to you by the firm of Erskine, Mansfield, Denham & Co., solicitors of Lincoln's Inn Fields, for the sum of 15,000*l*. due to the heirs of Lord Harry Norland in respect of an insurance effected upon his life.'

'The claim, gentlemen,' said the Chairman, 'was duly acknow. ledged and paid some weeks later. It was a heavy loss; but these things will occur, and there seemed no reason to doubt the facts alleged, or to dispute the claim.'

'I write this letter,' the Secretary continued reading, 'in order to inform you that the claim was fraudulent, inasmuch as Lord Harry Norland was at the time, and is still, actually living.'

Fraudulent! The man still living! At this point there was a sudden awakening. Everybody sat up and listened with all their ears.

'I may tell you, gentlemen,' the Chairman explained, 'that the writer of this remarkable letter is none other than Lord Harry Norland himself. We will now proceed without further interruption.'

'In conjunction with another person, I devised and carried out successfully a plan by which I was enabled to touch at once, and without the disagreeable necessity of previously expiring and being buried, the whole of the money for which I was insured. Other people have attempted the same design, I believe, but the thing has hitherto been managed clumsily. In my own case, it has been managed with great dexterity and artistic skill. As you will naturally be curious on a subject which interests you so closely I have no objection to reveal the method. It is not enough to write to your office and state that a certain person is dead. One must be prepared with proofs of the death should any doubt arise. No proof of death is quite satisfactory without evidence as to the disposal of the dead body. With that object, we procured from the Hôtel Dieu a patient apparently in an advanced state of consumption. My accomplice, being a medical man, highly recommended, was able to do this without suspicion. We nursed him ostentatiously. During the latter part of the illness he was nursed under the name of Lord Harry Norland. He died. His name was entered in the official register as Lord Harry Norland. He was buried in the cemetery at Auteuil, near Paris, as Lord Harry Norland. A headstone marks his grave, which is purchased in perpetuity. The doctor certified the cause of his death, and communicated the fact to the deceased's brother, Lord Malven, and to the deceased's solicitors. The death was also announced to the papers. The difficulties attendant on the successful conduct of the business are so great that you need not fear a repetition. Nobody, in order to assist a fraud, will consent to die and lend his own body. It is seldom, indeed, that a sick man can be found—a foreigner and friendless—whose death will cause no curiosity and raise no questions. Add to this, it is extremely difficult, as I have now experienced, to find the necessary assistance without encountering the objections of conscience.'

'Upon my word!' cried one of the Directors, 'this is a most wonderful letter. I beg your pardon. Pray go on.'

'We began very well. We buried our man under the name of Lord Harry Norland, as I have said. The difficulty then arose as to the presentation of the claim. It was most desirable that the claim should be made by the person who would most naturally be the deceased's heir and after proving his will and by his own solicitor.

'I am married. I have no children. I have not lived on good terms with my family. It was, therefore, quite reasonable to expect that I should leave my wife sole heir and executrix. It was also natural that she should go to my solicitors—the family solicitors—and ask them to manage her affairs.

'With this object I confessed to my wife as much of the conspiracy as was necessary. Like many women, she possesses, in addition to every virtue, a blessed devotion to her husband. Where he is concerned she is easily led even from the paths of honour. I practised on that devotion ; I used all the arguments and persuasions based on that devotion necessary to convert a woman of honour into the accomplice of a conspiracy. In brief, I made my wife join in the fraud. She consented to act for me, persuaded that if she did not the conspiracy would be discovered. The business has, therefore, been carried through with the greatest success. You have paid the claim in full without question. For me there was left the very comfortable provision of 15,000*l.*, with the consciousness of a daring and successful swindle. Unfortunately, my wife has now discovered that her conscience will give her no peace or rest until full restitution of the money has been made. She has informed me of her intention to send back without delay that part of it which lies at her bank in her own name—that is to say, five thousand pounds.

'I do not suppose that, as gentlemen, you would be disposed to subject a woman who thus desires to repair a wrong to the degradation of a public prosecution. No useful end, in fact, will be served in so doing. It is, in fact, in the conviction that you will take no proceedings that I write this letter.

'Further, as I wish my wife's scruples of conscience to be completely set at rest, I am prepared, on an assurance that the matter will be allowed to drop, to forward to you the remainder of the money, less two thousand pounds, which I have reason to believe will be sent to you in course of time. I am also prepared to instruct my wife, as my heir, in the event of my death to make no claim on the Company; and I have requested my solicitor to cease paying the annual premium. The Company will, therefore, be the gainers of the whole premiums which have been paid—namely, 300*l.* a year for ten years : that is to say, 3,000*l.*

'As for myself, I will take the necessary steps as soon as you have given me that letter of assurance. As regards the other principal in the conspiracy, it is hardly worth your while to search after him. I shall be obliged if you will be so good as to acknowledge this letter without delay, with any assurance which you may be able to make as regards the person whom I have dragged into the affair. I send you an address where a letter will find me. You may wish to watch the house. I assure you beforehand that it is useless. I shall not go there.—I remain, Gentlemen,

'Your obedient servant,
'HARRY NORLAND.'

'Perhaps,' said the Secretary, 'it is in connection with this letter that I have this day received a packet of bank-notes amounting in all to the sum of five thousand pounds. The packet is endorsed "Restitution money."'

'Bank-notes, gentlemen,' said the Chairman significantly, 'may be traced if necessary.'

The Directors looked at each other. This was, indeed, a very remarkable story, and one never before brought to the notice of any Board.

'Gentlemen,' said the Chairman, 'you have heard the letter; you now have the case before you. I should like to hear your views.'

'We are likely to get most of our money back,' said one of the Directors, 'it seems to me, by holding our tongues. That is the main thing.'

'If we could get Lord Harry himself,' said another, 'I should say : Go for him, but not for his wife. I wonder we ever took his life at all. If all stories are true about him he is as bad as they make 'em. He ran away when he was a boy, and went to sea: he was a strolling actor after that: he went out to the States and was reported to have been seen in the West: he has been a ship's steward: he has been on the turf. What has he not been?'

'We have got the money,' said another; 'that is the great thing. We must remember that we should never have found out the thing unless——'

'The Company must not compound a felony,' said the Chairman.

'Certainly not. By no means. At the same time, would any good purpose be served by public scandal in connection with a noble House?'

'The noble House,' said another Director, who was a Radical, 'may very well take care of itself. Question is, Would it do any good to anybody if we ran in the wife?'

'Who is she?'

'You would expect a ruffian like Lord Harry to marry a woman like himself. Not at all. He married a most charming creature named Henley—Iris Henley—father very well known in the City. I heard of it at the time. She would have him—infatuated about him—sad business. Mr. Chairman, I submit that it is quite impossible for us to take proceedings against this unfortunate lady, who is doing her utmost to make restitution.'

'The Company must not compound a felony,' the Chairman repeated.

'Even if we do not get back that two thousand pounds,' said the Secretary, 'the Company will lose nothing. The surrender value must be considered.'

Then another of the Directors spoke. 'We do not know where this lady is to be found. She is probably passing under another name. It is not our business to hunt her down.'

'And if we found her we should have to prove the case, and her guilty knowledge of the conspiracy,' said another. 'How would this precious letter be taken as evidence? Why, we do not even know that it is true. We might exhume the body: what would that prove after three months? We might open up the case, and spend a heap of money, and create a great scandal, and be none the better for it afterwards. My advice is, let the thing drop.'

'Well, but,' objected another, 'suppose we admit that the man is still living. He may die, and then there would be another claim upon us.'

'Of that,' said the Chairman, 'I think there need be no apprehension whatever. You have heard his letter. But, I repeat, we must not compound a felony!'

'I submit, Mr. Chairman,' said one who had not spoken—and he was a barrister—'that the Company knows nothing at all about Lady Harry Norland. We have had to deal with the firm of Erskine, Mansfield, Denham & Co., of Lincoln's Inn Fields: and a most

He came in, old, eminently respectable, but shaken.

respectable firm too. On their representations we paid the money. If it can be ascertained that we have been defrauded we must look to them. If we have to prosecute anybody it must be that respectable firm.'

'Good,' said the Chairman.

'I propose, therefore, that the Secretary write to Lord Harry Norland, informing him that the Company have had nothing at all to do with his wife, and do not recognise her action in any way. We shall then see what happens, and can proceed in accordance.'

At this moment a card was brought in. It was that of Mr. Erskine himself, senior partner in the very firm.

He came in, old, eminently respectable, but shaken. He was greatly shaken. 'Gentlemen,' he said nervously, 'I hasten to bring you a communication, a most extraordinary communication, which I have just received. It is nothing less than a confession—a full confession—from a person whom I had every reason to believe was dead. It is from Lord Harry Norland.'

'We know already,' said the Chairman, superior, 'the main facts which you are going to lay before us. We are met to-day in order to discuss our action in view of these facts. There has been a conspiracy of a very artful and ingenious character. It has been successful so far through the action of a woman. By the action of the same woman it is sought to make restitution. The hand of justice, however——'

'Perhaps,' said the lawyer, 'you will oblige me by allowing me to read the letter.'

'Pray read it'—the Chairman bowed—'though I do not suppose it will add to the information we already possess.'

'Gentlemen'—the lawyer read—'You will be surprised and pained to learn that I am not—as you were given to understand—dead; but on the other hand, living and in the enjoyment of rude health. I see no reason why my life should not be prolonged to threescore years and ten.

'The claim, therefore, which you sent in to the Royal Unicorn Life Insurance Company was fraudulent. It was the result of a deep-laid conspiracy. You have been made the innocent accomplice of a great crime.

'My wife, who now knows the whole truth, is most anxious for restitution to be made. She is about to restore that portion of the money which lies in her name. Most of the rest will be sent back by myself, on certain conditions.

'In communicating the fact of my being still alive to the head of my family you will please also to inform him that I authorise the discontinuance of the premium. This will save the family 300*l.* a year. This will be a solatium to him for the fact that his brother still lives to disgrace the name. If I should die before the next premium is due I order my heirs not to claim the money.—I remain, Gentlemen, your obedient servant,

'HARRY NORLAND.'

'The premium which should have been paid under ordinary circumstances,' said the Secretary, 'was due six weeks ago. The policy has therefore expired.'

'It is a characteristic letter,' said the lawyer. 'Lord Harry was born to be a trouble to his family. There has never been a time, so far as I remember, when he was not a trouble and a disgrace. Hitherto, however, he has avoided actual crime—at least, actual detection. Now, I suppose, the game is up. Yet, gentlemen, the letter is not that of an utter villain.'

. 'He will not be caught,' observed the Chairman. 'The letter is from too cool a hand. He has prepared a retreat. I dare say by this time he is in some safe and convenient disguise. We are only concerned—are we not?—for the moment with the lady. She has received the money from you. We paid it to you on your represen-tations.'

'Observe,' said the lawyer, 'that the moment she learns the truth she hastens to make restitution.'

'Humph!' said the Director, turning over Lord Harry's letter so that the lawyer should not be able to read the contents. 'Have you seen her?'

'I have not. I expect to do so before long. She will certainly call upon me.'

'She will be ill-advised,' said the Chairman, 'if she calls upon anybody just at present. Well, sir, I confess that I should be sorry —every member of this Board would be sorry—to see that lady placed in the dock beside her husband.'

'In the interests of the noble family concerned, I hope that neither of them will be placed in the dock.'

'Do you know who is the other man—the second principal?'

'I can guess. I do not know, however, where he is. All I know is what I have communicated to you—the contents of this letter.'

'One would like to get hold of the other man,' said the Chair-man. 'Presumably he does not belong to a noble family. Well, sir, I don't know what may be done; but this Company cannot, I repeat, compound a felony.'

'Certainly not. Most certainly not. At present, however, you have got very little to go upon. And unless evidence is forth-coming——'

'We will not discuss that part of the business,' said the Chair-man. 'A conspiracy has been undoubtedly entered into. We may be compelled to bring an action of some kind against your firm, Mr. Erskine. As regards the lady, if she is guilty——'

'No—no,' said the lawyer, 'upon my life! Sinned against—not guilty.'

The Chairman folded up Lord Harry's letter and gave it to the Secretary.

'We are much obliged to you, sir, for your prompt action. It is, of course, only what we should have expected of your firm.

Meantime, remember that the claim was made by you, that you received the money, and—but we will communicate with you in a few days.'

The Secretary wrote such a letter as was suggested. By return of post a cheque was sent, signed by one William Linville, for the sum of eight thousand pounds. The Company had, therefore, recovered thirteen out of fifteen thousand pounds. The Secretary had another interview with Mr. Erskine, the result of which was that the Company recovered the remaining two thousand pounds.

Every firm of solicitors contains its own secrets and keeps them. Therefore, we need not inquire whether it was intended that this money should be paid by the firm or by the noble family to which Lord Harry Norland belonged. It is, however, certain that a few days afterwards Mr. Hugh Mountjoy called at the office and had a long conversation with the senior partner, and that he left behind him a very big cheque.

The subject has never been brought before the Directors again. It was, indeed, privately discussed, and that frequently. Perhaps the story was whispered about outside the Board-room. These things do get about. There has been, however, a feeling that the thing, which would have been perfectly successful but for the conscience of a woman concerned, might be repeated with less tender consciences, and so the Companies be defrauded. Now the wickedness of the world is already so great that it needs no more teaching to make it worse. On the whole, the less said the better.

Besides, the tragic event which happened a day or two later effectively prevented any further step. That in itself was sufficient to wipe out the whole business.

CHAPTER LXIII

A REFUGE

T was all over. Iris had sent in her money. She was in a small lodging found for her by Fanny Mere, who called her cousin. She stayed indoors all day long, afraid of stirring abroad; afraid to read the papers; afraid that her husband was arrested on the charge of conspiracy and fraud; afraid that some kind of hue and cry might be out after her.

Therefore, when she heard a manly step on the stair, she started and turned pale, expecting nothing short of an armed messenger of the law. She never was in this danger for a single minute, but conscience made a coward of her.

The step was that of Hugh Mountjoy.

'I found you out,' he said, 'by means of Fanny. The girl knew that she was safe in letting me know your secret. Why are you in concealment?'

'You cannot know all, or you would not ask me that.'

'I do know all; and again I ask, why are you in concealment?'

'Because—— Oh, Hugh—spare me!'

'I know all, which is the reason why I cannot choose but come to see you. Come out of this poor place; resume your own name. There is no reason why you should not. You were not present at Passy when this conspiracy was hatched; you got there after the funeral. You, naturally, went to see the family solicitors. Iris, what has the conspiracy to do with you?' It will be observed that Hugh had not read the letter written to the Directors of the Company.

'Do you know about the money?'

'Certainly. You sent back all that you could—five thousand pounds. That showed your own innocence——'

'Hugh, you know that I am guilty.'

'The world will think that you are innocent. At any rate, you can come out and go about without fear. Tell me, what are your plans?'

'I have no plans. I only want to hide my head—somewhere.'

'Yes; we will talk about that presently. Meantime, I have some news for you.'

'News? What news?'

'Really good news. I have to tell you a thing which will sur-prise you.'

'Good news? What good news is there for me?'

'Your husband has sent back the whole of the money.'

'Sent back? To the Insurance Office?'

'All has been sent back. He wrote two letters—one to the solicitors and the other to the Insurance Company. It is not likely now that anything can be said, because the Directors have accepted the money. Moreover, it appears that they might have proceeded against the lawyers for the recovery of the money, but that they have nothing to do either with you or with Lord Harry Norland. That is a difficult point, however. Somebody, it seems, has compounded—or is going to compound—a felony. I do not understand exactly what this means, or what dreadful consequences might follow; but I am assured by the lawyers that we need apprehend nothing more. All is over.'

Iris heaved a profound sigh.

'Then he is safe?' she said.

'You think of him first,' said Hugh, jealously. 'Yes: he is safe; and, I do hope, gone away, out of the country, never to come back any more. The more important thing is that you should be safe from him. As for the doctor—but I cannot speak of the doctor with common patience. Let him be left to the end which always awaits such men. It is to be hoped that he will never, wherever he goes, feel himself in safety.'

'I am safe,' said Iris, 'not only from my husband, but from what else beside? You know what I mean. You mean that I, as well as my husband, am safe from that. Oh! the fear of it has never left me—never for one moment. You tell me that I am safe from public disgrace, and I rejoice—when I ought to sink into the earth with shame!' She covered her face with her hands.

'Iris, we know what you have done. We also know why you did it. What need we say more? The thing is finished and done with. Let us never again allude to it. The question now is—what will you do next? Where will you live?'

'I do not know. I have got Fanny Mere with me. Mrs. Vimpany is also anxious to live with me. I am rich, indeed, since I have two faithful dependants and one friend.'

'In such wealth, Iris, you will always be rich. Now listen seriously. I have a villa in the country. It is far away from London, in the Scottish Lowlands—quite out of the way—remote even from tourists and travellers. It is a very lonely place, but there is a pretty house, with a great garden behind and a stretch of sand and seashore in front. There one may live completely isolated. I offer you that villa for your residence. Take it; live in it as long as you please.'

'No, no. I must not accept such a gift.'

'You must, Iris—you shall. I ask it of you as a proof of friendship, and nothing more. Only, I fear that you will get tired of the loneliness.'

'No—no,' she said. 'I cannot get tired of loneliness: it is all I want.'

'There is no society at all.'

'Society?　Society for me?'

'I go to the neighbourhood sometimes for fishing.　You will let me call upon you?'

'Who else has such a right?'

'Then you will accept my offer?'

'I feel that I must.　Yes, Hugh; yes, with deepest gratitude.'

The next day she went down by the night-mail to Scotland. With her travelled Mrs. Vimpany and Fanny Mere.

CHAPTER LXIV

THE INVINCIBLES

THE proceedings of Lord Harry after he had sent off that cheque were most remarkable. If he had invited—actually courted—what followed—he could not have acted differently.

He left London and crossed over to Dublin.

Arrived there, he went to a small hotel entirely frequented by Irish Americans and their friends. It was suspected of being the principal place of resort of the Invincibles. It was known to be a house entirely given up to the Nationalists. He made no attempt to conceal his name. He entered the hotel, greeted the landlord cheerfully, saluted the head waiter, ordered his dinner, and took no notice of the sullen looks with which he was received or the scowls which followed him about the coffee-room, where half a dozen men were sitting and talking, for the most part in whispers.

He slept there that night.

The next day, still openly and as if there was nothing to fear, either from England or from Ireland, he walked to the station and took his ticket, paying no attention to what all the world might have seen and understood—that he was watched. When he had taken his ticket two men immediately afterwards took tickets to the same place. The place where he was going was that part of Kerry where the Invincibles had formerly assassinated Arthur Mountjoy.

The two men who followed him—who took their tickets for the same place—who got into the same carriage with him—were two members of that same fraternity. It is well known that he who joins that body and afterwards leaves it, or disobeys its order, or is supposed to betray its secrets, incurs the penalty of death.

On the unexpected arrival of Lord Harry at this hotel, there had been hurriedly called together a meeting of those members then in Dublin. It was resolved that the traitor must be removed. Lots were cast, and the lot fell upon one who remembered past acts of kindness done by Lord Harry to his own people. He would fain have been spared this business, but the rules of the society are imperative. He must obey.

It is the practice of the society when a murder has been resolved upon to appoint a second man, whose duty it is to accompany the murderer and to see that he executes his task.

In the afternoon, about an hour before sunset, the train arrived at the station where Lord Harry was to get down. The station-master recognised him, and touched his hat. Then he saw the two other men get down after him, and he turned pale.

'I will leave my portmanteau,' said Lord Harry, 'in the cloak-room. It will be called for.'

Afterwards the station-master remembered those words. Lord Harry did not say 'I will call for it,' but 'It will be called for.' Ominous words.

The weather was cold; a drizzling rain fell; the day was drawing in. Lord Harry left the station, and started with quick step along the road, which stretched across a dreary desolate piece of country.

The two men walked after him. One presently quickened his step, leaving the second man twenty yards behind.

The station-master looked after them till he could see them no longer. Then he shook his head and returned to his office.

Lord Harry walking along the road knew that the two men were following him. Presently he became aware that one of them was quickening his pace.

He walked on. Perhaps his cheeks paled and his lips were set close, because he knew that he was walking to his death.

The steps behind him approached faster—faster. Lord Harry never even turned his head. The man was close behind him. The man was beside him.

'Mickey O'Flynn it is,' said Lord Harry.

''Tis a —— traitor, you are,' said the man.

'Your friends the Invincibles told you that, Mickey. Why, do you think I don't know, man, what are you here for? Well?' he stopped. 'I am unarmed. You have got a revolver in your hand—the hand behind your back. What are you stopping for?'

'I cannot,' said the man.

'You must, Mickey O'Flynn—you must; or it's murdered you'll be yourself,' said Lord Harry, coolly. 'Why, man, 'tis but to lift your hand. And then you'll be a murderer for life. I am another—we shall both be murderers then. Why don't you fire, man.'

'By —— I cannot!' said Mickey. He held the revolver behind him, but he did not lift his arm. His eyes started: his mouth was open; the horror of the murderer was upon him before the murder was committed. Then he started. 'Look!' he cried. 'Look behind you, my lord!'

Lord Harry turned. The second man was upon him. He bent forward and peered in his face.

'Arthur Mountjoy's murderer!' he cried, and sprang at his throat.

One, two, three shots rang out in the evening air. Those who heard them in the roadside cabin, at the railway-station on the road, shuddered. They knew the meaning of those shots. One more murder to load the soul of Ireland.

But Lord Harry lay dead in the middle of the road.

The second man got up and felt at his throat.

'Faith!' he said, 'I thought I was murdered outright. Come, Mick, let us drag him to the roadside.'

They did so, and then with bent heads and slouched hats, they made their way across country to another station where they would not be recognised as the two who had followed Lord Harry down the road.

Two mounted men of the Constabulary rode along an hour later and found the body lying where it had been left.

They searched the pockets. They found a purse with a few sovereigns; the portrait of a lady—the murdered man's wife—a sealed envelope addressed to Hugh Mountjoy, Esq , care of his London hotel ; and a card-case : nothing of any importance.

'It is Lord Harry Norland,' said one. 'The wild lord—he has met his end at last.'

The letter to Iris was brief. It said:

'Farewell! I am going to meet the death of one who is called a Traitor to the Cause. I am the Traitor of a Cause far higher. May the end that is already plotted for me be accepted as an atonement ! Forgive me, Iris ! Think of me as kindly as you can. But I charge you—it is my latest word—mourn not for one who has done his best to poison your life and to ruin your soul.'

In the other letter he said :

'I know the affection you have always entertained for Iris. She will tell you what she pleases about the past. If she tells you nothing about her late husband, think the worst and you will not be wrong. Remember that whatever she has done was done for me and at my instigation. She ought to have married you instead of me.

'I am in the presence of Death. The men who are going to kill me are under this very roof. They will kill me, perhaps to-night. Perhaps they will wait for a quieter and a safer place. But they will kill me.

'In the presence of Death, I rise superior to the pitiful jealousy with which I have always regarded you. I now despise it. I ask your pardon for it. Help Iris to forget the action of her life of which she has most reason to be ashamed. Show that you forgive me—when you have forgiven her—and when you have helped her in the warmth and strength of your love to drive me out of your thoughts for ever.

'H N.'

EPILOGUE

T is two years after the murder of Lord Harry Norland, the last event connected with this history.

Iris, when she accepted Hugh Mountjoy's offer of his Scotch villa, went there resolved to hide herself from the world. Too many people, she thought, knew her history, and what she had done. It was not likely that the Directors of the Insurance Company would all hold their tongues about a scandal so very unusual. Even if they did not charge her with complicity, as they could, they would certainly tell the story—all the more readily since Lord Harry's murder—of the conspiracy and its success. She could never again, she told herself, be seen in the world.

She was accompanied by her friend and maid—the woman whose fidelity to her had been so abundantly proved—and by Mrs. Vimpany, who acted as housekeeper.

After a decent interval, Hugh Mountjoy joined her. She was now a widow. She understood very well what he wished to say, and she anticipated him. She informed him that nothing would ever induce her to become the wife of any other man after her degradation. Hugh received this intimation without a remark. He remained in the neighbourhood, however, calling upon her frequently and offering no word of love. But he became necessary to her. The frequent visits became daily; the afternoon visits were paid in the morning: the visitor stayed all day. When the time came for Iris to yield, and he left the house no more, there seemed to be no change. But still they continued their retired life, and now I do not think they will ever change it again.

Their villa was situated on the north shore of the Solway Firth, close to the outfall of the Annan River, but on the west bank, opposite to the little town of Annan. At the back was a large garden, the front looked out upon the stretch of sand at low tide and the water at high tide. The house was provided with a good library. Iris attended to her garden, walked on the sands, read, or worked. They were a quiet household. Husband and wife talked little. They walked about in the garden, his arm about her waist, or hand in hand. The past, if not forgotten, was ceasing to trouble them; it seemed a dreadful, terrible dream. It left its mark in a gentle melancholy which had never belonged to Iris in the old days.

And then happened the last event which the chronicler of this history has to relate.

It began in the morning with a letter.

Mrs. Vimpany received it. She knew the handwriting, started, and hid it quickly in her bosom. As soon as she could get away to her own room she opened and read it.

'Good and Tender Creature,—I ascertained, a good while ago, thinking that probably I might have to make this kind of application to you, where you were living and with whom. It was not difficult; I only had to connect you with Mr. Hugh Mountjoy and to find out where he lived. I congratulate you on being so well able to take care of yourself. You are probably settled for life in a comfortable home. I feel as happy about it as if I had myself contributed to this satisfactory result.

'I have no intention of making myself more disagreeable than I am obliged to do. Necessity, however, knows no law. You will understand me when I tell you that I have spent all my money. I do not regret the manner in which the money has been spent, but the fact that it has all gone. This it is which cuts me to the heart.

'I have also discovered that the late lamented Lord Harry, whose death I myself have the greatest reasons to deplore, played me a scurvy trick in regard to certain sums of money. The amount for which he was insured was not less than 15,000*l.* The amount as he stated it to me was only 4,000*l.* In return for certain services rendered at a particular juncture I was to receive the half of the insurance money. I only received 2,000*l.*, consequently there is still due to me the sum of 5,500*l.* This is a large lump of money. But Mr. Mountjoy is, I believe, a wealthy man. He will, doubtless, see the necessity of paying this money to me without further question or delay.

'You will, therefore, seek his presence—he is now, I hear, at home. You may read to him any part of this letter that you please, and you will let him know that I am in earnest. A man with empty pockets cannot choose but be in earnest.

'He may very possibly object.

'Very good. In that case you will tell him that a fraud has been committed in connection with which I am prepared to make a full confession. I consented, on the death of my patient, and at the earnest entreaty of Lord Harry Norland, to represent the dead man as his lordship. I then went away, resolving to have nothing more to do with the further villainy which I believe was carried on to the obtaining of the whole amount for which he was insured.

'The murder of Lord Harry immediately afterwards caused the Company to drop their intended prosecution. I shall reveal to them the present residence of his widow, and shall place my evidence at their disposition. Whatever happens I shall make the facts of the case public. This done, nothing can hurt me; while, whether the Public Prosecutor intervenes or not, neither Mr. Hugh Mountjoy nor his wife can ever show face to the world again.

'Tell Mr. Mountjoy, I say, whatever you please, except that I am joking. You must not tell him that. I shall call to-morrow morning, and shall expect to find the business as good as done.

'A. V.'

Mrs. Vimpany dropped the letter in dismay. Her husband had vanished out of her life for more than two years. She hoped that she was effectually hidden; she hoped that he had gone away to some far-off country where he would never more return. Alas! This world of ours has no far-off country left, and, even if the wicked man turneth away from his wickedness so far as to go to the Rocky Mountains, an express train and a swift boat will bring him back to his wickedness whenever he desires a little more enjoyment and the society of his old friends.

Mr. Vimpany was back again. What should she do? What would Iris do? What would Mr. Mountjoy do?

She read the letter again.

Two things were obvious: first, that he had no clue of the restitution; and, next, that he had no idea of the evidence against him for the murder of the Dane. She resolved to communicate the latter fact only. She was braver now than she had been formerly. She saw more clearly that the way of the wicked man is not always so easy for him. If he knew that his crime could be brought home to him; that he would certainly be charged with murder if he dared to show himself, or if he asked for money, he would desist. Before such a danger the most hardened villain would shrink.

She also understood that it was desirable to hide from him the nature of the evidence and the name of the only witness against him. She would calmly tell him what would happen, and bid him begone, or take the consequences.

Yet even if he were driven off he would return. She would live henceforth in continual apprehension of his return. Her tranquillity was gone.

Heavens! That a man should have such power over the lives of others!

She passed the most wretched day of her whole life. She saw in anticipation the happiness of that household broken up. She pictured his coming, but she could not picture his departure. For she had never seen him baffled and defeated.

He would come in, big, burly, with his farmer-like manner: confident, bullying, masterful. He would ask her what she had done; he would swear at her when he learned that she had done nothing; he would throw himself into the most comfortable chair, stretch out his legs, and order her to go and fetch Mr. Mountjoy. Would she be subdued by him as of old? Would she find the courage to stand up to him? For the sake of Iris—yes. For the sake of the man who had been so kind to her—yes.

In the evening, the two women—Mrs. Vimpany and Fanny— were seated in the housekeeper's room. Both had work in their laps : neither was doing any work. The autumnal day had been boisterous ; the wind was getting higher.

' What are you thinking of ? ' asked Fanny.

' I was thinking of my husband. If he were to come back, Fanny—if he were to threaten——'

' You would loose my tongue—you would let me speak ? '

' Yes ; for her sake. I would have shielded him once—if I could. But not now. I know, at last, that there is no single good thing left in him.'

' You have heard from him. I saw the letter this morning, in the box. I knew the handwriting. I have been waiting for you to speak.'

' Hush ! Yes, Fanny ; I have heard from him. He wants money. He will come here to-morrow morning, and will threaten Mr. Mountjoy. Keep your mistress in her own room. Persuade her to lie in bed—anything.'

' He does not know what I have seen. Charge him with the murder of the Dane. Tell him,' said Fanny, her lips stiffening, ' that if he dares to come again—if he does not go away—he shall be arrested for murder. I will keep silence no longer ! '

' I will—I am resolved ! Oh ! who will rid us of this monster ? '

Outside, the gale rose higher—higher still. They heard it howling, grinding branches together ; they heard the roaring and the rushing of the waters as the rising tide was driven over the shallow sands, like a mountain reservoir at loose among the valleys below.

In the midst of the tempest there came a sudden lull. Wind and water alike seemed hushed. And out of the lull, as if in answer to the woman's question, there came a loud cry—the shriek of a man in deadly peril.

The two women caught each other by the hand and rushed to the window. They threw it open ; the tempest began again ; a fresh gust drove them back ; the waters roared : the wind howled ; they heard the voice no more. They closed the window and put up the shutters.

It was long past midnight when they dared to go to bed. One of them lay awake the whole night long. In the roaring tempest she had seen an omen of the wrath of Heaven about to fall once more upon her mistress.

She was wrong. The wrath of Heaven fell upon one far more guilty.

In the morning, with the ebbing tide, a dead body was found lashed to the posts of one of the standing nets in the Solway. It was recognised by Hugh, who went out to look at it, and found it the body of Vimpany.

Whether he was on his way back to Annan, or whether he in-tended to call at the villa that evening instead of next morning, no one can tell. His wife shed tears, but they were tears of relief. The man was buried as a stranger. Hugh kept his counsel. Mrs.

Vimpany put the letter in the fire. Neither of them thought it wise to disturb the mind of Iris by any mention of the man. Some days later, however, Mrs. Vimpany came downstairs in a widow's cap.

To Iris's look of interrogation she replied calmly, ' Yes, I heard the other day. He is dead. Is it not better—even for him, perhaps —that he should be dead ? He can do no more wickedness ; he can bring misery into no more households. He is dead.'

Iris made no reply. Better—better far—that he was dead. But how she had been delivered from the man, to what new dangers she had been exposed, she knew not, and will never know.

She has one secret—and only one—which she keeps from her husband. In her desk she preserves a lock of Lord Harry's hair. Why ? I know not. Blind Love doth never wholly die.

THE END

A CATALOG OF
SELECTED DOVER BOOKS
IN ALL FIELDS OF INTEREST

A CATALOG OF SELECTED DOVER BOOKS IN ALL FIELDS OF INTEREST

CONCERNING THE SPIRITUAL IN ART, Wassily Kandinsky. Pioneering work by father of abstract art. Thoughts on color theory, nature of art. Analysis of earlier masters. 12 illustrations. 80pp. of text. 5⅜ × 8½. 23411-8 Pa. $2.50

LEONARDO ON THE HUMAN BODY, Leonardo da Vinci. More than 1200 of Leonardo's anatomical drawings on 215 plates. Leonardo's text, which accompanies the drawings, has been translated into English. 506pp. 8⅜ × 11¾. 24483-0 Pa. $10.95

GOBLIN MARKET, Christina Rossetti. Best-known work by poet comparable to Emily Dickinson, Alfred Tennyson. With 46 delightfully grotesque illustrations by Laurence Housman. 64pp. 4 × 6¾. 24516-0 Pa. $2.50

THE HEART OF THOREAU'S JOURNALS, edited by Odell Shepard. Selections from *Journal*, ranging over full gamut of interests. 228pp. 5⅜ × 8½. 20741-2 Pa. $4.50

MR. LINCOLN'S CAMERA MAN: MATHEW B. BRADY, Roy Meredith. Over 300 Brady photos reproduced directly from original negatives, photos. Lively commentary. 368pp. 8⅜ × 11¼. 23021-X Pa. $11.95

PHOTOGRAPHIC VIEWS OF SHERMAN'S CAMPAIGN, George N. Barnard. Reprint of landmark 1866 volume with 61 plates: battlefield of New Hope Church, the Etawah Bridge, the capture of Atlanta, etc. 80pp. 9 × 12. 23445-2 Pa. $6.00

A SHORT HISTORY OF ANATOMY AND PHYSIOLOGY FROM THE GREEKS TO HARVEY, Dr. Charles Singer. Thoroughly engrossing non-technical survey. 270 illustrations. 211pp. 5⅜ × 8½. 20389-1 Pa. $4.50

REDOUTE ROSES IRON-ON TRANSFER PATTERNS, Barbara Christopher. Redouté was botanical painter to the Empress Josephine; transfer his famous roses onto fabric with these 24 transfer patterns. 80pp. 8¼ × 10⅞. 24292-7 Pa. $3.50

THE FIVE BOOKS OF ARCHITECTURE, Sebastiano Serlio. Architectural milestone, first (1611) English translation of Renaissance classic. Unabridged reproduction of original edition includes over 300 woodcut illustrations. 416pp. 9⅜ × 12¼. 24349-4 Pa. $14.95

CARLSON'S GUIDE TO LANDSCAPE PAINTING, John F. Carlson. Authoritative, comprehensive guide covers, every aspect of landscape painting. 34 reproductions of paintings by author; 58 explanatory diagrams. 144pp. 8⅜ × 11. 22927-0 Pa. $4.95

101 PUZZLES IN THOUGHT AND LOGIC, C.R. Wylie, Jr. Solve murders, robberies, see which fishermen are liars—purely by reasoning! 107pp. 5⅜ × 8½. 20367-0 Pa. $2.00

TEST YOUR LOGIC, George J. Summers. 50 more truly new puzzles with new turns of thought, new subtleties of inference. 100pp. 5⅜ × 8½. 22877-0 Pa. $2.25

THE MURDER BOOK OF J.G. REEDER, Edgar Wallace. Eight suspenseful stories by bestselling mystery writer of 20s and 30s. Features the donnish Mr. J.G. Reeder of Public Prosecutor's Office. 128pp. 5⅜ × 8½. (Available in U.S. only)
24374-5 Pa. $3.50

ANNE ORR'S CHARTED DESIGNS, Anne Orr. Best designs by premier needlework designer, all on charts: flowers, borders, birds, children, alphabets, etc. Over 100 charts, 10 in color. Total of 40pp. 8¼ × 11. 23704-4 Pa. $2.25

BASIC CONSTRUCTION TECHNIQUES FOR HOUSES AND SMALL BUILDINGS SIMPLY EXPLAINED, U.S. Bureau of Naval Personnel. Grading, masonry, woodworking, floor and wall framing, roof framing, plastering, tile setting, much more. Over 675 illustrations. 568pp. 6½ × 9¼. 20242-9 Pa. $8.95

MATISSE LINE DRAWINGS AND PRINTS, Henri Matisse. Representative collection of female nudes, faces, still lifes, experimental works, etc., from 1898 to 1948. 50 illustrations. 48pp. 8⅜ × 11¼. 23877-6 Pa. $2.50

HOW TO PLAY THE CHESS OPENINGS, Eugene Znosko-Borovsky. Clear, profound examinations of just what each opening is intended to do and how opponent can counter. Many sample games. 147pp. 5⅜ × 8½. 22795-2 Pa. $2.95

DUPLICATE BRIDGE, Alfred Sheinwold. Clear, thorough, easily followed account: rules, etiquette, scoring, strategy, bidding; Goren's point-count system, Blackwood and Gerber conventions, etc. 158pp. 5⅜ × 8½. 22741-3 Pa. $3.00

SARGENT PORTRAIT DRAWINGS, J.S. Sargent. Collection of 42 portraits reveals technical skill and intuitive eye of noted American portrait painter, John Singer Sargent. 48pp. 8¼ × 11⅛. 24524-1 Pa. $2.95

ENTERTAINING SCIENCE EXPERIMENTS WITH EVERYDAY OBJECTS, Martin Gardner. Over 100 experiments for youngsters. Will amuse, astonish, teach, and entertain. Over 100 illustrations. 127pp. 5⅜ × 8½. 24201-3 Pa. $2.50

TEDDY BEAR PAPER DOLLS IN FULL COLOR: A Family of Four Bears and Their Costumes, Crystal Collins. A family of four Teddy Bear paper dolls and nearly 60 cut-out costumes. Full color, printed one side only. 32pp. 9¼ × 12¼.
24550-0 Pa. $3.50

NEW CALLIGRAPHIC ORNAMENTS AND FLOURISHES, Arthur Baker. Unusual, multi-useable material: arrows, pointing hands, brackets and frames, ovals, swirls, birds, etc. Nearly 700 illustrations. 80pp. 8⅜ × 11¼.
24095-9 Pa. $3.75

DINOSAUR DIORAMAS TO CUT & ASSEMBLE, M. Kalmenoff. Two complete three-dimensional scenes in full color, with 31 cut-out animals and plants. Excellent educational toy for youngsters. Instructions; 2 assembly diagrams. 32pp. 9¼ × 12¼. 24541-1 Pa. $3.95

SILHOUETTES: A PICTORIAL ARCHIVE OF VARIED ILLUSTRATIONS, edited by Carol Belanger Grafton. Over 600 silhouettes from the 18th to 20th centuries. Profiles and full figures of men, women, children, birds, animals, groups and scenes, nature, ships, an alphabet. 144pp. 8⅜ × 11¼. 23781-8 Pa. $4.95

25 KITES THAT FLY, Leslie Hunt. Full, easy-to-follow instructions for kites made from inexpensive materials. Many novelties. 70 illustrations. 110pp. 5⅜ × 8½.
22550-X Pa. $2.25

PIANO TUNING, J. Cree Fischer. Clearest, best book for beginner, amateur. Simple repairs, raising dropped notes, tuning by easy method of flattened fifths. No previous skills needed. 4 illustrations. 201pp. 5⅜ × 8½. 23267-0 Pa. $3.50

EARLY AMERICAN IRON-ON TRANSFER PATTERNS, edited by Rita Weiss. 75 designs, borders, alphabets, from traditional American sources. 48pp. 8¼ × 11.
23162-3 Pa. $1.95

CROCHETING EDGINGS, edited by Rita Weiss. Over 100 of the best designs for these lovely trims for a host of household items. Complete instructions, illustrations. 48pp. 8¼ × 11. 24031-2 Pa. $2.25

FINGER PLAYS FOR NURSERY AND KINDERGARTEN, Emilie Poulsson. 18 finger plays with music (voice and piano); entertaining, instructive. Counting, nature lore, etc. Victorian classic. 53 illustrations. 80pp. 6½ × 9¼. 22588-7 Pa. $1.95

BOSTON THEN AND NOW, Peter Vanderwarker. Here in 59 side-by-side views are photographic documentations of the city's past and present. 119 photographs. Full captions. 122pp. 8¼ × 11. 24312-5 Pa. $6.95

CROCHETING BEDSPREADS, edited by Rita Weiss. 22 patterns, originally published in three instruction books 1939-41. 39 photos, 8 charts. Instructions. 48pp. 8¼ × 11. 23610-2 Pa. $2.00

HAWTHORNE ON PAINTING, Charles W. Hawthorne. Collected from notes taken by students at famous Cape Cod School; hundreds of direct, personal *apercus*, ideas, suggestions. 91pp. 5⅜ × 8½. 20653-X Pa. $2.50

THERMODYNAMICS, Enrico Fermi. A classic of modern science. Clear, organized treatment of systems, first and second laws, entropy, thermodynamic potentials, etc. Calculus required. 160pp. 5⅜ × 8½. 60361-X Pa. $4.00

TEN BOOKS ON ARCHITECTURE, Vitruvius. The most important book ever written on architecture. Early Roman aesthetics, technology, classical orders, site selection, all other aspects. Morgan translation. 331pp. 5⅜ × 8½. 20645-9 Pa. $5.50

THE CORNELL BREAD BOOK, Clive M. McCay and Jeanette B. McCay. Famed high-protein recipe incorporated into breads, rolls, buns, coffee cakes, pizza, pie crusts, more. Nearly 50 illustrations. 48pp. 8¼ × 11. 23995-0 Pa. $2.00

THE CRAFTSMAN'S HANDBOOK, Cennino Cennini. 15th-century handbook, school of Giotto, explains applying gold, silver leaf; gesso; fresco painting, grinding pigments, etc. 142pp. 6⅛ × 9¼. 20054-X Pa. $3.50

FRANK LLOYD WRIGHT'S FALLINGWATER, Donald Hoffmann. Full story of Wright's masterwork at Bear Run, Pa. 100 photographs of site, construction, and details of completed structure. 112pp. 9¼ × 10. 23671-4 Pa. $6.50

OVAL STAINED GLASS PATTERN BOOK, C. Eaton. 60 new designs framed in shape of an oval. Greater complexity, challenge with sinuous cats, birds, mandalas framed in antique shape. 64pp. 8¼ × 11. 24519-5 Pa. $3.50

THE BOOK OF WOOD CARVING, Charles Marshall Sayers. Still finest book for beginning student. Fundamentals, technique; gives 34 designs, over 34 projects for panels, bookends, mirrors, etc. 33 photos. 118pp. 7¾ × 10⅝.   23654-4 Pa. $3.95

CARVING COUNTRY CHARACTERS, Bill Higginbotham. Expert advice for beginning, advanced carvers on materials, techniques for creating 18 projects—mirthful panorama of American characters. 105 illustrations. 80pp. 8⅜ × 11.
24135-1 Pa. $2.50

300 ART NOUVEAU DESIGNS AND MOTIFS IN FULL COLOR, C.B. Grafton. 44 full-page plates display swirling lines and muted colors typical of Art Nouveau. Borders, frames, panels, cartouches, dingbats, etc. 48pp. 9⅜ × 12¼.
24354-0 Pa. $6.00

SELF-WORKING CARD TRICKS, Karl Fulves. Editor of *Pallbearer* offers 72 tricks that work automatically through nature of card deck. No sleight of hand needed. Often spectacular. 42 illustrations. 113pp. 5⅜ × 8½.   23334-0 Pa. $3.50

CUT AND ASSEMBLE A WESTERN FRONTIER TOWN, Edmund V. Gillon, Jr. Ten authentic full-color buildings on heavy cardboard stock in H-O scale. Sheriff's Office and Jail, Saloon, Wells Fargo, Opera House, others. 48pp. 9¼ × 12¼.
23736-2 Pa. $3.95

CUT AND ASSEMBLE AN EARLY NEW ENGLAND VILLAGE, Edmund V. Gillon, Jr. Printed in full color on heavy cardboard stock. 12 authentic buildings in H-O scale: Adams home in Quincy, Mass., Oliver Wight house in Sturbridge, smithy, store, church, others. 48pp. 9¼ × 12¼.   23536-X Pa. $3.95

THE TALE OF TWO BAD MICE, Beatrix Potter. Tom Thumb and Hunca Munca squeeze out of their hole and go exploring. 27 full-color Potter illustrations. 59pp. 4¼ × 5½. (Available in U.S. only)   23065-1 Pa. $1.50

CARVING FIGURE CARICATURES IN THE OZARK STYLE, Harold L. Enlow. Instructions and illustrations for ten delightful projects, plus general carving instructions. 22 drawings and 47 photographs altogether. 39pp. 8⅜ × 11.
23151-8 Pa. $2.50

A TREASURY OF FLOWER DESIGNS FOR ARTISTS, EMBROIDERERS AND CRAFTSMEN, Susan Gaber. 100 garden favorites lushly rendered by artist for artists, craftsmen, needleworkers. Many form frames, borders. 80pp. 8¼ × 11.
24096-7 Pa. $3.50

CUT & ASSEMBLE A TOY THEATER/THE NUTCRACKER BALLET, Tom Tierney. Model of a complete, full-color production of Tchaikovsky's classic. 6 backdrops, dozens of characters, familiar dance sequences. 32pp. 9⅜ × 12¼.
24194-7 Pa. $4.50

ANIMALS: 1,419 COPYRIGHT-FREE ILLUSTRATIONS OF MAMMALS, BIRDS, FISH, INSECTS, ETC., edited by Jim Harter. Clear wood engravings present, in extremely lifelike poses, over 1,000 species of animals. 284pp. 9 × 12.
23766-4 Pa. $9.95

MORE HAND SHADOWS, Henry Bursill. For those at their 'finger ends,'' 16 more effects—Shakespeare, a hare, a squirrel, Mr. Punch, and twelve more—each explained by a full-page illustration. Considerable period charm. 30pp. 6½ × 9¼.
21384-6 Pa. $1.95

SURREAL STICKERS AND UNREAL STAMPS, William Rowe. 224 haunting, hilarious stamps on gummed, perforated stock, with images of elephants, geisha girls, George Washington, etc. 16pp. one side. 8¼ × 11.   24371-0 Pa. $3.50

GOURMET KITCHEN LABELS, Ed Sibbett, Jr. 112 full-color labels (4 copies each of 28 designs). Fruit, bread, other culinary motifs. Gummed and perforated. 16pp. 8¼ × 11.   24087-8 Pa. $2.95

PATTERNS AND INSTRUCTIONS FOR CARVING AUTHENTIC BIRDS, H.D. Green. Detailed instructions, 27 diagrams, 85 photographs for carving 15 species of birds so life-like, they'll seem ready to fly! 8¼ × 11.   24222-6 Pa. $2.75

FLATLAND, E.A. Abbott. Science-fiction classic explores life of 2-D being in 3-D world. 16 illustrations. 103pp. 5⅜ × 8.   20001-9 Pa. $2.00

DRIED FLOWERS, Sarah Whitlock and Martha Rankin. Concise, clear, practical guide to dehydration, glycerinizing, pressing plant material, and more. Covers use of silica gel. 12 drawings. 32pp. 5⅜ × 8½.   21802-3 Pa. $1.00

EASY-TO-MAKE CANDLES, Gary V. Guy. Learn how easy it is to make all kinds of decorative candles. Step-by-step instructions. 82 illustrations. 48pp. 8¼ × 11.
23881-4 Pa. $2.50

SUPER STICKERS FOR KIDS, Carolyn Bracken. 128 gummed and perforated full-color stickers: GIRL WANTED, KEEP OUT, BORED OF EDUCATION, X-RATED, COMBAT ZONE, many others. 16pp. 8¼ × 11.   24092-4 Pa. $2.50

CUT AND COLOR PAPER MASKS, Michael Grater. Clowns, animals, funny faces...simply color them in, cut them out, and put them together, and you have 9 paper masks to play with and enjoy. 32pp. 8¼ × 11.   23171-2 Pa. $2.25

A CHRISTMAS CAROL: THE ORIGINAL MANUSCRIPT, Charles Dickens. Clear facsimile of Dickens manuscript, on facing pages with final printed text. 8 illustrations by John Leech, 4 in color on covers. 144pp. 8⅜ × 11¼.
20980-6 Pa. $5.95

CARVING SHOREBIRDS, Harry V. Shourds & Anthony Hillman. 16 full-size patterns (all double-page spreads) for 19 North American shorebirds with step-by-step instructions. 72pp. 9¼ × 12¼.   24287-0 Pa. $4.95

THE GENTLE ART OF MATHEMATICS, Dan Pedoe. Mathematical games, probability, the question of infinity, topology, how the laws of algebra work, problems of irrational numbers, and more. 42 figures. 143pp. 5⅜ × 8½. (EBE)
22949-1 Pa. $3.50

READY-TO-USE DOLLHOUSE WALLPAPER, Katzenbach & Warren, Inc. Stripe, 2 floral stripes, 2 allover florals, polka dot; all in full color. 4 sheets (350 sq. in.) of each, enough for average room. 48pp. 8¼ × 11.   23495-9 Pa. $2.95

MINIATURE IRON-ON TRANSFER PATTERNS FOR DOLLHOUSES, DOLLS, AND SMALL PROJECTS, Rita Weiss and Frank Fontana. Over 100 miniature patterns: rugs, bedspreads, quilts, chair seats, etc. In standard dollhouse size. 48pp. 8¼ × 11.   23741-9 Pa. $1.95

THE DINOSAUR COLORING BOOK, Anthony Rao. 45 renderings of dinosaurs, fossil birds, turtles, other creatures of Mesozoic Era. Scientifically accurate. Captions. 48pp. 8¼ × 11.   24022-3 Pa. $2.25

JAPANESE DESIGN MOTIFS, Matsuya Co. Mon, or heraldic designs. Over 4000 typical, beautiful designs: birds, animals, flowers, swords, fans, geometrics; all beautifully stylized. 213pp. 11⅜ × 8¼. 22874-6 Pa. $7.95

THE TALE OF BENJAMIN BUNNY, Beatrix Potter. Peter Rabbit's cousin coaxes him back into Mr. McGregor's garden for a whole new set of adventures. All 27 full-color illustrations. 59pp. 4¼ × 5½. (Available in U.S. only) 21102-9 Pa. $1.50

THE TALE OF PETER RABBIT AND OTHER FAVORITE STORIES BOXED SET, Beatrix Potter. Seven of Beatrix Potter's best-loved tales including Peter Rabbit in a specially designed, durable boxed set. 4¼ × 5½. Total of 447pp. 158 color illustrations. (Available in U.S. only) 23903-9 Pa. $10.80

PRACTICAL MENTAL MAGIC, Theodore Annemann. Nearly 200 astonishing feats of mental magic revealed in step-by-step detail. Complete advice on staging, patter, etc. Illustrated. 320pp. 5⅜ × 8½. 24426-1 Pa. $5.95

CELEBRATED CASES OF JUDGE DEE (DEE GOONG AN), translated by Robert Van Gulik. Authentic 18th-century Chinese detective novel; Dee and associates solve three interlocked cases. Led to van Gulik's own stories with same characters. Extensive introduction. 9 illustrations. 237pp. 5⅜ × 8½. 23337-5 Pa. $4.50

CUT & FOLD EXTRATERRESTRIAL INVADERS THAT FLY, M. Grater. Stage your own lilliputian space battles.By following the step-by-step instructions and explanatory diagrams you can launch 22 full-color fliers into space. 36pp. 8¼ × 11. 24478-4 Pa. $2.95

CUT & ASSEMBLE VICTORIAN HOUSES, Edmund V. Gillon, Jr. Printed in full color on heavy cardboard stock, 4 authentic Victorian houses in H-O scale: Italian-style Villa, Octagon, Second Empire, Stick Style. 48pp. 9¼ × 12¼. 23849-0 Pa. $3.95

BEST SCIENCE FICTION STORIES OF H.G. WELLS, H.G. Wells. Full novel *The Invisible Man,* plus 17 short stories: "The Crystal Egg," "Aepyornis Island," "The Strange Orchid," etc. 303pp. 5⅜ × 8½. (Available in U.S. only) 21531-8 Pa. $4.95

TRADEMARK DESIGNS OF THE WORLD, Yusaku Kamekura. A lavish collection of nearly 700 trademarks, the work of Wright, Loewy, Klee, Binder, hundreds of others. 160pp. 8¾ × 8. (Available in U.S. only) 24191-2 Pa. $5.00

THE ARTIST'S AND CRAFTSMAN'S GUIDE TO REDUCING, ENLARGING AND TRANSFERRING DESIGNS, Rita Weiss. Discover, reduce, enlarge, transfer designs from any objects to any craft project. 12pp. plus 16 sheets special graph paper. 8¼ × 11. 24142-4 Pa. $3.25

TREASURY OF JAPANESE DESIGNS AND MOTIFS FOR ARTISTS AND CRAFTSMEN, edited by Carol Belanger Grafton. Indispensable collection of 360 traditional Japanese designs and motifs redrawn in clean, crisp black-and-white, copyright-free illustrations. 96pp. 8¼ × 11. 24435-0 Pa. $3.95

CHANCERY CURSIVE STROKE BY STROKE, Arthur Baker. Instructions and illustrations for each stroke of each letter (upper and lower case) and numerals. 54 full-page plates. 64pp. 8¼ × 11. 24278-1 Pa. $2.50

THE ENJOYMENT AND USE OF COLOR, Walter Sargent. Color relationships, values, intensities; complementary colors, illumination, similar topics. Color in nature and art. 7 color plates, 29 illustrations. 274pp. 5⅜ × 8½. 20944-X Pa. $4.50

SCULPTURE PRINCIPLES AND PRACTICE, Louis Slobodkin. Step-by-step approach to clay, plaster, metals, stone; classical and modern. 253 drawings, photos. 255pp. 8⅛ × 11. 22960-2 Pa. $7.50

VICTORIAN FASHION PAPER DOLLS FROM HARPER'S BAZAR, 1867-1898, Theodore Menten. Four female dolls with 28 elegant high fashion costumes, printed in full color. 32pp. 9¼ × 12¼. 23453-3 Pa. $3.50

FLOPSY, MOPSY AND COTTONTAIL: A Little Book of Paper Dolls in Full Color, Susan LaBelle. Three dolls and 21 costumes (7 for each doll) show Peter Rabbit's siblings dressed for holidays, gardening, hiking, etc. Charming borders, captions. 48pp. 4¼ × 5½. 24376-1 Pa. $2.25

NATIONAL LEAGUE BASEBALL CARD CLASSICS, Bert Randolph Sugar. 83 big-leaguers from 1909-69 on facsimile cards. Hubbell, Dean, Spahn, Brock plus advertising, info, no duplications. Perforated, detachable. 16pp. 8¼ × 11. 24308-7 Pa. $2.95

THE LOGICAL APPROACH TO CHESS, Dr. Max Euwe, et al. First-rate text of comprehensive strategy, tactics, theory for the amateur. No gambits to memorize, just a clear, logical approach. 224pp. 5⅜ × 8½. 24353-2 Pa. $4.50

MAGICK IN THEORY AND PRACTICE, Aleister Crowley. The summation of the thought and practice of the century's most famous necromancer, long hard to find. Crowley's best book. 436pp. 5⅜ × 8½. (Available in U.S. only) 23295-6 Pa. $6.50

THE HAUNTED HOTEL, Wilkie Collins. Collins' last great tale; doom and destiny in a Venetian palace. Praised by T.S. Eliot. 127pp. 5⅜ × 8½. 24333-8 Pa. $3.00

ART DECO DISPLAY ALPHABETS, Dan X. Solo. Wide variety of bold yet elegant lettering in handsome Art Deco styles. 100 complete fonts, with numerals, punctuation, more. 104pp. 8⅛ × 11. 24372-9 Pa. $4.00

CALLIGRAPHIC ALPHABETS, Arthur Baker. Nearly 150 complete alphabets by outstanding contemporary. Stimulating ideas; useful source for unique effects. 154 plates. 157pp. 8⅜ × 11¼. 21045-6 Pa. $4.95

ARTHUR BAKER'S HISTORIC CALLIGRAPHIC ALPHABETS, Arthur Baker. From monumental capitals of first-century Rome to humanistic cursive of 16th century, 33 alphabets in fresh interpretations. 88 plates. 96pp. 9 × 12. 24054-1 Pa. $4.50

LETTIE LANE PAPER DOLLS, Sheila Young. Genteel turn-of-the-century family very popular then and now. 24 paper dolls. 16 plates in full color. 32pp. 9¼ × 12¼. 24089-4 Pa. $3.50

KEYBOARD WORKS FOR SOLO INSTRUMENTS, G.F. Handel. 35 neglected works from Handel's vast oeuvre, originally jotted down as improvisations. Includes Eight Great Suites, others. New sequence. 174pp. 9⅜ × 12¼.

24338-9 Pa. $7.50

AMERICAN LEAGUE BASEBALL CARD CLASSICS, Bert Randolph Sugar. 82 stars from 1900s to 60s on facsimile cards. Ruth, Cobb, Mantle, Williams, plus advertising, info, no duplications. Perforated, detachable. 16pp. 8¼ × 11.

24286-2 Pa. $2.95

A TREASURY OF CHARTED DESIGNS FOR NEEDLEWORKERS, Georgia Gorham and Jeanne Warth. 141 charted designs: owl, cat with yarn, tulips, piano, spinning wheel, covered bridge, Victorian house and many others. 48pp. 8¼ × 11.

23558-0 Pa. $1.95

DANISH FLORAL CHARTED DESIGNS, Gerda Bengtsson. Exquisite collection of over 40 different florals: anemone, Iceland poppy, wild fruit, pansies, many others. 45 illustrations. 48pp. 8¼ × 11.

23957-8 Pa. $1.75

OLD PHILADELPHIA IN EARLY PHOTOGRAPHS 1839-1914, Robert F. Looney. 215 photographs: panoramas, street scenes, landmarks, President-elect Lincoln's visit, 1876 Centennial Exposition, much more. 230pp. 8⅞ × 11¾.

23345-6 Pa. $9.95

PRELUDE TO MATHEMATICS, W.W. Sawyer. Noted mathematician's lively, stimulating account of non-Euclidean geometry, matrices, determinants, group theory, other topics. Emphasis on novel, striking aspects. 224pp. 5⅜ × 8½.

24401-6 Pa. $4.50

ADVENTURES WITH A MICROSCOPE, Richard Headstrom. 59 adventures with clothing fibers, protozoa, ferns and lichens, roots and leaves, much more. 142 illustrations. 232pp. 5⅜ × 8½.

23471-1 Pa. $3.95

IDENTIFYING ANIMAL TRACKS: MAMMALS, BIRDS, AND OTHER ANIMALS OF THE EASTERN UNITED STATES, Richard Headstrom. For hunters, naturalists, scouts, nature-lovers. Diagrams of tracks, tips on identification. 128pp. 5⅜ × 8.

24442-3 Pa. $3.50

VICTORIAN FASHIONS AND COSTUMES FROM HARPER'S BAZAR, 1867-1898, edited by Stella Blum. Day costumes, evening wear, sports clothes, shoes, hats, other accessories in over 1,000 detailed engravings. 320pp. 9⅜ × 12¼.

22990-4 Pa. $9.95

EVERYDAY FASHIONS OF THE TWENTIES AS PICTURED IN SEARS AND OTHER CATALOGS, edited by Stella Blum. Actual dress of the Roaring Twenties, with text by Stella Blum. Over 750 illustrations, captions. 156pp. 9 × 12.

24134-3 Pa. $8.50

HALL OF FAME BASEBALL CARDS, edited by Bert Randolph Sugar. Cy Young, Ted Williams, Lou Gehrig, and many other Hall of Fame greats on 92 full-color, detachable reprints of early baseball cards. No duplication of cards with *Classic Baseball Cards.* 16pp. 8¼ × 11.

23624-2 Pa. $3.50

THE ART OF HAND LETTERING, Helm Wotzkow. Course in hand lettering, Roman, Gothic, Italic, Block, Script. Tools, proportions, optical aspects, individual variation. Very quality conscious. Hundreds of specimens. 320pp. 5⅜ × 8½.

21797-3 Pa. $4.95

HOW THE OTHER HALF LIVES, Jacob A. Riis. Journalistic record of filth, degradation, upward drive in New York immigrant slums, shops, around 1900. New edition includes 100 original Riis photos, monuments of early photography. 233pp. 10 × 7⅞. 22012-5 Pa. $7.95

CHINA AND ITS PEOPLE IN EARLY PHOTOGRAPHS, John Thomson. In 200 black-and-white photographs of exceptional quality photographic pioneer Thomson captures the mountains, dwellings, monuments and people of 19th-century China. 272pp. 9⅜ × 12¼. 24393-1 Pa. $12.95

GODEY COSTUME PLATES IN COLOR FOR DECOUPAGE AND FRAMING, edited by Eleanor Hasbrouk Rawlings. 24 full-color engravings depicting 19th-century Parisian haute couture. Printed on one side only. 56pp. 8¼ × 11. 23879-2 Pa. $3.95

ART NOUVEAU STAINED GLASS PATTERN BOOK, Ed Sibbett, Jr. 104 projects using well-known themes of Art Nouveau: swirling forms, florals, peacocks, and sensuous women. 60pp. 8¼ × 11. 23577-7 Pa. $3.50

QUICK AND EASY PATCHWORK ON THE SEWING MACHINE: Susan Aylsworth Murwin and Suzzy Payne. Instructions, diagrams show exactly how to machine sew 12 quilts. 48pp. of templates. 50 figures. 80pp. 8¼ × 11. 23770-2 Pa. $3.50

THE STANDARD BOOK OF QUILT MAKING AND COLLECTING, Marguerite Ickis. Full information, full-sized patterns for making 46 traditional quilts, also 150 other patterns. 483 illustrations. 273pp. 6⅞ × 9⅝. 20582-7 Pa. $5.95

LETTERING AND ALPHABETS, J. Albert Cavanagh. 85 complete alphabets lettered in various styles; instructions for spacing, roughs, brushwork. 121pp. 8¾ × 8. 20053-1 Pa. $3.75

LETTER FORMS: 110 COMPLETE ALPHABETS, Frederick Lambert. 110 sets of capital letters; 16 lower case alphabets; 70 sets of numbers and other symbols. 110pp. 8⅛ × 11. 22872-X Pa. $4.50

ORCHIDS AS HOUSE PLANTS, Rebecca Tyson Northen. Grow cattleyas and many other kinds of orchids—in a window, in a case, or under artificial light. 63 illustrations. 148pp. 5⅜ × 8½. 23261-1 Pa. $2.95

THE MUSHROOM HANDBOOK, Louis C.C. Krieger. Still the best popular handbook. Full descriptions of 259 species, extremely thorough text, poisons, folklore, etc. 32 color plates; 126 other illustrations. 560pp. 5⅜ × 8½. 21861-9 Pa. $8.50

THE DORÉ BIBLE ILLUSTRATIONS, Gustave Doré. All wonderful, detailed plates: Adam and Eve, Flood, Babylon, life of Jesus, etc. Brief King James text with each plate. 241 plates. 241pp. 9 × 12. 23004-X Pa. $8.95

THE BOOK OF KELLS: Selected Plates in Full Color, edited by Blanche Cirker. 32 full-page plates from greatest manuscript-icon of early Middle Ages. Fantastic, mysterious. Publisher's Note. Captions. 32pp. 9¾ × 12¼. 24345-1 Pa. $4.50

THE PERFECT WAGNERITE, George Bernard Shaw. Brilliant criticism of the Ring Cycle, with provocative interpretation of politics, economic theories behind the Ring. 136pp. 5⅜ × 8½. (Available in U.S. only) 21707-8 Pa. $3.00

THE RIME OF THE ANCIENT MARINER, Gustave Doré, S.T. Coleridge. Doré's finest work, 34 plates capture moods, subtleties of poem. Full text. 77pp. 9¼ × 12.
22305-1 Pa. $4.95

SONGS OF INNOCENCE, William Blake. The first and most popular of Blake's famous "Illuminated Books," in a facsimile edition reproducing all 31 brightly colored plates. Additional printed text of each poem. 64pp. 5¼ × 7.
22764-2 Pa. $3.00

AN INTRODUCTION TO INFORMATION THEORY, J.R. Pierce. Second (1980) edition of most impressive non-technical account available. Encoding, entropy, noisy channel, related areas, etc. 320pp. 5⅜ × 8½.
24061-4 Pa. $4.95

THE DIVINE PROPORTION: A STUDY IN MATHEMATICAL BEAUTY, H.E. Huntley. "Divine proportion" or "golden ratio" in poetry, Pascal's triangle, philosophy, psychology, music, mathematical figures, etc. Excellent bridge between science and art. 58 figures. 185pp. 5⅜ × 8½.
22254-3 Pa. $3.95

THE DOVER NEW YORK WALKING GUIDE: From the Battery to Wall Street, Mary J. Shapiro. Superb inexpensive guide to historic buildings and locales in lower Manhattan: Trinity Church, Bowling Green, more. Complete Text; maps. 36 illustrations. 48pp. 3⅞ × 9¼.
24225-0 Pa. $2.50

NEW YORK THEN AND NOW, Edward B. Watson, Edmund V. Gillon, Jr. 83 important Manhattan sites: on facing pages early photographs (1875-1925) and 1976 photos by Gillon. 172 illustrations. 171pp. 9¼ × 10.
23361-8 Pa. $7.95

HISTORIC COSTUME IN PICTURES, Braun & Schneider. Over 1450 costumed figures from dawn of civilization to end of 19th century. English captions. 125 plates. 256pp. 8⅜ × 11¼.
23150-X Pa. $7.50

VICTORIAN AND EDWARDIAN FASHION: A Photographic Survey, Alison Gernsheim. First fashion history completely illustrated by contemporary photographs. Full text plus 235 photos, 1840-1914, in which many celebrities appear. 240pp. 6½ × 9¼.
24205-6 Pa. $6.00

CHARTED CHRISTMAS DESIGNS FOR COUNTED CROSS-STITCH AND OTHER NEEDLECRAFTS, Lindberg Press. Charted designs for 45 beautiful needlecraft projects with many yuletide and wintertime motifs. 48pp. 8¼ × 11.
24356-7 Pa. $1.95

101 FOLK DESIGNS FOR COUNTED CROSS-STITCH AND OTHER NEEDLE-CRAFTS, Carter Houck. 101 authentic charted folk designs in a wide array of lovely representations with many suggestions for effective use. 48pp. 8¼ × 11.
24369-9 Pa. $2.25

FIVE ACRES AND INDEPENDENCE, Maurice G. Kains. Great back-to-the-land classic explains basics of self-sufficient farming. The one book to get. 95 illustrations. 397pp. 5⅜ × 8½.
20974-1 Pa. $4.95

A MODERN HERBAL, Margaret Grieve. Much the fullest, most exact, most useful compilation of herbal material. Gigantic alphabetical encyclopedia, from aconite to zedoary, gives botanical information, medical properties, folklore, economic uses, and much else. Indispensable to serious reader. 161 illustrations. 888pp. 6½ × 9¼. (Available in U.S. only)
22798-7, 22799-5 Pa., Two-vol. set $16.45

DECORATIVE NAPKIN FOLDING FOR BEGINNERS, Lillian Oppenheimer and Natalie Epstein. 22 different napkin folds in the shape of a heart, clown's hat, love knot, etc. 63 drawings. 48pp. 8¼ × 11. 23797-4 Pa. $1.95

DECORATIVE LABELS FOR HOME CANNING, PRESERVING, AND OTHER HOUSEHOLD AND GIFT USES, Theodore Menten. 128 gummed, perforated labels, beautifully printed in 2 colors. 12 versions. Adhere to metal, glass, wood, ceramics. 24pp. 8¼ × 11. 23219-0 Pa. $2.95

EARLY AMERICAN STENCILS ON WALLS AND FURNITURE, Janet Waring. Thorough coverage of 19th-century folk art: techniques, artifacts, surviving specimens. 166 illustrations, 7 in color. 147pp. of text. 7⅞ × 10¾. 21906-2 Pa. $9.95

AMERICAN ANTIQUE WEATHERVANES, A.B. & W.T. Westervelt. Extensively illustrated 1883 catalog exhibiting over 550 copper weathervanes and finials. Excellent primary source by one of the principal manufacturers. 104pp. 6⅛ × 9¼. 24396-6 Pa. $3.95

ART STUDENTS' ANATOMY, Edmond J. Farris. Long favorite in art schools. Basic elements, common positions, actions. Full text, 158 illustrations. 159pp. 5⅜ × 8½. 20744-7 Pa. $3.95

BRIDGMAN'S LIFE DRAWING, George B. Bridgman. More than 500 drawings and text teach you to abstract the body into its major masses. Also specific areas of anatomy. 192pp. 6½ × 9¼. (EA) 22710-3 Pa. $4.50

COMPLETE PRELUDES AND ETUDES FOR SOLO PIANO, Frederic Chopin. All 26 Preludes, all 27 Etudes by greatest composer of piano music. Authoritative Paderewski edition. 224pp. 9 × 12. (Available in U.S. only) 24052-5 Pa. $7.50

PIANO MUSIC 1888-1905, Claude Debussy. Deux Arabesques, Suite Bergamesque, Masques, 1st series of Images, etc. 9 others, in corrected editions. 175pp. 9⅜ × 12¼. (ECE) 22771-5 Pa. $5.95

TEDDY BEAR IRON-ON TRANSFER PATTERNS, Ted Menten. 80 iron-on transfer patterns of male and female Teddys in a wide variety of activities, poses, sizes. 48pp. 8¼ × 11. 24596-9 Pa. $2.25

A PICTURE HISTORY OF THE BROOKLYN BRIDGE, M.J. Shapiro. Profusely illustrated account of greatest engineering achievement of 19th century. 167 rare photos & engravings recall construction, human drama. Extensive, detailed text. 122pp. 8¼ × 11. 24403-2 Pa. $7.95

NEW YORK IN THE THIRTIES, Berenice Abbott. Noted photographer's fascinating study shows new buildings that have become famous and old sights that have disappeared forever. 97 photographs. 97pp. 11⅜ × 10. 22967-X Pa. $6.50

MATHEMATICAL TABLES AND FORMULAS, Robert D. Carmichael and Edwin R. Smith. Logarithms, sines, tangents, trig functions, powers, roots, reciprocals, exponential and hyperbolic functions, formulas and theorems. 269pp. 5⅜ × 8½. 60111-0 Pa. $3.75

HANDBOOK OF MATHEMATICAL FUNCTIONS WITH FORMULAS, GRAPHS, AND MATHEMATICAL TABLES, edited by Milton Abramowitz and Irene A. Stegun. Vast compendium: 29 sets of tables, some to as high as 20 places. 1,046pp. 8 × 10½. 61272-4 Pa. $19.95

REASON IN ART, George Santayana. Renowned philosopher's provocative, seminal treatment of basis of art in instinct and experience. Volume Four of *The Life of Reason*. 230pp. 5⅜ × 8. 24358-3 Pa. $4.50

LANGUAGE, TRUTH AND LOGIC, Alfred J. Ayer. Famous, clear introduction to Vienna, Cambridge schools of Logical Positivism. Role of philosophy, elimination of metaphysics, nature of analysis, etc. 160pp. 5⅜ × 8½. (USCO) 20010-8 Pa. $2.75

BASIC ELECTRONICS, U.S. Bureau of Naval Personnel. Electron tubes, circuits, antennas, AM, FM, and CW transmission and receiving, etc. 560 illustrations. 567pp. 6½ × 9¼. 21076-6 Pa. $8.95

THE ART DECO STYLE, edited by Theodore Menten. Furniture, jewelry, metalwork, ceramics, fabrics, lighting fixtures, interior decors, exteriors, graphics from pure French sources. Over 400 photographs. 183pp. 8⅜ × 11¼. 22824-X Pa. $6.95

THE FOUR BOOKS OF ARCHITECTURE, Andrea Palladio. 16th-century classic covers classical architectural remains, Renaissance revivals, classical orders, etc. 1738 Ware English edition. 216 plates. 110pp. of text. 9½ × 12¾. 21308-0 Pa. $11.50

THE WIT AND HUMOR OF OSCAR WILDE, edited by Alvin Redman. More than 1000 ripostes, paradoxes, wisecracks: Work is the curse of the drinking classes, I can resist everything except temptations, etc. 258pp. 5⅜ × 8½. (USCO) 20602-5 Pa. $3.50

THE DEVIL'S DICTIONARY, Ambrose Bierce. Barbed, bitter, brilliant witticisms in the form of a dictionary. Best, most ferocious satire America has produced. 145pp. 5⅜ × 8½. 20487-1 Pa. $2.50

ERTÉ'S FASHION DESIGNS, Erté. 210 black-and-white inventions from *Harper's Bazar*, 1918-32, plus 8pp. full-color covers. Captions. 88pp. 9 × 12. 24203-X Pa. $6.50

ERTÉ GRAPHICS, Erté. Collection of striking color graphics: *Seasons, Alphabet, Numerals, Aces* and *Precious Stones*. 50 plates, including 4 on covers. 48pp. 9⅜ × 12¼. 23580-7 Pa. $6.95

PAPER FOLDING FOR BEGINNERS, William D. Murray and Francis J. Rigney. Clearest book for making origami sail boats, roosters, frogs that move legs, etc. 40 projects. More than 275 illustrations. 94pp. 5⅜ × 8½. 20713-7 Pa. $2.25

ORIGAMI FOR THE ENTHUSIAST, John Montroll. Fish, ostrich, peacock, squirrel, rhinoceros, Pegasus, 19 other intricate subjects. Instructions. Diagrams. 128pp. 9 × 12. 23799-0 Pa. $4.95

CROCHETING NOVELTY POT HOLDERS, edited by Linda Macho. 64 useful, whimsical pot holders feature kitchen themes, animals, flowers, other novelties. Surprisingly easy to crochet. Complete instructions. 48pp. 8¼ × 11. 24296-X Pa. $1.95

CROCHETING DOILIES, edited by Rita Weiss. Irish Crochet, Jewel, Star Wheel, Vanity Fair and more. Also luncheon and console sets, runners and centerpieces. 51 illustrations. 48pp. 8¼ × 11. 23424-X Pa. $2.00

YUCATAN BEFORE AND AFTER THE CONQUEST, Diego de Landa. Only significant account of Yucatan written in the early post-Conquest era. Translated by William Gates. Over 120 illustrations. 162pp. 5⅜ × 8½.   23622-6 Pa. $3.50

ORNATE PICTORIAL CALLIGRAPHY, E.A. Lupfer. Complete instructions, over 150 examples help you create magnificent "flourishes" from which beautiful animals and objects gracefully emerge. 8⅛ × 11.   21957-7 Pa. $2.95

DOLLY DINGLE PAPER DOLLS, Grace Drayton. Cute chubby children by same artist who did Campbell Kids. Rare plates from 1910s. 30 paper dolls and over 100 outfits reproduced in full color. 32pp. 9¼ × 12¼.   23711-7 Pa. $3.50

CURIOUS GEORGE PAPER DOLLS IN FULL COLOR, H. A. Rey, Kathy Allert. Naughty little monkey-hero of children's books in two doll figures, plus 48 full-color costumes: pirate, Indian chief, fireman, more. 32pp. 9¼ × 12¼.
24386-9 Pa. $3.50

GERMAN: HOW TO SPEAK AND WRITE IT, Joseph Rosenberg. Like *French, How to Speak and Write It.* Very rich modern course, with a wealth of pictorial material. 330 illustrations. 384pp. 5⅜ × 8½. (USUKO)   20271-2 Pa. $4.75

CATS AND KITTENS: 24 Ready-to-Mail Color Photo Postcards, D. Holby. Handsome collection; feline in a variety of adorable poses. Identifications. 12pp. on postcard stock. 8¼ × 11.   24469-5 Pa. $2.95

MARILYN MONROE PAPER DOLLS, Tom Tierney. 31 full-color designs on heavy stock, from *The Asphalt Jungle, Gentlemen Prefer Blondes,* 22 others. 1 doll. 16 plates. 32pp. 9⅜ × 12¼.   23769-9 Pa. $3.50

FUNDAMENTALS OF LAYOUT, F.H. Wills. All phases of layout design discussed and illustrated in 121 illustrations. Indispensable as student's text or handbook for professional. 124pp. 8⅛ × 11.   21279-3 Pa. $4.50

FANTASTIC SUPER STICKERS, Ed Sibbett, Jr. 75 colorful pressure-sensitive stickers. Peel off and place for a touch of pizzazz: clowns, penguins, teddy bears, etc. Full color. 16pp. 8¼ × 11.   24471-7 Pa. $2.95

LABELS FOR ALL OCCASIONS, Ed Sibbett, Jr. 6 labels each of 16 different designs—baroque, art nouveau, art deco, Pennsylvania Dutch, etc.—in full color. 24pp. 8¼ × 11.   23688-9 Pa. $2.95

HOW TO CALCULATE QUICKLY: RAPID METHODS IN BASIC MATHE-MATICS, Henry Sticker. Addition, subtraction, multiplication, division, checks, etc. More than 8000 problems, solutions. 185pp. 5 × 7¼.   20295-X Pa. $2.95

THE CAT COLORING BOOK, Karen Baldauski. Handsome, realistic renderings of 40 splendid felines, from American shorthair to exotic types. 44 plates. Captions. 48pp. 8¼ × 11.   24011-8 Pa. $2.25

THE TALE OF PETER RABBIT, Beatrix Potter. The inimitable Peter's terrifying adventure in Mr. McGregor's garden, with all 27 wonderful, full-color Potter illustrations. 55pp. 4¼ × 5½. (Available in U.S. only)   22827-4 Pa. $1.60

BASIC ELECTRICITY, U.S. Bureau of Naval Personnel. Batteries, circuits, conductors, AC and DC, inductance and capacitance, generators, motors, trans-formers, amplifiers, etc. 349 illustrations. 448pp. 6½ × 9¼.   20973-3 Pa. $7.95

SOURCE BOOK OF MEDICAL HISTORY, edited by Logan Clendening, M.D. Original accounts ranging from Ancient Egypt and Greece to discovery of X-rays: Galen, Pasteur, Lavoisier, Harvey, Parkinson, others. 685pp. 5⅜ × 8½.

20621-1 Pa. $10.95

THE ROSE AND THE KEY, J.S. Lefanu. Superb mystery novel from Irish master. Dark doings among an ancient and aristocratic English family. Well-drawn characters; capital suspense. Introduction by N. Donaldson. 448pp. 5⅜ × 8½.

24377-X Pa. $6.95

SOUTH WIND, Norman Douglas. Witty, elegant novel of ideas set on languorous Mediterranean island of Nepenthe. Elegant prose, glittering epigrams, mordant satire. 1917 masterpiece. 416pp. 5⅜ × 8½. (Available in U.S. only)

24361-3 Pa. $5.95

RUSSELL'S CIVIL WAR PHOTOGRAPHS, Capt. A.J. Russell. 116 rare Civil War Photos: Bull Run, Virginia campaigns, bridges, railroads, Richmond, Lincoln's funeral car. Many never seen before. Captions. 128pp. 9⅜ × 12¼.

24283-8 Pa. $6.95

PHOTOGRAPHS BY MAN RAY: 105 Works, 1920-1934. Nudes, still lifes, landscapes, women's faces, celebrity portraits (Dali, Matisse, Picasso, others), rayographs. Reprinted from rare gravure edition. 128pp. 9⅜ × 12¼. (Available in U.S. only)

23842-3 Pa. $6.95

STAR NAMES: THEIR LORE AND MEANING, Richard H. Allen. Star names, the zodiac, constellations: folklore and literature associated with heavens. The basic book of its field, fascinating reading. 563pp. 5⅜ × 8½.   21079-0 Pa. $7.95

BURNHAM'S CELESTIAL HANDBOOK, Robert Burnham, Jr. Thorough guide to the stars beyond our solar system. Exhaustive treatment. Alphabetical by constellation: Andromeda to Cetus in Vol. 1; Chamaeleon to Orion in Vol. 2; and Pavo to Vulpecula in Vol. 3. Hundreds of illustrations. Index in Vol. 3. 2000pp. 6⅛ × 9¼.   23567-X, 23568-8, 23673-0 Pa. Three-vol. set $36.85

THE ART NOUVEAU STYLE BOOK OF ALPHONSE MUCHA, Alphonse Mucha. All 72 plates from *Documents Decoratifs* in original color. Stunning, essential work of Art Nouveau. 80pp. 9⅜ × 12¼.   24044-4 Pa. $7.95

DESIGNS BY ERTE; FASHION DRAWINGS AND ILLUSTRATIONS FROM "HARPER'S BAZAR," Erte. 310 fabulous line drawings and 14 *Harper's Bazar* covers, 8 in full color. Erte's exotic temptresses with tassels, fur muffs, long trains, coifs, more. 129pp. 9⅜ × 12¼.   23397-9 Pa. $6.95

HISTORY OF STRENGTH OF MATERIALS, Stephen P. Timoshenko. Excellent historical survey of the strength of materials with many references to the theories of elasticity and structure. 245 figures. 452pp. 5⅜ × 8½.   61187-6 Pa. $8.95